Jung on Ignatius of Loyola's *Spiritual Exercises*

A list of Jung's works appears at the back of the volume.

Jung on Ignatius of Loyola's *Spiritual Exercises*

LECTURES DELIVERED AT THE ETH ZURICH
VOLUME 7: 1939–1940

C. G. JUNG

EDITED BY MARTIN LIEBSCHER

Translated by Caitlin Stephens

ⓅPHILEMON SERIES
Published with the support of the Philemon Foundation
This book is part of the Philemon Series of the Philemon Foundation

PRINCETON UNIVERSITY PRESS
PRINCETON AND OXFORD

Princeton University Press is committed to the protection of copyright and the
intellectual property our authors entrust to us. Copyright promotes the progress
and integrity of knowledge. Thank you for supporting free speech and the global
exchange of ideas by purchasing an authorized edition of this book. If you wish
to reproduce or distribute any part of it in any form, please obtain permission.

Requests for permission to reproduce material from this work
should be sent to permissions@press.princeton.edu

Published by Princeton University Press
41 William Street, Princeton, New Jersey 08540
99 Banbury Road, Oxford OX2 6JX

press.princeton.edu

All Rights Reserved

ISBN 9780691244167
ISBN (e-book) 9780691244600

Library of Congress Control Number: 2022943024

British Library Cataloging-in-Publication Data is available

Editorial: Fred Appel and James Collier
Production Editorial: Karen Carter
Text Design: Carmina Alvarez
Jacket/Cover Design: Katie Osborne
Production: Erin Suydam
Jacket/Cover Credit: Jacket image by Pictorial Press Ltd / Alamy Stock Photo

This book has been composed in Sabon LT Std

Printed on acid-free paper. ∞

Printed in the United States of America

10 9 8 7 6 5 4 3 2 1

Contents

WINTER SEMESTER 1939/40

General Introduction

ERNST FALZEDER, MARTIN LIEBSCHER, AND
SONU SHAMDASANI

BETWEEN 1933 AND 1941, C. G. Jung lectured at the Swiss Federal Institute for Technology (ETH). He was appointed a professor there in 1935. This represented a resumption of his university career after a long hiatus, as he had resigned his post as a lecturer in the medical faculty at the University of Zurich in 1914. In the intervening period, Jung's teaching activity had principally consisted in a series of seminars at the Psychology Club in Zurich, which were restricted to a membership consisting of his own students or followers. The lectures at ETH were open, and the audience for the lectures was made up of students at ETH, the general public, and Jung's followers. The attendance at each lecture was in the hundreds: Josef Lang, in a letter to Hermann Hesse, spoke of six hundred participants at the end of 1933,[1] Jung counted four hundred in October 1935.[2] Kurt Binswanger, who attended the lectures, recalled that people often could not find a seat and that the listeners "were of all ages and of all social classes: students [. . .]; middle-aged people; also many older people; many ladies who were once in analysis with Jung."[3] Jung himself attributed this success to the novelty of his lectures and expected a gradual decline in numbers: "Because of the huge crowd my lectures have to be held in the *auditorium maximum*. It is of course their sensational nature that entices people to come. As soon as people realize that these lectures are concerned with serious matters, the numbers will become more modest."[4]

---

[1] Josef Bernhard Lang to Hermann Hesse, end of November 1933 (Hesse, 2006, p. 299).

[2] Jung (1987), p. 87.

[3] Interview with Gene Nameche [JOHA], p. 6.

[4] Jung to Jolande Jacobi, 9 January 1934 [JA].

Because of this context, the language of the lectures is far more accessible than that of Jung's published works at this time. Binswanger also noted that "Jung prepared each of those lectures extremely carefully. After the lectures, a part of the audience always remained to ask questions, in a totally natural and relaxed situation. It was also pleasant that Jung never appeared at the last minute, as so many other lecturers did. He, on the contrary, was already present before the lecture, sat on one of the benches in the corridor; and people could go and sit with him. He was communicative and open."[5]

The lectures usually took place on Fridays between 6 and 7 p.m. The audience consisted of regular students of technical disciplines, who were expected to attend additional courses from a subject of the humanities. But as it was possible to register as a guest auditor, many of those who had come to Zurich to study with Jung or undertake therapy attended the lectures as an introduction to Analytical Psychology. In addition, Jung held ETH seminars with limited numbers of participants, in which he would further elaborate on the topics of the lectures. During the eight years of his lectures—which were only interrupted in 1937, when Jung traveled to India—he covered a wide range of topics. These lectures are at the center of Jung's intellectual activity in the 1930s, and furthermore provide the basis of his work in the 1940s and 1950s. Thus, they form a critical part of Jung's oeuvre, one that has yet to be accorded the attention and study that it deserves. The subjects that Jung addressed in ETH lectures are probably even more significant to present-day scholars, psychologists, psychotherapists, and the general public than they were to those to whom they were first delivered. The passing years have seen a mushrooming of interest in Eastern thought, Western hermeticism, and mystical traditions, the rise of the psychological types industry and the dream work movement, and the emergence of a discipline of the history of psychology.

CONTENTS OF THE LECTURES

Volume 1: History of Modern Psychology (Winter Semester 1933/1934)

The first semester, from 20 October 1933 to 23 February 1934, consists of sixteen lectures on what Jung called the history of "modern psychology," by which he meant psychology as "a conscious science," not one that

---

[5] Interview with Gene Nameche [JOHA], p. 6.

projects the psyche into the stars or alchemical processes, for instance. His account starts at the dawn of the age of Enlightenment, and presents a comparative study of movements in French, German, and British thought. He placed particular emphasis on the development of concepts of the unconscious in nineteenth-century German Idealism. Turning to England and France, Jung traced the emergence of the empirical tradition and of psychophysical research, and how these in turn were taken up in Germany and led to the emergence of experimental psychology. He reconstructed the rise of scientific psychology in France and in the United States. He then turned to the significance of spiritualism and psychical research in the rise of psychology, paying particular attention to the work of Justinus Kerner and Théodore Flournoy. Jung devoted five lectures to a detailed study of Kerner's work *The Seeress of Prevorst* (1829),[6] and two lectures to a detailed study of Flournoy's *From India to the Planet Mars* (1899).[7] These works initially had a considerable impact on Jung. As well as elucidating their historical significance, his consideration of them enables us to understand the role that his reading of them played in his early work. Unusually, in this section Jung eschewed a conventional history of ideas approach, and placed special emphasis on the role of patients and subjects in the constitution of psychology. In the course of his reading of these works, Jung developed a detailed taxonomy of the scope of human consciousness, which he presented in a series of diagrams. He then presented a further series of illustrative case studies of historical individuals in terms of this model: Niklaus von der Flüe, Goethe, Nietzsche, Freud, John D. Rockefeller, and the "so-called normal man."

Of the major figures in twentieth-century psychology, Jung was arguably the most historically and philosophically minded. These lectures thus have a twofold significance. On the one hand, they present a seminal contribution to the history of psychology, and hence to the current historiography of psychology. On the other hand, it is clear that the developments that Jung reconstructed culminate teleologically in his own "complex psychology" (his preferred designation for his work), and thus present his own understanding of its emergence. This account provides a critical correction to the prevailing Freudocentric accounts of the development of Jung's work, which were already in circulation at this time. The detailed taxonomy of consciousness that he presented in the second part of this

---

[6] Kerner (1829).
[7] Flournoy (1900 [1899]).

semester was not documented in any of his published works. In presenting it, he noted he had been led to undertake it in response to the difficulties which he had encountered with his project for a psychological typology. Thus these lectures present critical aspects of Jung's mature thought that are unavailable elsewhere.

Volume 2: Consciousness and the Unconscious
(Summer Semester 1934)

This volume presents twelve lectures from 20 April 1934 to 13 July 1934. Jung commenced with lectures on the problematic status of psychology, and attempted to give an account as to how the various views of psychology in its history, which he had presented in the first semester, had been generated. This led him to account for national differences in ideas and outlook, and to reflect on different characteristics and difficulties of the English, French, and German languages when it came to expressing psychological materials. Reflecting on the significance of linguistic ambiguity led Jung to give an account of the status of the concept of the unconscious, which he illustrated with several cases. Following these general reflections, he presented his conception of the psychological functions and types, illustrated by practical examples of their interaction. He then gave an account of his concept of the collective unconscious. Filling a lacuna in his earlier accounts, he gave a detailed map of the differentiation and stratification of its contents, in particular as regards cultural and "racial" differences. Jung then turned to describing methods for rendering accessible the contents of the unconscious: the association experiment, the psycho-galvanic method, and dream analysis. In his account of these methods, he revised his previous work in the light of his present understanding. In particular, he gave a detailed account of how the study of associations in families enabled the psychic structure of families and the functioning of the complexes to be studied. The semester concluded with an overview of the topic of dreams and the study of several dreams.

On the basis of his reconstruction of the history of psychology, Jung then devoted the rest of this and the following semesters to an account of his "complex psychology." As in the other semesters, he was confronted with a general audience, a context that gave him a unique opportunity to present a full and generally accessible account of his work, as he could not presuppose prior knowledge of psychology. Thus we find here the most detailed, and perhaps most accessible, introduction to his own theory. This is by no means just an introduction to previous work, however, but a full-scale reworking of his early work in terms of his current understanding, and it presents models of the personality that cannot be found anywhere else in his work. Thus, this volume is Jung's most up-to-date account of his theory of complexes, association experiments, understanding of dreams, the structure of the personality, and the nature of psychology.

Volume 3: Modern Psychology and Dreams (Winter Semester 1934/1935 and Summer Semester 1935)

The third volume presents lectures from two consecutive semesters: seventeen lectures from 26 October 1934 to 8 March 1935, and eleven lectures from 3 May 1935 to 12 July 1935, here collected in one volume as they all deal primarily with possible methods to access, and try to determine the content of, the unconscious. Jung starts with a detailed description of Freud's and, to a somewhat lesser extent, Adler's theories and methods of analyzing dreams, and then proceeds to his own views (dreams are "pure nature" and of a complementary/compensatory character) and technique (context, amplification). He focuses particularly on three short dream series, the first from the Nobel Prize winner Wolfgang Pauli, the second from a young homosexual man, and the third from a psychotic person, using them to describe and interpret special symbolisms. In the following semester, he concludes the discussion of the mechanism, function, and use of dreams as a method to enlighten us and to get to know the unconscious, and then draws attention to "Eastern parallels," such as yoga, while warning against their indiscriminate use by Westerners. Instead he devotes the rest of the semester to a detailed example of "active imagination," or "active phantasizing," as he calls it here, with the help of the case of a fifty-five-year-old American lady: the same case that he discussed at length in the German seminar of 1931.

This volume gives a detailed account of Jung's understanding of Freud's and Adler's dream theories, shedding interesting light on the points in which he concurred and in which he differed, and how he developed his own theory and method in contradistinction to those. Since he was dealing with a general audience, a fact of which he was very much aware, he tried to stay on a level as basic as possible—which is also of great help to the contemporaneous, nonspecialized reader. This is also true for his method of active imagination, as exemplified in one long example. Although he used material also presented elsewhere, the present account is highly interesting precisely because it is tailored to a most varied general audience, and differs accordingly from presentations given to the hand-picked participants in his "private" seminars, or in specialized books.

Volume 4: Psychological Typology (Winter Semester 1935/1936 and Summer Semester 1936)

The fourth volume also combines lectures from two semesters: fifteen lectures from 25 October 1935 to 6 March 1936, and thirteen lectures from 1 May 1936 to 10 July 1936. The winter semester gives a general introduction into the history of typologies, and typology in intellectual and religious history, from antiquity to Gnosticism and Christianity, from Chinese philosophy (yin/yang) to Persian religion and philosophy (Ahriman/Lucifer), from the French Revolution (déesse raison) to Schiller's Letters on the Aesthetic Education of Man. Jung introduces and describes in detail the two attitudes (introversion and extraversion) and the four functions (thinking and feeling as rational functions, sensation and intuition as irrational functions). In the summer semester, he focuses on the interplay between the attitudes and the various functions, detailing the possible combinations (extraverted and introverted feeling, thinking, sensation, and intuition), with the help of many examples.

This volume offers an excellent, first-hand introduction to Jung's typology, and is *the* alternative for contemporary readers who are looking for a basic, while authentic text, as opposed to Jung's magnum opus *Psychological Types*, which, as it were, hides the sleeping beauty behind a thick barrier of thorny bushes, namely, its four hundred-plus pages of "introduction," only after which Jung deals with his own typology proper. As in the previous volumes, readers will benefit from the fact that Jung was compelled to give a basic introduction to, and overview of, his views.

Volume 5: Psychology of the Unconscious (Summer Semester 1937 and Summer Semester 1938)

Jung dedicated his lectures of summer 1937 (23 April–9 July; eleven lectures) and summer 1938 (29 April–8 July; ten lectures) to the psychology of the unconscious. The understanding of the sociological and historical dependency of the psyche and the relativity of consciousness form the basis to familiarize the audience with different manifestations of the unconscious related to hypnotic states and cryptomnesia, unconscious affects and motivation, memory and forgetting. Jung shows the normal and pathological forms of invasions of unconscious contents into consciousness, and outlines the methodologies to bring unconscious material to the surface. This includes methods such as the association experiment, dream analysis, and active imagination, as well as different forms of creative expression, but also ancient tools of divination including astrology and the I-Ching. The summer semester of 1938 returned to the dream series of the young homosexual man discussed in detail in the lectures of 1935, this time highlighting Jung's method of dream interpretation on an individual and a symbolic level.

Jung illustrates his lectures with several diagrams and clinical cases to make it more accessible to nonpsychologists. In some instances the lectures provide welcome additional information to published articles, as Jung was not obliged to restrict his material to a confined space. For example, he elaborated on the famous case of the so-called moon-patient, which was so important for his understanding of psychic reality and psychosis, or gave a very personal introduction to the use of the I-Ching. The lectures also shed a new historical light on his journeys to Africa, India, and New Mexico and his reception of psychology, philosophy, and literature.

Volume 6: Psychology of Yoga and Meditation (Winter Semester 1938/1939 and Summer Semester 1939; Plus the First Two Lectures of the Winter Semester 1940/1941)

The lecture series of the winter semester 1938/39 (28 October–3 March; fifteen lectures) and the first half of the summer semester 1939 (28 April–9 June; six lectures) are concerned with Eastern spirituality. Starting out with the psychological concept of active imagination, Jung seeks to find parallels in Eastern meditative practices. His focus is directed on meditation as taught by different yogic traditions and in Buddhist practice. The texts for Jung's interpretation are Patañjali's *Yoga Sûtra*, according to the latest research written around 400 CE,[8] and regarded as one of the most important sources for our knowledge of yoga today, the *Amitâyur-dhyâna-sûtra* from the Chinese Pure Land Buddhist tradition, translated from Sanskrit to Chinese by Kâlayasas in 424 CE,[9] and the *Shrî-chakra-sambhâra Tantra*, a scripture related to tantric yoga, translated and published in English by Arthur Avalon (Sir John Woodroffe) in 1919.[10] Nowhere else in Jung's works can one find such detailed psychological interpretations of these three spiritual texts. In their importance for understanding Jung's take on

[8] Maas (2006).
[9] Müller (1894), pp. xx–xxi.
[10] Avalon (1919).

Eastern mysticism, the lectures of 1938/39 can only be compared to his reading of the *Secret of the Golden Flower*[11] or the seminars on Kundalini Yoga.[12]

In the winter semester 1940/41, Jung summarizes the arguments of his lectures on Eastern meditation. The summary is published as an addendum at the end of this volume.

Volume 7: Spiritual Exercises of Ignatius of Loyola *(Summer Semester 1939 and Winter Semester 1939/1940; in Addition: Lecture 3, Winter Semester 1940/1941)*

The second half of the summer semester 1939 (16 June–7 July; four lectures) and the winter semester 1939/40 (3 November–8 March; sixteen lectures) were dedicated to the *Exercitia spiritualia*[13] of Ignatius of Loyala, the founder and first general superior of the Society of Jesus (Jesuits). As a knight and soldier, Ignatius was injured in the battle of Pamplona (1521), in the aftermath of which he experienced a spiritual conversion. Subsequently he renounced his worldly life and devoted himself to the service of God. In March 1522, the Virgin Mary and the infant Jesus appeared to him at the shrine of Montserrat, which led him to search for solitude in a cave near Manresa. There he prayed for seven hours a day and wrote down his experiences for others to follow. This collection of prayers, meditations, and mental exercises built the foundation of the *Exercitia spiritualia* (1522–24). In this text, Jung saw the equivalent to the meditative practice of the Eastern spiritual tradition. He provides a psychological reading of it, comparing it to the modern Jesuit understanding of theologians such as Erich Przywara.

Jung's considerations on the *Exercitia spiritualia* follow the lectures on Eastern meditation of the previous year. Nowhere else in his writings is there to be found a similarly intense comparison between oriental and occidental spiritualism. Its approach corresponds to the aim of the annual Eranos conference: namely, to open up a dialogue between the East and the West. Jung's critical remarks about the embrace of Eastern mysticism by modern Europeans and his suggestion to the latter to come back to their own traditions are illuminated through these lectures.

---

[11] Wilhelm and Jung (1929; 1931).
[12] Jung (1996 [1932]).
[13] Ignatius of Loyola (1996 [1522–24]).

In the winter semester 1940/41, Jung dedicated the third lecture to a summary of his lectures on the *Exercitia spiritualia*. This summary is included as an addendum to Volume 7.

Volume 8: The Psychology of Alchemy *(Winter Semester 1940/1941 and Summer Semester 1941)*

The lectures of the winter semester 1940/41 (from lecture 4 onward; 29 November–28 February; twelve lectures) and the summer semester 1941 (2 May–11 July; eleven lectures) provide an introduction to Jung's psychological understanding of alchemy. He explained the theory of alchemy, outlined the basic concepts, and gave an account of psychological research into it. He showed the relevance of alchemy for the understanding of the psychological process of individuation. The alchemical texts that Jung talked about included, beyond famous examples such as the *Tabula smaragdina* and the *Rosarium philosophorum*, many lesser-known alchemical treatises.

The lectures on alchemy built a cornerstone in the development of Jung's psychological theory. His Eranos lectures from 1935 and 1936 were dedicated to the psychological meaning of alchemy and were later merged together in *Psychology and Alchemy* (1944). The ETH lectures on alchemy highlight the way Jung's thinking on alchemy developed through those years. As an introduction to alchemy, they provide an indispensable tool in order to understand the complexity of his late works such as *Mysterium Coniunctionis*.

REFERENCES

Avalon, Arthur [Sir John Woodroffe], ed. (1919): *Shrî-chakra-sambhâra Tantra*, trans. Kazi Dawa-Samdup (Tantrik Texts 7) (London: Luzac & Co.; Calcutta: Thacker, Spink & Co.).

Flournoy, Théodore (1900 [1899]): *Des Indes à la planète Mars: Étude sur un cas de somnambulisme avec glossolalie* (Paris: F. Alcan, Ch. Eggimann); English translation as *From India to the Planet Mars: A Case of Multiple Personality with Imaginary Languages*, with a foreword by C. G. Jung and commentary by Mireille Cifali, trans. Daniel B. Vermilye (1901), ed. and introduced by Sonu Shamdasani (Princeton, NJ: Princeton University Press, 1994).

Hesse, Hermann (2006). *"Die dunkle und wilde Seite der Seele": Briefwechsel mit seinem Psychoanalytiker Josef Bernhard Lang, 1916–1944*, ed. Thomas Feitknecht (Frankfurt am Main: Suhrkamp).

(Saint) Ignatius of Loyola (1996 [1522–24]). "The Spiritual Exercises," in *Personal Writings: Reminiscences, Spiritual Diary, Selected Letters including the Text of* The Spiritual Exercises, trans. with introduction and notes by Joseph A. Munitiz and Philip Endean (London: Penguin Books, pp. 281–328).

Jung, C. G. (1929). Commentary on "The Secret of the Golden Flower," *CW* 13.

Jung, C. G. (1987). *C. G. Jung Speaking: Interviews and Encounters*, ed. William McGuire and R.F.C. Hull (Bollingen Series 97) (Princeton, NJ: Princeton University Press).

Jung, C. G. (1996 [1932]). *The Psychology of Kundalini Yoga: Notes of the Seminar Given in 1932 by C. G. Jung*, ed. Sonu Shamdasani (Bollingen Series 99) (Princeton, NJ: Princeton University Press).

Kerner, Justinus Andreas Christian (1829): *Die Seherin von Prevorst: Eröffnungen über das innere Leben und über das Hineinragen einer Geisterwelt in die unsere*, 2 vols (Stuttgart and Tübingen: J. G. Cotta'schen Buchhandlung; reprint: Kiel: J. F. Steinkopf Verlag, 2012); English translation as *The Seeress of Prevorst, Being Revelations Concerning the Inner-Life of Man, and the Inter-Diffusion of a World of Spirits in the One We Inhabit*, trans. Catherine Crowe (London: J. C. Moore, 1845; digital reprint: Cambridge: Cambridge University Press, 2011).

Maas, Philipp A. (2006). *Samâdhipâda: Das erste Kapitel des Pâtañjalayogaśâstra zum ersten Mal kritisch ediert* (Aachen: Shaker Verlag).

Müller, F. Max (1894). "Introduction," in *The Buddhist Mahâyâna Texts*, ed. F. Max Müller (The Sacred Books of The East 49) (Oxford: The Clarendon Press).

Editorial Guidelines

WITH THE EXCEPTION of a few preparatory notes, there is no written text by Jung. The present text has been reconstructed by the editors through several notes by participants of Jung's lectures. Through the use of short-hand, the notes taken by Eduard Sidler, a Swiss engineer, and Rivkah Schärf—who later became a well-known religious scholar, psychotherapist, and collaborator of Jung—provide a fairly accurate first basis for the compilation of the lectures. (The shorthand method used is outdated and had to be transcribed by experts in the field.)

Together with the recently discovered scripts by Otto Karthaus, who made a career as one of the first scientific vocational counselors in Switzerland, Bertha Bleuler, and Lucie Stutz-Meyer, the gymnastics teacher of the Jung family, these notes enable us not only to regain access to the contents of Jung's orally delivered lectures, but also to get a feeling for the fascination of the audience with Jung the orator.

There also exists a set of mimeographed notes in English that have been privately published and circulated in limited numbers. These were edited and translated by an English-speaking group in Zurich around Barbara Hannah and Elizabeth Welsh, and present more of a résumé than an attempt at a verbatim account of the content of the lectures. For the first years, Hannah's edition relied only on the notes by Marie-Jeanne Schmid, Jung's secretary at the time; for the later lectures the script of Rivkah Schärf provided the only source for most of the text. The edition was disseminated in private imprints from 1938 to 1968.

The Hannah edition does deviate from Jung's original spoken text as recorded in the other notes. Hannah and Welsh stated in their "Prefatory Note" that their compilation did "not claim to be a verbatim report or literal translation." Hannah was mainly interested in the creation of a readable and consistent text and did not shy away from adding or omitting passages for that purpose. As her edition was only based on one set of notes she could not correct passages where Schmid or Schärf rendered Jung's text wrongly. But as Hannah had the advantage of talking to Jung in person, when she was not sure about the content of a certain passage, her English compilation is sometimes useful to provide additional information to the readers of our edition.

In contrast to a critical edition, it is not intended to provide the differing variations in a separate critical apparatus. Had we faithfully listed all the minor or major variants in the scripts, the text would have become virtually unreadable and thus would have lost the accessibility that is the hallmark of Jung's presentation. For the most part, however, we can be reasonably certain that the compilation accurately reflects what Jung said, although he may have used different words or formulations. Moreover, in quite a number of key passages it was even possible to reconstruct the verbatim content: for example, when different note takers identified certain passages as direct quotes. Variations often do not add to the content and intelligibility, and often originated in errors or lack of understanding by the participant taking notes. In their compilation, the editors have worked according to the principle that as much information as possible should be extracted from the manuscripts. If there are obvious contradictions that cannot be decided by the editor, or, as might be the case, clear errors on behalf of Jung or the listener, this will be clarified by the editor's annotation.

Of the note takers, Eduard Sidler, whose background was in engineering, had the least understanding of Jungian psychology at the beginning, although naturally he became more familiar with it over time. In any case, he did try to protocol faithfully as much as he could, making his the most detailed notes. Sometimes he could no longer follow, however, or clearly misunderstood what was said. On the other hand, we have Welsh and Hannah's version, which in itself was already a collation and obviously heavily edited, but is (at least for the first semesters) the most consistent manuscript and also contains things that are missing in other notes. Moreover, Welsh and Hannah state that "Prof. Jung himself [. . .] has been kind enough to help us with certain passages," although we do not know which these are. In addition, over the course of the years, and also for individual lectures, the quality, accuracy, and reliability of the scripts by the different note takers vary, as is only natural. In short, the best we can do is try to find an approximation to what Jung actually said. In essence, it will always have to be a judgment call how to collate those notes.

It is thus impossible to establish exact editorial principles for each and every situation, such that different editors would inevitably arrive at exactly the same formulations. We have been able only to adhere to some general guidelines, such as "Interfere as little as possible, and as much as necessary," or "Try to establish what the most likely thing was for Jung to have said, on the basis of all the sources available" (including the *Collected Works*, autobiographical works or interviews, other seminars, interviews, etc.). If two transcripts concur, and the third is different, it is usually safe to go with the first two. In some cases, however, it is clear from the context that the two are wrong, and the third is correct; or if all three of them are unclear, it is sometimes possible to "clean up" the text by having recourse to the literature: for instance, when Jung summarizes Kerner's story of the Seeress of Prevorst. As with all scholarly works of this kind, there is no explicit recipe that can be fully spelled out: one has to rely on one's scholarly judgment.

These difficulties not only concern the establishment of the text of Jung's ETH lectures, but also pertain to notes of his seminars in general, many of which have already appeared in print without addressing this problem. For instance, the introduction to the *Dream Analysis* seminar mentions the number of people who were involved in preparing the notes, but there is no account of how they worked, or how they established the text (Jung, 1984, pp. x–xi). Some manuscript notes in the library of the Analytical Psychology Club in Los Angeles indicate that the compilation of the notes involved significant "processing by committee." It is interesting in this regard to compare the sentence structure of the *Dream Analysis* seminar with the 1925 seminar, which was checked by Jung. On 19 October 1925, Jung wrote to Cary Baynes, after checking her notes and acknowledging her literary input, "I faithfully worked through the notes as you will see. I think they are as a whole very accurate. Certain lectures are even fluent, namely those which you could not stop your libido from flowing in" (Cary Baynes papers, contemporary medical archives, Wellcome Library, London).

Our specific situation seems to be a "luxury" problem, as it were, because we have several transcripts, which was often not the case in other seminars. We also have the disadvantage, however, of no longer being able to ask Jung himself, as for instance Cary Baynes, Barbara Hannah, Marie-Jeanne Schmid, or Mary Foote could do. We can only work as best we can, and caution the reader that there is no guarantee that this is "verbatim Jung," although we have tried to come as close as possible to what he actually said.

Acknowledgments

THE PREPARATION FOR publication of these lectures, from thousands of pages of auditors' notes, has involved a long gestation. Like a complex jigsaw puzzle assembled by numerous hands over many years, this work would not have been possible without the contributions of many individuals to whom thanks are due. The Philemon Foundation, under its past presidents Steve Martin, Judith Harris, and Richard Skues, past copresident, Nancy Furlotti, and present president, Caterina Vezzoli, has been responsible for this project since 2004. Without the contributions of its donors, none of the editorial work would have been possible or come to fruition. From 2012 to 2020, the project was supported by Judith Harris at UCL. From 2004 to 2011, the project was principally supported by Carolyn Fay, the C. G. Jung Educational Center of Houston, the MSST Foundation, and the Furlotti Family Foundation. The project was also supported by research grants from the International Association for Analytical Psychology in 2006, 2007, 2008, and 2009.

This publication project was commenced by the former Society of Heirs of C. G. Jung (now the Foundation of the Works of C. G. Jung), between 1993 and 1998. Since its inception, Ulrich Hoerni has been involved in nearly every phase of the project, actively supported between 1993 and 1998 by Peter Jung. The executive committee of the Society of Heirs of C. G. Jung released the scripts for publication. At ETH Zurich, the former head of the archives, Beat Glaus, made scripts available and supervised transcriptions. Ida Baumgartner and Silvia Bandel transcribed shorthand notes of the lectures; C. A. Meier provided general information about the lectures; Marie-Louise von Franz provided information about the editing of Barbara Hannah's scripts; Helga Egner and Sonu Shamdasani gave editorial advice; at the Jung Family Archives, Franz Jung and Andreas Jung made scripts and related materials available; at the Archives of the Psychological Club, the former chairman, Alfred Ribi, and the librarian, Gudrun Seel, made lecture notes available; Sonu Shamdasani found notes taken by Lucie Stutz-Meyer. Rolf Auf der Maur and Leo La Rosa provided legal advice and managed contracts.

In 2004, the Philemon Foundation took on the project, in collaboration with the Society of Heirs of C. G. Jung, and since 2007, its successor organization the Foundation of the Works of C. G. Jung, and the ETH Zurich Archives. At the Foundation of the Works of C. G. Jung, Ulrich Hoerni, former president and executive director, Daniel Niehus, president, Thomas Fischer, past executive director, and Carl Christian Jung, present executive director, oversaw the project, and Ulrich Hoerni, Thomas Fischer, and Bettina Kaufmann, editorial assistant, reviewed the manuscript. Since 2007, Peter Fritz of the Paul & Peter Fritz Agency has been responsible for managing contracts. At the ETH Zurich Archives, Rudolf Mumenthaler, Michael Gasser, former directors, Christian Huber, director, and Yvonne Voegeli made scripts and related documents available. Nomi Kluger-Nash provided Rivkah Schärf's shorthand notes of some of the lectures, which were then transcribed by Silvia Bandel. Steve Martin provided Bertha Bleuler's shorthand notes of some of the lectures.

The editorial work has been overseen by Sonu Shamdasani, general editor of the Philemon Foundation. From 2012 the compilation and editorial work has been undertaken by Ernst Falzeder and Martin Liebscher at the Health Humanities Centre and German Department at UCL. They were joined by Christopher Wagner in 2018.

The editor of this volume, Martin Liebscher, would like to express his gratitude to the board of the Philemon Foundation, and in particular Judith Harris for her ongoing support throughout the work on this project; to Sonu Shamdasani for his scholarly guidance and help; to Thomas Fischer, Ulrich Hoerni, and Bettina Kaufmann from the Foundation of the Works of C. G. Jung; to the collaborators on the edition of Jung's ETH lectures, Ernst Falzeder and Christopher Wagner; to Fred Appel and his team at Princeton University Press; to Caitlin Stephens for her excellent translation and the George Sand reference; to Francesca Bugliani Knox; to Florent Serina for sharing his expertise on the French reception of Jung; to Jens Schlieter, Hans Gerald Hödl, and the Yggdrasill list for religious studies; to Tommaso Priviero for the translation from Italian; to Thomas Wilks for his transcription work; to Yvonne Voegeli from the C. G. Jung archive at the ETH library; to Tony Woolfson; and, especially, to his wife, Luz Nelly.

COMPILED BY ERNST FALZEDER,
MARTIN LIEBSCHER, AND SONU SHAMDASANI

Date	Events in Jung's Career	World Events
1933		
January	Jung continues his English seminar on Christiana Morgan's visions, on Wednesday mornings.	
30 January		Hitler is appointed Reich chancellor in Germany by the president, Paul von Hindenburg.
February	Jung lectures in Germany (Cologne and Essen) on "The Meaning of Psychology for Modern Man" (*CW* 10).	
27 February		Reichstag fire in Berlin. The fire, possibly a false flag operation, was used as evidence by the Nazis that the Communists were plotting against the German government, and the event is seen as pivotal in the establishment of Nazi Germany. Many arrests of leftists. On 28 February, the most important basic rights of the Weimar republic were suspended.
4 March		"Self-dissolution" of the Austrian parliament, and authoritarian regime under Chancellor Engelbert Dollfuß established.
5 March		In the German federal elections, the National Socialists become the strongest party, with 43.9% of the vote.

Date	Events in Jung's Career	World Events
13 March–6 April	Jung accepts the invitation of Hans Eduard Fierz to accompany him on a cruise in the Mediterranean, including a visit to Palestine.	
18–19 March	Athens. Visits the Parthenon and the theatre of Dionysus.	
23 March		The German parliament passes the *Ermächtigungsgesetz* (Enabling Act), according to which the government is empowered to enact laws without the consent of the parliament or the president of the Reich—a self-disempowerment of the parliament.
25–27 March	Jung and Fierz visit Jerusalem, Bethlehem, and the Dead Sea.	
28–31 March	Egypt, with visits to Gizeh and Luxor.	
March to June		Franklin D. Roosevelt starts the "New Deal" in the United States.
1 April		Nationwide boycott of Jewish shops in Germany.
5 April	Via Corfu and Ragusa, the *General von Steuben* arrives in Venice, from where Jung and Fierz take the train to Zurich.	
6 April	Ernst Kretschmer resigns from the presidency of the General Medical Society for Psychotherapy (GMSP) in protest against "political influences." Jung, as vice-president, accepts the acting presidency and editorship of the society's journal, the *Zentralblatt für Psychotherapie*.	
7 April		The German parliament passes a law that excludes Jews and dissidents from the civil service.

Date	Events in Jung's Career	World Events
22 April		In Germany, "non-Aryan" teachers are excluded from their professional organizations; "non-Aryan" and "Marxist" physicians lose their national health insurance accreditation.
26 April		Foundation of the Gestapo.
1–10 May		Ban on trade unions in Germany.
10 May		Public burning of books, including those of Freud, in Berlin and other German cities.
14 May	The *Berliner Börsen-Zeitung* publishes "Against Psychoanalysis," describing Jung as the reformer of psychotherapy.	
22 May		Sándor Ferenczi dies in Budapest.
27 May–1 June		The German government imposes the so-called Thousand Mark Ban, an economic sanction against Austria, whereby German citizens have to pay a fee of 1,000 Reichsmarks (the equivalent of about $5,000 in 2015) to enter Austria.
21 June	Jung accepts the presidency of the GMSP.	
26 June	Interview with Jung on Radio Berlin, conducted by Adolf Weizsäcker.	
26 June–1 July	Jung gives the "Berlin Seminar," opened by a lecture by Heinrich Zimmer on 25 June.	
14 July		"Law for the prevention of hereditarily diseased offspring" in Germany, which allows the compulsory sterilization of any citizen with alleged hereditary diseases.
14 July		In Germany, all parties with the exception of the NSDAP are banned or dissolve themselves.

Date	Events in Jung's Career	World Events
August	Jung's first attendance at the Eranos meeting in Ascona, giving a talk on "On the Empirical Knowledge of the Individuation Process" (retitled, CW 9.1).	
15 September	Foundation of a new German chapter of the GMSP, whose statutes demand unconditional loyalty to Hitler. Matthias H. Göring, a cousin of Hermann Göring, is named its president.	
22 September		Law on the "Reich Chamber of Culture" in Germany, enforces conformity (*Gleichschaltung*) of culture in general, tantamount to an occupational ban on Jews and artists who produce "degenerate" art.
7–8 October	Meeting of the Swiss Academy of Medical Science at Prangins. Jung presents a contribution on hallucination (CW 18).	
20 October	Jung's first lecture on "Modern Psychology" at ETH.	
5 December		Repeal of Prohibition in the United States with the passage of the Twenty-First Amendment.
10 December		Nobel Prize in Physics awarded to Erwin Schrödinger and Paul A. M. Dirac "for the discovery of new productive forms of atomic theory."
December	Jung publishes an editorial in the *Zentralblatt* of the GMSP, in which he contrasts "Germanic" with "Jewish" psychology (CW 10). The same issue contains a manifesto of Nazi principles by Matthias Göring that, be it by oversight or on purpose, also appears in the international, not only the German, edition, against Jung's wishes. Jung threatens to resign from the presidency, but ultimately stays on.	

Date	Events in Jung's Career	World Events

Other publications in 1933:

"Crime and Soul," *CW* 18

"On Psychology," revised version in *CW* 8

"Brother Klaus," *CW* 11

Foreword to Esther Harding, *The Way of All Women*, *CW* 18

Review of Gustav Richard Heyer's *Der Organismus der Seele*, *CW* 18

1934

Date	Events in Jung's Career	World Events
20 January		German "Work Order Act" and introduction of the "Führer principle" in the economy.
12–16 February		Civil war in Austria, resulting in a ban on all social-democratic parties and organizations, mass arrests, and summary executions.
23 February	Jung's last lecture at ETH in the winter semester of 1933/34.	
27 February	Gustav Bally publishes a letter to the editor of the *Neue Zürcher Zeitung* ("Psychotherapy of German Origin?"), in which he strongly criticizes Jung for his alleged Nazi leanings and antisemitic views.	
Spring	Beginning of Jung's serious and detailed study of alchemy, assisted by Marie-Louise von Franz.	
13–14 March	Jung publishes a rejoinder to Bally in the *Neue Zürcher Zeitung* ("Contemporary Events," *CW* 10).	
16 March	Publication of B. Cohen, "Is C. G. Jung 'Conformed'?" in *Israelitisches Wochenblatt für die Schweiz*.	
21 March	Jung's last seminar on Christiana Morgan's visions. The participants opt for continuing the English Wednesday morning seminars with one on Nietzsche's *Zarathustra*.	

Date	Events in Jung's Career	World Events
March–April	Publication of Jung's *The Reality of the Soul: Applications and Advances of Modern Psychology*, with contributions from Hugo Rosenthal, Emma Jung, and W. Müller Kranefeldt	
April	Jung publishes "Soul and Death" (*CW* 8).	
April	Interview with Jung, "Does the World Stand on the Verge of Spiritual Rebirth?" (*Hearst's International-Cosmopolitan*, New York).	
ca. April	Jung publishes "On the Present Position of Psychotherapy" in the *Zentralblatt* (*CW* 10).	
20 April	Jung's first ETH lecture in the summer semester.	
2 May	Jung starts the English seminar on Nietzsche's *Zarathustra* (until 15 February 1939).	
5 May	Jung's inaugural lecture at ETH, "A General Review of Complex Theory" (*CW* 8).	
10–13 May	Jung presides at the Seventh Congress for Psychotherapy in Bad Nauheim, Germany, organised by the GMSP, and repeats his talk on complex theory. Foundation of an international umbrella society, the IGMSP, organized in national groups that are free to make their own regulations. On Jung's suggestion, statutes are passed that (1) provide that no single national society can command more than 40% of the votes, and (2) allow that individuals who are banned from the German Society (that is, Jews) can join the International Society as "individual members." Jung is confirmed as president and as editor of the *Zentralblatt*.	

Date	Events in Jung's Career	World Events
29 May	James Kirsch, "The Jewish Question in Psychotherapy: A Few Remarks on an Essay by C. G. Jung," in the *Jüdische Rundschau*.	
31 May		The "Barmen Declaration," mainly instigated by Karl Barth, openly repudiates the Nazi ideology. It becomes one of the founding documents of the Confessing Church, the spiritual resistance against National Socialism.
15 June	Erich Neumann, letter to the *Jüdische Rundschau* regarding Kirsch's "The Jewish Question in Psychotherapy."	
30 June/ 1 July		The so-called Night of the Long Knives, or Röhm purge: SA leader Ernst Röhm, other high-ranking SA members, and alleged political opponents are executed on Hitler's direct orders, among them Röhm's personal physician Karl-Günther Heimsoth, a longstanding member of the IGMSP and a personal acquaintance of Jung.
13 July	Jung's last ETH lecture in the summer semester.	
25 July		Failed putsch attempt by the Nazis in Austria, in which the Austrian chancellor Engelbert Dollfuß is murdered.
29 July		New government in Austria under chancellor Kurt Schuschnigg, who tries to control the Nazi movement by his own authoritarian, right-wing regime.
2 August		Death of Reich president Paul von Hindenburg. Hitler assumes chancellorship and presidency in a personal union, as well as supreme command of the Wehrmacht.
3 August	Gerhard Adler, "Is Jung an Antisemite?," in the *Jüdische Rundschau*.	

Date	Events in Jung's Career	World Events
August	Eranos meeting in Ascona. Jung talks on "The Archetypes of the Collective Unconscious" (CW 9.1).	
1–7 October	Jung gives a seminar at the Société de Psychologie in Basel.	
26 October	First ETH lecture of the winter semester 1934/35.	

Other publications in 1934:

With M. H. Göring, "Geheimrat Sommer on his 70th Birthday," *Zentralblatt* 7

Circular letter, *Zentralblatt*, CW 10

Addendum to "Zeitgenössisches," CW 10

Foreword to Carl Ludwig Schleich, *Die Wunder der Seele*, CW 18

Foreword to Gerhard Adler, *Entdeckung der Seele*, CW 18

Review of Hermann Keyserling, *La Révolution mondiale*, CW 10

1935

Date	Events in Jung's Career	World Events
n.d.	Jung becomes titular professor at ETH.	
	Jung completes his tower at Bollingen, by adding a courtyard and a loggia.	
19 January	Jung accepts an invitation to lecture in Holland.	
22 January	Foundation of the Swiss chapter of the IGMSP.	
24 February		Swiss extend the period of military training.
1 March		Saarland reunited with Germany, marking the beginning of German territorial expansion under the National Socialists.
8 March	Final ETH lecture of the winter semester 1934/35.	

Date	Events in Jung's Career	World Events
16 March		The German government officially renounces its future adherence to the disarmament clauses of the Versailles Treaty.
26 March		Switzerland bans slanderous criticisms of state institutions in the press.
27–30 March	Eighth Congress of the IGMSP in Bad Nauheim (CW 10).	
2 May		Franco–Russian Alliance.
3 May	First ETH lecture of the summer semester 1935.	
May	Jung attends and lectures at an IGMSP symposium on "Psychotherapy in Switzerland."	
5 June		The Swiss government introduces an extensive armament expansion program.
11 June		Disarmament conference in Geneva ends in failure.
28 June	Publication of Jung's contribution at the May IGMSP symposium, "What Is Psychotherapy?" in the *Schweizerische Ärztezeitung für Standesfragen* (CW 16).	
12 July	Jung's last ETH lecture in the summer semester.	
August	Eranos lecture on "Dream Symbols of the Individuation Process" (CW 9.1).	
15 September		Passing of the so-called Nuremberg Laws in Germany depriving Jews (defined as all those one-quarter Jewish or more) and other non-"Aryans" of German citizenship, and prohibiting sexual relations and marriage between Germans and Jews.

Date	Events in Jung's Career	World Events
30 September–4 October	Jung gives five lectures at the Institute of Medical Psychology in London, to an audience of around one hundred (CW 18).	
October		Conclusion of the "Long March" in China.
2 October	Publication of Jung's "The Psychology of Dying" (a shortened version of "Soul and Death") in the *Münchner Neueste Nachrichten* (CW 8).	
2–3 October		Italian invasion of Ethiopia.
25 October	First ETH lecture of the winter semester 1935/36.	
6 October	Interview with Jung, "Man's Immortal Mind," *The Observer*.	
8 November		Switzerland tightens banking secrecy laws (leading to the introduction of numbered bank accounts).
December		Nobel Peace Prize awarded to the leftist German journalist and editor Carl von Ossietzky. Hitler forbids Germans to accept Nobel Prizes.
15 October	The Dutch national group of the IGMSP retracts its offer to host its next international congress, because of events in Nazi Germany. In his answer, Jung states that this "compromises the ultimate purpose of our international association," and declares that he will resign as its president, but does not do so.	

Date	Events in Jung's Career	World Events

Other publications in 1935:

The Relations between the I and the Unconscious, 7th edition, CW 7

Introduction and psychological commentary on the *The Tibetan Book of the Dead*, CW 11

"Votum C. G. Jung", CW 10

"Editorial" (*Zentralblatt* 8), CW 10

"Editorial Note" (*Zentralblatt* 8), CW 10

"Fundamentals of Practical Psychotherapy", CW 16

Foreword to Olga von Koenig-Fachsenfeld, *Wandlungen des Traumproblems von der Romantik bis zur Gegenwart*, CW 18

Foreword to Rose Mehlich, *J. H. Fichtes Seelenlehre und ihre Beziehung zur Gegenwart*, CW 18

1936

Date	Events in Jung's Career	World Events
February	"Yoga and the West" (CW 11).	
February	"Psychological Typology" (CW 6).	
27 February		Death of Iwan Pawlow.
Spring	Formation of the Analytical Psychology Club in New York City.	
March	Jung publishes "Wotan" in the *Neue Schweizer Rundschau* (CW 10).	
6 March	Final ETH lecture of the winter semester 1935/36.	
7 March		German military forces enter the Rhineland, violating the terms of the Treaty of Versailles and the Locarno Treaties. This remilitarization shifts power in Europe away from France and toward Germany.
28 March		The property of the Internationaler Psychoanalytischer Verlag, and all its stock of books and journals, are confiscated.

Date	Events in Jung's Career	World Events
May		Foundation of the Deutsches Institut für psychologische Forschung und Psychotherapie in Berlin, headed by M. H. Göring ("Göring Institute"), with working groups of Jungian, Adlerian, and Freudian orientation. Psychoanalysis was tolerated, but on the condition that its terminology be altered.
May	"Concerning the Archetypes, with Special Consideration of the Anima Concept," in the *Zentralblatt* (CW 9.1).	
1 May	First ETH lecture of the summer semester 1936.	
July		Beginning of Spanish Civil War.
10 July	Final ETH lecture of the summer semester 1936.	
19 July	Jung and Göring attend a meeting of psychotherapists in Basel, with representatives of different depth-psychological schools (among others, Ernest Jones for the International Psycho-Analytical Association).	
August	Eranos meeting; Jung speaks on "Representations of Redemption in Alchemy" (CW 12).	
1–16 August		Summer Olympics in Berlin. Germans who are Jewish or Roma are virtually barred from participating.
21–30 August	Jung travels on board the *Georgia* from Le Havre to New York City. Upon arrival in New York, he releases a "Press Communiqué on Visiting the United States," setting forth his political—or, as he insisted, his nonpolitical—position.	

Date	Events in Jung's Career	World Events
September	Jung lectures at the Harvard Tercentenary Conference on Arts and Sciences, on "Psychological Factors Determining Human Behavior" (*CW* 8), and receives an honorary degree. His invitation had given rise to controversy.	
12–15 September	Jung is guest of the Anglican bishop James De Wolf Perry in Providence, Rhode Island, addresses the organization The American Way, and then leaves for Milton, Mass., where he is guest of G. Stanley Cobb.	
ca. 19 September	Jung starts a seminar on Bailey Island, based on Wolfgang Pauli's dreams.	
2 October	Jung gives a public lecture at the Plaza Hotel in New York City, privately published by the New York Analytical Psychology Club under the title, "The Concept of the Collective Unconscious." (*CW* 9.1).	
3 October	Jung leaves New York City.	
4 October	Interview with Jung, "Roosevelt 'Great,' Is Jung's Analysis," *New York Times* (later published under the title, "The 2,000,000-Year-Old-Man").	
14 October	Jung lectures at the Institute of Medical Psychology, London, on "Psychology and National Problems" (*CW* 18).	
15 October	Interview with Jung, "Why the World Is in a Mess. Dr. Jung Tells Us How Nature Is Changing Modern Woman," *Daily Sketch*.	
18 October	Interview with Jung, "The Psychology of Dictatorship," *The Observer*.	

Date	Events in Jung's Career	World Events
19 October	Jung lectures before the Abernethian Society, St. Bartholomew's Hospital, London, on the concept of the collective unconscious (CW 9.1).	
25 October		Secret peace treaty between Germany and Italy.
27 October	Jung begins his seminars at ETH on children's dreams and old books on dream interpretation.	
3 November		Franklin D. Roosevelt is re-elected for his second term.
25 November		Anti-Comintern Pact between Germany and the Empire of Japan, directed against the Third (Communist) International.
10 December		Abdication of Edward VIII in the United Kingdom.

Other publications in 1936:

Review of Gustav Richard Heyer, *Praktische Seelenheilkunde*, CW 18

1937

Date	Events in Jung's Career	World Events
3–5 January	Jung participates in the workshop of the Köngener Kreis (1–6 January) in Königsfeld (Black Forest, Germany), on "Grundfragen der Seelenkunde und Seelenführung" (Fundamental questions of the study and guidance of the soul).	
30 January		Hitler formally withdraws Germany from the Versailles Treaty, and thus from making reparation payments, and demands a return of Germany's colonies.
23 April 1937	After a break in the winter semester, Jung's ETH lectures recommence.	

Date	Events in Jung's Career	World Events
26 April		Germany and Italy are allied with Franco and the fascists in Spain. German and Italian airplanes bomb the city of Guernica, killing more than 1,600.
23 May		Death of John D. Rockefeller.
28 May		Death of Alfred Adler in Aberdeen.
9 July	Final ETH lecture of the summer semester 1937.	
19 July		The Nazi Party's exhibition on "Degenerate Art" opens at the Institute of Archaeology, Munich.
August	Eranos lecture on "The Visions of Zosimos" (CW 13).	
2–4 October	Ninth International Medical Congress for Psychotherapy in Copenhagen, under the presidency of Jung (CW 10).	
October	Jung is invited to Yale University to deliver the fifteenth series of "Lectures on Religion in the Light of Science and Philosophy" under the auspices of the Dwight Harrington Terry Foundation (published as Psychology and Religion, CW 11). Dream seminar (continuation from the Bailey Island seminars), Analytical Psychology Club, New York.	
December	Jung is invited by the British government to take part in the celebrations of the 25th anniversary of the founding of the Indian Science Congress Association at the University of Calcutta. He is accompanied by Harold Fowler McCormick Jr. (1898–1973) and travels through India for three months.	

Date	Events in Jung's Career	World Events
13 December		In China, Nanjing falls to the Japanese. In the six weeks to follow, the Japanese troops commit war crimes against the civilian population, known as the Nanjing Massacre.
17 December	Jung's arrival in Bombay by the P&O liner *Cathay*.	
19 December	Jung reaches Hyderabad, where he is awarded an honorary doctorate by Osmania University in Hyderabad; night train to Aurangabad.	
20 December	Aurangabad: visits the Kailash Temple at Ellora, and Daulatabad.	
21 December	Visits the caves at Ajanta.	
22 December	Sanchi, Bhopal: visits the Great Stupa.	
23 December	Taj Mahal, Agra.	
27 December	Benares; visits Sarnath.	
28 December	Jung is awarded the D.Litt. (honoris causa) degree by the Benares Hindu University; gives presentation at the Philosophy Department: "Fundamental Conceptions Of Analytical Psychology"; guest of Swiss interpreter of Indian art Alice Boner; visits the Vishvanatha Śiva Temple.	
29 December	Calcutta.	
31 December	Travels to Darjeeling.	

Other publications in 1937:

"On the Psychological Diagnosis of Facts: The Fact Experiment in the Näf Court Case," CW 2

Date	Events in Jung's Career	World Events
1938		
1 January	Three-hour conversation with Rimpotche Lingdam Gomchen at the Bhutia Busty monastery.	
3 January	Opening of the 25th anniversary of the founding of the Indian Science Congress Association at the University of Calcutta.	
	Jung is treated in hospital in Calcutta.	
7 January	Jung is awarded (in absentia) the degree of Doctor of Law (honoris causa) by the University of Calcutta.	
10 January	Lecture at the College of Science, University of Calcutta: "Archetypes of the Collective Unconscious."	
11 January	Lecture at the Ashutosh College, University of Calcutta: "The Conceptions of Analytical Psychology."	
13 January	Visits the Temple of Konark ("Black Pagoda").	
21 January	Visits the Chennakesava Temple (also called the Kesava Temple) and the temple of Somanathapur (Mysore).	
26 January	Jung in Trivandrum; lecture at the University of Travancore: "The Collective Unconscious."	
27 January	Lecture at the University of Travancore: "Historical Developments of the Idea of the Unconscious."	
28 January	Ferry to Ceylon (Sri Lanka).	
29 January	Colombo.	

Date	Events in Jung's Career	World Events
30 January	Train to Kandy.	
1 February	Return to Colombo.	
2 February	Embarks on the SS *Corfu* to return to Europe.	
12 March		Annexation of Austria by Nazi Germany.
27 April		Edmund Husserl, the founding philosopher of phenomenology, dies in Freiburg.
May		The League of Nations acknowledges the neutral status of Switzerland.
29 April	After his return from India, Jung's ETH lecture series recommences.	
4 June		Sigmund Freud leaves Vienna; after a stop in Paris, he arrives in London two days later.
8 July	Final ETH lecture of the summer semester 1938.	
29 July– 2 August	Tenth International Medical Congress for Psychotherapy, at Balliol College, Oxford, under the presidency of Jung; awarded honorary doctorate by the University of Oxford. Gives "Presidential Address" (CW 10).	
August	Eranos lecture on "Psychological Aspects of the Mother Archetype" (CW 9.1).	
29 September		Munich Pact permits Nazi Germany the immediate occupation of the Sudentenland.
		Agreement between Switzerland and Germany concerning the stamping of German Jewish passports with "J."
28 October	First ETH lecture of the winter semester 1938/39.	

Date	Events in Jung's Career	World Events
October	Jung's ETH seminar series on the psychological interpretation of children's dreams commences in the winter term of 1938/39.	
9 November		A Swiss theology student, Maurice Bavaud, fails to assassinate Hitler at a Nazi parade in Munich, and is guillotined.
9/10 November		Pogrom against Jews in Nazi Germany ("Kristallnacht").
23 November	Jung gives his witness statement at the retrial of the murder case of Hans Näf.	

Other publications in 1938:

With Richard Wilhelm, *The Secret of the Golden Flower*, 2nd edition, CW 13

"On the *Rosarium philosophorum*," CW 18

Foreword to Gertrud Gilli, *Der dunkle Bruder*, CW 18

1939

January 1939	"Diagnosing the Dictators," interview with H. R. Knicker-bocker, *Hearst's International-Cosmopolitan*.	
15 February	The last of Jung's seminars on Nietzsche's *Zarathustra*, and hence of his regular English-language seminars.	
3 March	Final ETH lecture of the winter semester 1938/39.	
28 March		Madrid surrenders to the Nationalists; Franco declares victory on 1 April.
April	Visits the West Country in England in connection with Emma Jung's Grail research.	
4 April	Lecture at the Royal Society of Medicine in London, "On the Psychogenesis of Schizophrenia" (CW 3).	

Date	Events in Jung's Career	World Events
5 April	Lecture at the Guild of Pastoral Psychology, London, on "The Symbolic Life."	
28 April	First ETH lecture of the summer semester 1939.	
May	Surendranath Dasgupta lectures on Patañjali's *Yoga Sûtra* in the Psychology Club Zurich.	
	Interview with Howard Philp, "Jung Diagnoses the Dictators," *Psychologist*.	
July	At a meeting of delegates of the International General Medical Society for Psychotherapy Jung offers his resignation.	
7 July	Final lecture of the summer semester 1939.	
August	Eranos lecture "Concerning Rebirth" (CW 9.1).	
1 September		German troops invade Poland; Britain and France declare war on Germany two days later: beginning of World War II.
		Switzerland proclaims neutrality.
23 September		Sigmund Freud dies in London at the age of eighty-three.
	Jung moves his family for safety to Saanen in the Bernese Oberland.	
1 October	Jung's obituary of Freud is published in the *Sonntagsblatt der Basler Nachrichten* (CW 15).	
3 November	First ETH lecture of the winter semester 1939/40.	

Date	Events in Jung's Career	World Events
October	Jung's ETH seminar series on the psychological interpretation of children's dreams commences in the winter term 1939/40.	

Other publications in 1939:

"Consciousness, Unconscious and Individuation," CW 9.1

"The Dreamlike World of India" and "What India Can Teach Us," CW 10

Foreword to Daisetz Teitaro Suzuki's *Introduction to Zen-Buddhism*, CW 10

1940

Date	Events in Jung's Career	World Events
8 March	Final ETH lecture of the winter semester 1939/40.	
9 April		German troops invade Norway and Denmark.
10 May		German invasion of Belgium, the Netherlands, and Luxembourg.
12 May		France is invaded by Germany.
14 June		German troops occupy Paris.
20 June	In a letter to Matthias Göring, Jung offers his resignation of the presidency of the International General Medical Society for Psychotherapy.	
12 July	Jung sends his final letter of resignation to M. Göring.	
19 July		Hermann Göring is appointed *Reichsmarschall*.
August	Eranos lecture on "A Psychological Approach to the Dogma of the Trinity" (CW 11).	
7 September		Germany begins bombing raids against London ("the Blitz," until May 1941).

Date	Events in Jung's Career	World Events
29 October	Jung's ETH seminar series on children's dreams commences in the winter semester 1940/41.	
8 November	First ETH lecture of the winter semester 1940/41.	

Other publications in 1940:

Foreword to Jolande Jacobi, *Die Psychologie von C. G. Jung*, CW 18

1941

13 January		Death of James Joyce in Zurich.
28 February	Final lecture of the winter semester 1940/41.	
2 May	First ETH lecture of the summer semester 1941.	
11 July	Jung's final ETH lecture.	
August	Eranos lecture on "Transformation Symbolism in the Mass" (*CW* 11).	
7 September	Presents a lecture on "Paracelsus as a Doctor" to the Swiss Society for the History of Medicine in Basel (*CW* 15).	
5 October	Presents a lecture on "Paracelsus as a Spiritual Phenomenon" in Einsiedeln, on the four-hundredth anniversary of the death of Paracelsus (*CW* 13).	

Other publications in 1941:

Essays on a Science of Mythology: The Myth of the Divine Child and the Mysteries of Eleusis, with Karl Kerényi, CW 9.1

"Return to the Simple Life," CW 18

MARTIN LIEBSCHER

When I was engrossed with psychology and alchemy—no, to be more precise, it was when I was giving the seminar on Ignatius of Loyola—once, in the night, I had a vision of Christ. One night I awoke and there, at the foot of the bed, I saw a crucifix. Not quite life-sized. It was very clear and couched in a bright light. In this light, Christ was hanging on the cross and then I saw that it was as if his entire body were made of gold, as if of green gold. It looked wonderful. I was scared to death by it. Just then I was particularly engrossed by the "Anima Christi" [prayer]. There is a very beautiful meditation by Ignatius on it.

—C. G. Jung, 27 June 1957[14]

FROM OCTOBER 1938 to June 1939 Carl Gustav Jung's weekly lectures at the Swiss Federal Institute of Technology Zurich (ETH) were dedicated to the practice of active imagination as part of the individuation process, and its parallels in Eastern meditative practice.[15] Jung discussed the understanding of meditation in texts such as the *Amitâyur-dhyâna-sûtra*, *Shrî-chakra-shambhâra Tantra* or Patañjali's *Yoga Sûtra*. Notwithstanding the professed focus on Eastern spirituality, his lectures were strongly comparative as between East and West, for he also discussed Christian meditative practice as depicted in works by mystics such as Meister Eckhart (ca. 1260–ca. 1328) or Richard of Saint Victor (d. 1173). However, it must have come as a surprise to the audience when Jung concluded his "remarks on Yoga" in the midst of the summer term on 9 June 1939 with a

---

[14] Jung and Jaffé (forthcoming).
[15] *JMP*, vol. 6 (2021).

quotation from *The Secret of the Golden Flower* in order to begin the next lecture of 16 June with a "turn Westward" and a "return to our own Europe." From that date until 8 March 1940, he developed an interpretation of Ignatius of Loyola's *Exercitia spiritualia*, a text that he regarded as the prime example of the description of a Christian practice comparable to Eastern meditative techniques.

The *Exercitia spiritualia* were probably written around 1524 when Ignatius, after his conversion experience in 1521 and a pilgrimage to Jerusalem, settled in Barcelona for a period of two years. They were published in a limited edition during his lifetime, but none of these copies survived. The earliest edition we have today is a Spanish text, known as "the Autograph," which was not in Ignatius's own handwriting, but contains his corrections and annotations. As today's editors of the English translation make clear, there was an understandable reluctance of Ignatius to disseminate the text to a wider audience "as it was always through the *spoken* word that he introduced people to the *Exercises*. Somebody is required to 'give' the exercises, and only persons who have experienced the process that set these exercises in motion can do this."[16] For the uninitiated, the text looks rather uninspiring and reads like a practical manual for spiritual advisors. It opens with a set of twenty annotations, followed by detailed instructions on how to guide and accompany the retreatant through the four weeks of exercises. Whereas the focus at the beginning is to remove any obstacles that might hinder a clear and honest prayer to God, the exercises increasingly center on the life and teachings of Jesus Christ. In the first week, the retreatant is asked mainly to reflect on their sins and to meditate on the whereabouts of sinners' souls after death. This needs to be done with the involvement of all the physical senses, to create the most vivid possible impression. It is with this same intensity that the retreatant is then instructed to follow the birth, death, and resurrection of Christ in the weeks that follow. This practice of imagining oneself into biblical settings prompted Jung to draw parallels with his own psychological method of active imagination, which formed the overarching topic of his ETH lectures at the time. It was in this that he saw the similarities with the aforementioned spiritual texts from the East, characterizing the *Spiritual Exercises* as a Western equivalent to yoga.

---

[16] *IPW*, p. 281.

JUNG'S SOURCES, REVEALED AND UNREVEALED

Within Jung's work, this thorough examination of the Ignatian exercises is unique, and the choice of this topic for an entire lecture series does come as a surprise; consequently these lectures on Ignatian meditation have aroused greater interest than the other ETH lecture series with a more commonly Jungian theme to them. The first two lectures on the *Exercises* were reprinted from Barbara Hannah's original notes,[17] which were based on the script by Rivkah Schärf, in an abridged form in the journal *Spring* in 1977 and 1978.[18] The major monograph by Kenneth L. Becker in 2001 entitled *Unlikely Companions* provides the hitherto most thorough interpretation of the lectures.[19] But neither Becker nor the *Spring* editors realized the extent to which Jung's Ignatius lectures are based on the recycling of existing scholarly literature. In particular, the two opening lectures of 16 and 23 July are an almost verbatim rendition of an unpublished German translation of the Swedish monograph by Bernhard Hegardt entitled *Religion och Själsträning. En Studie i Jesuiternas Andliga Övingar*, from 1937.[20] Almost the entire historical and thematic introduction to Jung's lecture on the *Exercitia spiritualia* can be found in Hegardt's study. The present editor located a typescript of this translation, which has a number of handwritten annotations by Jung, in the Jung archive. The identity of the translator is as yet unknown. He or she was probably someone from the Jung's Zurich circle with a command of Swedish; or Jung may have paid a professional translator to render the text into German. Although Jung recommended the book at the beginning of the third lecture, he did not reveal to his audience how heavily he had relied on this source in the previous lectures.

Another important source that formed the basis of Jung's lectures was Philipp Funk's *Ignatius von Loyola*.[21] Funk (1884–1937) was a Catholic theologian and historian, who left the seminary twice due to his support of Catholic modernism. His collection of essays *Von der Kirche des Geistes* (On the Church of the spirit) (1913) was put on the Index. His translation of Ignatius's writings was published with a German Protestant publisher in 1913 as part of Gustav Pfannmüller's series *Die Klassiker der*

---

[17] BH, vol. 2, pp. 153–59.
[18] *Spring: Annual of Archetypal Psychology and Jungian Thought* (Zurich, 1977), pp. 183–201; (Zurich, 1978), pp. 28–36.
[19] Becker (2001).
[20] Hegardt (1937).
[21] Funk (1913a).

Religion (The classics of religion). The volume consists of a lengthy introduction, a translation of the *Exercitia spiritualia* based on the Latin edition by the Institutum Societatis Iesu from 1893, the "Rules to Understand the Movement of the Soul," usually published as an addendum to the exercises, and the autobiography of Ignatius known as *Reminiscences*. Jung used Funk's edition as the textual basis for his lectures, together with the *Praxis exercitiorum spiritualium*, a Latin commentary on the *Exercitia* by Sebastián Izquierdo, from 1695.[22] He observed,

> I must give you some literature about the Ignatian exercises. There is a slim, highly recommended book by Funk which came out in 1913 and is available in the Zentralbibliothek [Zurich central library]: *Ignatius von Loyola*. [. . .] There's a huge amount of literature about Ignatius and his exercises written by the Jesuits themselves, as well as by other Catholic scholars. Many Protestants have also written about them. But it's pointless for me to swamp you with literature.[23]

In his lectures, Jung used Funk's edition to quote from Ignatius's autobiography, especially those passages that concerned the visions, and from the annotations to the exercises.

CATHOLIC MODERNISM

Philipp Funk was not the only representative of Catholic modernism who played a significant role in forming Jung's view of Ignatius and the *Exercitia spiritualia* as depicted in the lectures of 1939/40. From 1933 onward, Jung had an opportunity to discuss the *Exercitia spiritualia* with Ernesto Buonaiuti (1881–1946) at the annual Eranos conferences in Ascona, where the former Catholic priest and historian of Christianity, who due to his defence of Catholic modernism was excommunicated in 1925,[24] lectured from 1933 to 1940. In 1935 he was asked to speak on the "The Exercises of Saint Ignatius of Loyola."[25] The image of Ignatius and the Jesuits that

---

[22] Izquierdo (1695). JLN contains a handwritten list: "Literature: 1. Izquierdo S.J./ 2. Phil. Funk: Ignatius v. Loyola 1913/ 3. Victoriner/ Thomas à Kempis: Imit. Christ."

[23] Summer semester 1939, Lecture 9 (see below).

[24] Buonaiuti was the author of *The Programme of Modernism* (Buonaiuti, 1908 [1907]) as a reply to the encyclical of Pius X *Pascendi Dominici gregis*, the pope's condemnation of modernism.

[25] Buonaiuti (1936). In his autobiography *Pellegrino di Roma* (1945), Buonaiuti commented on the reception of his lecture at the Eraonos conference: "In Ascona, I was dealing with Ignatius's exercises in front on an audience which almost in its totality was extra-

Jung received from Buonaiuti was, not surprisingly, rather negative. According to Buonaiuti, the *Exercitia spiritualia* had pushed the Church in a direction contrary to authentic Christian teachings: "Even the introductory 'Annotationes' of the *Exercitia* of Saint Ignatius give away their novelty and their original sin against the traditional and specific teachings of the Christian spiritual life and even more generally, let us say, compared with the whole dualistic tradition of religious spirituality."[26] Though he regarded the *Exercitia* as a logical development from Scholasticism and Aristotelian gnoseology, Buonaiuti held them accountable for creating an irreparable rift between empirical realism and mystic idealism, of which he saw the latest consequences in the pope's rejection of modernism.[27]

In contrast Funk's attack does not concern the *Exercitia spiritualia* as such, but Ignatius as the papal defender in Rome, who wrote the *Rules* as guidance to the exercises:

> The eighteen rules that Ignatius compiled for the masters and practitioners of the exercises contain the essence of the entire religious side of the Counter-Reformation. And the ultra-Montanism of the modern era, contrasting with medieval Catholicism, which did not exclude individualities and individual critique of the authorities, can be found in sentences such as "Every commandment of the church must be welcomed and defended and should not be attacked under any circumstances"—in principle, one must praise and defend all regulation and even the lifestyle of the Church superiors; even if there was reason for reprimand, it must not be addressed publicly—scholasticism must be upheld; what is white on the basis of one's own judgement must be acknowledged as black, if the Church decides so [. . .]. Neither the order of the Jesuits in its later effectiveness nor its founder Ignatius can be spared the accusation of having created a new Catholicism on the basis of a falsification of the pledge to obey and the rules of faith.[28]

Catholic and very likely astray from any practical form of Christianity. Well, I was not a little surprised when some of the best-known, well-credited, and best prepared of them with regard to psychological and pedagogical matters assailed me with lively and persistent critiques, almost as if I made myself responsible for an irreverent attack upon a methodological tradition of spiritual education, the Jesuit one, which is taken as a milestone of wisdom, prudence, and capacity." (2008 [1945], p. 407; translation by Tommaso Priviero (slightly revised)).

[26] Buonaiuti (1936), p. 315.

[27] Ibid., p. 319.

[28] Funk (1913a), pp. 24–25.

On 25 April 1955, Jung used the same argument against the Jesuit priest Raymond Hostie whose book *Du mythe à la religion* had enraged him:[29]

> I must express the assumption that I do an injustice to *you person-ally*, if I understand your critique as a distortion. In the end you are a member of an order that is based on the principle "quod oculis nostris apparet album, nigrum illa esse definierit, debemus itidem, quod nigrum sit, pronuntiare [We have to pronounce as black what appears to our eyes white if she [the Church] calls it black]."[30]

Already, in a letter to Père Bruno de Jésus-Marie of 30 November 1953, Jung had expressed his reservation regarding Hostie as a member of the Jesuit order:

> I know Père Hostie quite well; he stayed here for a few weeks fol-lowing courses at our institute. He is writing a thesis on my psychol-ogy. He possesses sufficient intelligence to understand psychology and is also capable of scientific honesty, good will and responsibil-ity, but he is a Jesuit, and as a Jesuit, my observations lose all sig-nificance, because he forces himself to suppress his true character to supplant it with what his superiors want him to be. Unfortunately, one must be doubtful, because one cannot hope to encounter a human being in him; rather he is an arrangement of machinations inspired by impersonal uncontrollable agents. I know a number of Jesuits and I regret to have to tell you that I have always had this ambiguous experience. I have learned that one is well advised to be prudent in dealings with representatives of this order. In any case, it seems reasonable not to rely too much on non-existent moral certainties.[31]

JUNG'S FEAR OF JESUITS AND ROMAN CATHOLICISM

This stereotypical image of the Jesuits which Jung expressed in the letter to Père Bruno and which he could also find in the texts of Catholic Mod-ernists such as Buonaiuti or Funk had been implanted in his childhood, when he developed an intense fear connected to everything Catholic. One

---

[29] Hostie (1955).

[30] Jung (1973), vol. 2, p. 245.

[31] Jung to Père Bruno de Jésus-Marie, 30 November 1953 (unpublished). I would like to express my gratitude to Florent Serina for pointing out this letter to me. Translated from the French.

day as a young boy he was gazing at a figure with "a strangely broad hat and a long black garment coming down from the wood":

> At the sight of him I was overcome with fear, which rapidly grew into deadly terror as the frightful recognition shot through my mind: "That is a Jesuit." Shortly before, I had overheard a conversation between my father and a visiting colleague concerning the nefarious activities of the Jesuits. From the half-irritated, half-fearful tone of my father's remarks I gathered that 'Jesuits' meant something especially dangerous, even for my father—Actually I had no idea what Jesuits were, but I was familiar with the word "Jesus" from my little prayer.[32]

In the protocols of his discussions with Aniela Jaffé, Jung expresses his childhood fear in even sharper terms: "I recalled how my father had spoken with colleagues about the danger of the Jesuits. I did not know what this was. But I knew the word 'Jesus' from my child's prayers. I thought, 'They are devils, that is why they are in disguise.' Then I had an anxious panic just as in the dream of the phallus. [. . .] The Jesuits, Catholics per se, are the 'completely other.'"[33] The negative Protestant image of the Jesuit as, in the words of Funk, the "anti-Lutheran" or "anti-Protestant" spearhead of the Counter-Reformation was particularly strong in Switzerland, where the Jesuits were expelled as a threat to the Republic in 1847 and the order was banned by constitutional law from 1848 until 1973. Funk's view in the introduction to his book, published in Berlin in 1913, does confirm this negative image and it comes as no surprise that Jung's lecture followed along those lines. A letter from Jung to Olga Fröbe-Kapteyn in 1943 concerning an invitation to the Jesuit theologian Hugo Rahner demonstrates how deeply this distrust toward the Jesuits was ingrained in Swiss society:

> Your idea of inviting Rahner to speak in Zurich is certainly tempting, but I must say I have reservations about whether he as a *Jesuit*, particularly in Zurich, could cause an undesirable furor for *political reasons*. The Jesuits as such are forbidden here and are not looked upon kindly even by the Catholic clergy. People are afraid of their

---

[32] Jung (1962), p. 11 (Germ.: p. 17).
[33] Jung and Jaffé (forthcoming), 18 January 1957.

disrupting the confessional peace, perhaps rightly, as they are a combative order.[34]

In the protocols, Jung reports how his childhood fear of the Jesuit priest led to a general mistrust of religious dogmas: "The Jesuit [. . .] belonged to this uncanny realm. From then on [. . .] a doubt always arose in me when religious doctrine was impressed on me: 'That is nice, that is good. Then I always thought: *but*, there is something else too, and people don't know it. This other was connected with the Catholic church. It was a *counterpoise*, the other extreme." It was many years later in Vienna that he was able to rid himself of this anxiety vis-à-vis the Catholic church, which he closely associated with the Jesuits:

> For years afterward I was unable to set foot inside a Catholic church without a secret fear of blood and falling and Jesuits. That was the aura or atmosphere that hung about it, but at the same time it always fascinated me. The proximity of a Catholic priest made me even more uneasy, if that were possible. Not until I was in my thirties was I able to confront Mater Ecclesia without this sense of oppression. The first time was in St. Stephen's Cathedral in Vienna.[35]

ROMAN CATHOLIC CONSERVATISM IN THE "EUROPÄISCHE KULTURBUND"

It is remarkable that it was a visit to St. Stephen's in Vienna that freed Jung of his anxiety. If the date given "in my thirties" is correct, it could have been during his visit to Freud in 1907, when the Jungs together with Ludwig Binswanger did some sightseeing. According to Jung, the midst of one's thirties plays a pivotal role in the development of an individual, as it marks the end of the contingency of birth and the turning toward the second half of life. However, Jung's first written draft of the chapter "Kinderjahre" provides a different version: "The first time I was able to confront the *Mater Ecclesia* without this sense of oppression was in St. Stephen's Cathedral in Vienna when I was in my fifties."[36] In that case, it might have been during one of Jung's visits to Vienna on the occasion of his lectures at the Europäischen Kulturbund on 22 February 1928 ("The

[34] Jung to Olga Fröbe-Kapteyn, 6 September 1943 [JA]. Translated from the German (emphasis as in the original).
[35] Jung (1962), p. 17 (Germ.: p. 23).
[36] Jung and Jaffé (forthcoming).

Structure of the Psyche"[37]), on 29 January 1931 ("The Unveiling of the Soul"[38]), or in November 1932, when he was invited by Jolande Jacobi, executive vice-president of the Kulturbund, who would later become one of his closest collaborators in Zurich.[39]

In 1928, Jung was quoted in the Viennese *Neue Freie Presse* as giving this positive assessment of Catholicism, which indicates that his St. Stephens experience might have happened during that visit to Vienna:

> In this connection I regard religious ideas as of the utmost importance, by which I do not, of course, mean any particular creed. Even so, as a Protestant, it is quite clear to me that, in its healing effects, no creed is as closely akin to psychoanalysis as Catholicism. The symbols of the Catholic liturgy offer the unconscious such a wealth of possibilities for expression that they act as an incomparable diet for the psyche.[40]

The Europäische Kulturbund was a conservative network of European intellectuals and writers founded by Karl Anton Prince Rohan (1898–1975) in 1922.[41] From Vienna, the Kulturbund spread quickly through several European countries linked by the notion of a shared cultural heritage and understanding. Rohan's movement was based on the ideal of a transnational and re-Catholicized Europe led by members of a class of elitist intellectual nobility.[42] Annual congresses and individual presentations were to establish the basis of this European network. Jung was involved in several ways in its activities: besides his 1928 lecture in Vienna, he participated in the Kulturbund conference in Prague that took place later that year, from 1 to 3 October, which was dedicated to the topic of "Elemente der modernen Zivilisation." His lecture concerned "The Spiritual Problem of Modern Man."[43] Since 1927, he had been a regular contributor to the *Europäische Revue*, the journal of the Kulturbund, in which he published significant articles such as "Woman in Europe,"[44] "The Structure

---

[37] "Die Struktur der Seele" (Jung, 1928b).

[38] "Die Entschleierung der Seele" (Jung, 1931b; Engl.: "Basic Postulates of Analytical Psychology," in Jung, 1931d).

[39] On Jung and the *Europäische Kulturbund*, see also Sherry (2010), pp. 83–88.

[40] "Das Reich des Unbewussten," *Neue Freie Presse*, 21 February 1928. In Jung (1987), p. 38.

[41] See Schulz (2010).

[42] Rohan (1923).

[43] Jung (1928c).

[44] Jung (1927).

of the Psyche,"[45] "Spiritual Problems of Modern Man,"[46] "Archaic Man,"[47] "The Unveiling of the Soul,"[48] "Ulysses,"[49] and "The Soul and Death."[50] Together with Richard Wilhelm he also published the introduction and commentary to the *Secret of the Golden Flower* entitled "Introduction to Ch'ang Sheng Shu (The Art of Prolonging Human Life)" in the *Europäische Revue*.[51] Jung's collaboration with the Kulturbund intensified in the early thirties, to the extent that at the Kulturbund conference in Zurich in 1932 he was chair for the first day's proceedings.[52]

The year 1932 held some significant developments with regard to the future orientation of the Kulturbund and the shape of its European ideal. That year, Rohan supported a European conference in the tradition of the Kulturbund in Rome, organised by the Italian Fascist government, and dedicated an entire volume of the *Europäische Revue* to the topic of Italian fascism. In his editorial, Rohan declared his support for and affirmation of the new Italy.[53] Also in 1932, another volume of the *Europäische Revue* appeared, on the question of Jewish culture and antisemitism, which included contributions from prominent Jewish intellectuals such as Leo Baeck (1873–1956), Jakob Wassermann (1873–1934) and Erich von Kahler (1885–1970). Alongside these, however, was also a cohort of antisemitic contributors such as the Germanist Josef Nadler (1884–1963) and the professor of law Wenzeslaus Graf Gleispach (1876–1944). Rohan stated in his introduction, "Einige Bemerkungen zur Judenfrage," that the "Jewish question is taboo at upper levels, and it therefore fills the streets below. It has always been thus in history: a problem emerges; the governing classes neglect it; they are afraid of dealing with it, or their brains are stuffed full of some ideology or other so that they do not even see the problem."[54] In April 1933, after the resignation of Ernst Kretschmer, Jung accepted the presidency of the General Medical Society of Psychotherapy. In his first editorial as the new president in the *Zentralblatt* he maintained

---

[45] Jung (1928b)
[46] Jung (1928c).
[47] Jung (1931a).
[48] Jung (1931b).
[49] Jung (1932)
[50] Jung (1934a).
[51] "Einleitung zu Tschang Schen Schu: Die Kunst, das menschliche Leben zu verlängern": Jung and Wilhelm (1929).
[52] "VIII. Jahrestagung des internationalen Verbandes für kulturelle Zusammenarbeit," Zurich, 30 May to 1 June 1932.
[53] Rohan (1932a), p. 667.
[54] Rohan (1932b), p. 453–54.

a position similar to Rohan's, stating that "the actual existing differences between the Germanic and the Jewish psychology, which reasonable people have long been aware of, should no longer be mixed."[55] In his defense against his critic GustavBally, he added, "I put the Jewish question on the table of the house. I have done this deliberately. My esteemed critic seems to have forgotten that the first principle of psychotherapy is to speak most comprehensively of all those things that are the most delicate, dangerous, and open to misunderstanding."[56] Jung's tone very much resembled that of Rohan, and suggests that he felt his argument to be consonant with the view of the European highbrow conservatism of his time.

JUNG'S READING OF ERICH PRZYWARA

One of the contributors to the Jewish volume of the *Europäische Revue* in 1932 was the prominent German-Polish Jesuit and theologian Erich Przywara (1889–1972), the editor of the *Stimmen der Zeit*. Przywara was one of the leading theological voices of his time. His philosophical knowledge and thinking made him a formidable and respected discussion partner for Catholics such as the saint and martyr Edith Stein, or leading Protestant theologians such as Karl Barth. In his theological contribution to the volume, "Jude, Heide, Christ," Przywara represented the Catholic position, ending on a note that was undoubtedly intended as an expression of his critical stance toward Hitler and the Nazi Party in Germany: "Thus the Catholic (who believes in the whole breadth of the Christian revelation) believes neither in a 'sacral nationalism' nor in a 'sacral internationalism,' but in the One God in the One Christ in the One Church, who as infinite being proclaims His infiniteness in the oscillating fullness of antithetical differences (Thomas of Aquinas, Compendium theol. e. 102)— i.e., here in the mystery of the cross."[57] In January 1933, Przywara warned again publicly against the looming Nazi Reich, calling it a distortion of the Christian Imperium of the past, a movement and leadership steeped in blood and intent on total power.[58] During the Nazi reign, Przywara continued to edit *Stimmen der Zeit*, providing a voice for critics of the regime and thus resisting Nazi propaganda. The journal was also a publishing home to Jewish thinkers such as Leo Baeck and Martin Buber. In March 1937, it

---

[55] Jung (1933c), § 1014.
[56] Jung (1934a), § 1024.
[57] Przywara (1932), p. 476.
[58] Przywara (1964), p. 169.

published the papal encyclical "*Mit brennender Sorge*. On the Church and the German Reich," condemning totalitarianism and the pseudo-scientific racism of Nazism. Consequently the journal was closed down, as was Przywara's Jesuit home. Critical lectures during the war raised Nazi suspicions, and the increasing pressure led to several episodes of mental and physical illness from which he barely recovered after the war.

According to Karl Rahner, it was Przywara who first made Ignatius of Loyola a "comprehended great of intellectual history" (verstandende Größe der Geistesgeschichte).[59] His main work on Ignatian theology was a three-volume commentary on the *Exercitia spiritualia* entitled *Deus semper maior*, published between 1938 and 1940,[60] and it was the first volume of this commentary that Jung used for his lecture series. As Kenneth Becker has rightly observed, Jung was probably not aware of the content of the second and third volumes, as they were only published at the time of the lecture series.[61] The first volume contains Przywara's interpretation of the "Anima Christi," the "Annotationes," the "Fundamentum," and the first week of exercises. Jung's heavy emphasis on these parts of the *Exercitia spiritualia* was not least due to his reliance on Przywara, which becomes particularly obvious through his focus on the "Anima Christi" prayer, in which Przywara finds an expression of the main content, the main direction, and the main meaning of the exercises.[62]

Przywara's writing style in *Deus semper maior* is a unique combination of theological concepts with modern philosophical language, a mixture of literary expressions with biblical citations and aspects of prayer. The style is at times highly abstract and requires deep knowledge of medieval scholastic and modern phenomenological philosophy on the one hand, whereas the complete lack of references and the associative argumentation that closely follows the Ignatian original text suggests a more reflective and devotional reading on the other. Perhaps it was Przywara's particular way of writing that prompted Jung to think of the book as a meditation, even as a prime example of the Ignatian exercises.[63]

Similarly to Jung, Przywara understands the human being as the union of opposites, in his existence as the union of body and spirit, in his creative becoming and activity as the union of man and woman, and in a

[59] Rahner (1968), p. 270.
[60] Przywara (1938).
[61] Becker (2001), p. 63.
[62] Pzrywara (1938), pp. 1–2.
[63] See p. 139. Cf. also Becker (2001), p. 63.

structural framework as a union of being a member and a cause.[64] These opposing forces are in mutual conflict, and in their struggle to overcome each other a rift opens up:

> Thus man as *human being* is obviously: as body and spirit the center of existence of the world (medium formale-materiale), as man-and-woman the center of the creation of the world (medium efficiens), as communal being the center of the order of the world (medium finale). But this triple center is an intersection of crossing movements (body to spirit, spirit to body; woman to man, man to woman; in to over, over to in). And it is not only an intersection, but a rift (body against spirit, spirit against body; woman against man, man against woman; in against over, over against in). The human as center, crossing, rift—thus the increasing realism of life experience appears.[65]

The human being as a crossing (*Kreuzung*) is a rift. As an image of God, the human is in the center of this crossing to proclaim God as the absolute center, which they cannot do of their own accord, but only through their *hanging in* God: "He is human, insofar as he is in God."[66] But the human being who thus participates in the divine nature by carrying God's center in their center of the crossing is tempted to abuse this hanging in God to become themself like God. This is the original sin that widens the rift and increases the tension that threatens to tear apart the human being and everything with them.[67] God's work of salvation is to step into this rift; and while being torn apart, He wins against the "prince of the world," and liberates the human being from servitude to sin. But in order to continue and fulfill the process of salvation, the members of the body of the torn crucified Son of God must be crucified with Him in the rift:

> Man as a crossing therefore means: man as crucifixion and the crucifixion of God. The hanging in God, as it essentially was to him as a crossing, is thus the hanging on the cross in God as the one hanging on the cross. Thus it is "curse" as "blessing": "Christ [. . .] being made a curse for us: for it is written, Cursed is every one that hangeth on a tree: That the blessing [. . .] might come [. . .] through Jesus Christ" (Gal. 3:13–14).

---

[64] Przywara (1938), p. 70.
[65] Ibid., p. 67.
[66] Ibid., p. 69.
[67] Ibid., p. 71.

The human, then, in ultimate concreteness means: cross-curse as cross-blessing. Man is (in this only-actual order of the supernatural salvation) a "real" person insofar as he hangs in this cross. But insofar as he hangs in this cross, as the inflation of the absolute center is torn apart in the reality of the nothingness of the rift and the misery of the rift is borne as blessedness of the atonement with God. In the measure of this duality, man is a "real" human.[68]

Jung must have felt a deep connection to this line of thought in Przywara. He himself had experienced this "hanging on the cross," the crucifixion with the crucified one in the rift that had opened between opposites. In 1913, he had started to be plagued by visions: frightful, terrifying images of terror emerged from his unconscious. As is widely known today, Jung described the visions in little black notebooks which would later form the basis of his *Liber Novus*. In an entry for 25 December 1913, one finds a remarkable description of a serpent coiled around the cross:

I see the cross—the removal of the cross[,] the mourning—how agonizing this sight is!

No longer do I yearn.

"You must."

I see the child, with the white serpent in his right hand, and the black serpent in his left hand.

I see the green mountain, the cross on it, and streams of blood flowing from the summit of the mountain.

I can look no longer—it is unbearable.

"You must."

I see the cross and Christ on it in his last hour and last torment. At the foot of the cross the black serpent has coiled itself.

I feel that the serpent of the prophet has wound itself around my feet and ties itself up tightly. The prophet looks at me with fiery gaze. I am contained and I spread my arms wide as if spellbound. Salome draws near from the right—The serpent has wound itself around my whole body, and it seems to me as if my countenance is that of a lion.

Salome says:

"Mary was the mother of Christ. Do you understand now?"

---

[68] Ibid.

I see that a terrible and incomprehensible power forces me to imitate the Lord in his final torment. But how can I presume to call Mary my mother?

"You are Christ."

I stand with outstretched arms like someone crucified, my body taut and horribly entwined by the serpent. Elijah looks at me with blazing eyes.

"You, Salome, say that I am Christ?"

It is as if I stood alone on a high mountain with stiff outstretched arms, the serpent squeezes my body in its terrible coils and the blood streams from my body, spilling down the mountainside.[69]

In the *Liber Novus*, this passage forms the last entry of the *Liber primus* entitled "Resolution." In the second layer to this entry Jung writes about the necessity to endure the mystery of Christ: "May the frightfulness become so great that it can turn men's eyes inward, so that their will no longer seeks the self in others but in themselves. I saw it, I know that this is the way. I saw the death of Christ and I saw his lament; I felt the agony of his dying, of the great dying. I saw a new God, a child, who subdued daimons in his hands. The God holds the separate principles in his powers, he unites them. The God develops through the union of the principles in me. He is their union."[70] Here Jung described what Przywara expressed many years later in his commentary on the *Exercitia spiritualita* of Ignatius: Christ's death on the cross as God's being torn apart in the process of salvation to reunify the opposites in the rift that has opened up in the crossing center of the human being. "Thus the human rift (as natural possibility) in reality is presented as salvation of the demonic rift (in the original sin) through the divine rift (in the cross)."[71]

Four month after Jung's vision, on 19 April 1914, he wrote, in what is known today as "Scrutinies," about his confrontation with the I, on which he depended "since the God has arisen and spreads himself in whichever fiery heavens."[72] He demands an improvement and threatens to torment the I: "Perhaps the whip will help? Now that goes under your skin, doesn't it? Take that—and that. What does it taste of? Of blood, presumably? Of the Middle Ages *in majorem Dei gloriam*?"[73] This phrase is commonly

---

[69] Jung (2020), vol. 2, pp. 194–95.
[70] Jung (2009), p. 104.
[71] Przywara (1938), p. 72.
[72] Jung (2009), p. 461.
[73] Ibid.

attributed to Ignatius of Loyola: "Ad maiorem Dei gloriam inque hominum salute" (To the greater glory of God and the salvation of mankind) and is used as an emblem of the Societas Iesu. Again we find the negative image of the Jesuits associated for Jung with blood, torment, and corporal punishment. What has also become clear at this stage is that Jung's reuniting God is not the Christian God Przywara is talking about in *Deus semper maior*.

THE VISION OF THE SERPENT AND THE CROSS

In the 1925 seminar, Jung emphasized the similarities of his vision to the initiation rites of the Mithraic cult:

> These images have so much reality that they recommend themselves, and such extraordinary meaning that one is caught. They form part of the ancient mysteries; in fact it is such fantasies that made the mysteries. Compare the mysteries of Isis as told in Apuleius, with the initiation and deification of the initiate. [. . .] One gets a peculiar feeling from being put through such an initiation. The important part that led up to the deification was the snake's encoiling of me. Salome's performance was deification. The animal face which I felt mine transformed into was the famous [Deus] Leontocephalus of the Mithraic mysteries, the figure which is represented with a snake coiled around the man, the snake's head resting on the man's head, and the face of the man that of a lion. [. . .] In this deification mystery you make yourself into the vessel, and are a vessel of creation in which the opposites reconcile.[74]

It is not entirely clear whether Jung had read Funk's collection in 1913. If so, it would have been his earliest reading of the *Exercitia spiritualia* and of the *Reminiscences*. In the *Reminiscences*, Ignatius described a series of visions which have remarkable similarities to Jung's own vision of the serpent and the cross. If he had come across these by 1913, his visions might have been informed not only by his knowledge of the Mithraic mysteries, but also by the images of Loyola's memories. In his lectures in 1939, Jung had a particular interest in the following visions of Ignatius:

> While he was in the almshouse something happened to him, many times: in full daylight he would see clearly something in the air

---

[74] Jung (2012), pp. 106–7.

alongside him, which would give him much consolation, because it was very beautiful, enormously so. He couldn't properly make out what it was an image of, but somehow it seemed to him that it had the shape of a serpent, and it had many things which shone like eyes, though they weren't eyes. He used to take much delight in and be consoled by seeing this thing, and the more times he saw it, the more his consolation would increase. And when that thing would disappear from his sight he would feel sad about it.[75]

According to Jung, Ignatius was incapable of reconciling this positive image of the serpent with Christian dogmatics that only seem to recognize it in its evil expression. But, Jung suggested, he could have thought of the serpent which Moses lifted up in the desert to protect his people from the plague of snakes.[76] In John 3:14, Jesus takes up this image to teach about the elevation of the Son of Man: "And as Moses lifted up the serpent in the wilderness, even so must the Son of Man be lifted up."[77] In the vision of Ignatius, Jung finds similarities to his own vision of the serpent in 1913, and supposes immediately that Ignatius struggled also with the moral dilemma involved in the reconciliation of the ethical opposites of good and evil. But this problem was Jung's own, whereas Ignatius seemed not to worry about the ethical quality of this visionary image; or at least, his reminiscences do not suggest so. Against the background of Jung's own visionary deification, of his becoming Christ, where the unification of the opposing serpent and the cross lead to his new God, Jung's understanding of Ignatius's ignorance about the identity of the serpent and Christ can be seen as a depiction of Jung's own struggle.

The particularity of the Ignatian serpent lies in its number of eyes. According to Jung, such a serpent symbolically represents the lower part of the nervous system, the medulla and the medulla oblongata. It is a symbol of the instincts, from which psychic life develops. Jung links it to the Kundalini snake of Indian yoga. It is a healing serpent:

[75] Ignatius, *Reminiscences*, in *IPW*, p. 20. Jung quoted from the German translation by Funk (1913a), pp. 57–58. See Jung's lecture of 30 June 1939.

[76] Numbers 21:6–9: "And the LORD sent fiery serpents among the people, and they bit the people; and much people of Israel died./ Therefore the people came to Moses, and said, We have sinned, for we have spoken against the LORD, and against thee; pray unto the LORD, that he take away the serpents from us. And Moses prayed for the people./ And the LORD said unto Moses, Make thee a fiery serpent, and set it upon a pole: and it shall come to pass, that every one that is bitten, when he looketh upon it, shall live./ And Moses made a serpent of brass, and put it upon a pole, and it came to pass, that if a serpent had bitten any man, when he beheld the serpent of brass, he lived" (*KJV*).

[77] John 3:14 (*KJV*).

When this serpent appears to us it means: I am reunited with my instincts. That is why the god of physicians, Asclepius, has a serpent. Because it all depends on reuniting the sick person with their own roots. Life will always cut us off from our roots. That is the danger of living solely in the conscious mind. One of the aims of the art of medicine, therefore, is to restore man to his own constitution in order for him to function according to his original foundations, to react, to live, in accordance with his own rules of life.[78]

According to Jung, Ignatius had injured himself through his physical practice of penitence. During his suffering, the healing serpent appeared, but he could not identify the serpent in its twofold nature: that is, as a symbol of venom and cure. Again, we see Jung's "resolution" in the mystery of Christ.

Jung discussed Ignatius's second vision concerning the serpent in the lecture of 7 July 1939. Here is Ignatius's text from the *Reminiscences*:

After this had lasted a good while, he went off to kneel at a cross which was nearby in order to give thanks to God. And there appeared to him there that vision which had often been appearing and which he had never recognized: i.e., that thing mentioned above which seemed very beautiful to him, with many eyes. But being in front of that cross he could well see that that thing of such beauty didn't have its normal colour, and he recognized very clearly, with strong backing from his will, that it was the devil. And in this form later the devil had a habit of appearing to him, often and for a long time, and he, by way of contempt would cast it aside with a staff he used to carry in his hand.[79]

The serpent appeared to Ignatius before the cross, and he identified it as the devil. The positive, undetermined tone associated with the first appearances of the serpent changed into the rejection of the serpent as evil. In his lecture, Jung emphasized the phrase "unter kräftiger Zustimmung seines Willens" (with strong backing from his will). The unconscious phenomenon per se would always be morally indifferent, and could be good or evil, Jung explained. It was only when it was placed in a certain conscious atmosphere (*Bewusstseinsatmosphäre*) that it would get determined in a moral sense. In this way, Jung was able to claim that Ignatius had

---

[78] See pp. 32–33.
[79] *RE*, p. 27.

been too dogmatic to reconcile the two visions. Jung instead had embraced the venomous serpent, the tempting pleasure in the appearance of Salome, and had reconciled it with the healing power of the cross, hence reaching a higher state through the union of the opposites: "Because I also want my being other, I must become a Christ. I am made into Christ, I must suffer it. Thus the redeeming blood flows. Through the self-sacrifice my pleasure is changed and goes above into its higher principles."[80] A valuable indication of how strongly Jung associated his own vision of 1913 with those of Ignatius is the reoccurrence of the Christ image in the aforementioned vision of Jung at the time of the lectures on Ignatius.[81]

Jung suggested that Ignatius had misunderstood his vision by giving it a moral value based on his belief in Christian dogma. This is the conscious atmosphere—*Bewusstseinsatmosphäre*—in which the healing serpent is replaced by the evil one of temptation. But is it possible that Jung was immune to such a conscious moral judgment in the case of his own visions? Here he is again, elaborating on his vision of the serpent and the cross in the 1925 seminar:

> Salome's approach and her worshipping of me is obviously that side of the inferior function which is surrounded by an aura of evil. I felt her insinuations as a most evil spell. One is assailed by the fear that perhaps this is madness. This is how madness begins, this *is* madness. [. . .] You cannot get conscious of these unconscious facts without giving yourself to them. If you can overcome your fear of the unconscious and can let yourself down, then these facts take on a life of their own. You can be gripped by these ideas so much that you really go mad, or nearly so.[82]

Clearly Jung here applies a conscious moral judgment to his visionary unconscious experience: "surrounded by the aura of evil", the "fear of madness," and so on. What then, one is tempted to ask, is the *Bewusstseinsatmosphäre* in which these moral determinations are made? It is the realm of science, of psychology. For many years after his visionary experiences, Jung tried to find a scientifically adequate expression to make his individual experience generally explicable and applicable. He thereby applied conscious moral judgments to his previously morally undetermined unconscious experience. "Unter kräftiger Zustimmung seines Willens" (with

---

[80] Jung (2009), p. 254.
[81] See p. xlvii.
[82] Jung (2012), pp. 105–6.

strong backing from his will), he tried hard to appease his visionary experiences with modern science, in the same way as Ignatius tried to do with Christian dogma.[83]

To summarize: Jung's choice to work through the Ignatian exercises in the lecture series of 1939/40, despite his lack of expert knowledge in the field, was triggered not least by his intention to compare his visionary experiences in the years from 1913 onward to the visions of Saint Ignatius. After the lecture series, the topic played a role once more, albeit a minor one, in a letter to the Dominican priest, and professor of dogmatic theology in Oxford, Victor White (1902–60), in which Jung asked about the nature of the "Anima Christi" prayer. During and after the war, Jung was also in contact with one of the leading Jesuit theologians and Church historians of his time, Hugo Rahner (1900–68), who, besides his research on patristics, was well known for his historically orientated theological studies of the life and work of Ignatius of Loyola. Rahner attended the Eranos conferences from 1943 to 1948. But notwithstanding his contact with such Jesuits as Rahner and Louis Beirnaert (1906–85)[84], Jung would never again undertake an attempt to lecture or write about the *Exercitia spiritualia*.

---

[83] Clearly Jung was taken by the similarities of his visionary experience to Przywara's description of the Christian God healing the opposites through his sacrifice on the cross, and by the similarities of his vision to those of Ignatius; but of similar importance for the amplification of his vision was his acquaintance with Mithraism and Orphism. In the lecture of 16 June 1939, Jung recommended Hans Leisegang's seminal study *Die Gnosis* (1924), which contains a lengthy chapter on the Ophites. At the time of this lecture series, Jung was probably already acquainted with Hans Leisegang's contribution to the Eranos yearbook of 1939 (published 1940), "Das Mysterium der Schlange" (The mystery of the serpent), in which Leisegang extended his previous research on the worship of the snake as part of the Orphic mysteries (Leisegang, 1940).

[84] On Jung and Beirnaert, see Florent Serina's doctoral thesis on the reception of Jung in France (2017), pp. 504–9. Ximena de Angulo reported a conversation between Jung and Beirnaert at the Eranos conference of 1950: "Apparently he asked Beirnaert point blank what he thought about the proclamation at this time, and Beirnaert had smiled and said he'd rather not say. From which C. G. assumed he was against it because it would make the work of men such as the Jesuits who are trained to deal with intellectuals much more difficult" (unpublished document, p. 6). See also Jung's letter to Hélène Kiener, 15 June 1955: Jung (1973), vol. 2, p. 265.

Translator's Note

ALL TRANSLATIONS PRESENT their own unique challenges, and this was no exception. In the case of these lectures it was not Jung's language in itself that was the most challenging feature—as these are the scripts of spoken lectures aimed at a lay audience, the language is in the main direct and uncomplicated. As I translated the lectures, I could at times really hear Jung's voice booming across the main auditorium at the ETH, and I hope I have succeeded in bringing this through in the translation.

Rather, the challenge in this particular lecture series came from the frequent changes in register and style between the different voices and the great variation in the age of the texts quoted. We have Jung's professorial but unpolished lecturing style of 1939/40; the somewhat unwieldy theological language of Jung's contemporary Erich Przywara with his unusual usage and neologisms; a Spanish Jesuit of the Middle Ages, Sebastián Izquierdo, whose text Jung translated himself from the Latin (and whose descriptions of hell are particularly vivid); and finally, some lengthy quotations from an ancient Gnostic text thrown in by Jung in the last lecture, as if to keep the translator on her toes. Running through it all, we hear the didactic medieval voice of Saint Ignatius as a constant background presence.

The English translations of quotations from the *Spiritual Exercises of Saint Ignatius of Loyola*, for which Jung used Philipp Funk's 1913 German translation, are here taken from the 1996 Penguin volume translated and edited by Joseph A. Munitiz and Philip Endean, and these Munitiz/Endean translations have a more modern feel than Funk's. Funk and Munitiz and Endean all translated directly from the Spanish, and there are occasional discrepancies between their translations. Where such discrepancies affect the thread of Jung's argument, I have supplied a literal translation from the German as quoted by Jung and noted this in the footnotes.

Where it is necessary for readers to know a German word in order to follow Jung's argument, I have supplied this in the text in square brackets.

This is the case in particular in lectures 9 and 10 (winter semester 1939/40), in which Jung discusses at length the etymology and meaning of the word *Geist*. This word always poses a problem for English translators, as it can be translated as either "spirit" or "mind," and the German term includes elements of both. Jung's longtime translator R.F.C. Hull too grappled with this problem, as can be seen from his translator's note in volume 8 of the *Collected Works*, in which he discusses the words *Geist* and *Seele*. Jung's examination of the word *Geist* here in lecture 10 is illuminating and hopefully also instructive for readers unfamiliar with German.

Finally, where an English word or phrase appears in italics in the text, this indicates that Jung said it in English.

Caitlin Stephens
Zurich, August 2021

Summer Semester 1939

Lecture 8[85]

16 JUNE 1939

IN THIS LECTURE we will now turn to a quite different chapter.[86] However, this chapter is once again about that great problem of the *imaginatio*, of the application,[87] the development, and the formation of the human capacity for imagination. After our rambling journey through the spiritual world of the East, we are returning to our Western world: that is, to Europe. This transition is no easy proposition. Nowadays one may well be able to travel physically by car from India to Europe in about three weeks, but making this journey intellectually is quite another matter. On arrival in the West one finds a completely different spiritual atmosphere.

In the East, despite the apparent abstraction, everything is simple, clear, and philosophical. It is about insight, differentiation, and understanding. It is essentially a spectacle that passes by, as it were, in a calm, peaceful[88] state and through which one changes or is changed. It is never a struggle, ordeal, or compulsion. It grows, blossoms, develops, and unfurls, and the yogi allows it to happen within him and through him, sees it in his visions, and experiences it in his body. But it is never unpredictable; there is no decision or torment. One hears nothing about conscience. Morality

---

[85] The text of this lecture is compiled from notes by LSM, ES, RS, and OK, as well as the English translation by BH. In addition Jung's preparatory typescripts, notes from JA were used (in the following abbreviated as JLN). These notes consist of an unpublished typewritten German translation of the Swedish monograph *Religion och själsträning: En studie i jesuiternas andliga övnigar* (1937) by Bernhard Hegardt. Jung noted, at the top of the first page, "Appendix to page 16e. Exercises."

[86] Jung began the lecture with an answer to a question concerning the previous lecture of 9 June 1939: see *JMP*, vol. 6, p. 253.

[87] ES and OK have "Verwandlung" (transformation) instead of "Verwendung" (application).

[88] LSM and ES have "freundlich" (friendly) instead of "friedlich" (peaceful).

comes into the picture only incidentally, in the form of a technical mistake, for example.

If you study Buddhism, which has a highly developed ethics, you see that not only the ways of life but also the ethical attitudes are highly humane. If someone becomes a monk and isn't happy being celibate, he can continue living outside the monastery as a lay or secular monk. If in this life something goes wrong because of your own imperfection, well yes, you incur a somewhat unpleasant and burdensome *karma*,[89] but you can make up for it in the next life. The next life will be slightly more difficult, due to your *karma*, but you can try to do things better next time, and *karma* gives you the opportunity to do that. The technical mistakes can be gradually eradicated through reincarnation. Buddha, before he became Buddha, also had countless previous stages, in which he existed as a plant, an animal, etc. and gradually developed to higher levels. It is like an ancient tree that in the course of hundreds of years exhibits the biggest, most beautiful blossoms. That is by and large the image of the psychological atmosphere of the East.

When we come to the West, however, we encounter a most unique religious and philosophical situation. Here we need to go back some way in history to understand how certain endeavors[90] came about, and we will then compare them with Eastern techniques. Specifically, I will explore with you the *Exercitia spiritualia* of Ignatius of Loyola. These were not developed until late in the sixteenth century, and there is a long religious and philosophical history behind them. Such efforts to alter the human psyche are age-old, and, as in the East, such things originally came from primitivism.[91] Among the primitives,[92] one already finds special times or

---

[89] *karman*; also *karma* (Sanskr.): "action," the mechanism by which conditional existence maintains itself through the circle of rebirth. "Through good and bad deeds the pot of living beings is produced; from the body, *karma* arises. This [the circle] revolves like a waterwheel. As the waterwheel moves up and down powered by the bullocks, so the psyche passes through life and death powered by *karma*" (*Gheranda-Samhitâ*, 1.6–1.7). Jung talks about the *karma* in his lecture of 4 November 1938 (*JMP*, vol. 6, p. 16). On *karma*, see Feuerstein (1997), pp. 149–50.

[90] LSM has "Bewegungen" (movements) instead of "Bemühungen" (endeavors).

[91] Jung improvised the following six paragraphs guided by his handwritten keynotes: "Primitive: Mag. Preparations, purification, initiation, instruction; ant. mystery cult: Eleusis. Egypt. Isis and Osiris; Hellenist. Syncretism, from which (Judaeo-Hellenism) Christianity" (JLN, p. 1).

[92] Jung's usage of the term "primitive" and its compounds is in line with classic phenomenological theories of religion (P. D. Chantepie de la Saussaye, W. B. Kristensen, E. Lehmann) and anthropological theories (E. B. Tylor) of his time. Geo Widengren argued that the phenomenological theories of Lehmann and others were an expression of the universal

phases in life: puberty rituals or later male rites of passage in which magic preparations are performed, initiations, instruction, ordeals, even mutilation and the like, for the purpose of achieving some kind of psychic transformation. From these primitive beginnings, which are found among all primitive peoples, as it were, the mysteries of antiquity gradually evolved. I refer above all to the ancient and holy cult of Eleusis, where the most significant magical and religious initiations took place throughout antiquity in the famous Eleusinian mysteries.[93]

These Eleusinian mysteries were performed until 392 CE, thus extending well into our Christian epoch, until they were abolished by a special edict of a Byzantine emperor.[94] They apparently disappeared without trace, meaning we actually have very little precise information about their content. But from the intimations of various writers and results of archaeological excavations we have been able to piece together most of it. These mysteries primarily altered the consciousness to such an extent that immortality was experienced—that is, an experience of unchanged existence in time. This is also expressed symbolically through time being suspended.

We find similar initiation rites in Egypt. The Eleusinian initiations most probably originated in Egypt and were brought to Greece along with the cultivation of grain around 1500 BCE. They were originally an agrarian mystery. The corresponding mysteries in Egypt were the Isis mysteries.[95] We have more recent information about those. I recommend the writings of Plutarch on these mysteries.[96] Well worth reading. He himself was an

---

evolutionary as well as theological and antitheological prejudices of their age (Widengren, 1974). For a critique of phenomenology of religion, see Evans-Pritchard (1965). On Jung and primitive mentality, see Shamdasani (2003), pp. 290–93.

[93] The Eleusinian mysteries were important ancient Greek initiation rites held annually in honor of Demeter and Persephone/Kore. In 1941, Jung and Karl Kerényi published a seminal study on the Eleusinian mysteries (Jung and Kerényi, 1941; Engl.: *Essays on a Science of Mythology: The Myth of the Divine Child and the Mysteries of Eleusis*, 1969). On the details of the Eleusinian cult, see Sourvinou-Inwood (2003).

[94] Theodosius I (347–95 CE; r. 379–95).

[95] Contrary to Jung's statement, the mysteries of Isis are of Graeco-Roman origin. The worship of the Egyptian goddess Isis developed during the Hellenistic period (323–31 BCE). The mysteries of Isis were modeled on the Eleusinian mysteries (see n. 93). The main source for today's knowledge of the secret initiation rites performed as part of the mystery cult is chapter 11 of the Latin novel *The Golden Ass* (actual title *Metamorphoses*) by Apuleius (see n. 97).

[96] Plutarch (Lucius Mestrius Plutarchus; ca. 46–ca. 120 CE) was a Greek biographer, author, and philosopher, who was also one of the two priests at the temple of Apollo in Delphi, the site of the famous oracle. His main works are *Parallel Lives* and *Moralia*. The latter consists of seventy-eight essays and contains an account of the mysteries

initiate. The well-known ancient novel by Apuleius, *Asinus aureus*, is also highly recommended, as at the end it describes a mystery rite.[97] The whole story is actually a mystery. It describes various changes that the initiate goes through before reaching the state of complete salvation.

There were of course many other mysteries as well as these ones. For instance, the Samothracian mysteries in which the Cabiri initiations took place.[98] Such mysteries became merged in around the first century before Christ, and together with neo-Pythagorean and Neoplatonic philosophy they formed Hellenistic syncretism, a conglomeration of the various religious and philosophical viewpoints. In practical terms, this resulted in numerous variations of the different mysteries. You can get a fuller picture in the book on Gnosis by Leisegang, for example.[99] There you will find many traces of these unique spiritual movements. I remind you again of Demeter and the Cabiri which I talked about after the dreams last year.[100]

Christianity arose out of these movements. In the West, we like to give the impression that Christianity fell straight from the sky with no prior history. That is inaccurate, historically. The main contents of Christianity,

---

entitled "Of Isis and Osiris, or the Ancient Religion and Philosophy of Egypt" (1878, vol. 4, pp. 65–139).

[97] Apuleius (Lucius Apuleius Madaurensis; ca. 124–ca. 170 CE) was a Platonic philosopher, rhetorician, and author, best known for the only Latin novel that survived in its entirety, *Metamorphoses* or *Asinus aureus* (*The Golden Ass*), which describes the fate of a man who is changed into a donkey for his misuse of magic. He only regains his original form through the worship of the Egyptian Goddess Isis and his subsequent initiation into her mysteries. Apuleius himself was an initiate of the Isis mysteries, and gave a detailed account of the initiation rites in the final chapter of his book. The text attracted the attention of Jungian psychologists such as Erich Neumann (Neumann, 1952) and Marie-Louise von Franz (Franz, 1970).

[98] The mysteries of Samothrace were, after the Eleusinian mysteries, the most famous initiation cult of antiquity. The sanctuary was dedicated to the worship of the Kabeiroi (Cabiri) or *megaloi theoi*, the great gods, of which four names are known: Axieros, Axiokersa, Axiokersos, and their servant Cadmilos or Casmilos. The initiation mysteries offered prosperity and safety to those traveling the seas. Jung had a keen interest in the Cabiri, endorsing the argument of Friedrich Creuzer (Creuzer, 1810–12) and Friedrich Wilhelm Joseph Schelling (Schelling, 1977 [1815]), according to which the Cabiri were the primal deities of Greek mythology. Jung himself wrote about the Cabiri in "Wandlungen und Symbole der Libido" (1911–12, §§ 209–11; Engl.: *A Study of the Transformations and Symbolisms of the Libido*, 1916; 1917) and in "Zur Psychologie der Trinitätsidee" (1942a, § 244; Engl.: "A Psychological Approach to the Dogma of the Trinity," CW 9). *Liber Novus* contains a dialogue between the "I" and the Cabiri, in which the Cabiri urge the "I" as "master of the lower nature" to cut through the brain and its entanglement with a sword, thereby sacrificing the Cabiri themselves: "The entanglement is your madness, the sword is the overcoming of madness" (Jung, 2009, pp. 425–28).

[99] Leisegang (1924).

[100] See Jung's lecture of 17 June 1938 (*JMP*, vol. 5).

which is rich in philosophical thought, were actually already present in this extraordinarily broad and to an extent very conscious constellation characterized on the one hand by Gnosticism and on the other hand by Neoplatonic philosophy. That in turn goes back to Pythagoras, Plato, and so forth.

From this specific syncretism, other special spiritual movements within Judaism also arose, but which then disappeared without trace due to dogmatic[101] rabbinic attitudes. The only remaining trace is the Kabbalah (Hebrew for "tradition" or "transmission"), a Gnosis that has survived to the present day.[102] Also the group known as the Sabians in the East. They are the Mandaeans in Basra and Kut al-Amara in Mesopotamia.[103] Also called the Christians of Saint John, they still exist today—Gnosticism lives on there.[104] There were also still Neoplatonic sects active in Baghdad until 1050, which were wiped out by Islamic persecution.[105]

[101] Only in BH.

[102] In February 1944, Jung suffered a severe heart attack. While he was in a twilight zone between life and death, he experienced a number of visions, one of which was of a Kabbalistic nature: "I myself was, so it seemed, in the Pardes Rimmonim, the garden of pomegranates, and the wedding of Tifereth with Malchuth was taking place. Or else I was Rabbi Simon ben Jochai, whose wedding in the afterlife was being celebrated. It was the mystic marriage as it appears in the Cabbalistic tradition. I cannot tell you how wonderful it was. I could only think continually, 'Now this is the garden of pomegranates! Now this is the marriage of Malchuth and Tifereth!' I do not know exactly what part I played in it. At bottom it was myself: I was the marriage. And my beatitude was that of a blissful wedding" (Jung, 1962, p. 294). The Kabbalistic marriage between the male and female aspect of God plays also a prominent part in Jung's *Mysterium Coniunctionis* (1955–56). Close collaborators of Jung's such as Rivkah Schärf-Kluger and Siegmund Hurwitz looked at the psychological aspects of the Kabbalah. Jung discussed Kabbalistic topics in letters to Ernst Fischer (21 December 1944: Jung [1973], vol. 1, pp. 355–56) and to Erich Neumann, (5 January 1952: Jung and Neumann [2015], pp. 280–84).

[103] The place names are given only in BH.

[104] The Sabians were a religious group mentioned three times alongside the Christians and the Jews in the Quran. They are often identified with the Mandaeans, believers of the Gnostic religion of Mandaeism. Known as Nasoreans, the Mandaeans left Palestine for Mesopotamia in the first century CE to escape persecution. During the Muslim conquest, they claimed one of their main prophets, Yahya ibn Zakariyya, to be identical with John the Baptist, which identified them as Sabians, who as "people of the book" enjoyed certain rights and protection. They reject Jesus as the Messiah and hold the teachings and the practice of baptism as rendered by John the Baptist in high regard. They have also been known as "Christians of Saint John" since the sixteenth century.

[105] The three most important centers of Neoplatonism after the Islamic conquest were Alexandria, Godeshapur, and Harran. All three made their impact on the learned culture of the city of Baghdad after its foundation in 762. Neoplatonic scholars from Godeshapur, a major center of Greek Byzantine culture and philosophy, made their mark on the philosophical debates in Baghdad, which with its famous libraries soon turned into the intellectual and cultural hub of the Islamic Golden Age. Another route of Neoplatonism infiltrating

In the West, little has remained, and only in secrecy. Most of it became incorporated into Christianity. It should therefore not surprise us that Christianity soon resumed those attempts that we encountered in the mystery cults, namely attempts at psychic transformation. This was particularly evident in the monasteries. The monasteries themselves, which were supposedly established on biblical authority, actually existed before Christ. We know that from Philo of Alexandria's descriptive tract *De vita contemplativa*.[106] In this he describes monastic communities which were wrongly assumed to be Christian by the old church, but which were actually Gnostic. However, they were precursors of the early Christian monasteries in Egypt. There in Alexandria we also find the first eremitic monastic communities, where the monks were able to devote themselves to their spiritual practice undisturbed. The monasteries were founded solely for this purpose.

These endeavors fundamentally to alter the human soul were pursued in monasteries before any kind of systematic processes or methods had been established. There are numerous examples of this. In the Middle Ages, a great number of books and tracts were produced containing instructions for prayer or meditation which had by then become more methodical.[107] One example is the *Goldene Büchlein* by Petrus of Alcántara.[108] Thomas à Kempis, who died in 1471, wrote *The Imitation of*

Islamic culture in Baghdad was via Harran in northern Syria, which was home to the Sabaeans. Their theology was also shaped by Neoplatonism, and merged with the thinking of Neoplatonist philosophers fleeing Alexandria in the third century. In the eighth century, Neoplatonism found its way from Harran to Baghdad.

[106] Philo Judaeus, also known as Philo of Alexandria (ca. 20 BCE–ca. 50 CE) was a Hellenistic Jewish philosopher, born in Alexandria. Philo brings together Greek philosophical traditions such as Platonism, Aristotelianism, Cynicism, and Stoicism with the Jewish exegesis of the Bible. As he combines religious revelation and philosophical reason, he has also been seen as a forerunner of Christian theology. In *De vita contemplativa* (*On the Contemplative Life, or On Suppliants*), Philo described the life of an ascetic religious community near Alexandria known as the Therapeutae (Philo, 1941, pp. 112–70). As Eusebius, in his commentary on Philo (*Historia ecclesiastica* [Eusebius, 1999] book 2, 17), identified their practice as Christian, Philo's account was seen as a description of a forerunner of Christian monastic life. More recent scholarship suggests that the way of life portrayed by Philo points more to a Jewish than a Christian sect. Given the negative valuation of Greek philosophy in the text, Philo's authorship of *De vita contemplativa* has also been disputed.

[107] From here, Jung closely follows the monograph of Bernhard Hegardt, *Religion och själsträning. En studie i jesuiternas andliga övningar* (1937). JLN contains a typewritten German translation of the Swedish original. Jung's translation, which builds the structure of his lecture, starts with Hegardt's p. 18.

[108] Saint Peter of Alcántara (1499–1562), born Juan Garabito Vilela de Sanabria, was a Spanish Franciscan friar and mystic. His sole publication is the *Tratado de la oración y meditación* (1556) (*Treatise of Prayer and Meditation*, 1926), known in German as the

Christ.[109] From more recent times, there is a very interesting spiritual work by Madame Guyon, *Moyen court et très-facile de faire oraison que tous peuvent pratiquer*. She was a French mystic whose famous confessor was Abbé Fénelon.[110] All these prayer instructions (*orationes*) are used for[111] meditation. They usually contain a description and analysis of the experiences that the person performing these exercises has had. Experiences of the spiritual life are examined, then strung together and arranged in stages corresponding to the ancient mysteries, in which there is also a ladder of progression. Jacob's ladder,[112] of the Old Testament, was often used to symbolize this climbing in stages up to the *unio mystica* with God.

Goldene Büchlein über die Betrachtung und das innerliche Gebet (1900), which was an important inspiration for other mystics such as Peter's spiritual heir Teresa of Ávila (1515–82).

[109] Thomas à Kempis (ca. 1380–1471), the best known member of the Brethren of the Common Life, a pietist Roman Catholic community founded by Gérard (de) Groote (1340–84) (see n. 116). Their simple way of living revolved around prayer and meditation, and is known as the *devotio moderna*. The *Imitation of Christ* consists of short texts with instructions for how to conduct a spiritual inner life following the example of Jesus Christ. Over the centuries, the book has maintained its popularity and has become one of the most successful books in Christianity. The book plays a prominent role in the chapter "Divine Folly" of Jung's *Liber Novus*, where its mediating truth is opposed to that of Nietzsche's philosophy, and where Jung reflects upon the imitation of Christ: "If I thus truly imitate Christ, I do not imitate anyone, I emulate no one, but go my own way, and I will also no longer call myself a Christian. Initially, I wanted to emulate and imitate Christ by living my life, while observing his precepts. A voice in me protested against this and wanted to remind me that my time also had its prophets who struggle against the yoke with which the past burdens us" (Jung, 2009, p. 332).

[110] Jeanne-Marie Bouvier de La Motte Guyon, Madame du Chesnoy (1648–1717), was a French mystic and author who was at the heart of the seventeenth-century controversy regarding quietism, which was declared as heretical by the papal bull *Coelestis pastor*. Although Guyon repeatedly retracted the propositions brought forward in her writings she was arrested in 1695 and not released until 1703. Her main work is *Moyen court et très-facile de faire oraison* (A short and easy method of prayer) written in 1685 (Guyon, 2007 [1685]). One of her disciples and defenders was François de Salignac de la Mothe-Fénelon (1651–1715), better known as François Fénelon, who met Madame Guyon for the first time in 1688. Fénelon was made archbishop of Cambrai in 1696 and royal tutor, a position he lost due to his role in the quietist controversy.

[111] RS and ES have "verstanden" (understood as) instead of "gebraucht" (used for).

[112] Genesis 28:12–17: "And he [Jacob] dreamed, and behold a ladder set up on the earth, and the top of it reached to heaven: and behold the angels of God ascending and descending on it./ And, behold, the Lord stood above it, and said, I am the Lord God of Abraham thy father, and the God of Isaac: the land whereon thou liest, to thee will I give it, and to thy seed;/ And thy seed shall be as the dust of the earth, and thou shalt spread abroad to the west, and to the east, and to the north, and to the south: and in thee and in thy seed shall all the families of the earth be blessed./ And, behold, I am with thee, and will keep thee in all places whither thou goest, and will bring thee again into this land; for I will not leave thee, until I have done that which I have spoken to thee of./ And Jacob awaked

These books, which deal with a kind of specific mystical union with God, were like manuals for monks who wanted to undertake the exercises. They not only give formal instructions about the time, place, manner, and method, but also about the content and material on which one should meditate. Thus in the Middle Ages a host of such religious meditation systems was created. The writings of the Victorines are good examples of this type of literature—Hugh of Saint Victor (1096–1141), for instance, wrote an interesting dialogue between the human being and the soul.[113] That is a typical Western meditation. Meditation was understood as an inner conversation between a person and their soul, with their good angel, or even with God. Ignatius also took up this approach in his exercises, in which an exercise often culminates in a *colloquy*—a discussion with one of the divine figures. So it's a prototype of this meditation. Hugh of Saint Victor gives us a good example of it. This inner debate, an inner conversation with oneself, is something that is very different from the approach in the East. With us it is all much more personalistic.

In the thirteenth century, after the Victorines, this system of meditation was developed further. The term "spiritual exercise" appears: the *exercitium*. At the same time the forms become somewhat more precise. During the fourteenth century, actual manuals or handbooks are produced with instructions of how to perform such exercises.[114] The purpose of all these exercises is the development in stages of the human consciousness, leading to a state of supposed perfection in which the experience of the *unio mystica*, the union with God, takes place. Originally there were usually three of these stages, but gradually the number of stages increased. There are even some tracts with up to forty stages. German medieval literature

---

out of his sleep, and he said, Surely the Lord is in this place; and I knew it not./ And he was afraid, and said, How dreadful is this place! this is none other but the house of God, and this is the gate of heaven" (*KJV*).

[113] Hugh of Saint Victor (1096–1141), medieval philosopher and mystical writer, laid the foundations for Scholastic theology; he became the head of the school of Saint Victor in 1133. He combined his philosophical and theological writings of an Aristotelian character with mystical teachings about the soul's journey to the union with God. His main work is entitled *De sacramentis Christianae fidei* (ca. 1134); his mystical writings include *De arca Noe morali* (Noah's moral ark) and *De arca Noe mystica* (Noah's mystical ark) (1125–30), *De vanitate mundi* (On the vanity of the world) and *Soliloquium de arrha animae* (Soliloquy on the earnest-money of the soul). Hugh's works are published as vols 175–77 of the Patrologia Latina (1854). On his psychology, see Ostler (1906). See also Jung's lecture of 28 October 1938 (*JMP*, vol. 6, pp. 7–8)

[114] Jung follows Hegardt (1937), p. 19; German translation in JLN, p. 2.

in particular excelled in expanding the methodical steps to such a degree that consciousness could be transcended.[115]

At the end of the fourteenth century, during a time when the moral and intellectual decline of monasteries was becoming noticeable, a kind of spiritual reformation movement occurred. This movement began in Holland, with Gérard de Groote (1340–84) and his followers.[116] They formed a group called the "Brethren of the Common Life." They followed the *devotio moderna* and were also called the *Devoti*. They dedicated themselves to pursuing a deep inner piety, an approach which had a great influence both on Catholicism and, later, on Protestantism. The Devoti produced some notable texts about such spiritual exercises. If you read *The Imitation of Christ* by Thomas à Kempis you will find a good example of the Devoti. They are evocative and exquisite religious meditations. This Devoti movement developed particularly during the fifteenth century. It became perhaps the most prestigious and popular spiritual movement of its time. Many outstanding characters belonged to the movement. The work they did was quite considerable. They took on a fundamental reform of the monasteries, which at that time had fallen into disrepute; in particular Johannes Busch (1399–1479)[117] in Germany, Johannes Mauburnus

---

[115] Jung here plays on the double meaning of the phrase "bis zur Bewusstlosigkeit," which literally means "as far as loss of consciousness," but also has the colloquial meaning of "to an excessive or ludicrous degree" or "ad nauseam."

[116] Gérard (de) Groote (1340–84), also Geert or Gerrit Groote, in Latin Gerardus Magnus, the Dutch founder of the Brethren of the Common Life, a pietist Roman Catholic community whose members imitated in their conduct of life the example of Jesus Christ. The new inward emphasis on prayer and meditation was called the *devotio moderna*. Groote was born in Deventer, near Utrecht, and studied scholastic philosophy and theology at the University of Paris. In 1347, he experienced a spiritual conversion that made him renounce his worldly goods and help the poor. He was ordained a deacon and became a highly popular missionary preacher. His teachings, often critical of the clergy, aroused anger, and an edict was issued that prohibited the preaching of laymen such as himself. Groote died of the plague at the age of forty-four, before this prohibition took effect. His spiritual direction was also informed by his contact with the mystic John Ruysbroeck (ca. 1293–1381) and led him to recommend the brethren to attach themselves to the canons regular of Saint Augustine. After Groote's death, a monastery was established in Windesheim, which became the center of the monastic reform movement of the fifteenth century.

[117] Johannes Busch (1399–1479), canon regular of the Windesheim congregation that was founded by disciples of Gérard de Groote two years after his death in 1386. Busch took the cloth in 1419 and made simple vows in 1420. He was later ordained as a priest in Cologne. His reform of canonical houses extended all the way from the canonries in the Netherlands to Saxony and Thuringia. He is the author of the *Chronicon Windeshemense* and *Liber de reformatione onasteriorum* (Busch, 1886).

(1460–1501)[118] in France, and Ludovico Barbo (1381–1443) in Italy, whom I mention because he was the one who finally brought these meditation methods and the spiritual writings to Spain. It is thanks to Barbo that Ignatius became at all familiar with this meditation movement. Barbo undertook, with great success, the reform of the Benedictine monasteries in Italy. He also wrote a text which he specifically referred to as a "modus meditandi et orandi."[119]

[120]These successes in cloister meditation became well known all over, and even reached as far as Spain, which at that time was rather distant from [the rest of] Europe. In 1442, Barbo and a few other monks came to the monastery at Monserrat near Barcelona.[121] This cloister is now famous on account of the time Ignatius spent there. Barbo initially led a thorough reform of the monastery, but after his death it quickly declined again. Later came another reformer, also from the *devotio moderna* movement. He was the abbot Cisneros (ca. 1455–1510), the teacher of Ignatius.[122] He once again implemented the *devotio moderna* very thoroughly, having brought much of the Devoti literature with him from France. I will mention here two titles: *Libellus de spiritualibus ascensionibus* (Little book about

---

[118] Johannes Mauburnus (1460–1501), also known as Jan Mombaer, was the last significant teacher of the *devotio moderna*. Born in Brussels, he became a canon regular of the Windesheim congregation at the age of seventeen. After his ordination, he was entrusted with the reform of canonical houses in the north of France. His most famous book is the *Rosetum exercitiorum spiritualium et sacrarum meditationum* (The rose-garden of spiritual exercises and holy meditations) (Mauburnus, 1494). The meditative practice described in this book was introduced to the Benedictine monastery of Montserrat by its abbot García de Cisneros (see n. 122), and thus was known to Ignatius.

[119] Ludovico Barbo (1381–1443), also known as Luigi Barbo, Italian reformer, canon regular, bishop of Treviso, Bendedictine monk. Barbo made contact with the northern European spiritual movement of the *devotio moderna* via the canon regular Paolo de Bernado (ca. 1330–93) of Rome. After the successful foundation and running of the Canons Regular of San Giorgi in Alga, he was asked to oversee the reform process of the monastic institutions in Italy. In 1408, he was appointed abbot of the Benedictine abbey of Santa Giustina in Padua and became a Benedictine monk. Balbo wrote to the monks of the cloister outlining the correct method of meditation and prayer (*Ad monachos Sanctae Justinae de Padua: Modus meditandi et orandi*). On Barbo, see Tassi (1952).

[120] Jung follows Hegardt (1937), p. 20; Germ.: JLN, p. 3.

[121] Santa Maria de Montserrat is a Benedictine abbey dating back to the eleventh century. Located on the mountain of Montserrat ("jagged mountain") in Catalonia, about fifty kilometers (thirty miles) west of Barcelona, the monastery was founded on the location where the Virgin of Montserrat had been venerated since the ninth century.

[122] García Ximénes de Cisneros (ca. 1455–1510), abbot of Santa Maria de Montserrat (see previous note), cousin of Cardinal Franciso Ximénes de Cisneros. Ignatius never met Cisneros, who had died twelve years prior to his own visit to the monastery in 1522. Jung refers here to the significance that Cisneros's teachings in the *Ejercitatorio de la vida espiritual* (1500; Engl.: *A Book of Spiritual Exercises*, 1876) held for Ignatius.

spiritual ascent),[123] and another by Mauburnus (whom I already mentioned), *Rosetum exercitiorum spiritualium et sacrarum meditationum*.[124] This is the first time we come across the expression "exercitium" [in the devotional literature].

Ignatius learned about the Devoti movement at the monastery in Montserrat from a book written by Cisneros himself, *Ejercitatorio de la vida spiritual*:[125] that is, exercise or drill rules. It fits in with our Western penchant for drills, military exercises, and so on. Abbot Cisneros, a great lover of order, had written the booklet for the pious pilgrims who came to the Montserrat—pilgrims whose conduct was apparently rather undisciplined and who needed to be brought into line by structured exercises. The booklet itself is a compilation of various methods combined into a meditation sequence. It is taken from the writings of the Devoti. One new aspect of it, connected to its military character, was that the meditation sequence was intended to be followed for period of thirty days. There was a daily spiritual task and the tasks had to be completed in thirty days, like in basic army training. The idea of retreats had already existed in antiquity. The word "retreat" was now used to describe a monk withdrawing to a hermitage near the monastery where he would not be disturbed even by the other brothers. The book set out a methodical process and precise regulations for such a retreat. So, when Ignatius, about whom we will hear more later, traveled to Manresa and stayed in the monastery, he came across this little book, these exercise rules for spiritual life, and it pleased him—he being a military officer to the core—inordinately, even though it was more difficult than anything he had ever encountered.

I would like to give you a small example of what these exercise rules were like. The whole thing was split into four weeks. The exercises had three distinct parts:

1. *Via purgativa*, that is, the path of purification;
2. *Via illuminativa*, that is, the path of enlightenment;
3. *Via unitativa*, that is, the path of union with God.

The fourth week was then spent contemplating the Lord's life and suffering. Essentially, that was supposed to support these three paths.

---

[123] The *Libellus de spiritualibus ascensionibus* (Engl.: *The Spiritual Ascent*, 1908) was written by Gerard Zerbolt of Zutphen (1367–98), a member of the Brethren of the Common Life.

[124] Mauburnus (1494). See n. 118.

[125] See n. 122.

So you see, even the order of thoughts is completely technical. The idea that they took from the Devoti and from even older spiritual exercises was that of the *unio mystica* with God. It had to be achieved, come hell or high water,[126] and via the technically correct routes, by a supreme effort of will. That is typical of the West—you don't find it in the East.

I will say some more about the three stages later. They find equivalence in occult philosophy, which was around at the same time as these exercises. The exercises represent the openly recognized, above-ground spiritual endeavors, all of which are characterized by enormous intellectual efforts of will. Concurrently there was also hermetic philosophy, which however was not recognized openly, in particular not as being a valid spiritual exercise. But the spiritual idea is exactly the same. However, one cannot say that the idea came from here—it is actually much older. All three stages correspond to a hermetic concept.

Here are some indications of how these exercises would be carried out:[127]

First week: *Via purgativa*

Monday: Begins with contemplating one's own sins and sin in general;
Tuesday: Contemplation of death, including one's own;
Wednesday: Hell and "I am hell";
Thursday: The Last Judgment;
Friday: The Passion of Christ;
Saturday: The sorrows of Mary;
Sunday: The glory of heaven, but with the thought that I, black, corrupt animal, can see the glory of God and perceive the difference.

Second week: *Via illuminativa*

Monday: Contemplation of God's beneficence, specifically of the creation of existence;
Tuesday: The blessing of God's forgiveness; that we might hope for God's grace;

---

[126] Trans. note: Jung used the German expression "in drei Teufels Namen" (in three devils' name) in reference to the three stages.

[127] The scheme that follows is taken from Hegardt (1937), pp. 21–22.

Wednesday: The blessing of being called to be a child of God; the idea of the *electio*;
Thursday: The justification before God;
Friday: Particular gifts received by the grace of God;
Saturday: The guidance of God under which we stand.[128]

Those are the individual parts of the *illuminatio*. Here, technical methods are used as a substitute for the actual experience: I imagine that I have a positive relationship to the creation, that I am happy to be alive, that I feel God's grace and feel myself called as a chosen one to lead a meaningful life, that I am justified in what I am, that I have a particular gift given to me by God, and that I moreover do not walk in darkness but am guided by the hand of God. That is the experience of the *illuminatio*. It is achieved here by these exercise techniques.

Then comes the third week, that of the *via unitativa*. The whole week is spent exclusively in contemplation of God.

Third week: *Via unitativa*

Monday: God as source and beginning of all things created;
Tuesday: God as the beauty of the universe; the Catholic church largely takes the standpoint that God can be seen through his revelation in nature;
Wednesday: God as the crowning glory;
Thursday: God from the perspective of the love of God, that He is all love; *sub specie amoris*;
Friday: God as the rule and law of all things, as the source of all laws and principles;
Saturday: God as the guide of the universe, the most tranquil guide;
Sunday: God as the most bountiful giver, as the one who gives everything.

This, therefore, is the technically correct substitute for the *unio mystica* which assumes that the mystical experience will be granted to one who meditates properly. Through these exercises, the mystical union is supposed to be achieved in a period of four weeks, in the same way that Buddhahood descends on the practicing yogi. And there are also the hermetic parallels.

---

[128] Jung omits Sunday. See Hegardt (1937), p. 21: "Sonntag: Die himmlischen Herrlichkeiten" (Sunday: the glory of heaven).

Lecture 9[129]

23 JUNE 1939

WE WILL NOW return to our actual topic.[130] I must give you some literature about the Ignatian exercises.[131] There is a slim, highly recommended book by Philipp Funk which came out in 1913 and is available in the Zentralbibliothek [Zurich central library]: *Ignatius von Loyola*.[132] In preparation for these talks on the Ignatian exercises, I used a Latin praxis: the *Praxis exercitiorum spiritualium* by the Spanish Jesuit Sebastián Izquierdo, from 1695.[133] It is a very good commentary on the Ignatian practices. There's a huge amount of literature about Ignatius and his exercises written by the Jesuits themselves, as well as by other Catholic scholars. Many Protestants have also written about them. But it's pointless for me to swamp you with literature.

Regarding the earlier meditations, I mentioned the Victorines, the writings of Hugh of Saint Victor. You can also get a good impression of the *devotio moderna* from the little prayer book by Thomas à Kempis, who died at the end of the fifteenth century. A prayer book which is universal: *The Imitation of Christ*.[134] It's a very nice medieval prayer book, which gives chapter-by-chapter meditations. A lot of it was carried over into Protestantism. In the Brethren's Congregation of Herrnhut there are daily meditation prompts, called watchwords. They used to issue a little book

---

[129] The text of this lecture is compiled from notes by LSM, ES, RS, and OK, the English translation by BH, and from JLN.

[130] Jung had dedicated the first half of the lecture to answering questions concerning the previous lectures on Eastern meditation. It is published in *JMP*, vol. 6.

[131] JLN contains handwritten literature lists on p. 1: "Literature: 1. Izquierdo S.J./ 2. Phil. Funk: Ignatius v. Loyola 1913/ 3. Victoriner/ Thomas à Kempis: Imit. Christ." and on p. 5: "Mention literature: Funk I.v.L 1913/ Thomas a Kempis (†1471)/ Sebastian Izquierdo. Praxis exercit. Spir. 1695".

[132] Funk (1913a).

[133] Izquierdo (1695).

[134] See n. 109.

every year with these meditation guides.[135] The brethren received a quotation, a watchword, on which they would meditate. These sorts of things are still flourishing today.

Last time I mentioned Cisneros's meditation series to you:

1. *Via purgativa*—Purification
2. *Via illuminativa*—Enlightenment
3. *Via unitativa*—Union, unification

This is a very typical series of stages which also underpins alchemical and hermetic meditations—although these are performed with chemical substances and not the prayer book. It is a very interesting comparison, because these things were amalgamated into the rituals of the Catholic church, specifically in the Mass.

There is a characteristic counterpart of the *via purgativa* in alchemy.[136] One only has to think of the subjects of the first week of purification: sin, death, hell, the Last Judgment, the Passion of Christ, the sorrows of Mary; and, finally, eternal glory—to provide a contrast to the impression of darkness and of suffering. It corresponds to the alchemical state of purgatory, hell, Hades; *tenebrositas*,[137] darkness, or *nigredo*, blackness; *melancholia*; torture. In this state, suffering and darkness prevail. It also involves a kind of death. It is the dead, unawakened state in which the mystics' little spark of the soul (the *scintilla*) is imprisoned in the darkness, in a dark state of suffering. Getting through this stage involves much effort and pain, and culminates in the *ablutio*, that is, the ablution or washing clean.

---

[135] This refers to the Herrnhuter Brüdergemeinde ("Brethren's Congregation of Herrnhut"), known in English as the Moravian Church, and formally as Unitas Fratrum, a faith movement that dates back to the Bohemian Reformation of the fifteenth century, linking it to the reformers Jan Hus and Petr Chelčický. In 1722, during the Counter-Reformation, a group of the brethren fled to Saxony, where they found refuge on the estate of Count Nikolaus Ludwig von Zinzendorf (1700–60), who later became bishop of the congregation. They founded a village nearby entitled Herrnhut. From there they successfully spread their theological teachings, close to both pietism and Calvinism, through missionary work around the world. Since 1731, without interruption, the *Losungen* (watchwords) have been published annually. The booklet contains a verse from the Old Testament for each day, selected annually by drawing lots, and an accompanying verse from the New Testament.

[136] On p. 5 of JLN, Jung contrasts the diagram of Hegardt (typewritten and translated into German) with alchemy. His handwritten notes on alchemy form the structure of his argument and read as follows: "Alchemie./ Chaos. Hades/ *nigredo* extraction animae (herm.-[xx]-mundi)/ *mors*/ Melancholie/ Tortur. Ablutio."

[137] *tenebrositas* (medieval Lat.): "darkness."

This then leads into the next state, the *illuminatio*, specifically the stage called the *albedo*, that is, the whitening, the whiteness.[138] This is compared in alchemy to the rising of the sun, early morning before dawn, the first light before the sun comes up. This is the moment when the blackness of sin is washed away, when the new light comes. It is also referred to as the *descensus animae*, the moment when the soul, which in this state was separated from the body (having first been hidden in the darkness of the body), descends. The body is washed and the whiteness enters it. Then the soul re-enters the body.

That is the second week in the meditation series. Here, the beneficence of creation (washing), God's forgiveness (descent), the calling (ensoulment), the justification (purification), then the gifts received by the grace of God, and finally God's guidance are meditated on. All this belongs to the whitening, the blessing of the reanimation (*revividatio*), but where one last thing is still missing: because now we have the dark, sinful state, and an enlightenment, a lightness, but this process has not actually generated a new quality yet—it is merely that the necessary insight into one's own sinfulness has been gained, but there is not yet a new way of being, no reconciliation, no union.

That is why it is followed by the *via unitativa*, that is, the path of union, the *unio mystica*.[139] It is the creation of a being that is free of all stains of the sins of the past.[140] This happens through the union in alchemy, the *conjunctio*, where two separate and different qualities are combined so that a complete, incorruptible creature comes about. In this *via unitativa*, the time is exclusively given over to meditating on the Godhead in all its aspects: as the creative source, as the beauty of the world, as the power and glory of the earth, then the aspect of love, of the law, the highest guide of the world and the giver of all goods and gifts. This meditation on the Godhead in its various aspects is the *unio*, the unification, the becoming-one. Because as a human one always remains imperfect. Man is transferred into the Godhead in a way. That is the eternal spotless and incorruptible state.

In alchemy, the *conjunctio* is defined as a union of a (this time alive) body which is *corpus*, and *anima* (soul). But it still lacks the spirit; that is still to come. And the spirit joins when the union of a masculine and a

---

[138] JLN, p. 5: "sol oriens/ *albedo* descensus animae./ *purificatio*."

[139] JLN, p. 5: "*conjunctio* spiritus cum corpore vivo et purificato. Messe!/ *Deus terrestris*./ Lapis = XP."

[140] RS has "und der Vergänglichkeit" (and transience) instead of "der Vergangenheit" (of the past).

feminine principle takes place. That is exactly what we have seen in Eastern philosophy. *Purusha* and *prakriti* always have to be reunified again and again, because they keep getting separated by the *sattvam*.[141] But in the conscious mind—*cittam*[142]—which separates and perceives the differences, we become aware, obtain the knowledge, that this and that is like that or like this. Our conscious minds continually split things, so that *purusha* and *prakriti* are separated. A curious psychological phenomenon occurs, which must be compensated for. We don't need to go into that further now.

In any case, in alchemy the *conjunctio* is the union of a female and a male principle, the spiritual and the material, as a result of which the perfect body arises, the *corpus glorificationis* of the Last Judgment, where we will all be resurrected with an immortal body.[143] The *subtle body*.[144]

---

[141] *purusha* (male), also *âtman* in the Vedanta tradition, the transcendental Self or pure Spirit, and *prakriti*, i.e., material nature. "In Classical Yoga the *purusha*, which is styled the 'power of Awareness' (*citishakti*) is conceived as being absolutely distinct from nature (*prakriti*), which lacks all awareness. Yet what we call consciousness is due to a curious correlation (*samyoga*) between the *purusha* and the *prakriti*" (Feuerstein, 1997, p. 236). Sir John Woodroffe (pseud. Arthur Avalon) described the *purusha* as "a center of limited consciousness—limited by the associated Prakrti and its products of Mind and Matter" (Avalon, 1919, p. 49). Jung discussed the *purusha* in the Kundalini seminar on 26 October 1932: "So *purusha* is identical with the psychical substance of thought and value, feeling. In the recognition of feelings and of ideas one sees the *purusha*. That is the first inkling of a being within your psychological or psychical existence that is not yourself—a being in which you are contained, which is greater and more important than you but which has an entirely psychical existence" (Jung, 1996 [1932], pp. 45–46). In his lectures of 2 June and 9 June 1939, Jung described the relationship between *purusha*, *prakriti*, and *sattvam* in detail. Of the latter he said, "These are *purusha* and *sattvam*. The difference between the *purusha* as the simple primal being and the *sattvam* which is a derivative combination or a functional result of the collision of *purusha* and *prakriti*. In other words, a differentiation of the self and the I" (*JMP*, vol. 6, p. 248).

[142] *citta/cittam* (Sanskr.): "mind" or "consciousness", from *cit* (to be conscious). See also Jung's lecture of 9 June 1939 (*JMP*, vol. 6, p. 248).

[143] 1 Corinthians 15:42–44: "So also is the resurrection of the dead. It is sown in corruption; it is raised in incorruption:/ It is sown in dishonour; it is raised in glory: it is sown in weakness; it is raised in power:/ It is sown a natural body; it is raised a spiritual body. There is a natural body, and there is a spiritual body" (*KJV*).

[144] Jung uses the English expression. In his lecture of 24 February 1938, he described the subtle body as "[a]n idea one also finds among primitives who differentiate the subtle body, the breath body, from the visible body. The subtle body is also described as anima. In Latin, *animus*, in Greek *anemos*, meaning wind or breath, thus a being of breath. This notation runs through the whole of alchemy. And you can find this idea the world over. Everywhere you have the idea of this subtle body, not as immaterial but of a finer quality (subtle), including the spirits" (*JMP*, vol. 6, pp. 156). He gave a detailed analysis of his understanding of the concept in his seminar on Nietzsche's *Zarathustra* (Jung, 1989 [1934–39], pp. 441–46, 449–50). Cf. also his lecture of 3 November 1933 (*JMP*, vol. 1, pp. 24–25) and

The *lapis philosophorum* is therefore also called the *lapis aetherius* and *invisibilis* (stone of invisibility). And the alchemists call this body which emerges from the *conjunctio* the *deus terrestris*, the earthly God, God of the earth. Now, the alchemists themselves draw an analogy between the *lapis* and Christ. That is very significant in alchemical philosophy, and led to the representation of the alchemical process as *missa*, as the Mass. I have brought a picture to show you how the alchemical process is depicted as a Mass [Fig. 1].[145]

Psychology and Religion (1938, § 160). In his private library, Jung had a copy of *The Doctrine of the Subtle Body in Western Traditions* (1919) by the historian, writer, and theosophist George Robert Stow Mead (1863–1933).
    [145] *The Artifex as Priest*, frontispiece to Melchior Cibinensis, *Symbolum*; from Maier (1617), p. 509. Also in Jung (1944) (*CW* 12, p. 397).

Lecture 10[146]

30 JUNE 1939

[147]I HAVE BEEN asked whether there is a written summary of my ideas about yoga philosophy. Regrettably, there is currently no such publication. I have only published one small thing about yoga: an examination and comparison of the Eastern attitude toward yoga and the Western psychological problem. This essay was published in an Indian journal in English: *Prabuddha Bharata*, that is, "Awakened India."[148] It is a modern philosophy journal devoted to yoga philosophy. I can't remember what year it was, but if you are interested, I can write and let you know. About the texts which I discussed with you, however, I have not published anything.

Last time we finished with an exposition of the alchemical parallels to this meditation series. I will remind you again briefly of the sequence:

> *via purgativa*;
> *via illuminativa*;
> *via unitativa*.

I compared the first two with the typical stages of the hermetic and alchemical process, and we got as far as the third phase, the *via unitativa*. I told you that the corresponding alchemical stage was called the *conjunctio*, the union of the spirit with the body. It is usually depicted in the form

---

[146] The text of this lecture is compiled from notes by LSM, ES, RS, and OK, as well as the English translation by BH.

[147] ES noted at the beginning: "*The psychological aspect of the mother archetype.* Lecture by C. G. Jung given at the Eranos conference in summer 1938 and published by the Psychology Club Zurich. A woman in front of me has this brochure with her. Another woman has a copy of a postscript to the last lecture, from which I take the following: ablutio = washing clean / albedo = whitening / conjunction = union of a live body which contains body and anima."

[148] Jung (1936a).

of the union of sun and moon, sometimes also of gold and silver: that is, precious metals.

I also mentioned that this typical *unio* of the alchemists is comparable with the purification rites of the Mass. We will examine this further today.

You know that hermetic philosophy, that curious medieval philosophy, was concurrent with the meditations of the Devoti. The body they sought was supposed to be produced by the mystical process which could only succeed by the grace of God, meaning the body became an analogy to Christ, which seems a gross absurdity to us today. But in the Middle Ages it was not absurd. It was not necessary to keep seeking an ultimate metaphysical truth. It was already there. Everything was completely certain. That God had created the world in seven days, and that the son of God had been born and God had become man—these were the ultimate truths beyond which there was nothing. As a result, the relationship of the chemical body could not be understood any other way than in the light of this metaphysics. If, therefore, a healing body was supposed to be found, it could not happen in any way other than through the grace of God, who had demonstrated this miraculous incarnation through his son. As a result, they attempted to frame the alchemical process according to the Christian dogmatic sequence of images: conception, birth, suffering and death of the Lord. This was imagined in material terms, and thus tried to effect the chemical transformation through material substances. That is why another name for this miraculous body, this *lapis philosophorum*, was the *salvator*, the savior—as a way of characterizing it as the physical savior in contrast to the spiritual one which was Christ. In the Middle Ages, Christ was by no means a historical figure, but rather a presence, as he still is today in the Catholic rites whereby the life and death of the Lord still take place in the Mass. In the Middle Ages, God was present everywhere, including in chemistry, and his presence was assumed to be in all things.

The stone was also referred to as the *pelicanus noster*.[149] The pelican feeds its young with its own blood. There are depictions of it piercing its breast with its beak in order to feed its young, in the same way as the Lord died for us and miraculously nourishes us with his blood. Because he is the bread and the wine.[150] Thus the *lapis* was also called the *cibus*

---

[149] *pelicanus noster* (Lat.): "our pelican." Cf. *JMP*, vol. 6, pp. 170–71.
[150] JLN, p. 5: "medicina catholica, aurum potabile."

immortalis,[151] *medicina catholica*,[152] panacea, *aurum potabile*,[153] or *sanguis spiritualis*.[154] One could assume that this particular development of the concept in hermetic philosophy clearly stems from the Church tradition. It was doubtless influenced by it. At that time there were also well-known alchemists within the Church, such as Albertus Magnus,[155] who took a close interest in these things. Certain treatises have also been ascribed to others, but it is all rather doubtful. But what is certain is that the language of the Church fathers plays a significant role in the whole symbolism of hermetic philosophy.

That would all be well and good were it not for the fact that these alchemical ideas began at the same time as the origins of Christianity. Many of these ideas are even found in pre-Christian times, particularly in China.[156] In this regard, there can be no possible doubt that the miraculous baptismal water in the Church is already anticipated in treatises from the first century AD. And they go back to pre-Christian sources. Back then a rich body of literature was already available, of which only a few excerpts remain, popping up as quotations. So we have here a case of ancient natural philosophy apparently exerting an influence on the beginnings of Christianity.

In the Mass, we find precisely these symbols of union, this *unio*, specifically in the Roman Catholic Mass with the act of breaking the Host: the bread is broken in half and the lower part of the left half is broken off again and mixed with the wine. That is the breaking of the body of Christ. Part of this body is mixed with the blood, that is, the wine. Wine is *spiritus* in both senses of the word, and thus body and spirit are reunified.

---

[151] *cibus immortalis* (Lat.): "immortal food."

[152] The English physician and occultist Robert Fludd (1574–1637) wrote a two-volume alchemical treatise entitled *Medicina catholica* (Fludd, 1629–31).

[153] *aurum potabile* (Lat.): "drinkable gold."

[154] *sanguis spiritualis* (Lat.): "spiritual blood."

[155] Albertus Magnus (ca. 1200–80), also known as Albert the Great, was a German Dominican friar and theologian, who is regarded as one of the most universal thinkers of his time. He left Paris in 1247 to become regent of studies in Cologne. In 1259, together with his student Thomas Aquinas (1225–74), he was involved in establishing a study program for the Dominican order, which involved the study of philosophy, and set the foundation for Dominican scholastic philosophy. Albert and Thomas were both instrumental in synthesizing Aristotelian philosophy with Christian doctrines. The alchemical text *Libellus de alchimia* was falsely ascribed to Albertus Magnus. See also *JMP*, vol. 6, pp. 189–90.

[156] In 1929, Jung wrote a psychological commentary on the Chinese Taoist alchemical text *The Secret of the Golden Flower* (Jung, 1929). This collaboration with the sinologist and former Christian missionary in China Richard Wilhelm (1873–30) coincided with the end of his work on *Liber Novus*.

The relevant part of the Mass goes (translated from the Latin), "May this commingling and consecrating of the Body and Blood of our Lord Jesus Christ avail us who receive it until life everlasting."[157] It is therefore the *cibus immortalis*, the immortal food. Even medieval philosophers interpreted it like this: that the *mixtio* was a symbol of unity, of the restoration of the living Christ. That, then, is the moment in the Mass when the Lord rises again, and moreover *vere realiter substaniarum*, that is, truly in reality and substance, which is construed as a resurrection. It is referred to directly as such.

In the Byzantine Mass of the Greek Orthodox Church, the breaking is done in an even more interesting way. There is still the Host, or a round piece of bread. But very often there is no Host, but behind the altar and the *iconostasis* (picture wall), on the *prothesis* (a table or a kind of sideboard) lies a loaf of bread. And there a priest carries out the supposed slaughter of Christ (*mactatio Christi*) by piercing the loaf with the silver spear in the same way that Christ was stabbed in the side by the soldier. In that way the priest makes sure that Christ is really dead. Then the actual transubstantiation takes place.[158] The Host bread is then divided not into two, but into four parts. These four parts are laid on the paten, a small silver plate. Arranged as follows [Fig. 2]:

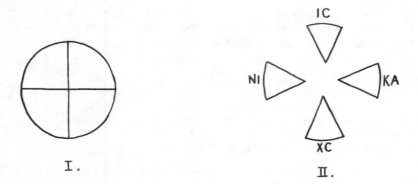

I.   II.

[157] Jung had the original Latin text written down amongst his lecture notes: "Byzant. Mass/ in this arrangement to discos patena./ Rom. *Commixtio./* Haec commixtio, et consecratio corporis et sanguinis Domini nostri Jesu Christi fiat accipientibus nobis in vitam aeternam. Amen./ *mixtio:* Symbol of unity and of *resurrection:* Blood and soul of the Lord combine with the dead body (vide Brinktrine: p. 244)/ Conciliation and salvation. Eph. 2, 1 & 14." (JLN, p. 5).

[158] According to the teachings of the Roman Catholic church, "transubstantiation" designates the conversion of the whole substance of the Eucharistic elements of bread and wine into the substance of the body and blood of Christ at consecration by the priest. (See Waterworth, 1848 [Council of Trent, session 13], p. 79). Jung gave a lecture on the transformational symbolism of the Mass at the Eranos conference of 1941 (Jung, 1942b).

```
                                        IC
                                        V

Jesus Christus nika =              NI >          < KA

Jesus Christ conquers                   ∧
                                        XC
```

That is the establishment of the quaternity. They are four individually existing pieces. It corresponds exactly to the quartering into the four elements in alchemy. Then they are put together again with the wine, as a result of which Christ is resurrected: the joining together of the separated. These ritual activities in the Mass correspond precisely to the alchemical processes which, in their late medieval form, were naturally greatly influenced by the Mass.

Many objections were raised by Protestants about the validity of the Mass. According to the Gospels, it was not warranted. But the ideas that were represented in the rituals of the Mass actually already appear in the Pauline epistles, which are known to be older than the Gospels. Thus, in the Epistle to the Ephesians, we find a passage which contains notions that correspond exactly to our meditation series:

> And you hath he quickened, who were dead in trespasses and sins;/
> Wherein in time past ye walked according to the course of this world,
> according to the prince of the power of the air, the spirit that now
> worketh in the children of disobedience[.][159]

That is the Gnostic notion of the lord of the world. It is presumably the actual Dêmiourgos[160] of the Gnostic systems, who in his vanity imagined he had created a world, and one day, when he had had enough of admiring his work, looked up and discovered a light above him that he had not created. And he traveled until he reached the light, which was always so far above him. And then he came to another world, and it suddenly dawned on him that worlds and worlds existed and had existed alongside the one he had created. This is a Gnostic myth and it is a psychological experience.

[159] Ephesians 2:1–2 (*KJV*).
[160] *Dêmiourgos*: Greek for "demiurge," according to Gnosticism the creator God of the world who is, due to his material imperfection, opposed to a higher spiritual deity. In the *Visions Seminar*, Jung identified the Gnostic God Abraxas, who plays a significant role in Jung's *Liber Novus*, with the demiurge (Jung, 1997 [1930–34], pp. 806–7). Cf. also Jung's lecture of 26 May 1939 (*JMP*, vol. 6, pp. 227–28).

He had to apprehend that he was only a lesser God. The religious communities of the time interpreted it as the Jewish God and even then made antisemitic corrections to the Old Testament. Then it continues,

> Among whom also we all had our conversation in times past in the lusts of our flesh, fulfilling the desires of the flesh and of the mind; and were by nature the children of wrath, even as others./ But God, who is rich in mercy, for his great love wherewith he loved us,/ Even when we were dead in sins, hath quickened us together with Christ, (by grace ye are saved;)[161]

Then a part about the Jews, who at least had a promise of the covenant with God, while the heathens had been without God.[162] It goes on,

> For he is our peace, who hath made both one, and hath broken down the middle wall of partition between us;/ Having abolished in his flesh the enmity, even the law of commandments contained in ordinances; for to make in himself of twain one new man, so making peace;/ And that he might reconcile both unto God in one body by the cross, having slain the enmity thereby[.][163]

The reconciliation of both parts in one body, with God through the cross. These are ideas that were present before any ritual was formed, and that certainly very much concerned the spirit of the early Christians, as such ideas were then incorporated into the Mass. Another such idea:

> Now therefore ye are no more strangers and foreigners, but fellow citizens with the saints, and of the household of God;/ And are built upon the foundation of the apostles and prophets, Jesus Christ himself being the chief corner stone;/ In whom all the building fitly framed together groweth unto an holy temple in the Lord:/ In whom ye also are builded together for an habitation of God through the Spirit.[164]

These ideas of spiritual temple-building continued to have a huge effect later. The last remains of it are the Freemasons, the final remnants of that philosophical secret sect of the Rosicrucians, who stemmed from the

---

[161] Ephesians 2:3–5 (*KJV*). Jung quoted from the Zürcher edition of the Bible of 1931.

[162] Jung refers to Ephesians 2:12: "That at that time ye were without Christ, being aliens from the commonwealth of Israel, and strangers from the covenants of promise, having no hope, and without God in the world[.]:" (*KJV*).

[163] Ephesians 2:14–16 (*KJV*).

[164] Ephesians 2:19–22 (*KJV*).

alchemists. They, therefore, are the last of the alchemists. Unfortunately, the Freemasons today no longer pay attention to their history, but focus instead on other things.

The development of the soul as a kind of temple-building is seen in the Eastern series of symbols in which the monastery (*vihâra*) is built[165], the building of a real temple where the highest Buddha is then enthroned.[166] These are perfectly parallel notions, namely the idea of the union of the two: of the one who was held in a certain way in the spiritual life by the covenant of God (by the messianic promise) with the one who was dead; that is, the union of the spiritual and unspiritual, which was then accomplished later in the ritual act. According to Paul's view, Christ himself united the dead and the spiritual and is therefore the savior from the law of death, because he united the opposites, and precisely because of that, he himself is freed from the law of death.

I would also like to give you a small example of the way in which these meditations of Cisneros were formulated.[167] It will serve as an example of these meditation texts which abounded in the Middle Ages. So here is a text in which you can see how different the people in the Middle Ages were (and we still are today) from their Eastern counterparts. As an example of his form of meditation we will choose the observations of the first week on "sin." Cisneros says,

> And then, withdrawing within thine own spirit, look on thyself as a guilty man; and standing before thy God with great fear, as before a severe Judge about to condemn thee, thou must exactly recall to mind and deeply consider how much God is offended by every sin. Thus, in order to pierce and rouse thyself to devotion [. . .] let thy heart at the beginning of thy prayer be wounded by the thought of thy sins; and thus, sharply reproaching thyself under the pricking of these thorns, say to thyself as follows, "O my soul, bethink thyself now most carefully, and strive with all thy might to feel how much even one sin is displeasing to God. See how pride cast down Lucifer from Heaven, disobedience drove Adam out of Paradise; Sodom and Gomorrah were burnt for luxury, and the whole world perished by the Flood."

---

165 RS added "oben" (above) here.
166 See *JMP*, vol. 6, pp. 132–33.
167 OK: "Dr. Jung then read from this text a long set of instructions by Cisneros that were used for the exercises."

Think how the Son of God, thy redeemer, underwent for sin a most bitter death that sin might not be unpunished, and God's justice might be duly satisfied. [. . .] Turn over likewise in thy mind the sins thou didst commit before thy conversion; how manifold they were [. . .] and indeed they were so many that thou canst not reckon up their number. [. . .] See how weighty they are, since thou hast offended God and crucified Christ afresh by them [. . .]; how little thou hast done to make amends for thy sins; how little thou hast grieved for them [. . .]. Where therefore thou, being a sinner, and above all if thou art a beginner, dost feel the arrows of fear in thy heart, and thy soul filled with grief, not through the fear of the Hell thou hast deserved, but because thou hast wronged thy most loving God, bow down thy soul, rest thy head on thy hands, thinking thyself unworthy to look up to Heaven, and, turning thy heart towards thy God, say, with bitter sorrow, "O most loving Father, I am the prodigal son who committed all these crimes against Thy boundless Majesty and I have been so thankless to Thee. [. . .]"

When, therefore, thy soul hath been after this manner tried in the first part of the way of purity, and is full of bitterness and grief at the painful thought of her sins, let her pass on to the second step, that is to say, to compunction [. . .].

And when thou hast after this manner humbled thyself with shame and compunction of heart, say this prayer: "O Lord Jesus Christ, my God, I am that unhappy man, of all sinners the vilest and most wretched, who hath done so many and such great crimes against Thy boundless Majesty, that I am not able to number them; for they are even above the sands of the sea, the number whereof no man can tell."

And when thou hast prayed thus, or in any other wise, as thy devotion or the sorrowing of thy heart shall move thee to do, try with all thy strength to bring forth sighs and groans from thy inmost heart [. . .].

Now when thou hast schooled thyself well in compunction of heart, despair not of God's mercy, but rouse thyself to hope, which lifting up of thy heart is the next part of thy work. With great confidence, I say, lift up thy head, which hitherto thou hadst held on thy knees; and rest a little while, recall thy thoughts, and with sweetness of soul lift thyself up to praise the Lord, imploring His mercy, considering His greatness and nobleness, pronouncing at the same time these five words, which will kindle great devotion within thee: "Good, beautiful, sweet, merciful Lord."[168]

In addition, he gives detailed instructions that one should make the sign of the cross every evening while standing or kneeling, appeal to the Holy Ghost, and do meditation exercises on the sins of the day. This examination of one's conscience must be short and succinct. Much store is set by discipline here.

These guidelines give you an approximate image of the spirit in which the meditations were carried out. If you now think back to the Eastern texts you have heard about, you will surely be struck by the enormous difference. We may well say: yes, but that is the Middle Ages. It was another era. But this spirit still exists, even if not in the same form. How do you think we would react if we encountered a Sanskrit text with such things in it? This pious fury at one's own sinfulness, the abasement before God, this contrition. We would think a lot more critically, we would say, "Yes, these Indian people are terribly arrogant, incredibly proud, real barbarians who need to beat themselves up so that they can function." Of course, we do not say that about ourselves. But it is so. You cannot imagine how the European appears from outside. I was interested in doing that once. It was one of the main reasons I wanted to travel. After the world war, my first concern was to go somewhere where there were no White people, in order to properly see the European to a certain degree. It is impossible to see it at home. In the oases of North Africa I caught a glimpse.[169] Then later with the Pueblo Indians I saw how the Europeans actually appear to others.[170] They are birds of prey, pirates, brigands; that's why there are such difficulties. We always want to rob and steal. We are seeing it again today. Of course, the people who have already stolen enough are very satisfied. The others, who have not yet stolen enough, they are

[168] Cisneros (1876 [1500]), pp. 46–51. Jung quoted an unpublished German translation (JLN, pp. 5–7) from Hegardt's Swedish version (Hegardt, 1937, p. 22).

[169] In March 1920, Jung accompanied his friend Hermann Sigg on a business trip to North Africa. They traveled from Algiers via Tunis to Sousse, where Jung parted from Sigg and continued his journey on his own to the oases of Tozeur and Nefta. Jung described the enormous impact this experience had on his soul in *Memories, Dreams, Reflections* (Jung, 1962, pp. 238–45). The *Black Books* reveal that a dream about an encounter that he had with an Arab prince in the Sahara desert held deep significance for him and preoccupied him for a long time after his return. See Shamdasani's introduction to the *Black Books* (Jung, 2020, pp. 75–78). On Jung's trip to North Africa, see Burleson (2005).

[170] In 1925, Jung visited a tribe of Native Americans at Taos pueblo, New Mexico. See Jung (1962), pp. 275–81. See also Jung's lectures of 17 November 1933 (*JMP*, vol. 1, p. 45) and 13 January 1939 (*JMP*, vol. 6, p. 90).

the bad ones. That is why we deserve such admonishments and moralizing discipline. It fits perfectly for the West. That's how we are. We cannot take credit for our morality at all. Heaven knows we need it! Anyone who gets so worked up talking about morality is always suspected of needing it.

Ignatius had come across these meditations. He went to Montserrat, where Cisneros's successor was already installed. There at Montserrat, Ignatius did a general confession. I'll give you his brief biography:[171] His name was Don Íñigo López de Recalde, he lived from 1491 to 1556, died in Rome, and was a Spanish nobleman. He was an army officer, a real soldier who had defended the fortress of Pamplona in the campaign against the French in 1521.[172] After being hit in the leg by a cannonball, the wound healed badly and he was bedridden for a time. Unable to wield the sword, he was given something to read. The then soldier was generally not much of a reader, but he was interested in what he had been given—it was a life of Jesus,[173] and a legend of the saints.[174] He immersed himself in these books and the ideas took hold of him. Because he could no longer fight with the sword, his warrior instinct turned itself against his sins, against the enemy within, against his own failings. The first thing which caused him conflict, therefore, was his worldliness. It concerned being a knight. He had promised a lady he would wear her glove, in true knightly fashion. It caused him a terrible conflict. He had devoted his services as a knight to her. But here was God demanding his service. He then found the solution: constructing a spiritual knighthood. He performed a general confession in the monastery at Montserrat. Then he went to the Dominican

---

[171] JLN, p. 8, contains biographical information about Ignatius in Jung's handwriting.

[172] The battle of Pamplona (or Pampeluna) took place on 20 May 1521. It was part of military campaign of the French-backed Navarrese against the Spanish, who had conquered the Iberian part of the Basque-based Kingdom of Navarre in 1512. The inhabitants of the city of Pamplona, the capital of Navarre, rose up against the Spanish. Loyala rejected the Spanish governor's plan to surrender and took shelter with his troops in the citadel of the castle. The fortress was besieged and finally conquered by the Navarrese.

[173] Ludolph of Saxony (ca. 1295–1348), also known as Ludolphus de Saxonia and Ludolph the Carthusian, was a German Roman Catholic theologian. His highly popular main work De vita Christi (1374) was translated into several languages. It contains not only a description of the life of Christ, but also commentaries, prayers, and meditations. His instructions to meditate by visualizing scenes from the Gospels bear similarities to the Exercitia spiritualia of Ignatius.

[174] The Legenda aurea (Golden Legend) (Voragine, 2012 [1260]) contained the life of the saints collected and told by Jacobus de Voragine (ca. 1230–89). It was one of the most important and widely read books in late medieval Europe. Ignatius used a Spanish translation from 1511 entitled Flos sanctorum.

cloister in Manresa, Catalonia, and subjected himself to strict exercises and acts of penance. He had very interesting visions while he was there. It is extraordinarily interesting, from a psychological point of view, to look in detail at such visions with a modern academic approach. I did this once with our national holy figure Nicholas of Flüe. The only reason he was not canonized was because it was not possible to get enough money together. Otherwise he would have become a real saint. You can read more about that in a piece I wrote for the *Neue Schweizer Rundschau*.[175]

I will quote these visions from Ignatius's biography, which he dictated himself when he was very old to his pupil Gonçalves da Câmara:[176]

> While he was in the almshouse something happened to him, many times: in full daylight he would see clearly something in the air along-side him, which would give him much consolation, because it was very beautiful, enormously so. He couldn't properly make out what it was an image of, but somehow it seemed to him that it had the shape of a serpent, and it had many things which shone like eyes, though they weren't eyes. He used to take much delight in and be consoled by seeing this thing, and the more times he saw it, the more his consolation would increase. And when that thing would dis-appear from his sight he would feel sad about it.[177]

Here there is not yet an interpretation, only a light attempt at interpreta-tion. He would actually have preferred this vision to have a different form. He had expected some kind of human figure such as Christ or Mary. But unfortunately it was a serpent. The serpent as a vision figure is not

---

[175] Nicholas of Flüe, or Brother Klaus (1417–87), Swiss hermit, ascetic, and visionary, who was canonized and declared patron saint of Switzerland by Pope Pius XII in 1947. Jung wrote an article about the saint for the *Neue Schweizer Rundschau* entitled "Bruder Klaus" in 1933 (Jung, 1933a). At the end of the first semester of the lectures at the ETH, on 23 February 1934, Jung gave a psychological account of Brother Klaus (*JMP*, vol. 1, pp. 133–34). See also Franz (1959).

[176] Luís Gonçalves da Câmara (ca. 1519–1575) joined the Society of Jesus in 1545. Between 1553 and 1555, Ignatius dictated his memories to him: what would later form the basis of the saint's semi-autobiographical account *Reminiscences*. In 1555, he was made director for the physical needs of the community in Rome and thus came into close con-tact with Ignatius for a period of seven months. During this time, Gonçalves noted down his observations of the everyday life of Ignatius, which together with some later reflections is known as the *Memoriale* (Câmara, 2004 [1904]). The text was not published before 1904 because Jesuit superiors were worried that it might present the saint in an all too human way.

[177] Ignatius, *Reminiscences*, in *IPW*, p. 20. Jung quoted from Funk's German transla-tion (1913a), pp. 57–58.

supported at all in Christian dogma. The only interpretation would be the serpent from paradise, but that is known to be the devil, the tempter, and is therefore ruled out. The second serpent that could be considered is the serpent made by Moses in the desert, which he set upon a pole to get rid of the plague of serpents.[178] That corresponds with what Christ later said: "And as Moses lifted up the serpent in the wilderness, even so must the Son of man be lifted up."[179] That is the image of the serpent twined around the cross. This symbol also occurs in alchemy. But apparently Ignatius did not know this fact, otherwise he would have immediately interpreted it as being Christ. But he was in the dark about that. But regarding the serpent as Christ, nowhere does it say that it was made of eyes. That is something distinctly new, something individual.

Now, in the Middle Ages it was generally the case that people, including the blessed Brother Klaus, who had a unique vision, very individual, would reframe it until it fitted into Christian dogma. It was no longer about the actual idea, but what could be valid in the Christian dogmatics. We would say, "What did you see?" He would answer, "A snake with glowing eyes." And we would answer, "That is what you saw. You can never prove that it is Christian. You only saw this image. It is something unique and individual."

But eye-serpents like that are by no means rare. I have come across similar images quite often. It is a basic symbol for the lower part of the nervous system. It encompasses the whole of the spinal cord and represents the lower center of the brain. It is the sphere of the instincts, the roots, from which the whole psychic life comes. That's why in Indian philosophy it is a healing serpent.[180] When this serpent appears to us it means "I am reunited with my instincts." That is why the God of physicians, Asclepius,

---

[178] Numbers 21:6–9: "And the LORD sent fiery serpents among the people, and they bit the people; and much people of Israel died./ Therefore the people came to Moses, and said, We have sinned, for we have spoken against the LORD, and against thee; pray unto the LORD, that he take away the serpents from us. And Moses prayed for the people./ And the LORD said unto Moses, Make thee a fiery serpent, and set it upon a pole: and it shall come to pass, that every one that is bitten, when he looketh upon it, shall live./ And Moses made a serpent of brass, and put it upon a pole, and it came to pass, that if a serpent had bitten any man, when he beheld the serpent of brass, he lived." (KJV).

[179] John 3:14 (KJV).

[180] In Tantric yoga, the *kundalini-shakti* (serpent power) is understood as a coiled serpent lying dormant in the *mûlâdhâra chakra* (root-prop wheel), the lowest of the seven *chakra*s (see n. 505). The aim of the yogic practitioner is to awaken the serpent-power in order to rise along the *sushumnâ-nâdî*, the central conduit connecting the chakras, from the base of the spine to the crown of the head. There Shakti unites with Shiva, leading to a blissful state of higher awareness. In 1932, Jung accompanied a seminar series on Kundal-

has a serpent.[181] Because it all depends on reuniting the sick person with their own roots. Life will always cut us off from our roots. That is the danger of living solely in the conscious mind. One of the aims of the art of medicine, therefore, is to restore man to his own constitution in order for him to function according to his original foundations; to react, to live, in accordance with his own rules of life.

Ignatius had been doing penance, his health had suffered, and then this healing serpent appeared to him. In the ancient world, it might have been interpreted as the giant serpent that was brought from Epidaurus to Rome in order to rid Rome of an epidemic. The serpent is the symbol both of venom and of healing. But Ignatius wasn't able to make that interpretation.

Another vision:

> He used to have great devotion to the Most Holy Trinity, and so used to pray each day to the three persons separately. And as he was also praying to the Most Holy Trinity as such, a thought used to occur to him: how was he making four prayers to the Trinity? But this thought troubled him little or not at all, as something of little importance[.][182]

A faint doubt arises here: after all, it ought to have troubled him.

---

ini yoga by the Tübingen Sanskrit scholar Jakob Wilhelm Hauer with a psychological commentary (Jung, 1996 [1932]).

[181] Asklêpios/Asclepius, Greek and (as Lat. Aesculapius) Roman God of medicine and healing, son of Apollo and Coronis, raised by the centaur Chiron, who taught him the art of healing. His cult was particularly strong in the third century BCE. In the so-called Asklepia, priests cured the sick of their ailments using a method called incubation. Asklêpios was worshipped throughout Greece, with the most famous sanctuary being in Epidaurus. His symbol, a staff entwined by a serpent, has long represented the profession of medicine.

[182] Ignatius, *Reminiscences*, in *IPW*, p. 25. Jung quoted from Funk's German translation (1913a) p. 63. In what follows, references to this text are abbreviated as *RE*.

Lecture 11[183]

I HAVE BEEN asked how one can best get hold of my article "Yoga and the West",[184] which I published in the journal *Prabuddha Bharata*. For that I refer you to Watkins publishing house in London.[185] The *Essays in Zen Buddhism* by Suzuki are going to be published in Germany.[186] The German translation is not out yet. It's difficult to predict these days—because there are decidedly higher powers in the world which even prevent publications, we cannot say exactly when it will come out.

In the last session, I mentioned the visions of the blessed Brother Klaus. There is an original publication about them by Father Alban Stöckli of Einsiedeln, which was published in Lucerne: *Die Visionen des seligen Bruder Klaus* [The visions of the Blessed Brother Klaus].[187] You may remember that I mentioned Nicholas of Flüe because he also had visions like Ignatius, and also interpreted his visions in this way: that is, according to dogmatic principles.

---

[183] The text of this lecture is compiled from notes by LSM, ES, RS, and OK, as well as the English translation by BH.

[184] Jung (1936a).

[185] A London-based book store and publishing house that specializes in spiritual literature, founded by the esoteric scholar John M. Watkins, a friend of Madame Blavatsky. The publishing enterprise started in March 1893; the book store was opened in 1897. Watkins printed the first English translation, by H. G. Baynes, of Jung's *Septem Sermones ad Mortuos* (1916), in 1925.

[186] Daisetz Teitaro Suzuki (1870–1966), Japanese philosopher and scholar of Buddhism, in particular Zen Buddhism. His books helped familiarize a wider Western audience with the theory and practice of Zen Buddhism. Suzuki participated in the Eranos conferences in Ascona in 1953 ("The Role of Nature in Zen Buddhism") and 1954 ("The Awakening of a New Consciousness in Zen"). Suzuki's book *Introduction to Zen Buddhism* was first published in Japan in 1934 (Suzuki, 1934b). The German translation with an introduction by Jung came out under the title *Die große Befreiung* in 1939 (Jung, 1939). The *Essays in Zen Buddhism* were published in three series by Luzac & Co. of London for The Eastern Buddhist Society of Kyoto in 1927, 1933, and 1934 (Suzuki, 1927; 1933; 1934a).

[187] Stöckli (1933).

Last time we ended with a discussion of the Ignatian visions.

And, one day, while praying the office of Our Lady on the steps of the abovementioned monastery, his understanding began to be raised up, in that he was seeing the Most Holy Trinity in the form of three keys on a keyboard[.][188]

These three keys on a keyboard he interpreted as the Holy Trinity. His biography refers to himself in the third person, because he dictated it. There it says,

and this with so many tears and so many sobs that he could not control himself. And on walking that morning in a procession which was leaving from there, at no point could he restrain his tears until the mealtime, nor after the meal could he stop talking, only about the Most Holy Trinity, and this with many comparisons, a great variety of them, as well as much relish and consolation, in such a way that the impression has remained with him for the whole of his life, and he feels great devotion when praying to the Most Holy Trinity.[189]

He translated this vision of the three piano keys directly into the Trinity in the dogmatic sense. Of course, to us such an interpretation seems extraordinarily arbitrary. If, however, we adopt the mindset of someone like Ignatius and of that time, the Trinity association is of course the first to come to mind. If he saw something with three parts, it naturally referred to the Trinity. Anyone at that time who saw a vision with any kind of division into three would come to this conclusion, never mind a theologian who writes about the Trinity.

Another episode reported in his biography is the following:

Similarly, while being in that town in the church of the said monastery, and hearing mass one day, as the body of the Lord was being raised, he saw with his interior eyes some things like white rays which were coming from above. And although after so long a time he cannot properly explain this, still what he saw clearly with his understanding was [. . .] how Jesus Christ Our Lord was present in that most holy sacrament.[190]

---

[188] *RE*, p. 25.
[189] Ibid., pp. 25–26.
[190] Ibid., p. 26.

What he actually saw was a bright white light coming down from above. He interpreted it as the presence of Christ in the sacrament of the altar, thus in the Host. This was one of the problems that preoccupied people throughout the Middle Ages—to what extent Christ could transubstantiate in the Host *vere, realiter et substantialiter*.[191] Again, Ignatius simply interpreted this vision to fit the dogmatic idea.

> Often, and for a long time, as he was in prayer, he used to see with his interior eyes the humanity of Christ[.][192]

Another important question in the Middle Ages was what Christ's body actually consisted of. After all, it was the abode of God and could not possibly have all the failings of a human body. The dogmatic formula is of course, "true God and man."[193] So one had to believe that Christ's body was also a human body. But that gave rise to all sorts of doubts which, combined with reason, made it very difficult to apply the dogma. No wonder the problem preoccupied him.

Another vision reads,

> As for the form that used to appear to him, it was like a white body, not very big nor very small, but he did not see any distinction of limbs. He saw this often in Manresa. Were he to say twenty or forty times, he wouldn't be so bold as to judge that this was a lie. He has seen it another time when he was in Jerusalem, and again when travelling to Padua[.][194]

What he saw was a kind of elongated light figure, but it could not be recognized as a human body, because no limbs could be seen. Essentially, then, a glowing shape.

> Our Lady too he has seen in a similar form, without distinguishing the parts. These things he has seen confirmed him back then, and they always gave him such great confirmation regarding the faith, that he has often thought to himself that if there weren't Scripture to

---

[191] *vere, realiter et substantialiter* (Lat.): "truly, really, and substantially." See Jung (1942a).

[192] *RE*, p. 26.

[193] The Council of Trent (1545–63) decreed on the most holy sacrament of the Eucharist that "in the august sacrament of the holy Eucharist, after the consecration of the bread and wine, our Lord Jesus Christ, true God and man, is truly, really, and substantially contained under the species of those sensible things" (Waterworth, 1848, p. 77).

[194] *RE*, p. 26.

teach us matters of the faith, he would be resolved to die for them solely on the basis of what he has seen.[195]

These are psychological facts that demand to be taken seriously. The visions immediately reminded him of the holiest of images, and to see them substantiated in this way moved him deeply, but it was the fact of the vision that moved him, not the interpretation. Such visions are in themselves capable of triggering an immediate invigorating effect in the person who sees them.

Another time he had an epiphany:

After this had lasted a good while, he went off to kneel at a cross which was nearby in order to give thanks to God. And there appeared to him there that vision which had oft been appearing and which he had never recognized: i.e., that thing mentioned above which seemed very beautiful to him, with many eyes. But being in front of that cross he could well see that that thing of such beauty didn't have its normal colour, and he recognized very clearly, with strong backing from his will, that it was the devil. And in this form later the devil had a habit of appearing to him, often and for a long time, and he, by way of contempt would cast it aside with a staff he used to carry in his hand.[196]

This vision, which at first had filled him with the highest spiritual rapture, suddenly gets a different interpretation. At first it was a manifestation of God, and then he suddenly realized, because it was not as brightly colored as usual, that it was evidently a bad spirit—though this realization came through "strong backing from his will." Of course, there is no evidence that it was first particularly good and later particularly bad. It was what it was: a vision, which of course can have both values.[197] The devil can also appear. There is no tangible reason why this thing should now be declared to be evil. But the fact is that it was declared to be evil: that is, a doubt arises from this vision. Actually we do not know what it is. It could be good but it could also be evil, and then comes a decision of will, which makes it into the aspect it is later presented as. That is to say, these unconscious phenomena are morally indifferent, and only when they enter into a particular conscious atmosphere are they identified by consciousness as this or that.

---

[195] Ibid.
[196] *RE*, p. 27.
[197] From this point in the text, one page from RS's manuscript is missing.

Then he had another kind of vision which is very strange:

[T]hey boarded the pilgrim ship. On to this ship too he brought nothing with which to feed himself beyond the hope he was placing in God, just as he had done on the other.[198]

He lived only from alms.

Throughout this time Our Lord often appeared to him, which gave him great consolation and energy. Moreover, it seemed to him he repeatedly saw a large round object, apparently of gold[.][199]

So, a golden ball, something round apparently of gold. And this was now the Lord. It's not easy to see, even from the perspective of Christian dogmatics, why it should particularly be the Lord.

[A]lways growing in devotion, i.e. in facility in finding God, and now more than ever in his whole life. And every time and hour he wanted to find God, he found him. And that now too he had visions often, especially those which have been talked about above, when he saw Christ like a sun. This often used to happen as he was going along talking about important things, and that would make him arrive at assurance.[200]

Psychologically, this means that a spontaneous manifestation of the unconscious always occurs in critical situations. Here it shows itself as a round apparition, like gold; another time it is described as being more like the sun. The analogy with the sun works very well for Christ, insofar as he is often identified with the sun, for example as *sanctus sol justitiae*, that is, the holy sun of righteousness: "But unto you that fear my name shall the Sun of righteousness arise with healing in his wings."[201]

At this point the visions are very authentic, precisely because of their undogmatic character. These are visions that other people could have too, people who wouldn't qualify as saints. One can also see such visions in mentally unbalanced people, of course—rather often actually, because such people are often in very critical situations which for normal people

---

[198] *RE*, p. 33.

[199] Ibid. Jung had typed the passages from *RE* in the translation by Philipp Funk (1913a) on a separate sheet. A handwritten annotation by Jung citing the Latin translation by Anibal du Coudray (from between 1559 and 1561) of the original Spanish and Italian manuscript reads, "res quaedam rotunda tanquam ex auro et magna."

[200] *RE*, p. 63.

[201] Malachi 4:2 (*KJV*).

are not so critical. For people with an unbalanced nervous system, however, such situations are so difficult and conflict-prone that they spiral into a
kind of panic or disintegration. Then such visions can occur, which bring
a kind of solution, rather like an epiphany. It is a concretized epiphany.
The result is then very often that a conscious conviction takes root, such
as the belief that God particularly helped the person by appearing right
at that very moment. Psychologically, this simply means that at certain
typical moments of human life, spontaneous manifestations of the unconscious occur which have this resolving effect. How such things are described
is left to the discretion of the individuals and their convictions. Thus you
might say that Jesus Christ, that is God, appeared to you in the form of
a sphere. But such interpretations often seem inelegant or contrived.

For example, Swedenborg, who made a great impression on Kant, had
his first vision at the age of fifty-six or fifty-seven.[202] He was in London
at the time, had dined very well, and as he sat there after dinner the whole
floor became a mass of wriggling worms. In the corner appeared a figure
with a red cape who said to him, "Don't eat so much!" It was a spontaneous
vision, an insight from the unconscious: "Now you have gorged yourself
too much." These writhing creatures were a projection of his struggling
digestion. The figure was his better self: "Now stop it and be sensible." He
saw it as divine advice, and the extraordinary impression was thus
firmly established. He then believed it had been the Lord himself.

If you study the visions of saints and others, you can roughly see which
visions are authentic. I now want to tell you one of Ignatius's visions
which I would not describe as authentic.

I am jumping ahead. When he already had pupils, he went to Rome
and was in much doubt about whether he would be received by the pope
for his founding of an order. In this state of mind, he had another vision.
He saw how God transferred the protection of the "Society of Jesus" to
his son bearing the cross, and he heard a voice which apparently came

[202] Emanuel Swedenborg (1688–1772), Swedish scientist, philosopher, and mystic, who
had a spiritual awakening in 1744, at the age of fifty-six. From that moment on, he experienced numerous visions and dreams in which Jesus Christ asked him to write *The Heavenly
Doctrine* in order to reform Christianity. In his book *Heaven and Its Wonders and Hell
from Things Heard and Seen* (1758), Swedenborg claimed to have been given access to
heaven and hell to describe the state after the days of the Last Judgment, which had already
happened in 1757. There are repeated references to Swedenborg in Jung's works (Jung,
1905, §§ 706–7; 1952, § 902). Swedenborg's experiences instigated Immanuel Kant to
write anonymously his *Träume eines Geistersehers* (1838 [1766]; Engl.: *Dreams of a Spirit-
Seer*, 1900). See Jung's lecture of 2 February 1934 (*JMP*, vol.1, p. 108).

from Jesus: "I will be favorable to you in Rome."[203] Even if this vision really happened this way and he also really heard the voice, it was a purely dogmatic vision, which I do not find authentic. He had acquired the habit of projection through these visions, which initially had been genuine, and had learned to make his own thoughts appear. If you practice, you can project certain thoughts on to yourself. It has also been said about Mohammed, for example, that he always had visions which fitted the situation and told him what he wanted to hear.

If a vision assumes this complex character, it is usually a projection of something hoped for or thought of. It is a projected fantasy, in other words a concretized fantasy. He thought of it, hoped for it, and let it appear. But that only works in a person who is already well practiced at dealing with the unconscious. First he observes spontaneous visions. Then these visions are revised in keeping with the dogma, and in this way he gradually gains practice in also letting thoughts appear that are now purely dogmatic and have nothing to do with the essence of the unconscious. The more complex the visions, the further they get from the unconscious, and the more questionable their authenticity becomes.

Of course I do not dispute that he had the experience, but the authentic visions are the ones that appear everywhere: also among primitives, for example, who describe the soul as a sphere. The soul's essence appears in the form of a sphere. These ideas can be found in many places around the world. Apparitions of light manifest in almost every spiritualist séance provided a halfway decent medium is present, and also in dreams, all over the world. One has to make a clear distinction between the element that

---

[203] "Ego vobis Romae propitius ero." This affirmation can also be found in a painting on the ceiling of Sant'Ignazio di Loyola in the Campo Marzio in Rome, after Il Gesù the second most important Jesuit church in Rome, which is dedicated to Saint Ignatius. There is no mention of this vision or phrase in RE. According to Pedro de Ribadeneira, the vision, which took place in La Storta, went as follows: "It happened that when they were approaching Rome, on entering an abandoned and isolated church, Ignatius was praying quite fervently. There, right off, his heart changed and the 'eyes of his mind' were so filled with brilliant light that he saw clearly how God the Father commended Ignatius and his companions in a loving way to God the Son as he was carrying the Cross, and put them under the protection of his invincible right hand. When Jesus had most graciously received them, turning to Ignatius with a mild and untroubled expression, even while he was with the Cross, he said, 'I will be favorable to you in Rome.' This quite amazing divine vision marvelously encouraged and strengthened Ignatius. He said to Fabre and Laínez after his prayer, 'What lies ahead for us in Rome I have no idea, whether God wants us to be put on a cross or on the wheel. But this I have discovered and know for sure: whatever outcome awaits us, Jesus Christ is going to be favorable to us.' He revealed his entire vision to his companions to raise their spirit and spur them on." (Ribadeneira, 1572 [2014], pp. 98–99)

is really perceived and the way it is interpreted at a particular time. The sphere naturally signifies the rounded whole. Your own wholeness is revealed to you, which naturally has a resolving effect. It immediately creates a sense of inner security. You have become one with your own doubt.[204] The opposites have united and the sphere is a symbol of that.

Back to the biography of Ignatius:[205] From Manresa he went to Barcelona, and in 1523 to Palestine. He got the money for the journey together by begging, as he was not allowed to have money or possessions, and he lived from alms. In Jerusalem he was expelled by the Franciscan provincial, who was the highest superior at that time in Jerusalem, because he had made himself unpopular with the Turks who were fighting there with the Saracens. He could only stay there a few days. He came back to Barcelona and realized that he needed to get some education. After all, he was a soldier, not a scholar. He began learning Latin, and had to conjugate the verb *amo*. He could not utter the word, because he kept lapsing into a state of *Gottesminne*, "love of God." He felt the total bliss of his love for God. It was not too good for his Latin studies, but a great experience for his piety. But he did not let that stymie his pursuit of knowledge. In Salamanca, he studied philosophy, and at the same time he kept on doing all kinds of proselytizing: speaking to people, that is, to help them. He regularly did the exercises with people whom he met by chance. In 1528, he set off for Paris, on foot, to go and properly study theology. Accompanied by a donkey to carry his books, he walked all the way to Paris, surviving on alms. Both before and after the journey he came into occasional conflict with the Inquisition due to his missionary activities. This was of course unpleasant—it was not an institution to be trifled with at that time. The stench of bodies burning at the stake was still common.

---

[204] ES has "Man ist seinen eigenen Zweifel los geworden" (you are freed from your own doubt) instead of "Man ist mit seinem eigenen Zweifel eins geworden" (become one with your own doubt), and LSM has "Da ist alles, woran man zweifeln könnte, nichts mehr" (all the doubts you may have are no more).

[205] Jung had prepared a handwritten note for this section (JLN, p. 8): "*Don Iñigo López de Recalde* [ed. note: this name was often wrongly given as Loyola's birth name], born 1491. Officer, defended Pamplona against the French in 1521. During illness reads a life of Jesus and a legend of the saints. Conflict with worldliness, esp. with the lady to whom he had dedicated his services. *Spiritual knighthood.* Then general confession at Montserrat. After that Dominican monastery in *Manresa*. Penance. *Visions.* (See *attached*!) Then Barcelona and 1523 Palestine. There expelled by Franciscan Provincial. Then Barcelona. Education attempts: when conjugating "amo" lapses into *Gottesminne*. In Alcalá philosophy. Keeps doing exercises alongside. 1528, with a donkey carrying books, goes to Paris. Always lives from alms. Conflict with Inquisition." From this point, Jung followed again the typewritten German translation by Hegardt (1937).

He was put on trial several times, for example in Salamanca. The people who had followed the exercises with him were questioned. From the files it seems they were mainly women.[206] The statement of a woman who took part in the exercises says that she asked Ignatius of her own volition to guide her and instruct her in how she could serve God. He answered her that she should speak to him often over the course of a month and during this month she should confess and go to communion every week. In the first week she would be very happy and enjoy it, without knowing why. In the second week she would be very sad, but he hoped she would feel great benefit from it. He also told her that he wanted to explain the exercise of the three powers of the soul to her. These are mentioned in the exercises. He also showed her the merit that one could earn in temptation. He spoke of venial sin, *peccatum veniale*, and how it could become mortal sin, *peccatum mortale*.[207] This is typical. First the venial sin, which then leads to mortal sin. He further spoke of the Ten Commandments, of the circumstances of the mortal sins, and of the five senses. He told her that if she entered into God's service, she would be plagued by temptations of evil.[208] He taught her how to examine her conscience, and told her she should do it twice a day, once after lunch and again after dinner, by kneeling down and saying, "My God, my Father, my Creator! I thank you and praise you for all the many blessings that you have bestowed upon me and, I hope, will still bestow upon me."[209] This prayer is typical

---

[206] Here, Jung continues to follow the unpublished German translation by Hegardt (1937), pp. 26–27: "One of the women involved reported to the investigating judges on 10 May 1527, 'that she asked Ignatius to guide her and instruct her in how she could serve God. And Don Iñigo responded that during this month she should confess and go to communion every week. He added that the first time she would be happy, without knowing why, that in the second week she would be very sad, but he trusted in God that she would feel great benefit from it [. . .]. He also said that he wanted to explain the exercise of the three powers of the soul. He also showed her the merit that one could earn in temptation; he spoke of venial sins, and how they could become mortal sins; and of the Ten Commandments, of the circumstances of the mortal sins, and of the five senses [. . .]. He told her that if she entered into God's service, she would be plagued by temptations of evil. He taught her how to examine her conscience, and said she should do it twice a day, once after lunch and again after dinner, by kneeling down and saying, My God, my Father, my Creator! I thank you and praise you for all the many blessings that you have bestowed upon me and, I hope, will still bestow upon me. I beg you on the merit of your suffering for the grace to be able to examine my conscience well.'"

[207] The Latin expressions have been added by Jung to the typewritten German translation of Hegardt (1937).

[208] Jung added the following comment to his Hegardt script: "In the eye there lives an unrecognized demon which drives the adepts mad (Antimimos in Zosimos)." (JLN, p. 8)

[209] Up to here, Jung was using the unpublished German translation of Hegardt (1937), pp. 26–27.

of the West: as I hope you will continue to bestow this and that upon me, and if you have already undertaken to do something for me this time, then, woe betide you if you do not help me further. That is something one still hears a lot today. That is Western religiosity. Asking God for everything in the most unashamed way, that is real Western religion. That reminds me of a somewhat crude story that I must tell you: in olden times there was a small chapel at the Spalentor in Basel. And when the people of Alsace came to the market in Basel to sell their wares, they would stop and pray there to the Mother of God for good business, that they would make at least enough to buy some food, perhaps just a little soup, and maybe also some herbs for the soup, and then perhaps also enough for a bit of cured meat, and so on. And when the baby Jesus then once asked a market woman what else she wanted, the praying lady answered, "Shut your mouth, I'm talking to your mother."[210] This is the kind of psychology that would have the saints beaten if it did not rain. It is a primitive psychology that is still present today, although this story is about fifty years old.

These experiences with the Inquisition and all sorts of rumors flying around about his spiritual activities, which were followed by so many women in particular, started to make things rather awkward for him.[211] Thus in 1528 he headed to Paris, where he stayed for a considerable number of years. There he devoted himself to providing spiritual guidance to Spanish students at the university in Paris, in the form of prayer meetings and confessions, as he had done in Salamanca. Of course the same rumors began circulating in Paris. There were a few unpleasant incidents. There was a series of young Spanish aristocrats, who under the influence of these exercises renounced all worldliness, gave away their possessions (which of course belonged to their parents), and begged for alms in imitation of their master. Ignatius was accused of having confused these young people with intellectual wizardry. He was denounced by the Inquisition. As soon as Ignatius heard about his denunciation, however, he went to the grand inquisitor Doctor Matthieu Ory and explained himself.[212] Ignatius, with

---

[210] North of Basel—Jung's home town—lies the broad Rhine Plain, and to the west of the Rhine is the Alsace region (today part of France), where some people speak a dialect of German similar to that of Basel. Alsace has very fertile land, and from ancient times Alsatian vegetable growers and market-women came to Basel to sell their wares. Their route into the city led through the historic Spalentor, a grand gate in the city walls dating from the fourteenth century. (Thanks to Ulrich Hoerni for this information.)

[211] Jung here continues to follow Hegardt (1937), pp. 27–29.

[212] Matthieu Ory (1492–1557), French Dominican friar and theologian, who was appointed inquisitor by Francis I in 1536 and grand inquisitor for France in 1539. The witness statement at the Roman trial against Ignatius and his companions in 1538 reports that

his winning manner, was able to convince Ory. After that he had no more problems from the Inquisition.

He stayed in Paris until 1530. During this time he worked as a *directeur de conscience*,[213] as spiritual director and guide. He gradually changed, began to withdraw from this activity and devote more time to his studies. He had several negative experiences, in particular when attempting to conduct the exercises with a large number of people all together at the same time. He now decided to do the exercises with just a few people, in peace and quiet, and became more methodical and careful in the selection of his penitents. He restricted his activity essentially to intelligent and educated men. But even with this limited group he was more cautious and avoided exercises. He did not lead his own exercises again until 1533. Then he encountered the people who would be instrumental to the fate of the Jesuit order. He met Peter Faber, who became one of his most important colleagues.[214] He led him through the exercises, and we know that Faber followed them with great success. As if by the wave of a magic wand, Faber was freed from his carnal nature, his temptations, and his character weaknesses. He was filled with spiritual strength and enthusiasm, more than he would ever have dreamed possible.

Ignatius also had similar success converting others, such as Francis Xavier,[215] who became well known through his Indian mission, and Diego

---

"having learnt of and seen their habits, way of life and teaching, he [i.e., Ory] declared them free from all suspicion of heresy, and drew up letters patent for the said Ignatius in his justification" (from the report of Ory's testimony, quoted in *IPW*, p. 373, n. 123). Ory was the author of *Ad haeresum redivivas affectiones Alexipharmacum* (Paris, 1544; Venice, 1551–58).

[213] *directeur de conscience* (Fr.): "spiritual director."

[214] Saint Peter Faber (1506–46), also known as Pierre Favre, born in Savoy in humble circumstances. His extraordinary intellectual talent led him to study philosophy and theology at the University of Paris in 1525. There he shared a room with Francis Xavier (see n. 215), and from 1529 onward also with Ignatius. Before he was ordained priest, Ignatius led him through the spiritual exercises. He was the only priest among those who pronounced the vows of poverty, chastity, and obedience on 15 August 1534 in the chapel of Saint-Denis in Montmartre. Pope Paul III appointed Faber to teach theology and scripture at the Sapienza University in Rome. He was later sent to Germany as part of a Catholic delegation to lead a dialogue for reunification with the Protestants. When these efforts failed, he was sent to Portugal to establish the Society there. On his way to the Council of Trent, where he was appointed one of the papal theologians, he was overcome by a fever in Rome. He died in the presence of Saint Ignatius. Peter Faber was canonized by Pope Francis in 2013. On Peter Faber, see Mary Purcell's biography *The Quiet Companion* (1970).

[215] Saint Francis Xavier (1506–52) was born as Francisco de Jasso y Azpilicueta in the Kingdom of Navarre. In 1525, he went to study at the University of Paris, where he and his friend Peter Faber (see n. 214) shared a room with Ignatius. After the completion of his studies in 1530, he taught Aristotelian philosophy at Beauvais College. Francis Xavier was

Laynez.[216] Thus in 1533 he initiated the Society of Jesus.[217] It was not an organized society, but a small conventicle.[218] They lived from alms, as they had taken vows of poverty and chastity. In 1535, Ignatius returned to Spain. In 1537, he arranged with his companions in Spain and France that they would meet in Venice to make a pilgrimage to the holy sepulcher in Palestine. However, the Turkish war made this sea journey to Jerusalem impossible.[219] In Venice, the suggestion of founding a monastery was made for the first time. He then headed for Rome. On the way he

---

among the seven men who on 15 August 1534 took a vow of poverty, chastity, and obedience in the chapel of Saint-Denis in Montmartre. Subsequently he studied theology and was ordained priest in 1537. Three years later, he was sent together with another co-founder of the Society of Jesus, Simão Rodrigues de Azevedo (1510–79), to the Portuguese colony of Goa in India, becoming de facto the first Jesuit missionary. His mission covered the south of India and Ceylon (modern Sri Lanka), Malacca, Amboina and Ternate, and Japan. He was struck down by a fever and died in 1552 while trying to enter mainland China. Francis Xavier was canonized in 1622. He is the patron saint of Catholic missions, co-patron saint of Navarre in Spain, and the patron saint of Australia, Borneo, China, East Indies, Goa, Japan, and New Zealand. His body remains in the Basilica of Bom Jesus in Goa, and is an object of veneration due to its undecayed state.

[216] Diego Laynez (1512–65), Spanish theologian of Jewish heritage and second superior general of the Society of Jesus. He met Ignatius during his studies at the University of Paris and was one of the seven who pronounced their vows of poverty, chastity, and obedience (see n. 217). Together with Alfonso Salmerón (1515–85), a co-founder of the Society of Jesus, he took part in the Council of Trent as a papal theologian and was instrumental in its outcome.

[217] The vow of Montmatre on 15 August 1534 was taken by seven men in the chapel of Saint-Denis: Ignatius of Loyola, Peter Faber (see n. 214), Francis Xavier (see n. 215), Diego Laynez (see n. 216), Alfonso Salmerón (1515–85), Nicolas Bobadilla (1511–90), and Simão Rodriguez de Azevedo (1510–79). The precise details of the vows are unknown, but they very likely included a life of poverty, chastity, and service to the pope, and a pilgrimage to Jerusalem.

[218] Jung added at the bottom of the typescript translation of Hegart's text the following keynotes: "They formed a small society. In Montmartre in 1534 they took vows of chastity and poverty and devoted themselves to missionary work. In 1535 R. [incorrect for Recalde] returned to Spain. In 1537 gathering of all companions in Venice for journey to Jerusalem. Turkish war. (Idea of forming monastery through contact with Theatines.) Therefore to Rome. Vision on the way: God puts society under protection of son carrying cross. 'Ego vobis Romae propitious ero.' Thus *Societas Jesu*. In 1540 Pope Paul III confirms founding (*Regimini militantis* bull). Ignatius becomes General (*locum Dei tenens*). After appointment goes happily to the kitchen to serve as kitchen hand." (JLN, p. 10)

[219] This refers to the Third Ottoman–Venetian war, between 1537 and 1540. King Francis I of France had formed an alliance with Sultan Süleyman I of the Ottoman Empire to defeat the Roman Holy Empire under the Emperor Charles V. In an attempt to invade the Apennine Peninsula, Ottoman troops conquered the Habsburg areas of Dalmatia and broke their peace treaty with the Republic of Venice by besieging Corfu. The worried Pope Paul III managed to appease France and the Holy Roman Empire and put together a Holy League to stop the Ottoman advances. After heavy losses on the side of the Holy League, a treaty was signed in 1540 to end the war.

had the vision that I already told you, about Christ helping him.[220] In Rome, after considerable initial difficulties, he was finally successful, and in 1540, Pope Paul III confirmed the founding of the Jesuit order with the papal bull *Regimini militantis ecclesiae*.[221] He had achieved his goal. He was appointed the first Jesuit general, specifically as *locum Dei tenens*.[222] It is characteristic of Ignatius that after being elevated to the status of general, he went straight to the kitchen and served as a kitchen hand to prove to himself that he was not too lofty. He was still the first Jesuit general when he died in Rome. That is the rough outline of his life.

I can't discuss the exercises in the short time that is left. It is a very extensive topic. I'll have to keep it for next semester. I'd just like to say something else about the exercises in general. Ignatius certainly broke with tradition in terms of the meditation exercises. The Devoti understood meditation as something that was actually quite close to the Eastern immersion, but of course based on a quite different dogmatic attitude. The purpose of such devotional exercises was an immersion in God, the generation of inner peace, inner stillness, cutting oneself off from the world and letting go—the typical goals of medieval meditation.

Remember what I read out from Meister Eckhart.[223] In contrast, Ignatius made the meditation exercises regimented. He called them exercises, which they had never been called before. They lasted thirty to forty days. Every contemplation lasted exactly one hour. Other ideas also come into these exercises: for example, the *electio*. For the Devoti, the meditations were nothing to do with being an *electus*, a chosen one. But for Ignatius that played a big role. That was his, the Jesuits', goal. His exercises also lack the mystical elements of the religiosity of the Devoti: the ecstasy, for example. The mystical phenomena are completely excluded. At most, certain mystical ideas or feelings are tolerated or allowed as stimuli, to get the will on to the right path. The path of the Devoti went completely

---

[220] See pp. 39–40.

[221] *Regimini militantis ecclesiae* (Lat.: "To the government of the church militant") (1938 [1540]), was a papal bull issued by Pope Paul III on 27 September 1540. The bull restricted the numbers of members to sixty. The restriction was only lifted with a revised text of the bull by Pope Julius III, *Exposcit debitum* (Lat.: "The duty requires") (1937 [1550]).

[222] *locum Dei tenens* (Lat): "representative of divine providence." Chapter 3 of *Exposcit debitum* states that "because of the great value of good order and for the sake of the constant practice of humility, never sufficiently praised, the individual subjects should not only be obliged to obey the general in all matters pertaining to the Society's Institute but also to recognize and properly venerate Christ as present in him" (Aldama, 1990).

[223] See *JMP*, vol. 6, pp. 235–44.

inwards, toward stillness, intimacy, and peace in God. With Ignatius, it is all directed outward: deeds, battle and argument, undertakings, attacks against the world. It is all active and goal-oriented. With Ignatius, the whole edification and mystical immersion are completely consumed in regulation, provisos, very specific instructions, for which reason he was also reproached for reducing everything to the drill rules of a commanding general. I will not venture an opinion about whether this reproach is justified, but I have to mention it. These particular qualities of the Ignatian exercises have a historical origin which comes not from Christianity, but from Arabic mysticism. I will begin with that next semester.

Winter Semester 1939/40

Lecture 1[224]

IN THE PREVIOUS semester we examined the nature of what I have called active imagination. Before I start on the actual topic for this semester, I'll give you a recap of what we discussed in this regard: "imagination" is understood as a way or means to change, improve, heal, elevate, or complete the personality. The word itself comes from the Latin *imago*, that is, image, and means the picturing, the imprinting, of an image or an idea. The word "idea" comes from the Greek *eidos*, which also means image. Through this imprinting of an image, we attempt to generate a transformation of the essence, specifically of the psychological essence, in other words of the human character.

You know that a person's original character is full of contradictions and marked by all manner of disturbances. The character is never, or seldom, a harmonious arrangement. There are always certain tensions present, which can increase considerably over a lifetime and give one the feeling of a disturbance or aberration. This results in difficulties in life and with other people, with regard to circumstances and relationships in our lives. All this results from the contradictions and tensions of the natural character, which is the result of the combination of two long lines of ancestors in which there are of course incompatibilities. After all, people are not just the products of their parents. Their parents are also the result of long lines of ancestors. When two distant tribes mix, it is to be expected that all kinds of incompatibilities will arise in the individuals. That's why, since time immemorial, we have deemed man to be in need of improvement. Admittedly, there are some people who believe that man is fundamentally

---

[224] The text of this lecture is compiled from notes by LSM, ES, RS, and OK, as well as the English translation by BH. ES remarked, "Lecture Jung, W.S. 1939/40 'The individuation process'/ I attended the 1st lecture [3.XI.39] but left my notes in the train, but later got them back."

good. But this view is contradicted by a great many opinions, experiences, and facts. That's why the Christian world view sees man as unfinished, in fact even as being in a state that is outside of grace. The possibility of entering a state of grace comes only after baptism. An unbaptized state is a natural state, uninitiated. This idea is found not only in Christianity, but also in many primitive tribes. For example, the African Kavirondo have the view that young people who have not yet been through the (often very harrowing) initiation rites are only animals, and not yet human.[225] That is how strong the conviction is that the original and natural man is not finished, is far from a state of perfection, or even is not yet a person, but only a creature of nature. This deep conviction gives rise, therefore, to efforts to improve or elevate the human being. At the primitive level, this takes place through initiation rites, which could also be called active imagination in a certain sense, because in these rites the young people are presented with images on which they then have to model themselves. Most of the time this is properly drummed into them, in the same way as the old schoolmasters, like the ones I had, would drum each letter of the alphabet into you with a triple-twisted three-foot willow rod. That's where the word *einbläuen*[226] comes from. On a primitive level, this is not only done directly, but also through hunger, thirst, and lack of sleep, through poisoning (for example, they were forced to drink some concoction which almost poisoned them), through wounding, and so on. Sometimes these creatures who were becoming "human" were in danger of losing their lives in the process, and others were almost driven crazy by such procedures. The sole purpose of these painful procedures was mnemonic, to ensure that the initiates remembered the tribal lore;[227] because along with all the magical procedures, they were taught the sacred tribal lore about how

[225] The term "Kavirondo" refers to the native people living in the valley of the Nzoia river, on the western side of Mount Elgon, and along the northeast coast of Lake Victoria. From October 1925 to April 1926, Jung traveled, together with Helton Godwin ("Peter") Baynes (1882–1943), George Beckwith (1896–1931), and Ruth Bailey to Mount Elgon (4,321 meters; 14,177 feet;), which lies at today's border between Kenya and Uganda. They stayed for a while with the local tribe of the Elgonyi. See Jung (1962), pp. 253–70 and Bailey (1969–70). See too the lecture of 24 February 1938 (*JMP*, vol. 6, p. 160).

[226] Trans. note: *einbläuen* means "to teach something through continued insistent repetition"; *bläuen* "to hit," or "to turn blue." Bruises are also called *blaue Flecken* (blue spots) in German.

[227] Friedrich Nietzsche (1844–1900) advanced a similar argument in his philosophical polemic *Zur Genealogie der Moral* (1887) (*KSA*, vol. 5; Engl.: 2006): "[P]erhaps there is nothing more terrible and strange in man's prehistory than his *technique of mnemonics*. 'A thing must be burnt in so that it stays in the memory: only something that continues to hurt stays in the memory'—that is a proposition from the oldest (and unfortunately the longest-lived) psychology on earth" (2006, p. 38).

the gods and their half-animalistic forebears originally created the earth, the humans, the animals, and the plants. In this way, humans are elevated to a higher state, through a secret knowledge. They become spirits, in a way. They have to go through a figurative death and are taught that they died and through rebirth have become spirits. That is how it is at the primitive level.

At higher levels, there are more complicated and more spiritual forms of transformation, and thus in the previous semesters we looked at the clearest forms of this type: for example, Eastern yoga traditions. I told you about classical yoga, about the *Yoga Sûtra* of Patañjali.[228] I also told you about two Buddhist texts which relate to this transformation.[229] In these, a series of aids of a symbolic nature are used, symbolic images that represent the transformation, and through the internalizing of the images, the individual is supposed to be transformed. Through contemplation one should be transformed into that which is the goal of Buddhism, that is, to become Buddha. We dealt very thoroughly with the series of symbols in the Buddhist rituals. I would like you to recall this series, because it is important that you keep this canon of symbolic transformation in mind for later, when we come to the Western parallels. In the course of the previous lectures I also gave you a Western parallel from the Middle Ages: namely, the hermetic or alchemical transformation series, which can be placed directly alongside the Eastern symbol series.

East:
1. Emptiness

West:
1. Chaos or *nigredo* (blackness)

In the East, "emptiness" means the mental discarding of thoughts. The training that leads to that is yoga training, which is done together with all kinds of physical exercises that are intended to lead to an emptying of the conscious mind. In contrast, in the West the "chaos" or "nigredo" is not thought of as a mental state, but as a material state. That is the big difference: Eastern mysticism is driven by the soul, while in the West it is matter. The Westerner sees all psychological experience first in matter. That is the initial state in Genesis: "And the earth was without form, and void; and darkness was upon the face of the deep."[230] That is this chaos. A state of deepest unconsciousness, devoid of thoughts, which is equivalent to the very origins of the world. Why is it like this in the West? It is actually a

---

[228] See the editor's introduction to *JMP*, vol. 6 (Liebscher, 2021, pp. xlvii–li).

[229] In the previous lectures series, Jung had spoken about the *Amitâyur-dhyâna-sûtra* and *Shrî-chakra-sambhâra Tantra*. See again the editor's introduction to *JMP*, vol. 6 (Liebscher, 2021, pp. li–lxix).

[230] Genesis 1:2 (*KJV*).

curious fact that in the West, a soul secret or soul state is discovered in matter. That shows you the extraordinary extraversion of the Western spirit toward the matter of the world. We see it in things, Eastern people see it inside, in the soul. The Easterner does not explain the chaotic state with something external.

| 2. Four elements | 2. Tetramery |

The symbols of quartering on the Eastern and Western side correspond to each other. When there is an empty or chaotic state, a process of division must set in. One thing must be differentiated from another. That is an act of consciousness, a differentiation. Consciousness arises out of the chaos. On the second day of the Creation, the *divisio* takes place, the separation of the upper and lower waters.[231]

| 3. Mount Meru | 3. *separatio* |

In the East, Meru, the cosmic mountain, rises up out of the absolute surface as the initial form. It symbolizes a definite something amid absolute indeterminacy. It is an anticipation of form. A form emerges. The *separatio* is the dividing of the liquid from the solid, according to Genesis. That would be the third day of the Creation.[232] What rises up out of the watery medium, or coagulates from it, are the *montes*, the mountains.

| 4. City | 4. *castrum* |

From the peak of this mountain, a well-enclosed city then emerges, built by human hands. It corresponds to the *castrum* (castle) in the medieval West, the fortress, the city or the *thesauria* (treasury). The mountain ultimately means form, in the last instance human form. At the top is the head, and within it consciousness. It is a sealed off mental space. In the same way, the *castrum* is apart and protected against the influence of the environment. From that comes a four-headed being, the

| 5. *vajra* | 5. *congelatio* |
| (diamond, thunderbolt) | (solidifying) |

---

[231] Genesis 1:6–8: "And God said, Let there be a firmament in the midst of the waters, and let it divide the waters from the waters./ And God made the firmament, and divided the waters which were under the firmament from the waters which were above the firmament: and it was so./ And God called the firmament Heaven. And the evening and the morning were the second day" (*KJV*).

[232] Genesis 1:9: "And God said, Let the waters under the heaven be gathered together unto one place, and let the dry land appear: and it was so" (*KJV*).

This *vajra* mainly appears in Tibetan Buddhism. It is the incorruptible substance, that which no longer changes. It is extremely valuable and corresponds to the *lapis philosophorum*, the philosopher's stone of the alchemists. The corresponding stage in the West is the *congelatio*, the freezing, becoming solid; the *quaternitas* or *quaternarium*, that is, the quaternity. The quaternity becomes solid; in other words, the four elements melt together. What was separate is joined together. There is now a solid unit, a center. But, we could say, this center already exists. It is the I. That would be the most obvious assumption, and in actual fact we do find numerous points in alchemy which indicate that this center is actually the I. But on the other hand, there are many more indications that it is not the I, but another center. It is as if, through this process, it is not the I, which already exists, that arises—otherwise it could not after all have been divided into four parts, as that itself would be a conscious act of will—but rather some other essence, a center that did not exist before, a new center of the personality. I have called this center the self. There is positive evidence of this in the Eastern texts, which make specific reference to it.

So what is the self? It is a center or a wholeness that consists not only, like consciousness, of the conscious psyche, but of both the conscious and unconscious parts of the psyche together. This self also comprises what we are but do not know we are. We are much more than we think, and sometimes also much more unpleasant, or indeed pleasant, than we know. We are not only that which we imagine ourselves to be—we are also the effect that we have on other people. On the whole, we are extraordinarily unaware of these other traits. But if we look at our dreams, for example, we find parts of our personality acting in ways that we're completely unaware of during the day, unless a good friend takes us aside and has a quiet word one day. We do not know the extent of the self, because the limits of the unconscious psyche cannot be determined. We need to realize that.

What appears here is thus an initial structure of the self. That is, the treasure that is hidden in the castle, guarded in the treasury. That is the big treasure, the solidified center of the personality that can no longer be changed. The I, on the other hand, is very changeable. The I includes all sorts of possibilities. In contrast to the I, this being or essence is as it is, and not as we wish it to be.

This essence is also characterized by four colors, which are always red, green, yellow, and blue. We find the same in the West. When the colors appear, the older masters say, then the *cauda pavonis*—the peacock's tail—appears.[233] They represent the qualities of this being. One old alchemist says so many colors appear that only God could have imagined them. That's because it is a supernatural being. It has not come about through natural processes, but only through this mystical procedure. At first it is an inanimate object. *Vajra* is simply a concentrated energy and is represented by the diamonds. The quaternity, the *quaternarium*, is static, with a crystalline form. Now the lotus makes an appearance:

6. Lotus	6. Golden flower, tree

The lotus is a plant, a flower, and corresponds to the alchemical idea of the golden flower. Another variant is the tree, the *arbor philosophica*.[234] The apparently inorganic essence, which has solidified and has four colors, now comes to life and is capable of growth and improvement.

7. Moon	7. *luna*

From the lotus emerges the moon. This corresponds to the alchemical stage of *luna*, or moon, and is also referred to as the silver (*argentum*).

8. Sun	8. *sol = aurum =* gold

The sun is also included as the masculine equivalent to the moon. The sun corresponds to the gold: *sol—aurum.*

These now again appear to be inorganic characteristics, but in fact are symbolic: as are the moon, the sun, this divine couple the sun-god and moon-goddess, philosophically speaking the masculine and feminine, the two forms of the lotus. This is a contrast that is developed at another stage. Here the lotus enters the picture again, but strictly in the feminine sense:

9. Lotus yoni	9. The white woman, *al-baida*

That is, the female genitals. This corresponds in alchemy to the "white woman," *al-baida*, which is Arabic for "the white one." She is also identified with silver. She is the *regina*, the queen, in elevated human form, as kings and queens are representatives of the gods.

10. Moon with lingam	10. *conjunctio*

This is the union of the feminine and the masculine, namely of the moon with the lingam. The lingam has a double meaning: it is the phallus, the

---

[233] See *JMP*, vol. 6, pp. 168, 199–200.
[234] See Jung (1954a).

male genitals, but it is also the *subtle body*,[235] the breath body, the spiritual body. The union of the two is of course thought of as a sexual union. In alchemy, it is the *conjunctio* that is always represented as a sexual act and which takes place between the white woman and the *servus rubeus*, the red slave. That is the *rex*, the king. These are the two famous alchemical colors: the white and the red, which represent precisely this *conjunctio*. Here the opposites, which are ultimately depicted as masculine and feminine, are brought together in union. The self, therefore, is a *coincidentia oppositorum*, a coming together of the opposites, the solution to the problem of the opposites. After all, that is why one strives for this goal, this unchangeable, inexorable unity.

| 11. *vihâra* | 11. *vas hermeticum* |

Vihâra, the cloister, is no longer a city, but a sacred[236] site in which the creature that arises out of this union will live. The union is fruitful. It produces a child who grows up in Vihâra. Vihâra corresponds to the famous *vas hermeticum* of hermetic philosophy, the container in which the transformation takes place. It is called the glass house and is identical with the retort in which the transformation takes place and in which the homunculus appears. In the East they call this living creature the Mahâsukha:

| 12. Mahâsukha | 12. hermaphrodite |

Mahâsukha, the lord of blessedness, is the Buddha. Here, on the other hand, it is referred to as a hermaphrodite: that is, a dual-sex creature that symbolizes the union of the opposites. It is sometimes depicted as the child of the sun and moon. That is the homunculus, the philosopher's stone, the *lapis philosophorum* which is said to be transparent, respectively invisible, an ethereal being, alive like a human being. It is also described as the great light, the *lux moderna*, the new light that illuminates the darkness: "lumen exortum in tenebris."[237] For the philosopher Zosimos,[238] it is the *phôteinós*, the person of light. According to Christian teachings, even back

---

[235] Jung used the English term.

[236] BH has "spiritual."

[237] "Exortum est in tenebris lumen rectis: misericors, et miserator, et justus" (*Vulgate*, Psalm 111:4). The *KJV* translation counted as Psalm 112:4 reads, "Unto the upright there ariseth light in the darkness: he is gracious, and full of compassion, and righteous."

[238] Zosimos of Panopolis (active around 300 CE), Greco-Egyptian alchemist. His authentic writings are grouped in *Authentic Memoirs*, the *Chapters to Eusebia*, the *Chapters to Theodore*, and *The Book of Sophe* (see Mertens, 2006, p. 209). Jung had a particular interest in the mystical aspect of his alchemy and wrote on three chapters from the *Authentic Memoirs* known as the *Visions*. See Jung (1954b), which is an extended version of his

then this figure was described as the second Adam.[239] The first is mortal, corrupted. He was sentenced to death because of his unfinished state. The second Adam, who is identified with Christ, is the sempiternal, the eternal, the incorruptible. For this reason he is also called *salvator noster*, "our redeemer," and *medicina catholica*, which heals people not only of their physical ailments, but also of their mental suffering. He is also referred to as *scintilla*, "the spark," in Greek *spitha*, or directly as *tò tês psychês phos*, "light of the soul": that is, a substance that brings enlightenment or initiation. It is therefore also known as Hermes, who is the great *psychagôgos* or *psychopompós*,[240] the guide of souls, the initiating priest of the mysteries. That is why there are also depictions of this creature enclosed in a transparent glass ball. Inside the ball is Hermes, the guide of souls, who leads men toward truth and enlightenment.

In the "Binding Love Spell of Astrapsoukos"[241] there is a sentence that reads, "Come to me Lord Hermes."[242] And at the end it says, "I am you and you are I."[243] And so there is a mutual recognition, despite being different:

1937 Eranos lecture entitled "Einige Bemerkungen zu den Visionen des Zosimos" (Some observations on the visions of Zosimos).

[239] In his epistle to the Romans and in his first epistle to the Corinthians, Saint Paul formulated his doctrine of the comparison between the first man Adam and the last or second Adam, i.e., Jesus Christ: "Wherefore, as by one man sin entered into the world, and death by sin; and so death passed upon all men, for that all have sinned:/ Therefore as by the offence of one judgment came upon all men to condemnation; even so by the righteousness of one the free gift came upon all men unto justification of life./ For as by one man's disobedience many were made sinners, so by the obedience of one shall many be made righteous" (Romans 5:12, 18–19); "And so it is written, The first Adam was made a living soul; the last Adam was made a quickening spirit./ Howbeit that was not first which is spiritual, but that which is natural; and afterward that which is spiritual./ The first man is of the earth, earthy; the second man is the Lord from heaven" (1 Cor. 15:45–47) (*KJV*).

[240] *Psychagôgos*, from Greek *psyche* (soul) and *agein* (to lead); *psychopompos*, from Greek *psyche* (soul) and *pempein* (to send, conduct). Jung uses the term to describe an archetypal figure guiding the soul through the archetypal world of the collective unconscious. It is often the "anima"/"animus" respectively or the "wise old man" that takes on this role of a mediator between the conscious and the unconscious and "points the way to the highest meaning" (Jung, 1935, § 60). Examples Jung uses frequently are Vergil or Beatrice in Dante's *Divine Comedy*, or Nietzsche's *Zarathustra* (Jung, 1935, § 77). In *Liber Novus*, Elijah and Philemon appear as such guides of the soul.

[241] *Papyri graecae magicae* 8.1–63 (Preisendanz, vol. 2, pp. 45–47; Engl.: pp. 145–46).

[242] "ἐλ[θ]ὲ μοι, κύριε Ἑρμῆ" (Preisendanz, vol. 2, p. 45; Engl.: p. 145).

[243] "σὺ γὰρ εἶ ἐγὼ χαὶ ἐγὼ σὺ" (Preisendanz, vol. 2, p. 47; Engl.: p. 146): "I know you, Hermes, and you know me. I am you and you are I. And so, do everything for me, and may you turn to me with Good Fortune and Good Daimon, immediately, immediately; quickly, quickly."

I am me and he is Hermes, but I am Hermes and Hermes is me. That is the relationship between the I and the self. Like the way in which a small circle enclosed within a larger circle is identical with the larger one: identical, but not the same. We can therefore see here how such symbolism leads to a conclusion that can only be called "becoming oneself", or individuation.

So, with that I completed my discussion of Eastern forms of yoga and moved on to a Western yoga form, if this word is applicable to the West at all: namely, the *Exercitia spiritualia* of Saint Ignatius of Loyola. I presented Ignatius's biography to you and also discussed the visions by which he was guided. We saw that the familiar symbols indicating individuation came up in those visions. At that time, of course, they were interpreted dogmatically. I also told you that our Swiss national holy figure, Nicholas of Flüe—the only reason he has not yet been canonized is due to lack of funds—also had such visions, which he also processed with a dogmatic lens until they fitted into the Christian world view. It was a completely justified process.

I brought it to your attention that the *exercitia spiritualia* did not appear out of the blue, but had already been practiced in the monasteries as meditation exercises in earlier times, specifically with the meditations of the Devoti. I mentioned the direct spiritual forefather of Ignatius: Abbot Cisneros of the Montserrat cloister near Barcelona. That's where Ignatius found the book by Cisneros. The title was *Das Exerzierreglement des geistigen Lebens*.[244] So even before Ignatius we see that this idea of discipline was present, that it had to be accomplished at all costs. That is the West for you. In the East there is no talk of will and discipline. There it all grows naturally. Even if people make the utmost efforts, if they don't get that far it doesn't really matter. After all, you have the whole of eternity ahead of you in which the things you have missed can still happen. You still have a hundred or a thousand incarnations to go, so there's no urgency. The tree can grow peacefully and naturally. In the West, we only have the *one* existence, so it's always urgent. It has to happen, whether it wants to or not. That also has its upsides.

The book by Cisneros includes instructions for a four-week *retraite* [retreat]. That is the *terminus technicus* for "withdrawal." I will briefly go through it again.

---

[244] "The exercise rules for spiritual life"; published in English as *A Book of Spiritual Exercises* (Cisneros, 1876 [1500]); see n. 122.

First week: *Via purgativa*, the path of purification. Here it starts, with the *nigredo*, the darkness of the natural sinful state of the unredeemed:

Monday: Contemplation of sins;
Tuesday: Contemplation of death;
Wednesday: Contemplation of hell;
Thursday: Contemplation of the Last Judgment;
Friday: Contemplation of the Passion of Christ;
Saturday: Contemplation of the sorrows of Mary;
Sunday: The sun rises. Meditation on the glory of heaven.

Second week: *Via illuminativa*. Here God's good deeds are contemplated:

Monday: The Creation;
Tuesday: God's forgiveness;
Wednesday: The calling;
Thursday: The justification;
Friday: Particular gifts received by the grace of God;
Saturday: The guidance of God.[245]

Third week: *Via unitativa*. In the first week we had the painful, dark, sinful state. In the second week we saw that God is well disposed to us. This naturally causes an enormous tension which is resolved in the third week, the path of union:

Monday: God as source and beginning of all things created;
Tuesday: God as the beauty of the universe;
Wednesday: God as the glory and honor of the world;
Thursday: God as love;
Friday: God as the rule and law of all things;
Saturday: God as the guide of the universe;
Sunday: God as the most bountiful giver, as the one who gives everything.

Here we see a significant difference from the East and from hermetic philosophy. In both of those traditions it is the self; in the Christian sphere it is God. Instead of the Buddha, the highest being, higher than all Gods, in the West is the Godhead and not the self.

Fourth week: In the fourth week there is contemplation of the life and suffering of the Lord, to support the previous contemplations. Here, God

[245] Hegardt (1937), p. 21: "Sunday: Die himmlischen Herrlichkeiten" (Sunday: The glory of heaven).

is specified as being man, as Christ is God incarnated as a man. Here the attention is turned to the God, who appeared in human form, who suffered, died, and was reborn. That leads to man, but to the God-man who is a person in the Trinity, who is not the self. He stands outside, whereas the Mahâsukha is inside. It is God in me. I am Buddha, that is, my self, that which I have become. Because my "I" is an illusion, it is *mâyâ*, it is dissolved. After that I read out another section from Cisneros's book.

Now, having learned about his forerunner, we come to Ignatius himself. He is a thoroughly original individual, although Cisneros certainly paved the way to a great extent. Cisneros is significantly less determinate; he is still strongly influenced by the meditations of the Devoti, whose main goal was the immersion in God.[246] To escape from the world into the peace of God was their goal. This path is the monastic ideal. But not for Ignatius. He has no monastic ideal, but rather a strong identification with the world and reality. This is a peculiar element in Ignatius, that has been— not unjustly—attributed to other teachers who seem very remote. But at that time in Spanish culture these teachers were still very well known— namely the Arabs. We find in Arabic mysticism—in contemporary and earlier times—a development that is very closely related to the Ignatian mentality. It begins with one particular master. His name is Al-Ghazâlî; he lived from 1059 to 1111. I will talk about him next time.

---

[246] From here, Jung followed again the private German translation of Hegardt (1937), pp. 32–33.

Lecture 2[247]

10 NOVEMBER 1939

AT THE END of the last lecture, I mentioned that the Ignatian exercise rules were strongly influenced by Arabic mysticism. There were similar endeavors within Islam. The name of the master who was actually the spiritual father of Islamic mysticism is Al-Ghazâlî, who lived from 1059 to 1111.[248] He was an Islamic theologian and also a Greek philosopher. He lived in Baghdad, where until 1050 there was a Neoplatonic community of Greek philosophers living under false names, who were still tolerated by Islam. They were highly cultured and thus much valued as physicians and philosophers. Al-Ghazâlî drew his knowledge of Greek philosophy from these philosophers. He understood and applied Greek philosophy and all the scientific knowledge of his time. We still have some of his writings and we know that he had a very peculiar point of view regarding the doctrine of causality, which is particularly characteristic of Islam and is remarkable for certain psychological reasons. I will outline it for you here. It is the notion that causality in any form whatsoever is the direct will of Allah. A bit like in Schopenhauer: a stone rolling down a slope is in accordance with the will [to live] in nature. And so for Al-Ghazâlî the causal connection of the event is the direct manifestation of the will of Allah. Al-Ghazâlî linked the theological tradition of Islam, which had already existed for four hundred years at that point, with Greek philosophy and the mystical experiences of individual saints. Thereby he became the de facto father of

---

[247] The text of this lecture is compiled from notes by LSM, ES, RS, and OK, as well as the English translation by BH. LSM noted on the upper margins of her script: "Have a good journey, enjoy yourself, careful, don't fall! Warm regards. L. S.-M."

[248] Jung's handwritten annotation to the typescript translation of Hegardt (1937) reads, "Al-Ghazâlî: 1059–1111 in Baghdad. The most important religious leader in Islam since Mohammed. Theology and philosophy. Uses Greek philosophy and all the knowledge of that time. Causality = the direct will of Allah. Brings tradition and mystical experience together. Since then Islam a mystical religion" (JLN, p. 11).

Islamic mysticism and it could be said that following him, Islam became a mystical religion. We know very little about that in the West.

His writings caused quite a commotion in the West. It was an era when occidental scholars, who were still a rare breed, were beginning to get wind of the treasures of Arabic literature. That was the time of the Moorish universities in Salamanca and Cordoba, when the Europeans got to know Greek writers via Arabic scholars.[249] Thus the Christian clerics came across devotional books and mystical books which made a tremendous impression on them. They translated whole pages, sometimes even whole books, into Latin. It was mainly the Dominicans who undertook this work. They were the scholars of the Church. You will therefore find Islamic influences in many prayer books or devotional books of the early Middle Ages. Al-Ghazâlî, for example, was cited as if he was one of the Church fathers, as a sacred authority.

In the Arabic and Sufi mysticism where he had the greatest influence, we can see things that have curious correspondences with the exercises of Ignatius. There too are the retreats, the exercise periods of thirty to forty days that we find with Ignatius. These exercises took place under the leadership of a religious teacher, of the sheikh, to whom the students owed absolute obedience. The exercitants had to fast, remain silent, and stay awake. They led an ascetic life. There was an absolute duty of confession. Everything that moved them, impressed them, they were obliged to confess to the sheikh. The burden of responsibility on the sheikh was considerable, as he was responsible for the healing of his pupils' souls, similar to the process in the Ignatian exercises. These exercises also included contemplation of sins, repentance, death and hell. A strict examination of one's conscience, the *examen particulare*, was also obligatory. And then one more little detail: the exercitants were instructed to keep a small notebook in which they noted, using points and lines, the spiritual improvements or deterioration they had achieved, so that one could actually convince oneself to some extent of the balance of one's moral account. A French researcher recently proved that in the Mohammedan orders of Algeria and Morocco such exercises are still practiced, which are very similar to these retreats.[250]

---

[249] From here, Jung continued to paraphrase his German translation of Hegardt's study (Hegardt, 1937, p. 33).

[250] Jung repeated Hegartdt's (1937, p. 33) reference to Herman Müller's study *Origines de la Compagnie de Jésus* (1898).

Ignatius had in common with the Arabs and Moors a certain fanaticism, as well as his spirit of military discipline, of unconditional obedience. The purpose is the absolute dictatorship of the sheikh,[251] to which one was required to submit without grumbling. Then the duration of the exercises, the meticulous instructions about posture, silence, awareness of the five senses, and many other points that go into far too much detail. All these things were already found in Islam before Ignatius's time, and we have the documentary proof, as it were, that Islam really did have a significant influence, even if it was denied by certain elements who even argued the opposite, that the Mohammedan monastic orders were influenced by Christianity. It is possible, of course, that that happened too, but in any case these things existed long before Ignatius.

Before we go into the actual exercises, I must make several general comments about them. There are two types of exercises: the small ones and the large ones. The large exercises usually extend over thirty days. The terminology is: the large exercises are "given," whereas the small ones that only last three days are "preached." The small ones are also called exercises, and conducted by an exercise director, but are more for laypersons. Everyone, so to speak, is permitted to do them, while the large ones are significantly more demanding. As a result, the selection of who is permitted is naturally somewhat more complicated. While the exercise director performs the role of a revivalist preacher in the small exercises, in the large exercises he is less a preacher than a soul guide, an actual spiritual advisor.

The small exercises are, practically speaking, something like a Methodist revival meeting or other gatherings for worship where the atmosphere plays an important role. They are mostly groups formed around a favorite preacher in which the emotions are strongly influenced. Now, of course there are those phenomena, familiar to all of you, in such religious groups. There is a certain intensity, highly miraculous conversions and effects that raise the spirits and are then taken as evidence of the goodness of the proclaimed truth.

The three-day exercises are of course very important for the Jesuit order. However, they were not always welcomed by the entire Church, and even among the Jesuits there is not always consensus about them. For example, one well-known Jesuit says of the smaller exercises, "The three-day exercises are flooding the land, they are our joy, our hope, and—our

---

[251] Hegardt (1937), p. 34: "schejkens absoluta diktatur."

affliction."[252] Well, you can imagine why. The effects that arise through the arousal of emotions sometimes have psychological consequences that are less pleasant for the revival preacher, as there is always a considerable number of women who react in a certain way.[253]

Even Ignatius had noticed, indeed expressly determined, that the large complete series of exercises was not suitable for the masses, but actually only for a few people. He had experiences very early on, as I mentioned to you last semester, that made him careful in this regard. He then gave up working with large groups, for these very reasons. Because in a group people are different from when they are alone. In a group, one becomes unconscious. You are unaware of what is happening to you when you are in the group. The collective person is elevated and strengthened to the detriment of individual consciousness, to the extent that you completely forget yourself. That is why the morality of a group is always below the level of individual morality and therefore generally of dubious quality. Large gatherings of people always tend toward mob psychology.

The great difficulties of our time come from the unrootedness of city dwellers. The urban population is always somewhat under par. They are too close together. They become collective. In addition, they are told by the priests that community is the only way to godliness. Then they experience a considerable disappointment. One only needs to be a member of a patriotic shooting club to see this. When one of them gives a speech, what fine fellows the Swiss shooters are. Each of them feels he too is a little William Tell and goes home in high spirits. But the next day he discovers that he is only Mr So-and-so who rents a room on the fourth floor of an apartment building and lives on three hundred francs a month. And his life is not exactly a great success. The whole William Tell feeling flies straight out the window. In such a communal life, one experiences disappointing effects. In the moment it seems as if everything is right with the world, and then comes the big disappointment: when the illusion evaporates. The crowd is terribly suggestible, they believe everything, but also do everything and not one person bears responsibility. Read the book by Le Bon sometime, *Psychologie des foules*.[254] Unfortunately I haven't got

---

[252] Jung repeated the citation in Hegardt (1937), p. 38. The quotation is from Böminghaus (1927), p. 1. The end of this and the next two paragraphs are Jung's own elaborations.

[253] ES noted, "general guffaws and approving drumming of feet."

[254] *Psychologie des foules* (1895), translated into English as *The Crowd: A Study of the Popular Mind* (1896), by Charles-Marie Gustave Le Bon (1841–1931) was a seminal study on crowd psychology, in which Le Bon observed that the individual immersed in a large crowd for a length of time is susceptible to influences unknown to him. Sigmund Freud

time to go into it more now. And I don't want to use any modern examples. This communal glorification is a real menace, a disaster. Community is something only for independent people, not for those who have no roots. Just take one hundred intelligent people and form a committee with them, and see what it becomes: a blundering behemoth. Intelligence is lost in the crowd, because each extinguishes the other. Everything sinks down to the level of that which we have in common. That is of course the collective man, and that is *Homo sapiens*. And do you think *Homo sapiens* is really sapient? I, at least, have never seen such a one.

Ignatius, therefore, was very wise to be cautious about selecting his exercitants. Where possible, he worked with them individually, though not in the large exercises. But even here, the director had to be available to the exercitants every hour, deal with each of them individually, answer every question, in order to have contact with them as individuals so as to avoid this group mentality taking effect, in which a merely stupid enthusiasm is whipped up that is worthless. That's why he wrote,

> The Exercises are to be adapted to the capabilities of those who want to engage in them, i.e., age, education or intelligence are to be taken into consideration. Hence someone uneducated or of poor health should not be given things that cannot be undertaken without fatigue and from which no profit is to be derived. Similarly, in order that each may feel more at ease and derive the best benefit, what is given to each exercitant should be in accordance with his or her dispositions. Hence, one who is hoping to gain some instruction and to reach a certain level of peace of soul can be given the particular examen, then the general examen; also together with this, for half an hour in the morning, the way of praying about the commandments, capital sins, etc. Such persons can also be recommended to confess their sins each week, and if possible to receive communion

---

based his understanding of group psychology in *Group Psychology and the Analysis of the Ego* (1921) on Le Bon's theory. Jung also refers to Le Bon in 1940, stating that "[t]he psychology of a large crowd sinks to the level of mob psychology" (Jung, 1940, § 225), as well as in his post-war explanation of the psychological fascination with National Socialism in Germany: "There are countless people who go a little bit beyond the scope of the normal, in one way or another, either temporarily or chronically. If they get together in large numbers—which is what happens in any crowd—abnormal phenomena appear. One need only read what Le Bon has to say on the 'psychology of crowds' to understand what I mean: man as a particle in the mass is psychically abnormal. Ignorance of this fact is no protection against it" (Jung, 1946, § 477).

every fortnight, and better still every week, if they are so inclined. This arrangement is more suited to unformed and uneducated people, to whom explanations can be given of each commandment, each of the capital sins, the precepts of the church, the five senses, and the works of mercy.[255]

So, a strict differentiation according to individual circumstances. This way of giving the exercises is of course a sermon. With the small exercises, it is mainly the skilled preacher who does the work, and the effect on the listener is essentially based on the speech by the exercise director. In the large exercises, while the work is also done by the exercise director, the main work is the responsibility of the individual. For that purpose, the exercitant is isolated, perhaps living in a single room, speaking to no one and performing daily contemplations without disturbances. Here the process is quite different.

I have a little note about a description of such exercises from the eighteenth century in Naples.[256] There it says that they gathered in the Jesuit house known as the "professed house" for this retreat. In the first instance the nobility, then the high-ranking clergy, and lastly the young students and others, of whatever status and walk of life, were invited to these assemblies:

All of these according to their rank/ gather twice a day in a large spacious room/ but otherwise comfortable place/ to attend the exercises for two hours in the morning/ and two hours in the evening. And as darkness and gloominess can contribute more than a little to helping one collect one's thoughts, all the windows are covered. The first thing/ one notices in entering the room/ is a large painful crucifix/ many skulls/ skeletons/ cross/ and crowns of braided thorns/ everything needed to move one to prayer: with the chime of the bell, the spiritual reading begins/ and from the most spiritual books/ that are to be had; [. . .]/ Following this, the points for contemplation are recited by the exercise leader with great spirit/ usually taken from the basic truths of the first weeks/ because these lend themselves best to purifying the soul and its desires: then the contemplation begins/ with

---

[255] Translation: *IPW*, p. 287. Jung quoted the first line from Funk (1913a), p. 133; and the rest from his German translation of Hegardt (1937), p. 39.

[256] Jung took this description from Hegardt (1937), pp. 42–43; Hegardt, in turn, had found it in Rosignoli (1737).

a series of deeds to be added: first repentance for sins committed: then a devout conversation with Christ the Lord/ with the added intention of a serious improvement. After the contemplation is completed, one proceeds to various pious exercises; comparable with/ pulling something out of a spiritual lucky dip or a catalogue of mortifications/ or a spiritual saying. For example: Fleeting is/ what there delights/ eternal/ what there tortures; or: Be ye therefore ready also/ for the Son of Man cometh at an hour when ye think not; or: They are always cheery and full of fun/ and in a moment go down to hell; or: He who considers that he will soon die/ will easily spurn everything. Finally/ and at the conclusion of the prayer/ each and every person kisses the five holy wounds/ receives the holy blessing and returns home in solitude.[257]

And although this gives only a faint impression of the large exercises, with this assembly it is like with "burning coals which alternately flare up, igniting and illuminating each other, so that soon all burn with the same fervor."[258]

These retreats were also supposed to have had the most wondrous moral effect on the participants. One can easily imagine it. The most amazing transformations would occur: drunkards stopped drinking, smokers ceased smoking, the lame and crippled walked away carrying their beds, and so on. Indeed, all the things that can be produced through group psychology and through autosuggestion happened. That is the shadow side of the small exercises. They are actually no different from the *revivals*. We don't need to spend any more time on them, because they have no parallels to the Eastern yoga forms.

We will move on to the large exercises. Before we get started I must tell you that I myself have never performed these exercises, and am therefore not in a position to tell you about them from my own experience. But I will try to give you information as objectively as possible using the literature, which is extensive. I see these exercises as an extraordinarily interesting parallel to the Eastern yoga practices, which is why I am interested in them. I will show you, with examples from modern Jesuit literature, how these exercise points are meditated on under the strictest conditions.

---

[257] Rosignoli (1737), pp. 366–68.
[258] This sentence is taken from Hegardt (1937), p. 43, who quoted Rosignoli (1737), p. 368. From here on, Jung deviates from his German translation of Hegardt.

The exercises are subject to certain general rules, called the "Annotations":[259]

1. The term "spiritual exercises" denotes a certain method of examining one's conscience, of meditating, contemplating, and praying with the aim of ridding the soul of its disordered attachments and finding the divine will in regard to the disposition of one's life and one's own healing.[260]

That is the official formulation, not mine.

2. The exercise director should provide an account of the events to be meditated upon or contemplated only, simply running over the salient points with brief or summary explanations. The exercitant should then continue working on the historical foundations and reflect on them rationally. If this throws some light on the matter, this personal finding will have a stronger effect and bear longer-lasting moral fruit.[261]

In this paragraph, we see the idea mentioned earlier, that in the large exercises the exercise director restricts himself to the most necessary explanation

[259] "Annotations (or notes) to provide some explanation of the Spiritual Exercises that follow. They are intended to be of assistance both to the person giving them and to the person who is to receive them" (*IPW*, pp. 282–88). These annotations were written by Ignatius and printed together with the *Spiritual Exercises*. On one occasion, he referred to them as a preface. Jung quoted them in the German translation by Funk (1913a).

[260] Funk (1913a), p. 130. The Funk text differs somewhat from the *IPW* text. A literal translation of Funk's German text as cited by Jung is given above. The *IPW* text runs, "The term 'spiritual exercises' denotes every way of examining one's conscience, of meditating, contemplating, praying vocally and mentally, and any other spiritual activity, as will be said later. For just as strolling, walking and running are exercises for the body, so 'spiritual exercises' is the name given to every way of preparing and disposing one's soul to rid herself of all disordered attachments, so that once rid of them one might seek and find the divine will in regard to the disposition of one's life for the good of the soul" (*IPW*, p. 282).

[261] Funk (1913a), p. 130; again, the Funk text differs from the *IPW* text, and a literal translation of Funk as cited by Jung is given above. The *IPW* text runs, "The person who gives to another a way and a plan for meditating or contemplating must provide a faithful account of the events to be meditated or contemplated, simply running over the salient points with brief or summary explanations. For if a person begins contemplating with a true historical foundation, and then goes over the historical narrative and reflects on it personally, one may by oneself come upon things that throw more light on the history or better bring home its meaning. Whether this results from one's own reasoning or from the enlightenment of divine grace, this is more gratifying and spiritually profitable than if the director had explained and developed at length the meaning of the history. For it is not so much knowledge that fills and satisfies the soul, but rather the intimate feeling and relishing of things" (*IPW*, p. 282).

of the points to be contemplated and gives them to the exercitant. It is the task of the exercitant, when meditating on the individual points, to draw those conclusions and find those applications that result in a moral improvement or psychological change.

> 3. In all the spiritual exercises that follow we bring the intellect into action in order to think and the will in order to stir the deeper affections. We should therefore note that the activity of the will, when we are speaking vocally or mentally with God Our Lord or with his Saints, requires greater reverence on our part than when we are using the intellect to understand.[262]

That is once again the official formulation. Here we see how much emphasis is placed on intellect and reason, and how affect arises by thinking things through. One sees, for example, one's own imperfection and is annoyed about it, is saddened or regretful. This affect is translated into the will. A new attitude of will arises which directs itself naturally to the practical level, insofar as one says, "All right, from now on I want to act like this or like that."

> 4. The exercises that follow are made up of four Weeks, corresponding to the four parts into which these exercises are divided: namely, the First is the consideration and contemplation of sins; the Second is the life of Christ our Lord up to, and including, Palm Sunday; the third, the Passion of Christ our Lord; the Fourth, the Resurrection and Ascension, with the three ways of praying.[263]

So, these are just general provisions.

> 12. The giver of the exercises should remind the receiver frequently that since an hour has to be spent in each of the five exercises or contemplations to be made each day, one should always try to find contentment in the thought that a full hour has indeed been spent in that exercise—and more, if anything, rather than less! For the enemy usually leaves nothing undone in his efforts to procure a shortening of the hour of contemplation, meditation or prayer.[264]

I will talk about the other rules when we get to the relevant points.

---

[262] *IPW*, p. 282.
[263] *IPW*, pp. 282–83.
[264] *IPW*, p. 285.

We are now getting to the essential part, the specificities of the exercises, and I want to focus heavily here on the main principle, and especially on the start of the exercise, which seems to me to be the most significant part from our point of view. Of course we are entering deep into Christian psychology here, and not just a Christian but a Catholic one, which for some of you may be far from your experience. Particularly to us Protestants it is extremely foreign and seems strange. But I would like to ask you, at any rate those of you who attended my other lectures, to follow my elaborations in the same spirit as you did previously, and perhaps to maintain that same naivety and openness that you displayed about the Eastern topics. We approach the Eastern things from a position of impartiality. We just let them work on us as something perhaps completely foreign. I'm sure you remember how the texts we discussed together were for us very outlandish. So now it would be good to approach these things not from the position of a Christian person with a Christian upbringing, but by imagining that you are from India and have never heard of such things. Then you will experience the intuitive effect that they have. When the word Christ crops up, you must not think that you know what that is, but imagine it is the Mahâsukha, the Shrî Heruka or one of the Buddhas.[265] Because actually we do not know what it really all means. Sometimes we regret having read the Bible as a child. If we were to read it now for the first time, we would have a different, a fresh and intuitive, impression. In the East, I saw how people in India discovered the New Testament and read it with quite different eyes and saw things in it that I had never noticed, and was only able to see when I looked at it through the Eastern lens. It would be good if you could remember the descriptions I gave you of tantra yoga. You will then immediately see striking differences and parallels at each point.

Before the actual exercise, it is introduced by the *praeparatio* (preparation), which generally consists of an *oratio* (prayer) or *meditatio*. Here I have an old Jesuit, from the classical school, who gives us an authentic message about the character of the *praeparatio*. Izquierdo gives a definition of the *oratio mentalis*, the mental prayer:

---

[265] *mahâsukha* (Sanskr.): "great joy," refers to the state of bliss at the moment of realization of enlightenment; here embodied as the lord of blessedness (see *JMP*, vol. 6, p. 278). Shrî Heruka, in Vajrayana Buddhism, is the Sanskrit name of enlightened beings or deities, who are associated with supreme bliss and the emptiness of all phenomena. In his lecture of 13 January 1939, Jung explained, "Psychologically, Mahâsukha or Heruka would correspond to what one describes as the self: namely, the whole that one assembles through ego consciousness and the totality of the unconscious" (*JMP*, vol. 6, p. 84).

Thus whoever goes to pray should know that it is nothing other than recalling a certain thing that was said or a deed, and reflecting rationally and with reason upon it, so that one thinks about the substance, the incidental and the circumstances of this recollection, and thereby moves the will to draw reasonable conclusions, to have the right affects and sacred resolutions. And that is now the fruit of this meditation.

So when a person goes to perform this *oratio* or *meditatio*, he should clearly envisage beforehand the points that he wants to deal with, and keep them in mind. [. . .]

And two steps before the place where he will perform this *oratio*, he should stop and raise his spirit, imagining vividly [That is now the active imagination; CGJ] that he is standing before the countenance of God who is listening to him benevolently. [. . .]

The position of the body in the *oratio* is usually kneeling. Or one can lay face down on the floor [That is called full prostration; CGJ] or stand upright, and if the body is too weak for anything else, one may also sit [. . .].

Then, in order to direct one's attention completely toward the meditation and keep one's fantasy reined in, one should do a *compositio loci*.[266]

So, one has to paint a precise picture in one's mind of the location of the event, the people, the *dramatis personae*, and all the specific circumstances. And he even says one should make an *imago corporea*, a physical image, of it. That is now the active imagination, specifically the act of very precisely physically ascertaining the thing and imagining it in order to make the

---

[266] Izquierdo (1695), pp. 8–9. Jung translated the Latin text into German for his audience, and this and subsequent passages quoted from Izquierdo's text are here directly translated from Jung's German translation of the Latin. For accuracy, we have provided the original Latin in the footnotes. Izquierdo's text here reads, "Oratio mentalis, sive Meditatio aliud non est, quam aliquod dictum, vel factum revocare in memoriam: & circa illud cum intellectu ratiocinari, ponderando substantiam, accidentia, & circumstantias eius, aliudque ex alio concludendo: sicque movere voluntatem ad sana consilia, probos affectus, & sancta proposita concipienda, in quo stat fructus orationis./ Antequam quis ad orationem accedat, puncta in illa meditanda debet praeparare, & secum in memoria ferre. [. . .]/Duobis circiter passibus ante locum, ubi est orandum, animum sursum elevet, confideretque habere se praesentem, ac spectatorem Deum, qui benigne ipsum, & magno salutis ipsius studio velit audire. [. . .]/ Situs corporis ut plurimum flexis genibus erit. Quod si tamen plus attentionis, aut devotionis percipiat pronus in terram, vel stans, ita faciat. Et si aliud non permittat infirmitas corporis, petita a Domino venia, sedere poterit./ [. . .] Deinde ad maiorem attentionem orationis, ad continendamque Phantasiam, eamque quando alio divertitur, colligendam. Compositionem loci faciet[.]"

situation as real as possible—the whole situation: the people, the place, and the individual circumstances.

From this description you can already see one thing—the striking difference from the East. The *praeparatio* is begun with the invocation, so to speak. You have a figure to talk to, a personal conversation partner. Instead of turning inward, you choose, perhaps from your memory, a point on which you want to reflect. For example, maybe a man committed a sin at a certain time, at a certain place, and against a certain person. He collects it from his memory, from his conscious mind. From his conscious mind, therefore, he takes only building blocks which he presents, in a manner of speaking, to a personal interlocutor to whom he turns. The meditation is directed therefore not toward oneself, but toward the other party. Thus the meditation as Ignatius conceived it bears no relation to meditation in the East, but is an *oratio* in the sense of a *petitio*, a request, an invocation, a turning to another party. That is a typical Western extraversion, in sharp contrast to the East.

I can't point out the Eastern parallels every time; I expect you to remember them. The Eastern meditation path traverses inner events. Everything takes place internally. No other party is ever called upon. There is no sense of a personal relationship. I saw that in practice in a temple in Ceylon.[267] I observed something strange during an evening service. It was seven o'clock, and the Buddhist service takes place every evening at this time. The temple was aglow with the light of the little coconut-oil lamps illuminating a golden picture of the Buddha—it was already nighttime, as the sun sets at six. Then a young girl came in carrying dishes full of jasmine blossoms broken off the stems. The temple was filled with the intoxicating scent. She scattered these blossoms on the altar before the Buddha while whispering a *mantra*. I was accompanied by a Buddhist monk, and I asked him, "Is that to honor the Buddha?" And his answer was, "Oh no, the Buddha does not exist, Buddha has entered the *maha nirvâna*, the great *nirvâna*, from whence there is no way back. He has completely vanished. There is no longer any Buddha." "What is she saying then?" I asked. "She is reciting the *mantram*: just as these flowers fade away, so our life is fleeting." That is an evening prayer for young people in Buddhism. It is not an invocation, but an admonishment to oneself.

---

[267] Until 1972, Sri Lanka was known as Ceylon.

Lecture 3[268]

17 NOVEMBER 1939

LAST TIME WE got as far as discussing the *praeparatio*: the introduction, the preparation. I want to recall your attention to the sentence that clearly shows us what is actually meant by this preparation: Specifically, the right attitude to the enterprise, the collecting of thoughts, the concentration and the evocation, the actual *imaginatio*, that is, the imagination, the formation of a concrete image that is intended to illustrate the subject of the meditation. Thus very much in keeping with the instructions in the Eastern texts that we looked at before on how to imagine the Buddha or Bodhisattva in detail. Except that here the subject is different.

I will turn again to the text of the old Spanish Jesuit who wrote a very instructive book about these exercises.[269] There he says,

> In order to pay more attention to the contemplation or *oratio* and rein in the fantasy so that you are not distracted by other thoughts, make a *compositio loci*. That means a particular physical image of those subjects about which you want to meditate. You should bring them all to life in your imagination, and precisely picture the things, people, places and all other circumstances that make up the event or memory on which you will meditate.
>
> If you manage to make a complete picture, the *petitio* follows, the invocation, namely asking God to give you the grace to collect yourself correctly and to obtain the right fruit from your contemplation.[. . .]
>
> For that purpose he takes one of the prepared points and reflects on it, using reason, by weighing up everything that relates to this

---

[268] The text of this lecture is compiled from notes by LSM, ES, RS, and OK, as well as the English translation by BH.

[269] Izquierdo (1695).

point. And he then directs his rational reflection to produce the corresponding will.[270]

The thoughts must thus lead to an action of will, so that the right affects are triggered. So you see, it is not sufficient to reflect coolly on these meditation points; one also has to draw certain conclusions, to illuminate the whole point and make decisions about it. This of course then leads to the production of affects. For example, the person meditating thinks of a sin which he has committed, and then presents to himself all the circumstances surrounding the event and decides that he no longer wants to behave in this way. At that point, he realizes that he is not in harmony, but that something inside him is saying, "Well, but perhaps you could do it again after all, let's not be so hasty!" The human being is weak and has all kinds of opposition to change. This then triggers an affect in him. He gets terribly afraid that he might not be able to keep his promise, and then he knows that he is moving from a venial sin to a mortal sin, because he would then have knowingly sinned again. This leads to a moral conflict, a moral situation, from which the *affectus probos*, the right affect, emerges.[271] He has to let it make an impression on him in order to get churned up inside. After being in this state of inner turmoil for a while, it is likely that he can eventually bring himself to make a decision after all.

And then comes the final part of the meditation, namely the part called the colloquy. About this he says,

This colloquy is nothing other than that one speaks in familiar terms with Christ the Lord or with the Mother of God or with the Holy Trinity or with one of the divine persons.[272]

It is most curious to think of holding such a conversation. He also says other things, specifically that one should then conduct this conversation

---

[270] Ibid., p. 9. Jung translated the first line into German slightly differently from at the end of the previous lecture. The original Latin text goes as follows: "Deinde ad maiorem attentionem orationis, ad continendamque Phantasiam, eamque quando alio divertitur, colligendam. Compositionem loci faciet, hoc est, imaginem aliquam corpoream eorum, quae meditaturus est, sibi effinget, repraesentantem res, personas, locum, & alias circumstantias, prout postulaverit materia meditationis./ Tum sequitur Petitio, qua petet a Deo lumen, & gratiam ad colligendum ex ea oratione fructum ipsius materiae consentaneum [. . .]./ Post haec proponent sibi unum ex punctis, quae praeparata fert, & circa illud ratiocinabitur, ponderans cuncta, quae ad ispum pertinent; suamque ratiocinationem, atque poderationem diriget ad excitandam, ac permovendam voluntatem[.]"

[271] Ibid., p. 9: "ut affectus probos eliciat."

[272] Ibid., p. 10: "Quod Colloquium aliud non est, quam familiariter loqui cum Christo Domino, cum Deipara, vel cum SS. Trinitate, aut aliqua ex Divinis Personis."

in a variety of ways, for example by "assigning different people" in the sense of masks, of roles, and that one should for example "speak as if one were the creature with the creator, or as the servant with the master, or as the son with the father, the pupil with the teacher, the patient with the doctor, the friend with the friend, or the beggar with the rich man," the purpose being to illuminate one's relationship with the Divinity from all sides.[273] When, for instance, one speaks as friend to friend, it is of course different from when one speaks as a beggar to a rich man. Thus the conversation gains a greater psychological character of reality, and a great many more aspects appear. The conversation consists of addressing someone. The Godhead is simply spoken to, but there is no one there who answers. The case is therefore something like—to give a banal example—the one in a little book by George Sand in which she presents conversations with her soul mate, but over the thirty pages only she speaks, we never hear what he says.[274] It is therefore a wholly one-sided conversation. It is only a talking *to*. The exercitant speaks to the Godhead and doesn't hear what the Godhead replies.

In antiquity it was similar. People also spoke to the god-images back then. In some places there was even a step next to the statue of a god, so that one could climb up and speak into the god's ear. But in those days the gods answered. People would gaze at the statues of the gods until they could perceive a visible sign: for example, the statue nodded its head. The honored object was certainly not inert. We know this also from the legends of saints, in which the saints depicted in paintings make certain gestures, or a voice is heard. The projection caused by my addressing the object brings about an animation of the object, so to speak, which then appears to be reacting. The statue of a god nods its head or some other sign occurs, the objectivity of which cannot be established. But that doesn't matter. The essential thing is that the connection with the Godhead has taken place for that particular person. Then it is completely irrelevant whether the statue really, in our sense of the word, nodded or not.

But in these exercises, we never hear about any kind of response, not even a trace of such an answer, apart from the indirect effect of the grace

273 Ibid., p. 10: "Idque varias interim sibi personas aptando; seu creaturae cum Creatore; seu servi cum Domino; filii cum Patre, discipuli cum Magistro, aegroti cum Medico, amici cum Amico, mendici cum Divite colloquentis[.]"

274 George Sand (1804–76), male pseudonym for Amandine Aurore Lucile Dupin, a hugely successful and prolific French author of the Romantic era, whose works impressed and inspired writers such as Victor Hugo, Fyodor Dostoevsky, and Marcel Proust. Jung referred here to Sand's "Daily Conversations with Dr. Piffoel," in *The Intimate Journal* (1929). See also Jung 1940, § 237. On Sand, see Harlan (2004).

which is thus understood as the fruit of the *oratio* and could be interpreted as the answer of the Godhead.

After the colloquy comes a spoken prayer, the *oratio vocalis*, as instructed here: "if the person concerned is on special terms with the Mother of God, it is good to say an 'Ave Maria,' or if it is the Holy Trinity, then one should say a 'Pater Noster,' and if it is Christ who is standing in front of you, you should say the 'Anima Christi.'"[275] It is most common to say the "Anima Christi." That is an old Church prayer that is meditated on very carefully in the modern exercises. I would like to use this prayer to give a basic description of the form the meditation takes. I need to show you how these things are meditated on in detail. Thus we will do the same as we already did with the Eastern texts. There we also went into the individual details of the meditations and saw what a unique spiritual constellation emerges from those Eastern symbols. We now want to do the same for the Christian spirit. Now, here too I would like to ask you again to listen objectively and to try to forget that you, some of you at least, have had a Christian upbringing.

The "Anima Christi" prayer is not by Ignatius, but is an old Church prayer:

Anima Christi, sanctifica me.
Corpus Christi, salva me.
Sanguis Christi, inebria me.
Aqua lateris Christi, lava me.
Passio Christi, conforta me.
O bone Jesu, exaudi me.
Intra tua vulnera absconde me.
Ne permittas me separari a te.
Ab hoste maligno defende me.
In hora mortis meae voca me
Et iube me venire ad te,
Ut cum Sanctis tuis laudem te
In saecula saeculorum. Amen.

(Soul of Christ, sanctify me.
Body of Christ, save me.
Blood of Christ, inebriate me.
Water from the side of Christ, wash me.

---

[275] Izquierdo (1695), pp. 10–11: "Huic Colloquio plerumque finem imponet oratio aliqua vocalis: puta, si cum Beata Virgine habitum est, *Ave Maria*, &c. si cum Santissima Trinitate, *Pater noster*, &c. si cum Christo Domino. *Anima Christi*, &c."

Passion of Christ, strengthen me.
O Good Jesus, hear me.
Within your wounds hide me.
Permit me not to be separated from you.
From the wicked foe, defend me.
At the hour of my death, call me
and bid me come to you
That with your saints I may praise you
For ever and ever. *Amen.*[276])

So that is how this short prayer goes. We now want to look at the individual parts of this meditation prayer, like we would with any text, and we should take a naive approach, as it were, to these contents that will partly seem so familiar to us, and yet are also so unfamiliar. Here I will follow the analysis by Erich Przywara.[277] He has written three volumes about the exercises, entitled *Deus semper maior*.[278] He says with regard to this "Anima Christi" that one should be subjectively aware that one's "soul is permeated by Christ" and one's "blood is perfused by the blood of the Passion of Christ."[279] Those are his words.

The *anima Christi* is actually a strange idea. Is the soul of Christ differentiated from Christ as a figure? It seems almost to be the case, because otherwise one would not speak of an *anima Christi*. But because Christ is the whole Godhead according to the dogma, one could surely not also separate him from his *anima*. But in this prayer, the *anima* and the *corpus* are distinct, are two different things. Przywara now says that the main content of the whole exercises actually lies in this intersection, namely in

---

[276] This translation is from *Finding God in All Things* (2005), pp. 89–90. Cf. the translation by John Henry Newman (*IPW*, p. 359): "Soul of Christ, be my sanctification; / Body of Christ, be my salvation; / Blood of Christ, fill all my veins; / Water from the side of Christ, wash out my stains; / May Christ's Passion strengthen me; / O good Jesus, hear me; / In your wounds I fain would hide, / Never to be parted from your side; / Guard me when my foes assail me, / Call me when my life shall fail me, / Command me then to come to thee, / That I for all eternity / With your saints may praise thee ./ Amen. The following German translation, given in the lecture, is probably by Jung: "Seele Christi, heilige mich. / Körper Christi, heile mich. / Blut Christi, berausche mich. / Wasser der Seite Christi, reinige mich. / Leiden Christi, stärke mich. / O, guter Jesu, erhöre mich. / In Deinen Wunden verbirg mich. / Gestatte nicht, dass ich von Dir getrennt werde. / Gegen den bösen Feind verteidige mich. / In der Stunde meines Todes rufe mich / Und lass mich zu Dir kommen, / Damit ich mit Deinen Heiligen Dich lobpreise / In alle Ewigkeit. Amen."

[277] Erich Przywara (1889–1972), Polish-German Jesuit priest, theologian, and philosopher. See Introduction to this volume, pp. lvii–lxii.

[278] Przywara (1938).

[279] Ibid., p. 3. All citations from Przywara are translated from the German.

the sentence "Christ lives in me."[280] He is referring to the part in Galatians where Paul says, "I am crucified with Christ: nevertheless I live; yet not I, but Christ liveth in me."[281]

Now one tries to somehow make this assertion true in the meditation, or to bring it into effect through *consideratio*—consideration, weighing up, reason; *meditatio*—reflection; *contemplatio*—contemplation, looking at; and fourth, through experiencing it through the senses. This is a typically Ignatian feature, that the human senses also have to be involved, otherwise this penetration by Christ has no entry point. And the result of these four stages or forms of meditation must be that Christ is seen, in a way, from the inside, almost as if he is *within* one. We could just as easily say, "I in Christ", which Przywara formulates like this: "From within Christ, to see with His eyes, to feel with His heart, to breathe with Him[.]"[282] In other words, a complete transposition[283] of the person into the Christ figure. This is a classic difference from how it is in the East. There, it is not about being transposed into the Buddha, but rather I *become* Buddha. But here, it is about something that Ignatius already called a "jumping out of oneself,"[284] a kind of jumping over into the Christ figure so that one leaves oneself behind, so to speak, or one dissolves fully in the physical and spiritual essence of Christ, with a complete stripping of the self. That is the opposite to what we saw in the East, where the self becomes the Buddha. At the end of our examination of the "Anima Christi," I will show you a few more Eastern texts in which you can clearly see the Eastern attitude.

Przywara now goes through the prayer line by line, word by word, saying what he thinks about it, what occurs to him. These interpretations are very interesting from the psychological standpoint. About the first line he says,

1. "Anima Christi, sanctifica me." (Soul of Christ, sanctify me.)
   The soul is the entity of the whole life. The soul of Christ is the entity of all that which is Christ. Out of the soul of Christ the life of Christ is formed, and therefore my life as Christ in me.[285]

---

[280] "In (1) the main content of the exercises is expressed: the personal realization that 'Christ lives in me.'" (Przywara, 1938, p. 3)

[281] Galatians 2:20 (*KJV*).

[282] Przywara (1938), p. 3.

[283] LSM has "Transformation" (transformation) instead of "Transposition" (transposition); ES has "Transgression" (transgression).

[284] See Przywara (1938), p. 4.

[285] Ibid., p. 5.

Soul, what is the soul? It is the form, the entity of Christ's being. A mold for all that which is Christ. From this form, the life of Christ is formed, and therefore also the life of the one who is contemplating Christ, who is meditating on Christ. And insofar as he allows his life to be formed thus, he is in a way also transferred over into this life of Christ, so that he now *vere, realiter et substantialiter*[286] no longer lives as himself, but as Christ.

This idea of the soul as form is a concept already found in the Middle Ages: that the soul is actually the form-giving principle of human beings which also forms their outer lives and their bodies. So when one meditates on the soul of Christ, one is meditating on the form. We find the same idea in the East. I visited a monastery at Belur Mutt, north of Calcutta, several times. It's a monastery of the Ramakrishna order.[287] There is a small chapel room which does not have an altar as we understand it, but rather a curtain under which is a kind of throne consisting purely of low silk cushions. On top of it is a photograph of Ramakrishna. It's terribly tasteless, but the people don't see that at all. They actually see Ramakrishna there. A daily meditative prayer is said before the photograph, not in order to honor Ramakrishna, but to adopt the form of Ramakrishna: to enter into the form of Ramakrishna. This is literally what they told me. I took part in this meditative ritual. What I found very interesting was that the monk who was the celebrant had to prepare the day before with a long meditation exercise until he had conceived of[288] the form and entered into the anima of the Ramakrishna. As such he was then able to lead the ceremony. The ceremony itself was very typical of Hinduism. They brought old Vedic offerings as symbols: for the earth, flowers; for light, fire; for the air, a frond to fan the altar seat; for water, a sprinkling, a libation of water. Then they sang Vedic hymns. All the monks sit on the floor in the lotus position throughout and often prostrate themselves at certain points as the offerings are made. Thus it is not an honoring of Ramakrishna

---

[286] See n. 191.

[287] Belûr Math or Belur Mutt was founded by Swami Vivekananda, a chief disciple of Ramakrishna Paramahamsa. It is located on the west bank of Hooghly river, Belûr, West Bengal. The temple was consecrated on 14 January 1938. Jung was present and described the ceremony in the seventh volume of the copybooks 'Excerpta' (p. 14): "On 14–15 Jan. the consecration of the Sri Rama Krishna temple in Belur Mutt (math) near Calcutta took place. A consecration hut was specially erected according to Vedic ritual on the eastern side of the new temple" (JL; facsimile in Shamdasani, 2012, p. 178); cf. *JMP*, vol. 6, pp. 19–20.

[288] RS has "erreicht" (reached) instead of "erdacht" (conceived of).

in the usual sense—rather, signs[289] are generated that are reminiscent of the form into which each individual enters: once again it is a very different concept from the Christian one, even though the basic idea of the soul as form is the same.

The *anima Christi* is now supposed, as a result of the meditation, to permeate through the exercitant so completely that his own life becomes the life of Christ himself. Then Przywara moves on to the second part of the first line. I will read this part out to you, because it is almost impossible to get across the unique emotion of the meditation:

> Therefore: *sanctifica me*, separate me out and set me apart like temple and temple utensils, which are separated out and set apart so that they either serve only the temple or must be destroyed, and in the service of the temple itself serve the altar, i.e., become the sacrifice. "Holy" means "with God," and yet also means "damned"— treading the fine line between blessing and curse—and herein completely surrendered. Christ lives in me—or I do not live. Christ is all—or is the curse into nothingness.[290]

That refers to this point: "Christ hath redeemed us from the curse of the law, being made a curse for us: for it is written, Cursed is every one that hangeth on a tree[.]"[291]

2. "Corpus Christi, salva me." (Body of Christ, save me.)
The life of Christ in me is the life of God which became the body, and whose body is the visible church.[292]

The Church is also the *corpus Christi*.

> It is not about invisible divinity, hidden interiority, unembodied spirituality, pure soulfulness, but about God who becomes man, inwardness that expresses itself in the work, spirituality that finds expression in the flesh, soul that is only visible as a body. Christ in the visible church, Christ in the visible work in the visible world. Because He should be everything, everything in me, everything through me and into the world.[293]

---

[289] ES has "Erinnerungsbilder" (memories, souvenir pictures) instead of "Erinnerungszeichnen" (mementos, memories, souvenir signs).
[290] Przywara (1938), p. 5.
[291] Galatians 3:13 (*KJV*).
[292] Przywara (1938), p. 5.
[293] Ibid.

That is now the method which I spoke of earlier, namely the inner realization that should lead to the eruption of affects. Then come ethical conclusions that lead to action; visible fruits, as it were.

So, this body of Christ which is meditated on here is the visible manifestation of the Lord who is to save me, specifically to make me whole. About that he says,

> Herein: *salva me*, save me. The body saves: Christ, by making him visible, human, flesh—through the humility of this impotence. Save me[294] [He has a peculiar style that I don't vouch for; CGJ] healed wound of the sins, healed blood of the sacrifice. The sin is redeemed in the sacrifice: *sanctifica me*. But the sacrifice is not the last. Because sacrifice is the most open wound. Sin is redeemed in the sacrifice in the body of Christ. The body of Christ is the salvation: *salva me*. Thus it is the perfect wholeness: spirit and flesh, God and creature are one in the "head and body one Christ," in every one of his limbs, in every life and working of these limbs.[295]

The *corpus Christi* is thus here thought of as the source of human wholeness. At the same time it is a reason why those meditating have in a way to take leave of themselves in order to enter completely into the form of Christ, through which they achieve that wholeness which Christ symbolizes for us. Namely, Christ is for us a symbol for the wholeness of the human being.

So you see how deep these meditations go. Of course, such depths are not reached in every case, but in the case of such an ingenious man as Przywara these things naturally go a lot further. In principle, that is how the things are carried out. Once again, it is extraordinarily striking that one finds here an explicit tendency toward visibility, toward concrete material reality, and not an evaporation into the spiritual realm, a renunciation of the body or the flesh; instead it is expressly the flesh, the body, the concrete that is emphasized. And again, that is something that we do not find at all in the East. It is totally unfamiliar. There, nothing becomes concrete, rather the concrete is all dissolved in *mâyâ*.[296] Everything is illusion.

---

[294] Trans. note: the German translation of "salva me" in the "Anima Christi" is "heile mich" (heal me *or* save me). Przywara writes "mache mich heil," which also means "make me whole."

[295] Przywara (1938), p. 5.

[296] *mâyâ* (Sanskr.): "she who measures," a Vedânta concept that denotes what stands in contrast to the absolute non-dual reality; often translated as "illusion." Cf. Jung's lecture of 19 May 1939: "This is the *materia*, from *mater*, the mother, mother earth. The mother is

If you do not know that, you have not even grasped the very basics of yoga philosophy. It is a real illusion. It is concrete, but this concreteness is illusion. There it is not a transcending of the body, but the body becoming illusory. Amid the reality, carnality, actuality of the body, this inner adjustment takes place through which one recognizes it as illusion. And then one is in another state.

Here, however, there is clear tendency to allow this inner experience to immediately also become an outer experience. This is now the aspect that contrasts most strongly with the earlier meditation exercises of the Devoti. This is specifically Ignatian: this orientation toward the realization *in concreto*, the becoming-real in the body of the Church. This unique emphasis on the physical could even make one wonder whether for us Westerners the physical is not actually an a priori reality at all, but first has to be preached, first has to become real. There are many things in our religion that point to this.

We only have time to touch on one other point, which is just as peculiar, namely the [third line of the "Anima Christi"]:

3. "Sanguis Christi, inebria me." (Blood of Christ, inebriate me.)

If you were to read such words in an Indian text you would think of a bloodlust, of a soma drink,[297] perhaps of an orgy at which blood was drunk. You might think of a Dionysian blood ceremony—at any rate certainly of something very primitive. But of course we are so used to these ideas that they no longer strike us as strange. The blood of Christ is so abstract and anemic that it no longer says anything to us. But imagine if we had never heard of it before. Like that Indian man who visited England and stated, "What the missionaries say is all a con. The English are actually animal worshippers! Everywhere they have doves, lions, eagles, oxen, and winged men." He had seen all these emblems in the Romanesque and Gothic churches and thought, "Aha, now we have it!" And we no longer even notice when we are in a church and see a lamb with a banner and

---

the first carrier of this symbol of the feminine which I describe as anima. Thus, the first projection naturally appears in the mother and later is extended on to matter; hence the name *materia*. This is the same as what the East calls *mâyâ*. Generally it is translated as "illusion" or "delusion," but comes from the root '*ma*,' i.e., to build, hence *mâyâ* is the building material. Whatever I can touch and perceive is *mâyâ*. It is a real illusion, an illusion that has become actual" (*JMP*, vol. 6, p. 209).

[297] *soma* (Sanskr..): "extract," is the name of a drink extracted from a plant of the same name, which gives immortality. It is mentioned in the *Rig-Veda* as well as the in the *Avesta*, the sacred text of Zoroastrianism. The precise nature of this intoxicating plant is still a subject of controversy.

cross or a *putto*[298] with a little angel's head and golden wings. But to a naive person, like the Indian man, it is striking. And the texts are also striking. The first time someone hears "blood of Christ, inebriate me", it sounds very dangerous. One has all sorts of suspicions and thinks, "What is meant by that?" What is it actually getting at? It awakens memories of ancient times past, when gruesome human sacrifices were made. Then you see a person being horribly crucified, a bleeding corpse so to speak. That is terribly shocking for the naive understanding. One asks oneself, "What sort of people must they be, to have such symbols?" That is typical of the West. In the East there is no blood and soil theory. Just imagine, a Catholic authority claims the ideas of blood and soil for itself. And that is also correct. This carnal outlook, these primordial instincts that come to the fore here, they originate with us. For example, just go and look in a gallery of medieval art. What do you actually see? One person is being roasted on the grill, another has his intestines pulled out, another is walking around with his head under his arm. If you come from the East, it seems extraordinary.

And what does that tell us? You know, blood and soil, that was just bait to catch the mice and rats, and now it has become reality in quite a different way.[299] That's how it goes with us. That's why, when one talks a lot about blood, then blood shall come. But also one talks about it because it is already there. It is in our nature. "Bloodlust"—you must have heard that word. We should also meditate on it, but more from the Eastern perspective, for our edification, a kind of bitter edification. However, the way Przywara meditates on it is of course in the Christian tradition, where the danger is already transformed into something intellectual and spiritual, so that one's primordial ideas somehow vanish. One no longer thinks of them at all. Thus he says,

> 3. "Sanguis Christi, inebria me." Because Christ is within one from the inside (*anima Christi*), because Christ is one's whole form (*corpus Christi*), therefore one is now also permeated, warmed, perfused by Him: not only the form of Christ as my form, but flowing in the flow of Christ, hunted to and fro in the bloodstream of Christ,

---

[298] *putto* (Ital.): a winged child-angel; in the ancient world, winged infants were able to influence human lives. The depiction of *putti* was revived by Italian Renaissance artists, in particular the sculptor Donatello (1386–1466), who merged them with Christian iconography.

[299] On 1 September 1939, German troops had invaded Poland, which marked the beginning of World War II.

restive in the restiveness of Christ, transformable in the transformation of Christ—in his body, which is the Church.

Therefore, "inebria me." The narrow and anxious "reasonableness" must become the intoxication of drunkenness, if my life is to be so swept away. The blood of Christ glows, the blood of Christ hunts—in the love that is beyond all measure, in its height and breadth and depth. Inebriate me![300]

"Inebria me" actually represents the inebriation through the sacrament of the wine. That in itself is already a diminishment—wine instead of blood. But the wine has a spiritual meaning in the Christian mystery, and as a result no longer signifies that dangerous aspect of inebriation. And the inebriation induced by the blood, by the wine, should now have the effect of sweeping the meditator into the *corpus Christi*, or into the *corpus mysticum*; through an act of violence as it were, through a drunken ecstasy, the meditator is swept on a wave up and over into the bloodstream of Christ. Some of these descriptions are found in Przywara.

[300] Przywara (1938), pp. 5–6.

Lecture 4[301]

LAST TIME WE began studying the "Anima Christi" meditation, and I want to continue with that today. We got as far as discussing the third line, "Sanguis Christi, inebria me"—"blood of Christ, inebriate me"—and we come now to the fourth line:

4. "Aqua lateris Christi, lava me." (Water from the side of Christ, wash me.)

This invoking of Christ refers to the fact that, according to the Gospel text, it was not just blood, but also water that flowed from the wound in Christ's side.[302] It is also a reference to the purification[303] of the wine with the water in the Eucharist. The blood and the water are meditated on separately, as having different meanings. The blood, which corresponds to the wine, causes the inebriation, the ecstasy, the delirium, this feeling of being swept into the figure of Christ, while the water signifies the opposite. That is what Przywara says in his meditation: that the water here actually counteracts the drunkenness that is caused by the blood and the wine, and thus represents a clarity.[304] He is of course referring to the purifying effect of the miraculous water from the wellspring of Christ. Such ideas played a significant role in the Middle Ages, as you perhaps already know from art history. The blood symbolizes the grace, and the water the *ablutio* or the dissolution of the blackness of sin.

---

[301] The text of this lecture is compiled from notes by LSM, ES, RS, and OK, as well as the English translation by BH.

[302] John 19:34: "But one of the soldiers with a spear pierced his side, and forthwith came there out blood and water" (*KJV*).

[303] RS and ES have "Mischung" (mixture) instead of "Reinigung" (purification).

[304] "Blood and water, drunkenness and clarity. Drunkenness of the dissipation, in which the eyes become clear, to look at God from clarity in clarity" (Przywara, 1938, p. 6).

This idea also comes up in hermetic philosophy, where this *ablutio* with the miraculous water also plays a significant role. This miraculous water is very often directly described as *sanguis*, blood. One of the basic concepts of hermetic philosophy is that one can extract this water from matter; because the savior is also hidden or slumbering in the matter. That is, he comes not just from heaven above, but also from the depths of matter.

Przywara here, after this invocation, has a section in which he divides these invocations into three parts. But we don't need to go further into his notion of the three parts. It would go too far and doesn't add much to the meaning.

Now we are coming to the further invocation of the second part [of the "Anima Christi"]:

5. "Passio Christi, conforta me." (Passion of Christ, strengthen me.)

Przywara now says here that the Passion, or suffering, is the actual mystery of Christ.[305] The suffering of God who now manifests himself. This is actually a central idea, which is also of psychological significance, that is unique to the West. In none of the major religions does one find this relationship to suffering that is found in Christianity, namely this willingness to suffer, in some cases a real desire to suffer. Think of the martyrs. A purpose is seen in suffering which we simply do not find in other religions and other cultures. The idea is that this mystery is a kind of sacred mystery. Rather than a human suffering, it is primarily the suffering of God that is meant. And the thinking goes that God debases himself to the level of men and through this debasing also experiences suffering, as if suffering were a characteristic of mankind. His incarnation is painful.

In the earlier lectures we saw often enough that the Western equivalent of the Eastern *âtman*, of the self, is Christ. The figure of Christ is a very precise equivalent. In the West as in the East, this "self" is sought, but through quite different paths. We have already talked about the Eastern path. The Western path is, however, totally different from the Eastern one. Namely, here one particular aspect is emphasized, which in the East is apparently completely overlooked: the aspect of suffering. Self-actualization, individuation, is a more intense process of suffering in the West; the Westerner, that is, experiences the psychological process in this way, and formulates it as the incarnation of a God. Such a formulation is not found in the East at all. In the East, the self grows out of the man, man grows into this self. Man takes on the form of this self, emerging

305 Przywara (1938), p. 7.

from his[306] own substance. That is why the conviction exists that the *âtman* is both a cosmic being and at the same time my own inner being, hence the expression, "Smaller than small, greater than great."[307] Or,

> The person (*purusha*), not larger than a thumb, dwelling within, always dwelling in the heart of man, is perceived by the heart, the thought, the mind; they who know it become immortal.

> The person (*purusha*) with a thousand heads, a thousand eyes, a thousand feet, having compassed the earth on every side, extends beyond it by ten fingers' breadth.[308]

In the East, man's innermost conscious being is expressed in this paradox. It is the thinker of thinking, the listener of listening, the seer of seeing, and so on. In the West, on the other hand, it is not an inner experience. It is not an individual psychological experience, but the experience of something external. This same self, this same *âtman*, approaches Western experience as an external powerful figure. It is not just a purely spiritual creation, but is also a historical occurrence, as it were. In the historical figure of Jesus, the self appears on the world scene. You know, the otherworldly Christ or even the mystical Christ is not very popular in Protestantism. Protestants like to speak of the historical Jesus, namely that figure who lived and existed, whom we know from tradition, from the Gospels, and who still acts, to a certain extent, as a role model for us. Only sectarian mysticism uses this idea of the inner Christ or the cosmic Christ. Those expressions have become almost obsolete within Protestantism, but they live on in Catholicism. There, the cosmic Christ is still upheld in all his glory.[309] He really acts as a god, so to speak. As such, *Ecce Deus*,[310] he approaches mankind, equipped with power, divine force, even excessive divine force over them, so that one can never say whether Christ has grown out of the person, or whether the person has grown up into Christ. Christ

---

[306] RS and ES here refer to "es" (it) rather than "er" (he) (rendered above by possessive "his").

[307] *Shvetâshvatara Upanishad* 8.3.20 (*SBE*, vol. 15, p. 248).

[308] *Shvetâshvatara Upanishad* 8.3.13–14 (*SBE* vol. 15, pp. 246–47). See Jung's lecture of 26 May 1939 (*JMP*, vol. 6, p. 223).

[309] According to Werner Thiede, the concept of a "cosmic Christ" originated only at the end of the nineteenth century within the theosophic movement, and was coined by Annie Besant (Thiede, 2001). Jung's erroneous claim of its Catholic origin stems from the increasing usage of the concept within the Catholic church. Jung mentioned Besant in his lecture of 4 November 1938 (*JMP*, vol. 6, p. 20).

[310] *Ecce Deus* (Lat.): "Behold God" (probably a play on Pontius Pilate's words referring to Christ in the Vulgate translation of John 19:5, "Ecce homo" [Behold the man]).

is there, and was always there, already there before all the world, and we can only jump out of ourselves and over into Christ, so to speak. We can only obliterate ourselves in order to transfer ourselves across into this Christ, not to become Christ. These meditations serve this very purpose: to release people from their mere humanity, so that they pass over into the divine form of grace, into which they are accepted and even merged, but in the way an atom merges with an infinitely greater mass: He is the body, we are his limbs.[311] He is the vine, we are the branches.[312] He is the whole, we are the parts.[313] In contrast, in the East it goes, I am the whole. I am the *âtman*. I am this world. Everything comes to me, everything wants to enter me. I am everything. *Tat tvam asi*.[314] To our Christian sensibilities, such ideas seem completely incomprehensible and strange. But it is simply a total reversal of our Western Christian perception.

Religions are after all formulations, expressions of a very specific mental attitude, of a psychological temperament. Our Western temperament is appropriately expressed by the Christian myth. Regardless of what some might say, the *consensus gentium*[315] shows that Christianity has been the appropriate formulation for us over the last fifteen centuries. Since the time of the Reformation, its effectiveness as an expression of our psychological condition has waned significantly. From that we must conclude that our psychological condition has altered in a peculiar way since around the sixteenth century, or perhaps even earlier, and that we therefore have a feeling of dissatisfaction. Now, it is hard to demonstrate psychologically what this dissatisfaction is based on and where it stems from. After all, we cannot simply accept the puerile statements of those who say: it is simply not true or impossible that a virgin can have a son. There are even some intellectuals who spout such banalities. That is not what it is about at all; it's about symbolic truths. The dogma is a symbolic truth. We ought not to think that our fathers, grandfathers, and great-grandfathers were fools and idiots; otherwise we would be so, too. We cannot let ourselves admit that. What's good for the goose is good for the gander. So we must

[311] 1 Corinthians 12:27: "Now ye are the body of Christ, and members in particular" (*KJV*).

[312] John 15:5: "I am the vine, ye are the branches: He that abideth in me, and I in him, the same bringeth forth much fruit: for without me ye can do nothing" (*KJV*).

[313] 1 Corinthians 12:12: "For as the body is one, and hath many members, and all the members of that one body, being many, are one body: so also is Christ" (*KJV*).

[314] *Khândogya Upanishad* 6.8.7 (*SBE*, vol. 1, p. 101): "Now that which is that subtle essence (the root of all), in it all that exists has its self. It is the True. It is the Self, and thou, O Svetaketu, art it." (Germ. transl: Deussen, 1897, p. 166).

[315] *consensus gentium* (Lat.): "common consent," lit. "agreement of the people."

accept that our forefathers meant something by these things and that we are perhaps the idiots, as we no longer understand what they actually meant, because for one reason or another we no longer have the language at our command. People who demand such stupid evidence of truth raise no real objection against the dogma.

It has never been about that. Our task should actually be to understand why people came up with claims like the virgin birth, the Trinity, and so on. There is the additional factor that such claims by no means occur only in Christianity. There are also virgin cults and births in other places which have nothing to do with Christ.[316] The idea of Trinities, that is, of triads of gods, goes back as far as the ancient Egyptians, and can also be found amongst the primitives. It is about the nature of humanity. The question is not why Christianity has established such absurd claims that cannot be proven by science, but rather why it is that mankind knows such things and that they are so valuable to us. What are these thoughts based on, and what do they mean in our psychological make-up? You can be certain that they mean something. There are religious people, thousands, millions, who will confirm to you that these things have great meaning for them. Men are not so crazy that something that is incredibly meaningful for one person means nothing at all to another. Well, it is actually like that nowadays, but that explains the tremendous decline of civilized humanity, because some people have beliefs, ideals, and goals that other people know nothing about and do not understand at all. We find ourselves in a veritable Tower of Babel, and I fear that the causes are the same as they have been since time immemorial. This confusion stems from the hubris, the arrogance of man: of human consciousness, that is, which now suddenly thinks it can divest itself of the task of reflecting on such things. If we no longer reflect on such things, we no longer think about our own reasons for existence, in other words about our inner experience. Then we think only about what is external, rational, which is certainly also important: bank balances or public appointments, for example. But what is the use of a healthy bank balance if you feel ill at ease in yourself? You would happily give away your hundreds and thousands just to feel comfortable in your skin for an hour. If you feel as if your psyche is somehow falling apart, then you go to the doctor, and you would gladly hand over your entire fortune if he could free you from an abominable neurosis. We

---

[316] At the 1938 Eranos conference dedicated to the "Figure and Cult of the Great Mother," Ernesto Buonaiuti spoke about "Mary and the Virgin Birth of Jesus" (Buonaiuti, 1939). The conference proceedings were published in 1939.

have forgotten what these ideas mean for the well-being of the human soul. We have completely forgotten what they meant for people in the Middle Ages. When we talk about the Middle Ages, we always think of the poor hygiene and the lack of international connections (as if ours were good), of miserable carriages with which one could not even travel as far as Belgrade. But—can we do that today? We cannot even travel from Holland to London with any degree of security. We think of diseases: leprosy, plague, and so on; of the "dark" Middle Ages, the Inquisition burning people alive. But shall I read you some statistics from the last twenty years? Our times are overall much worse than the Middle Ages, make no mistake. The Middle Ages were harmless in comparison to what is going on today. We read in horror about the poisonings in the courts of the Borgias.[317] But that is child's play compared to the things we are experiencing today. We have no grounds to hold forth about the consciousness of people in the Middle Ages. This consciousness has simply been lost from our field of vision, and we no longer know about the preoccupations of medieval man. But you just have to flick through medieval books to see immediately how people thought about these things, the effect they had on their lives. Then we suddenly see the psychological healing significance of such ideas. These beliefs actually have the effect of calming and pacifying the whole person. Man and his existence thus gain a meaning that goes far beyond the sacred bank balance, so far that it even extends beyond suffering.

Suffering for us no longer has any meaning and has to be cured straight away, because it is wrong. One should not accept suffering, it should be rejected, healed, avoided. We don't even want to hear about it, because it is unseemly. These medieval people knew, however, firstly that suffering is unavoidable, and secondly that it is a blessing because it is full of meaning. It has a meaning and a purpose. It sets something in motion. Imagine, for example, a sick person who can accept that his neurosis has a meaning; he may not understand it, but God has sent him this trouble for a specific purpose, namely to remind him that he has to suffer for a specific meaningful reason, and it is thus significant. In his own suffering, he even identifies with the suffering of God. Then you see immediately what

[317] The House of Borgia was an Italian-Spanish noble family that rose to fame during the Italian Renaissance. Two Borgias were elected pope: Alfons de Borja, who ruled as Pope Callixtus III (1455–58), and Rodrigo Lanzol Borgia, Pope Alexander VI (1492–1503). The latter fathered several illegitimate children, amongst them Cesare Borgia (ca. 1475–1507) and Lucrezia Borgia (1480–1519), whose names have become almost synonymous with ruthless power politics. Rumors link them to incest, poisoning, and murder.

a wealth of meaning is gained from his belief in a suffering God. He knows that this suffering is the image of God himself becoming man. He knows that suffering is part of the path toward his own self. He knows that without this suffering his self can never come into being. Then he can accept it. If he can accept that, the sting is taken out of it. People can bear anything if they can see the meaning in it.[318] But we have completely lost the meaning. In this regard we are less, not more, advanced than the Middle Ages. So we have no grounds at all to put ourselves on a particularly high pedestal. Our Western model is Christianity and it says, God— that is, the self—can only come into being through suffering. The self emerges from suffering, so accept your suffering, then you are on the way to Christ, to the self.[319]

The East, as I already said, has a quite different attitude in this regard. It seeks only the liberation from pleasure and suffering. Pleasure and suffering are deemed equal. In the East, the only aim is to free oneself from these opposites. They do not have that militant attitude of Western people who want to conquer desire, to win, who do all they can to avoid suffering, to achieve pleasure, who want to battle with and overcome suffering. For people in the East, because they live close to nature, close to the earth,[320] pleasure and suffering are so interwoven that they know these two things balance each other. Pleasure cannot be avoided, suffering cannot be avoided. The Easterner knows that redemption lies only in freeing oneself from both. One frees oneself not only from the bad, but also from the good. One frees oneself from these two, becomes *nirdvandva*: that is, free of opposites.

---

[318] Cf. Nietzsche (1889) (*KSA*, vol. 6; Engl.: 2005): "If you have your 'why?' in life, you can get along with almost any 'how?'. People don't strive for happiness, only the English do" (2005, p. 157).

[319] The German pastor and theologian Walter Uhsadel visited Jung in Küsnacht on 29 May 1938 and gave the following account of their meeting (Uhsadel, 1966, pp. 120–21.): "As I took my leave, he led me into a small room in which he treated his patients. He had in this room a copy of a very lovely Gothic stained-glass window of the Crucifixion. Through this the room had acquired the character of a spiritual place. While Jung was pointing to this window he said to me, 'Just look, this is the crucial thing for us.' When I asked him why he said this, he replied in his calm, collected way, 'I have just returned from India, where this problem has arisen for me anew. Mankind has to cope with the problem of suffering. Eastern man wishes to free himself from the problem of suffering by stripping off life. Western man, on the other hand, attempts to suppress suffering with drugs. However, suffering must be overcome insofar as one endures it. This we learn solely from him.' And with this he pointed to the Crucified One." On Jung and Uhsadel, see Liebscher (2020)

[320] RS has "ursprüngliches, organisches" (primordial, organic) instead of "naturbedingtes, erdnahes" (natural, close to the earth).

This unique way of experiencing things is based on a different psychological temperament. Its starting point is completely different from the Western one. In the West, a largely masculine, combative attitude prevails. We strive for pleasure and get it too, in direct or indirect ways. Suffering is avoided or overcome. In the East, they cannot defend themselves against either pole. The East has a feminine attitude toward the world. The world is an awesome drama, in which one is helplessly swept up, powerless to do anything about it. Everything is a matter of course, is at one with the gods. Every accomplishment in daily life is a piece of the divine, awesome life, and that is how people live. Every banal part of the daily routine is a ritual and is accompanied with ritual beliefs. I once told you[321] how the cart drivers in Ceylon[322] ritually solve the problem when two carts crash into one another. Here we would hear terrible cursing and swearing, but in the East one driver says a *mantra* to the other: "All disturbance is temporary, no soul." That is: problems pass, it is only temporary. It is not real. One has no soul. There is nothing there that reacts. You are illusion. Your cart, your donkey, your soul; none of that happened at all. In other words, it means nothing, it is just the world. With that the most ordinary of mere mortals free themselves from any kind of difficulty by quickly saying, "Everything is temporary, there is no disturbance, there is no soul, there is no I." That is the Eastern attitude.

We can now assume, or even know, for very specific psychological reasons, that when the outer attitude to the world is a feminine, suffering, passive one, then the inner attitude is totally masculine. And vice versa: where the outer attitude is combative, the inner one is feminine, namely a peculiar receptivity, willingness, submissiveness, an acceptance, surrendering. Now, you'll find that expressed very clearly in medieval Christianity in the idea of surrendering to the overarching figure of Christ, of *âtman*, in relation to whom I am like a vessel or something which actually does not have its own existence, but only finds a purpose when filled by him.

In the East, on the other hand—one finds this in every person in the East—there is an inner strength, a masculinity, that pushes itself up toward the cosmic mountain and carries the crown of the universe above: I am the world, and that is illusion. That is an inner masculine attitude which explains a lot about Eastern people: specifically their deep, unyielding nature. Their eyes have the quality of a dark gemstone which one cannot

---

[321] Jung's lecture of 16 December 1938 (*JPM*, vol. 6, p. 72).
[322] See n. 267.

see into. It's always a puzzle for us, while our eyes are as telltale as a woman's glance. One sees right in, one feels accepted, one feels somehow drawn in. That's why the world sinks into the Western soul and poisons it at the roots. That's why we lap up everything to do with the East. We have Buddhist temples and study the teachings zealously, while the Easterner, at best, says, "Well then, your Christ was a very nice man, said very good things, very useful. We have no objections there. He's probably an incarnation of Vishnu." They accord him his place. "The Gospels are a very good book. There are even things in there that are really similar to the *Upanishads*.[323] Of course we've known all that for ages." They don't absorb it in the same way that we do. It doesn't take hold of them in the same way as it does us. For example, the cult of Mary is very popular there, especially in south India. Right down in the south there's a temple of the virgin mother goddesses. At the southernmost tip of India, the Jesuits wanted to found a mission, in a place where there was a temple of Mariamman.[324] Then they discovered that this goddess is a virgin mother goddess. So they said, "It is the Virgin Mary." Then all was well, plain sailing. You may say that it was a piece of holy deceit. But it didn't hurt the local people, because they deceived and allowed themselves to be deceived. At the end of the day it doesn't matter, because I am also the gods. You can't cause any nonsense with the gods, because I am them. Next time, I'll show you an Indian text where you can hear all of that from the source, so to speak.

From that you can see how different our attitude is from the Eastern one. For us, the central figure is endowed with a penetrative power. You have to invoke this figure and then it reveals its powerful effect. We wait and hope for the powerful effect of the figure. It is already charged, a priori, with masculine power to which our inner being relates in a feminine way, submissively. This also explains why the West is particularly prone

---

[323] *Upanishads*, from Sanskrit *sat* (to sit), prefixed by *upa* and *ni*, meaning "to sit down close to (one's teacher)": a collection of more than two hundred Indian texts (though traditionally 108 are mentioned, in accordance with the holy Hindu number), the earliest dating back to the second millennium BCE. They were regarded as secret teachings that were rendered orally from teacher to student. The *Upanishads* can be seen as commentaries to and refinements of the teachings of the four ancient Vedas; hence they are also referred to as *Vedanta* (the end of the Veda). Jung's first written engagement with the *Upanishads* can be found in his "Wandlungen und Symbole der Libido" (1911–12, §§ 208, 243–45, 677–80), in which he gives a psychological reading of passages from the *Upanishads* and the *Rig-Veda*.

[324] Mâri, also known as Mariamman or Mariaai, meaning Mother Mari, is a Hindu goddess of rain, worshipped particularly in the south of India.

to psychological epidemics. The East has never had follies like the children's crusade.[325] They deceive and let themselves be deceived, the holy men too. If someone tells you a fib, that's perfectly all right. I am only an illusion, and the other is too. There is no category for lying or being swindled. Of course it is convention among decent people not to be coarse about it, but to do it in a refined way. But if you go to the East with ideas of categories of truth, you'll be very disappointed. Europeans have found themselves sorely disappointed in this regard. Then they say, "These holy men are mere con men." Take the great Gandhi.[326] In India he is called Mahatma, the great soul. He is a saint, a holy man. And he fasts for weeks on end to push some demand through with the government. The famous *Secret Service*, which you are hearing about yet again, discovered that the Mahatma eats dextrose tablets. He lives on them. He calls that fasting, and keeps himself going with them, saying they are not real food, but medicine.[327] We say, "What an impostor!" But in the East, it's as broad as it is long. It is taken for granted. They accept it because the world is an illusion. If someone came along and said, "I am the God of Europe!" they would say, "Okay then. There are so many crazy people and so many holy ones, why not this one?" Thus Easterners are singularly well protected against psychological epidemics. They stand on a solid foundation of the self. We have the self outside. Woe betide us when the convincing powerful figure comes from outside, or stands somewhere outside of us. They

[325] The term "children's crusade" is an English translation from Latin *peregrinatio puerorum*, and refers to the failed crusade of mainly youths and young adults in 1212. Inspired by alleged miraculous visions and miracles, young people from Germany and France, overwhelmingly from impoverished backgrounds, took vows to regain Jerusalem from the Saracens. They were led in Germany by the shepherd Nicholas of Cologne and in France by the twelve-year-old Stephen of Cloyes. Unarmed and underfunded, both undertakings failed bitterly and never made it to the Holy Land. Many participants died of hunger and exhaustion; others were sold as slaves to the Saracens.

[326] Mohandas Karamchand, called "Mahatma" (great soul, venerable) Gandhi (1869–1948), leader of the Indian independence movement in its peaceful protest (*satyagraha*, lit. "truth force") against British colonial rule, "father" of the Indian nation. On Gandhi, see his autobiography *The Story of My Experiments with Truth* (1993), which covers his life until 1921 and was published in the magazine *Navjivan* from 1925 to 1928; also Gandhi (1962).

[327] There is no evidence for Jung's claim; however, the Central Bureau of Intelligence in the Indian Home Office and the Information Department of the India Office in London provided only limited and selected access to the British press, which reported mainly on two of Gandhi's nine hunger strikes, those in 1932 and 1943. Using nutritional experts, the British press became increasingly critical of Gandhi's method, culminating in an article in the *Daily Express* on 1 March 1943, where it was revealed that Gandhi had at least once taken a lime juice sweetened with sugar during his fast, which would have marked the end of previous fasts (p. 1). See Pratt and Vernon (2005).

only need to have one success, a good bank balance is enough for us to think, "He must be right, because he is successful." Then we believe it and are crushed—in a really feminine way. When the big strong man comes along, showing off—yes, then! Then he is convincing. Pay attention to that word.

I have experienced this myself and it really knocked me sideways. When I was a very young lecturer at the university and lectured on primitive psychology,[328] as I was going down the stairs afterwards I heard one student say to another, "I didn't understand a word." And her friend answered, "Neither did I, but he must be right, he's so forceful." That really is a Western attitude, even though it was a woman who said it, who ought to have had a certain inner masculinity. But it applies to everyone. In the East, that would be far from the truth. Because for an Eastern woman it goes without saying: if someone is powerful, he is a man, and he is convincing. *Überzeugend* [convincing]. Listen to that word![329] That is accepted in the East, and not with us, but here it is hidden behind a curtain. Easterners accept what it is to be human. Their a priori conviction is that we are all deluded, are weak, that we are tangled up in the world and its events in a terrible way. There is nothing one can do about it, unless one gets off the spinning wheel of the *samsâra*, the wheel of rebirth;[330] unless one says, "I know. I recognize it. I know that I am *âtman*, that I am the world." That releases the Easterner. Because for people from the East, suffering is not meaningful, but is simply the opposite of pleasure. And pleasure is as bad as pain. Suffering is the end of the Nidâna chain, about which the "Nidâna-Samyutta" says,

> Thus I have heard. On one occasion the Blessed One was dwelling at Sâvatthî in Jeta's Grove, Anâthapindika's Park. There the Blessed One addressed the bhikkhus thus: "Bhikkhus!"—"Yes, venerable sir," those bhikkhus replied. The Blessed One said this: "Bhikkhus, I will teach you dependent origination. Listen to that and attend

[328] Jung lectured at the University of Zurich from 1905 to 1913. He resigned as a lecturer on 30 April 1914. See Hoerni (2019), p. xiv. Although there was no lecture announced under the title "Primitive Psychology," Jung did refer to this as a topic of his lectures also on other occasions: "I lectured on psychopathology, and, naturally, also on the foundations of Freudian psychoanalysis, as well as on the psychology of primitives. These were my principal subjects." (Jung, 1963, p. 117; Jung and Jaffé, forthcoming).

[329] Trans. note: the German word "überzeugend" (convincing) is a composite of the words "über" (over) and "zeugen" (to sire/father a child *or* to attest to something).

[330] *samsâra* (Sanskr.): "flow", is a term used to describe the instability and flux of the phenomenal world. See also Jung's lecture of 26 May 1939 (*JMP*, vol. 6, p. 223).

closely, I will speak."—"Yes, venerable sir," those bhikkhus replied. The Blessed One said this: "And what, bhikkhus, is dependent origination? With ignorance as condition, volitional formations [come to be]; with volitional formations as condition, consciousness; with consciousness as condition, name-and-form; with name-and-form as condition, the six sense bases; with the six sense bases as condition, contact; with contact as condition, feeling; with feeling as condition, craving; with craving as condition, clinging; with clinging as condition, existence; with existence as condition, birth; with birth as condition, aging-and-death, sorrow, lamentation, pain, displeasure, and despair come to be. Such is the origin of this whole mass of suffering. This, bhikkhus, is called dependent origination."[331]

And we release ourselves from this condition of suffering through the knowledge: I am the self, the *âtman* and the world.

---

[331] Bhikkhu Bodhi (2000), p. 533. Jung quoted this passage from Geiger (1922), p. 5. See also Jung's lecture of 17 February 1939 (*JMP*, p. 139).

Lecture 5[332]

LAST TIME WE dealt with the fifth verse [of the "Anima Christi"]:

"Passio Christi, conforta me." (Passion of Christ, strengthen me.)

I highlighted that suffering and the attitude to suffering is one of the classic differences between the Eastern and Western standpoints. As I said, in the East there is a quite different psychological temperament. The Easterner says, "I am the *âtman*" or, "Through enlightenment I become Buddha," while the Westerner's entire standpoint is that one's own life and one's own autonomy lie in the figure of Christ. Thus the Western person says, "My life disappears into the life of Christ, I am permeated and overpowered by him." It is notable that the East has an essentially negative attitude to suffering. Suffering belongs to illusion. The world is a place of suffering, but one leaves this state by freeing oneself from conflicts.[333] Meanwhile, this growing into the life of Christ leads one to receive[334] the mystery of Christ: in other words, to perceive the suffering of the God who is becoming or has become man, as Przywara says.[335] If we then think that Christ is the corresponding figure of the self for the Westerner, then this realization that the God-man, or the God-become-man, suffers actually means that the process of individuation, of becoming oneself, is a

---

[332] The text of this lecture is compiled from notes by LSM, ES, RS, and OK, as well as the English translation by BH.

[333] LSM and OK have "Gegensätze" (opposites) instead of "Konflikte" (conflicts).

[334] ES has "Empfindung" (sensation, perception) instead of "Empfang" (reception).

[335] "*Passio Christi, conforta me*—the soul of Christ is the inside of Christ. Christ, however, is nothing 'if not the crucified' (1 Cor. 2:2). Thus the suffering of Christ is the soul of the soul of Christ and the interior of the interior of Christ: the actual mystery of Christ. The mystery of Christ: because it is unheard of that the all-powerful God should suffer, that the ever-blessed God is abject, that the ever-holy God is wounded, that the eternal immortal God is dying. The mystery of Christ—because herein the hidden tenderest aspect of God's love becomes visible: the tabernacle of the inner divine life" (Przywara, 1938, p. 7).

painful affair that causes suffering. This suffering is not expressed as my personal suffering, but as the suffering of God. So we could say that it is projected into the divine figure. We do not find this concept in the East. The person becoming Buddha is even, to the extent that that person is enlightened, freed from suffering. Suffering disappears like the clouds of *mâyâ*.[336]

This peculiar Western attitude means, therefore, that the more perfect figure, the bigger person, the more comprehensive, future man who towers above the present one, is a God who, so to speak, becomes man and in so doing experiences suffering. We could thus also flip the sentence around—by developing myself into this divine or perfect state, I go through a process of suffering. This condition of suffering is of course also a human condition: that is, my state of suffering; but that is secondary, in that it repeats the suffering of Christ in a way. The essential element here is not my suffering, but the suffering of Christ, which is always present, always happening. This is one of those concepts that is difficult to grasp, which you will also find in the psychology of the Mass:[337] namely, that the sacrifice of Christ is not a repeated sacrifice, but is ongoing, always present, a sacrifice that took place outside of time and in some way is always happening, because it took place in eternity, that is, beyond time, and seems always to repeat itself. The Passion of Christ is the same. It is an eternal suffering, a permanent suffering, but it is also continuously resolved through the glorification and transfiguration of Christ, and by the return of Christ to the purely divine state as the second figure in the Trinity.

This formulation seems to sit well with the Western temperament, otherwise we in the West would probably have come up with something quite different. It must in some way fit our temperament, otherwise it would not have been possible for such an objectionable concept as that of a suffering God to have gained such a following.

If you think about it, in the ancient world, the idea that a God suffers must have seemed totally shocking. And indeed it is. That counted against Christianity, and yet the idea still managed to assert itself with such force that the Western mind has been captivated by it for fifteen hundred years. There is no other idea in the West that could come nearly as close to expressing the Western mindset, and hence our fascination with it. Now, gradually, mankind is beginning to somehow slough off this fascination, and

[336] See n. 296.
[337] At the Eranos conference of 1941, Jung lectured on the "Transformation Symbolism in the Mass" (Jung, 1942b).

to that extent also our understanding of these statements is collapsing and they are apparently losing effectiveness, which represents a great loss.

I would like to provide you with more information about the Christian concept, because it is of fundamental importance for an understanding of the *Exercitia spiritualia*. As you know, our Protestant concepts are not completely in agreement with the Catholic ideas, because in Protestantism the strict concept of the Trinity has disappeared to a large degree. You may have read recently in the *Neue Zürcher Zeitung* about the decisions regarding the ecumenical council of churches.[338] This story reveals a piece of medieval religious history, namely a discussion about whether to sign a document asserting that Christ is God. A host of voices were raised against it. Apparently one can also hold the view that Christ is not God. This notion shows what the present situation is like, at least in reformed Protestantism. We cannot even acknowledge Christ as the Godhead, even though he himself said he was the Son of God. This position of Son of God played a considerable role, after all, and as you perhaps remember from the New Testament, the Jews wanted to stone Jesus for saying such a thing. John says in chapter 10 [of his Gospel],

> Jesus answered them, Is it not written in your law, I said, Ye are gods?/ If he called them gods, unto whom the word of God came, and the scripture cannot be broken;/ Say ye of him, whom the Father hath sanctified, and sent into the world, Thou blasphemest; because I said, I am the Son of God?/ If I do not the works of my Father, believe me not./ But if I do, though ye believe not me, believe the

---

[338] On 29 and 30 November 1939, the *Neue Zürcher Zeitung* reported on the meeting of the Kirchensynode des Kanton Zürichs (Church synod of the canton of Zurich), which took place on 29 November 1939. The synod discussed whether the Swiss churches should become members of the Ökumenischer Rat der Kirchen (Ecumenical Council of the Churches; from 1948, World Council of Churches), and accept the constitution that had been drafted in Utrecht in 1938. The Utrecht meeting saw the unification of the two main ecumenical organizations, Life and Work and Faith and Order. In its constitution, the Ecumenical Council stated that it was a union of churches that acknowledge Jesus Christ as their God and savior. The Zurich synod controversially discussed the formulation "as God" and voted for a declaration in which it recommended the acceptance of the Utrecht constitution, but only with the caveat that "Jesus Christ alone is also the Lord and head of our Swiss church, but that our participation in the work of the Ecumenical Council may not be bound to denominational formulations." (*Neue Zürcher Zeitung*, 30 November 1939, no. 2028).

works: that ye may know, and believe, that the Father is in me, and
I in him.[339]

Christ refers here to Psalm 82, where it says, "I have said, Ye are gods;
and all of you are children of the most High."[340] This statement is very
curious and very obscure, and people have often wondered what is actually meant by it.[341] But with a literal reading, there is really no other way
to understand it than that we are children of God, or related to God. All
other interpretative gymnastics are just that. Because there are also other
parts in the New Testament that provide evidence that such a statement
was meant, that man is related to God, and that Christ's assertion that he
was the Son of God was not so absurd after all. For example, in the second epistle to the Corinthians we find the following: "Know ye not your
own selves, how that Jesus Christ is in you, except ye be reprobates?"[342]
Then another passage at Galatians 2:20: "I live; not I, but Christ lives in
me."[343] That is the literal translation. There are some Protestant theologians now publishing Bible translations in which it does not say Christ is
"in you" but "between you", "among you",[344] so that one doesn't get the

---

[339] John 10:34–38 (KJV). Jung quoted from the Luther Bible edition of 1912.

[340] Psalm 82:6 (KJV). Jung again quoted from the Luther translation.

[341] Irenaeus writes about this passage, "We were not made gods at our beginning, but
first we were made men, then in the end, gods. God does this out of the purity of his goodness so that none may think him envious or ungenerous. 'I have said, You are gods, and all
of you are children of the Highest.' So he speaks, but since we are not able to bear the
power of divinity, he goes on to say, 'But you will die like men.' Thus he expresses both the
generosity of his giving, and our weakness, and the fact that we are possessed of free will.
For because of his kindness he bestowed his gift upon us, and made men free, as he is free.
Because of his foresight he knew men's weakness, and the results of that weakness; but
because of his love and his goodness he will overcome [the weakness of] the nature of created man. It was necessary that [the weakness of men's] nature should first be shown and
afterwards be overcome, and mortality be swallowed up by immortality, corruptibility by
incorruptibility, and man become conformed to the image and likeness of God, having received the knowledge of good and evil" (Adversus haereses, 4.37.4; in Bettenson [1956],
p. 69).

[342] 2 Corinthians 13:5 (KJV). The scripts render the text from the Zürcher edition of
the Bible.

[343] Galatians 2:20. Jung translated this line from Greek to German. The English translation follows his rendering. Jung's translation is closest to the Luther translation: "Ich lebe
aber; doch nun nicht ich, sondern Christus lebt in mir." The KJV reads "[N]evertheless I
live; yet not I, but Christ liveth in me."

[344] An example for this kind of translation during Jung's time was the Textbibel des
Alten und Neuen Testaments (Kautzsch, 1899): "oder erkennet ihr nicht an euch selbst, daß
Christus Jesus unter euch ist?" (or do you not recognize in yourselves that Jesus Christ is
among you?). The translation was provided by a team of Protestant theologians under the
editorship of Emil Kautzsch (1841–1910). The translation of the New Testament was taken

idea that Christ could be the inner Christ, that it is a case of an inner relation with God. It's hard to understand why anyone would have such resistance to the idea, but one has one's suspicions.

I would like to give you a parallel from the ancient world. South of Cairo in Oxyrhynchus, papyri from the first century were unearthed that were apparently notes from a kind of collection of anecdotes about Jesus. They probably predate the canonical Gospels, which came very late.[345] In the Gospels it says, "For where two or three are gathered together in my name, there am I in the midst of them."[346] That would be the between. But the original[347] version says, "Wheresoever there are (two, they are not without) God: and where there is one alone I say I am with him."[348] It seems that the text was subsequently edited,[349] to take away the one and add it to the two. Then there are three. That's enough for an association, for a church in fact. One alone cannot make a church, despite what Coleridge once said: "I believe in the one and only true church of which I am presently the only member."[350] You see what considerations are at play here: namely, consideration for the church. One alone does not have grace; there needs to be a club of members already. That is of course clearly intended to discourage lone mavericks and activities that are too individualistic. But inevitably,

---

from the ninth edition of Carl Heinrich von Weizsäcker's (1822–99) *Das Neue Testament* (first edition, 1875). Weizsäcker was a leading exponent of the historical-critical school of Bible exegesis. Jung's critical view of this method might explain his derogatory, somewhat cryptic remark that follows in the lecture.

[345] Bernard P. Grenfell and Arthur S. Hunt, who discovered these papyri in Oxyrhynchus in 1897, stated in their edition that "they were earlier than 140 AD, and might go back to the first century" (Grenfell and Hunt, 1898, p. 3), which might support Jung's theory that these logia predated the canonical Gospels. However, recent scholarship dates the "the Oxyrhynchus sayings of Jesus" to between 150 and 300 CE.

[346] Matthew 18:20 (*KJV*).

[347] See n. 345.

[348] Oxyrhynchus papyrus 1.10, in "The Oxyrhynchus Sayings of Jesus" (Rhodes James, 1924, p. 27).

[349] See n. 345.

[350] This quotation is wrongly attributed to the English poet, philosopher, and theologian Samuel Taylor Coleridge (1772–1834). It is in fact from another member of the circle of the so-called Lake Poets, the essayist and literary critic Thomas de Quincey (1785–1859), who was for a while a friend of Coleridge. In his main work, *Confessions of an English Opium Eater* (1821), De Quincey wrote, "This is the doctrine of the true church on the subject of opium: of which church I acknowledge myself to be the only member—the alpha and the omega: but then it is to be recollected that I speak from the ground of a large and profound personal experience: whereas most of the unscientific authors who have at all treated of opium, and even of those who have written expressly on the materia medica, make it evident, from the horror they express of it, that their experimental knowledge of its action is none at all" (De Quincey, 2013 [1821], p. 41). I thank Jens Schlieter for pointing this out to me.

it still has an effect in the church today. That's why one point, I believe, was translated completely incorrectly. It is not at all that Christ is "among you," but that he is actually "in you." Paul acknowledges that "Christ liveth in me."[351] Paul no longer lives, Christ lives. He is the body. If I fit in anywhere at all, I am merely an accessory. There is also a passage in the Acts of the Apostles: "For in him we live, and move, and have our being; [. . .] For we are also his offspring."[352] That is: we have a divine lineage.

Here we see the roots and seeds of an original primordial view which in the course of Christianity's history have not developed; instead the whole autonomy of the human-divine being has become concentrated in Christ, and man has been left empty-handed, so to speak. These seeds have not developed, and yet these are the seeds from which the Eastern belief developed: I am the *âtman*, I am the world. In the West, this process was reversed, as you can see. Man sank down and is only significant as a member of a community. As an individual, a man has no divine right, but must wait for the grace of the church. Then why are we surprised when a martial[353] age finally erupts and this idea is already prepared in our culture, where there is then not even any God left to turn to? What is man then? There is no longer a church, but there is a crowd, there is the state, and the individual no longer exists. That is a catastrophe, both spiritual and human, of the greatest magnitude. Then we can no longer allow ourselves to have organizations, to form groups of people—because we have no form other than the state, which is nothing but a conglomeration of human individuals, and which, although it is man-made, does not come from our deepest nature, but is a protective device that is intended always to remain in human hands. Then, of course, the mob mentality emerges. Each person regresses to the subhuman level, because they are no longer an individual, a personality. The individual can no longer be heard, because now the beast roars. Only someone who can roar louder than the beast can still be heard. We have the loss of the church structure to thank for that. But it is also due to the fact that education has historically been solely the domain of the church that the civilized European has sunk to this level. Nowadays the church should know that it can no longer subordinate the individual exclusively to the church. That nullifies a person, and if the

---

[351] Galatians 2:20 (*KJV*).

[352] Acts 17:28 (*KJV*). Jung shortened the German quotation and seems to have paraphrased the text.

[353] ES and OK have "materialistisch" (materialistic) instead of "martialisch" (martial).

church walls cave in there is nothing left but rubble, and the individual no longer even exists. Instead of developing these seeds, which are clearly sown and articulated in the Holy Scripture, the church developed its power, its strength as an institution for human welfare. Our entire culture, after all, is essentially Christian.[354] That we can say for sure, because had the Catholic church not existed where would we be now? We would be absolutely nowhere. But we got stuck with the church as an institution, and didn't incorporate the original confessions. Thanks to this situation, we have never been able to comprehend the East. Because all we do is dismiss the Eastern ideas as so-called megalomania. Who here knows that Christ said, "You are gods"? Have you ever heard a sermon about that? I haven't. There are still many points in the New Testament on which no sermons have been given.

I must tell you about another point. In the Acts of the Apostles, you'll find that depiction of the pouring forth of the Holy Ghost which is psychologically significant.[355] Christ says, "I want to leave you a paraclete, a comforter."[356] That is, he wants to leave the Spirit of God for these children of God whom he is now leaving. There the Spirit of God falls from heaven as fiery tongues. These fiery flames do not fall "between" people, but upon each individual figure. Each of them receives the paraclete and can then say, "I have received the spirit of God. I am the abode, another aspect of the Godhead." That is the third in the Trinity. The whole Godhead is received in the Holy Ghost. It also simply makes sense logically. But it was never followed up, thanks to the Inquisition. If one man says he has received the spirit of God, that he is the *theos*, what can one say to that? There's nothing more to say. Because then he could proclaim anything, the worst kind of heresy. That's what the so-called *Schwarmgeister* did.[357] Then the

---

[354] LSM has "kirchlich" (clerical) instead of "christlich" (Christian).

[355] Acts 2:2–4: "And suddenly there came a sound from heaven as of a rushing mighty wind, and it filled all the house where they were sitting./ And there appeared unto them cloven tongues like as of fire, and it sat upon each of them./ And they were all filled with the Holy Ghost, and began to speak with other tongues, as the Spirit gave them utterance" (*KJV*).

[356] John 14:16: "And I will pray the Father, and he shall give you another Comforter, that he may abide with you for ever"; John 14:26: "But the Comforter, which is the Holy Ghost, whom the Father will send in my name, he shall teach you all things, and bring all things to your remembrance, whatsoever I have said unto you" (*KJV*).

[357] *Schwarmgeister* or *Schwärmer* (Ger.): "enthusiasts": this refers to radical pietist groups in the wake of the Reformation, who "by false appeal to the Holy Spirit pay inadequate regard to the *extra nos* of Christian salvation" (Leppin, Enns, and Stroh, 2011). Luther used the term in his dispute with the Zwickau prophets. See Hilliard (2011); Makari (2016), pp. 78–86.

whole institution of the church crumbles, so we have to understand that it was impossible for the church to deal with this problem. But this problem is an eternal truth, and becomes acute at those moments when the church cannot keep its flock together any longer, when cracks appear in the church walls. Then we should remind ourselves of these assertions. They are not empty words, but basic psychological truths, without which we do not have any kind of buttress against the problems of today. If as individuals we do not manage to remember our own divinity, so to speak, we degenerate helplessly into the herd-animal mindset. Someone simply saying "I" is not enough;[358] such people are seen as mere egoists or individualists, and rightly so. But as for an individual person remembering his original divinity, that is a completely different story. Such a pronouncement expresses the deepest foundations on which we stand. It concerns the whole person, only a tiny part of which is found in our consciousness. This statement concerns the human self. It is not he, not the I, who is God: the self is the God within, and this self is, as the whole, significantly superior to the part, namely consciousness. In Christian philosophy, we hear virtually nothing about this self, because it is kept hidden. But we would have heard about it if the church had been able, when it was still all-powerful, to develop the religion of the Holy Ghost: to rise up out of Christ, that is, as he said himself. Because if he is the Son of God, and he calls us the children of God, then we would be his brothers and sisters. If the Holy Spirit as the third person of the Trinity descends on everyone, then lots of people are in exactly the same spiritual state as Christ was when the Spirit of God descended on him in the baptism.

But this idea was too difficult. It is still far too difficult for the church today. In the Middle Ages, one would have been burnt to death immediately for voicing such criticism. But we can never accept and perceive as true our spiritual connection with the East, we can never assimilate the East, if we do not also consider this Christian predisposition in us, when we do not know that this assertion was also already present in the original texts of Christianity. We are suffering from a *développement arrêté*.[359] Our spiritual development in the West has been somewhat stunted, while in the East it has become hypertrophic, because they did not have institutions that could be compared in any way to the Catholic church. Buddhism is far from being a church in this sense.

---

[358] ES has "gilt" (applies) instead of "genügt" (is enough).
[359] *développement arrêté* (Fr.): "arrested development."

I would like briefly to quote an author who suffered from this Western problem, wrestled with it, and was felled by it. I mean, the problem of the collapse of the church, of traditional Christianity, that unfortunately cannot be denied. Optimistic souls want to think and believe that it can still be saved, but if we look at the facts, if we count the number of people who are *extra ecclesiam*,[360] we must admit that Christianity is in bad shape nowadays. That person is Friedrich Nietzsche. He made the pronouncement, "God is dead."[361] God has died. And he didn't realize that in proclaiming this he was actually within the dogma, that it was a Christian pronouncement. Because God has died. He is always dying, and the death of Christ is one of the mysteries of Christianity. The death of God is preached to us, after all. That much we know: God has died. But Nietzsche didn't mean it like that; he meant: God has come to an end. With that, God coming to an end and having no successor, something very special happened for the world. Nietzsche didn't know that *he* would become God's successor. Then when mental illness got the better of him, he signed his letters with names such as "the crucified one" or "Dionysos", or "Zagreus"—that is, the mutilated one, who was also a god, also a deceased god. And this fate was played out in him. In *Zarathustra*, he prophesied it himself, when he says to the dying tightrope walker, "Your soul will be dead even before your body."[362] Eleven years after his soul died, Nietzsche's body died.[363]

---

[360] *extra ecclesiam* (Lat.): "outside of the church."

[361] Nietzsche, in aphorism 125 of *Die fröhliche Wissenschaft* (1882) (*KSA*, vol. 3; Engl.: 1974), had a madman announce the death of God: "God is dead. God remains dead. And we have killed him. How shall we comfort ourselves, the murderers of all murderers? What was holiest and mightiest of all that the world has yet owned has bled to death under our knives: who will wipe this blood off us?" (1974, p. 181). However, Nietzsche was not the first to declare the demise of the Judaeo-Christian God. This was a common trope amongst German romantic poets and philosophers such as Georg Friedrich Wilhelm Hegel (1977 [1802]), Heinrich Heine (2007 [1834]) or Jean Paul (1845 [1796–97]).

[362] Nietzsche (1883–85) (*KSA*, vol. 4, p. 22; Engl.: 1961, p. 48).

[363] Friedrich Nietzsche's mental breakdown took place around the end of 1888, in Turin. At that time he started writing letters to friends and to public figures such as King Umberto I of Italy that showed clear signs of a mental collapse. These were signed "Dionysos" or "the Crucified," thus linking them to the ultimate line of the author's previously completed philosophical autobiography *Ecce Homo*: "Dionysos versus the Crucified." After receiving such a letter, Jakob Burckhardt was so alarmed that he contacted Nietzsche's friend Franz Overbeck, who went to Turin on 7 January 1889 to fetch his friend. Subsequently, Nietzsche was sectioned in the Friedmatt clinic in Basel from 10 to 17 January 1889. His mother Franziska Oehler-Nietzsche then brought him to the asylum in Jena, where he remained until 24 March 1890, when he was released into the custodianship of his mother. After her death in 1897, his sister Elisabeth Förster-Nietzsche moved her brother from Naumburg to the Villa Silverblick in Weimar, where Nietzsche then lived until

No wonder that in his most significant, far-reaching book, his confessional work *Thus Spoke Zarathustra*, there are many parts which are thoroughly Christian. He moves within a thoroughly Christian world view—how consciously, is hard to say—but he has a Western psychology and simply cannot escape this Western world view. He simply has to extend his thinking within these Christian categories, and thus he also dealt with the motif of the suffering God in *Zarathustra*. I would like to present it to you as a *document humain*.[364] Pay attention to the unique symbolism that Nietzsche uses. You will find these points in the section called "The Intoxicated Song":[365]

God's woe is deeper, you strange world! Reach out for God's woe, not for me! What am I? An intoxicated, sweet lyre
—a midnight lyre, a croaking bell which no one understands but which *has* to speak before deaf people, you Higher Men! For you do not understand me!
Gone! Gone! Oh youth! Oh noontide! Oh afternoon! Now come evening and midnight; the dog howls, the wind:
is the wind not a dog? It whines, it yelps, it howls. Ah! Ah! how it sighs! how it laughs, how it rasps and gasps, the midnight hour!

---

his death on 25 August 1900. The cause of Nietzsche mental demise is unclear; most probably it was the result of a syphilitic infection. In his seminar on Nietzsche's *Thus Spoke Zarathustra*, Jung claimed to have known the doctor who treated Nietzsche: "[T]hat exceedingly sensitive nervous man [sc. Nietzsche] had a syphilitic infection. That is a historical fact—I know the doctor who took care of him. It was when [the doctor] was twenty-three years old" (Jung, 1989 [1934–39], p. 609). Jung most likely referred to Otto Binswanger, whose nephew Ludwig had been Jung's assistant at the Burghölzli clinic. On Nietzsche's disease, see Volz (1990).

[364] *document humain* (Fr.): "testimony of human life."

[365] Jung quoted here from the section "The Intoxicated Song" from the fourth part of *Thus Spoke Zarathustra*, where the famous originally unnamed "Midnight Song" from the third part is repeated, and thus often comes under the different title "Das Nachtwandler Lied" (Somnambulist song). Regarding these different titles, Werner Stegmaier writes, "It sometimes comes under the title 'Das andere Tanzlied' [The other dance song] which, however, in *Za[rathustra]* III refers to the preceding prose text, sometimes under the title 'Das Nachtwanderer-Lied' [Somnambulist song], probably because in *Za* IV it is repeated in full, sometimes under the title 'Das trunkene Lied' [The intoxicated song]: that is how Nietzsche referred to it in his annotated copy (cf. Mazzino Montinari, commentary on the *KSA*, *KSA*, vol. 14, [p.] 343) and it then appeared under this title in the GOA, the KA and the SA. Instead we call it by the first line or, for reasons that will be outlined below, by the name that is also commonly used, 'Mitternachts-Lied' [Midnight song]. That leaves open, which is of some importance for the interpretation, whether the song is only heard at midnight or whether it is also spoken or sung by [the midnight hour]." (Stegmaier, 2013, p. 88, n. 7).

How it now speaks soberly, this intoxicated poet! perhaps it has
overdrunk its drunkenness? perhaps it has grown over-wakeful?
perhaps it ruminates?
it ruminates upon its woe in dreams, the ancient, deep midnight
hour, and still more upon its joy. For joy, though woe be deep: *Joy
is deeper than heart's agony.*

You grape-vine! Why do you praise me? For I cut you! I am cruel,
you bleed: what means your praise of my intoxicated cruelty?
"What has become perfect, everything ripe—wants to die!" thus
you speak. Blessed, blessed be the vine-knife! But everything
unripe wants to live: alas!

Who is the grape-vine that has ripened, that wants to die? And who holds
the knife? It is Nietzsche himself who is the sacrificer, and Christ the bleeding sacrifice.

Woe says: 'Fade! Be gone, woe!'

That is really Western: overcoming suffering.

But everything that suffers wants to live, that it may grow ripe and
merry and passionate, [. . .]

Here comes the other side of Western man, the *concupiscentia.*[366]

[. . .] passionate for remoter, higher, brighter things. "I want heirs,"
thus speaks everything that suffers, "I want children, I do not want
myself."
Joy, however, does not want heirs or children, joy wants itself,
wants eternity, wants recurrence, wants everything eternally the
same.
Woe says: 'Break, bleed, heart! Walk, legs! Wings, fly! Upward!
Upward, pain!' Very well! Come on! my old heart: *Woe says:
Fade! Go!*

What do you think, you Higher Men? Am I a prophet? A
dreamer? A drunkard? An interpreter of dreams? A midnight bell?
A drop of dew? An odour and scent of eternity? Do you not hear
it? Do you not smell it? My world has just become perfect,
midnight is also noonday,

---

[366] *concupiscentia* (Lat.): "longing, desire."

pain is also joy, a curse is also a blessing, the night is also a sun—
be gone, or you will learn: a wise man is also a fool.
Did you ever say Yes to one joy? O my friends, then you said Yes
to *all* woe as well. All things are chained and entwined together, all
things are in love;
if ever you wanted one moment twice, if ever you said: 'You please
me, happiness, instant, moment!' then you wanted *everything* to
return!
you wanted everything anew, everything eternal, everything
chained, entwined together, everything in love, O that is how you
loved the world,
you everlasting men, loved it eternally and for all time: and you
say even to woe: 'Go, but return!' *For all joy wants -eternity!*

———————

All joy wants the eternity of all things, wants honey, wants dregs,
wants intoxicated midnight, wants graves, wants the consolation
of graveside tears, wants gilded sunsets,
what does joy not want! it is thirstier, warmer, hungrier, more
fearful, more secret than all woe, it wants *itself*; it bites into *itself*,
the will of the ring wrestles within it,
it wants love, it wants hatred, it is superabundant, it gives, throws
away, begs for someone to take it, thanks him who takes, it would
like to be hated;
so rich is joy that it thirsts for woe, for Hell, for hatred, for shame,
for the lame, for the *world*—for it knows, oh it knows this world!
You Higher Men, joy longs for you, joy the intractable, blissful—
for your woe, you ill-constituted! All eternal joy longs for the
ill-constituted.
For all joy wants itself, therefore it also wants heart's agony!
O happiness! O pain! Oh break, heart! You Higher Men, learn
this, learn that joy wants eternity,
joy wants the eternity of all things, *wants deep, deep, deep
eternity!*[367]

In this avowal you can see the strange transition from the Christian
psychology of suffering, the suffering of the sacrificed God, into something
unholy, namely joy, which ultimately seeks itself, but it becomes this desire for itself. Joy is actually a bad word, it is an immoral desire that

———————

[367] Nietzsche (1883–85) (*KSA*, vol. 4, pp. 401–3; Engl.: 1961, pp. 330–32).

seeks the wayward, the ill-constituted. And it has to seek the ill-constituted if it seeks itself. That is part of it. That's why Nietzsche also calls the higher men, for whom he so longs, the ill-constituted. He symbolizes joy as the search for eternity, for the dragon biting its tail, the image of the ring of eternity. That is a symbol of the self. He does not mean the desire for his I, but for the eternal element in man, the timeless, the divine.

Now we will leave the "Passio Christi" and turn to the next verse [of the "Anima Christi"]:

6. "O bone Jesu, exaudi me." (Oh good Jesus, hear me.)

This is once again an invocation and a call to the figure of Christ with his autonomous activity. Now we will hear Przywara's meditation on this. Namely, he says that Christ listens to him.[368] Precisely speaking, that is not what it says in the invocation. There it simply says: "Exaudi me." "Hear me." That does not yet mean that God does hear, but the Jesuit meditation transfers the whole activity so much into Christ that Przywara makes it quite clear, here and in the contemplation, that God listens to him, that God relates to him, not he to God. As if he had not previously said, "Exaudi me." As if God were listening to him from the beginning. "Whatever I say to Him, whatever He hears, whatever I express, whatever He takes in: I am it."[369] With that he wants to express that he offers up his I to Christ, as it were. He leaves it completely in the hands of the invoked figure of Christ.

These ideas continue even more clearly in the next verse:

7. "Intra tua vulnera absconde me." (Within your wounds hide me.)

Here we see a general Christian idea, that the wounds somehow signify protection for people, that men are somehow absorbed into Christ's wounds. Now imagine that in real life. Imagine a little person placed into the wound of another person, or as Przywara says, the grain is plunged into the earth.[370] So here the body of Christ is in a way treated like the plowed earth, as if it were opened up for this purpose, in order for people to enter into the body.

---

[368] "In the suffering of Christ the spell is broken: I know that God is listening, and I know that I can say everything. *Ex-audi.* It is a listening that lifts me out of my enchantment. And it is therefore an authority to which I give myself over" (Przywara, 1938, p. 7).

[369] Ibid.: "Was immer ich Ihm sage, was immer Er hört, was immer ich heraus-sage, was immer Er in Sich hinein hört: ich bin's."

[370] "Because the suffering of Christ in the Christian person, and of the Christian in Christ, is not earthy heroism, but a sinking, as the grain of wheat disappears down into the earth" (Przywara, 1938, p. 8).

These ideas have always played a certain role, but they reached a climax with Zinzendorf's mysticism.[371] Zinzendorf created a downright obscene affair out of the side-wound of Christ. It is really revolting, what he made of it. The most innocent Sunday-school child can see that. There is no need for any kind of analytical interpretative gymnastics here.[372] It is quite obvious that he thought of the side-wound of Christ as some kind of maternal genitalia into which one would plunge in order to be incubated in it and reborn in the blood. I'm not making a bad joke here; it's a fact. You see the same thoughts in Przywara's meditation too, only sanitized and less offensive, as a furrow of earth in which a seed is sown. There are Etruscan plows that are phallus-shaped. Well into the last century it was still the custom in many places for the farmer to take his wife out to the field on a moonlit night and sleep with her there, in order to ensure that the fields would be fertile. I'm not talking about some primitives performing rites which in comparison have an unmistakable meaning. Now, these thoughts always crop up with this wound mysticism, and the strange thing is that Christ has a male body. Christ is now, most curiously, if we apply the Catholic notions strictly, not only male, but also female. One speaks of the androgyny of Christ, of the male femininity. In chapter 14 of Revelation it says, "These are they which were not defiled with women; for they are virgins. These are they which follow the Lamb whithersoever he goeth."[373] It refers to holy men who have not been tainted by contact with females. Priests, for example, who live in celibacy. They are actually

---

[371] Christian Renatus (or Christel) von Zinzendorf (1727–52), son of the founder and bishop of the Brethren's Congregation of Herrnhut (Moravian Church) Nikolaus Ludwig von Zinzendorf (1700–1760) (see n. 135). Christian Renatus became the leader of the Single Brethren's Choir in Herrnhaag, then one of the centers of the Moravian Church, where he was venerated as the representative of Christ. At a festival in 1748, Christian Renatus and his co-elder Joachim Rubusch (1717–73) proclaimed themselves to be the living side-wound of Christ. Brothers who were present believed they were kissing the actual side-wound of Christ. Following his father's teaching, according to which all souls are female, Christian Renatus also spoke of his marriage with the side-wound of Christ, and declared all Single Brethren to be the brides of Christ. The events in Herrnhaag caused a scandal within the Moravian Church and beyond, and led to the shutting down of the community in Herrnhaag. Nikolaus Ludwig took his son with him to England, where Christian Renatus died at the age of twenty-five.

[372] Jung probably refers here to Oskar Pfister's study on Nikolaus Ludwig von Zinzendorf from 1910, which he dedicated to Jung. Pfister argues that Zinzendorf's description of the side-wound of Christ is equivalent to that of the female genital, "as the organ of birth on the one hand and the place of the maximal satisfaction of the the religious eros endowed with all markers of the primary homosexual act or of a homosexuality pushed into the religious realm on the other hand" (Pfister, 1910, p. 58).

[373] Revelation 14:4 (KJV).

parthenoi.[374] They are men and yet they are female. And this characteristic is also applied to Christ, specifically with reference to Genesis, where it says that Eve, the first woman, was created from the side of Adam. So there must have been a wound there, a birth canal out of which came Eve. That is the *Ecclesiae* archetype, the archetype of the emergence of the church out of the side-wound of Christ. The birth of the church was therefore in a way like the birth of Eve, out of the side-wound of Christ. Thus the side-wound somehow signifies the maternal gateway.

[374] *parthenoi* (Gk. παρθένοι): "maidens."

Lecture 6[375]

8 DECEMBER 1939

LAST TIME WE talked about the seventh invocation [of the "Anima Christi"]:

7. "Intra tua vulnera absconde me." (Within your wounds hide me.)

I told you that these *vulnera*, from *vulnus*, the wound, are mainly understood in connection with the side-wound. And that this side-wound is traditionally a kind of feminine characteristic of the *corpus Christi*. This female aspect of Christ is clearly expressed in the iconography. He is often represented with feminine features, as is his cousin Mithras, as it happens. At the moment of the *tauroktonos*, the killing of the bull,[376] Mithras is depicted with very feminine features, and Cumont who is the great authority on Mithraism even says that there is something quite hysterical about his features.[377] Evidently a certain male femininity is also attributed

---

[375] The text of this lecture is compiled from notes by LSM, ES, RS, and OK, as well as the English translation by BH.

[376] *tauroktonos* (Gk. ταυροκτόνος): "bull-killing."

[377] Mithraism was a mystery religion in the Roman Empire of the first to the fourth century CE that centred on the worship of the god Mithras and involved a rite of initiation of seven grades. It was particularily popular amongst members of the Roman army. The worship took place in underground temples called *mithraea*. Jung was familiar with Mithraism through Albrecht's Dieterich's *A Mithras-Lithurgy* (1903), from which he quoted in "Wandlungen und Symbole der Libido" (1911–12, § 173) to show the similarities between this ancient mythological belief and the delusions of the Burghölzli patient Emile Schwyzer (1862–1931) (See also Jung's lecture of 16 December 1938, *JMP*, vol. 6, pp. 66–67; and Shamdasani, 2003, p. 216; 1990). One of Jung's earlier sources on the Mithras cult was Georg Friedrich Creuzer's *Symbolik und Mythologie der alten Völker, besonders der Griechen* (Symbolism and mythology of the ancient peoples, particularly the Greeks) (Creuzer, 1810–12); but the main authority in the field of Mithraism was the Belgian archaeologist and historian Franz Cumont (1868–1947), who argued that the Roman worship of Mithras originated from Persian Mazdaism, a theory that has been contested by more recent scholarship. Amongst other writings of Cumont, Jung had a copy of *Textes et monuments figurés relatifs aux mystères de Mithra* (1894–99) (*The Mysteries of Mithra*, 1903), arguably Cumont's most important contribution to the study of Mithraism.

to him. This male femininity of Christ is also referred to as androgyny. From *aner* and *gyné*.[378] This androgyny is not unique to the Christ figure: from the field of comparative religion we know that most of the chthonic[379] gods have an androgynous character.

I would like to quote a Catholic writer to you, Georg Koepgen. He wrote a book called *Die Gnosis des Christentums*.[380] It is very reliable; it was given the episcopal imprimatur.[381] In it, he says that the masculine and the feminine are united in Christ: "His voluntary accedence to immolation is feminine,"[382] and in him the male femininity became obvious. For Koepgen, Christ is an androgynous being. He also says the Church is androgynous, in that the Church is the *corpus mysticum Christi*, and that the celibacy of priests is evidence of the male maidenhood of the soul. This view, while not dogmatic, is tolerated in the Church. Now, it is of course significant that the figure of Christ is thought of as male–female. Because this male femininity of Christ has a function of uniting the opposites, in that the male figure sort of represents the bridegroom for the woman. For example, in the Catholic church, there is the notion that the unmarried woman is a bride of Christ. He is her bridegroom. For the man he is female—for the man's consciousness that is. We must of course assume that the opposite is true when it comes to the unconscious relationship with this figure.

Przywara stresses that the wounds are open, and that they are open in order that we, the worshipers, the meditators, can "be enveloped within the unsealed God."[383] Those are his words. The suffering in Christ, says Przywara, is a kind of descent, like the grain of wheat sinking into the furrow of the soil. He says, "And it cannot show itself at all, because it is

---

[378] *aner* (Gk. ἀνήρ): "man"; *gyné* (Gk. γυνή): "woman."

[379] Only in ES. From *chthon* (Gk. χθών): "earth."

[380] Koepgen (1939). See Becker (2001), p. 62. Jung also refers to Koepgen's theory of Christ's androgyny in *Mysterium Coniunctionis*: "In recent time the theme of androgyny has been subjected to quite a special treatment in a book by a Catholic writer which merits our attention. This is *Die Gnosis des Christentums*, by Georg Koepgen, an important work that appeared in 1939 with the episcopal imprimatur in Salzburg, and since then has been placed on the Index" (Jung, 1955–56, § 537).

[381] The book was banned by the Roman Catholic Church in 1941. See *Index librorum prohibitorum, anno 1946: Appendix in qua recensentur libri proscripti ab anno 1940 usque ad annum 1945 inclusive.*

[382] Koepgen (1939), p. 316.

[383] "All wounds that I bear are Christian wounds, that is into Christ. In this time there is no healing of the wounds, but they are *vulnera*, open wounds, because they close themselves autonomously in death and resurrection, that we may be enveloped within the unsealed God." (Przywara, 1938, p. 8).

the suffering of the immature child that can only hide itself in the womb from whence it once came."[384] It couldn't be said more clearly. This idea is symbolically necessary to reveal and explain the interpenetration between the faithful and Christ. This mutual penetration is already attested to in the Gospels. Think of the part in John where it says, "He that eateth my flesh, and drinketh my blood, dwelleth in me, and I in him."[385] At this point too you see that the inner Christ is authentically acknowledged. Similarly at the end of John chapter 17, in the part referred to as the high priestly prayer of Jesus, we read, "And I have declared unto them thy name, and will declare it: that the love wherewith thou hast loved me may be in them, and I in them."[386] In these words, the idea of the interpenetration between the faithful and Christ is very clearly expressed, but of course always with the stress laid on the activity of Christ and not on the side of the faithful, who are not ascribed any autonomous efficacy of their own. In the Christian view, of course, Christ as God-man has absolute autonomy. He is the complete center of activity.

As we have seen in the course of these lectures—I am referring back to the earlier semesters[387]—Christ is a Western formulation of what in the East is called self, *âtman* or Buddha. He symbolizes—if we can consider him a symbol—the self. So when the dogma says that Christ as God became man, then in psychological terms it means that the self entered human consciousness; or that consciousness began to recognize the self as a human component—and in a most unique form. Namely, it is as if it entered me from outside, through its own autonomy and not through my own realization. It is not I who realize a self in me—as the Easterner does—but the

---

[384] Ibid.

[385] John 6:56 (*KJV*) (Germ.: Züricher Bibelübersetzung, 1931).

[386] John 17:26 (*KJV*) (Germ.: Züricher Bibelübersetzung, 1931).

[387] See Jung's lecture of 9 December 1938 (*JMP*, vol. 6, p. 63): "At the end of last time I drew your attention to the parallels that exist between the inner sun in the *Amitâyur-dhyâna-sûtra* and the mystical idea of the inner Christ. In Indian philosophy, there is a substantial parallel: the philosophy of the *âtman*. The word *âtman* is related to the German word *Atem* meaning breath, also our *Odem*, the breath of life that runs through all things, corresponding to the essence of the Buddha. The one, the great, that is also described as Prajâpati, i.e., the creator of the world. Both these terms are identical in their use and have similar terms of reference: the *âtman* is the absolute origin of being. The particular: that he is not only the universal being like that of the highest Buddha, the essence of the world itself, but he is also a personal being. Everyone has a personal self, this *âtman* within, but this is only one aspect of the universal. Whoever immerses himself in the practice of yoga, flows in a way out of the personal *âtman* into the general, and then considers himself a universal being. There are exactly the same preconditions as in Buddhism. The being of one's own self, as the text also shows, is at the same time a universal being."

self enters the Westerner from outside, as a historic event, even. That we can accept, that it was a historic event, the life of Christ, I mean. And thus that figure historically entered the field of vision of human consciousness and was recognized as the divine figure of the self, namely the self as that indescribable and indefinable figure that is greater than us, in which a person readily feels contained.

In the East, naturally, the process is different. There, this self is first recognized as something residing in the cave of the heart, something very tiny which is contained in me. In contrast, in the Western psychological experience, the self is recognized as something voluminous, as something that encloses me or should enclose me, that presents itself to me with the complete and absolute power[388] of a divine being. And this presentation is simply the act of it becoming conscious. Mankind to an extent became conscious that this man, this teacher, this rabbi, this prophet Jesus was a God-man. So all those notions about Osiris which the Egyptians had been preparing for thousands of years combined with the messianic notions and settled upon these people, as it were—if you want to look at it like that from a psychological point of view.

Of course it wasn't that people discussed and agreed among themselves: "We want to call him the God-man." Jesus probably exerted such an effect that his disciples were immediately convinced that he was filled with God's spirit, that he was a prophet. We know that from the Gospels, that initially he was seen as a prophet. Then gradually a public perception formed that he was the realization of all these notions that were floating around at that time and were extremely popular.[389] After all, that was anyway a time full of miraculous deeds and mysterious characters. We find other such messianic figures in Christ's immediate vicinity, and in the Hellenic world there were other figures of this kind who came after Christ too.

Moreover, this kind of condensation process of public opinion had often happened before. Look at Empedocles, who claimed to be a divine human, a god so to speak, and when he traveled from one town to another he was followed by thousands of people. He was hailed wherever he went as a savior, and when he could no longer save himself from the people, he went to Etna to withdraw from the world. When they apparently

---

[388] RS has "Machtentfaltung" (evolving power) instead of "Machtvollkommenheit" (absolute power).

[389] RS has "betont" (emphasized) instead of "beliebt" (popular).

even followed him there, he jumped into the volcano to get away from them and find peace.[390]

Pythagoras,[391] too, was believed to incarnate divinity. In early antiquity that was nothing special, as people believed that the gods still roamed the earth and it was not impossible to bump into one now and again. People in the ancient world were still able to regard those with godlike qualities as gods, and so they could compress all their existing ideas into that figure, particularly if that person apparently had all the qualities that would justify an attribution of godliness.

The dogma predicates further that the figure of the savior is a figure of suffering, that he was slandered, derided, murdered, wounded; in other words, that the act of becoming human is an act of suffering, or an event that is characterized by suffering. That is to say, the process of individuation, of becoming oneself, of the self becoming conscious, is a divine suffering. It is as though the figure that presents itself as the self suffers in this process; a figure of suffering that is characterized in particular by the side-wound, by the mysteriously implied androgyny. Now we realize that for the Western consciousness, which has such an exquisitely masculine attitude, the feminine aspect entering a male organism through individuation of course has a wounding effect. Because then one's masculinity is wounded. It also explains why this idea is completely unknown in the East: because their attitude to the outer world is passive, feminine, resigned, while their masculinity is internal and is then actualized in the individuation process. Hence the Eastern credo: it is me, I make the world.

---

[390] Empedocles (ca. 495–ca. 435 BCE), statesman, physician, philosopher, and poet; born in Acagras in Sicily, Empedocles played an important role as a democratic statesman after the death of the tyrant Theron. He was praised by Aristotle as the inventor of rhetoric and by Galen as the founder of the Italian school of medicine. But he was also a charismatic religious teacher with a large following and claimed to be a god. According to John Burnet, it is likely that Empedocles preached a form of Pythagoreanism that was not considered orthodox by the heads of the Pythagorean Order, from which he was expelled (Burnet, 1892, p. 200). Legend has it that Empedocles ended his life by leaping into the crater of the Etna, which is most unlikely, as according to ancient sources he did not die in Sicily.

[391] Pythagoras (ca. 570–ca. 495 BCE), philosopher from Samos, founded a philosophical school in Croton where he arrived in 530 BCE. Initiates took an oath of secrecy and lived together in a community following an ascetic lifestyle. Pythagoras is associated with many teachings, particularly related to mathematics and scientific discoveries; however, his own authorship is not certain, as many of these findings were probably by followers or members of his school. His most prominent doctrine is that of the transmigration of the souls (metempsychosis), according to which souls are immortal and take on a new body after death. During Pythagoras's lifetime legends were already told about his supernatural powers and his ability to perform miracles. Later Roman legends have it that he was the son of Apollo. On Pythagoras, see Burkert (1962).

This wounding, this side-wound, this feminization of God or suffering figure of God is also found in Germanic mythology. One part in particular in the *Edda* is very representative of this. I don't know whether you know it. It is from the *Hávamál Edda*. Odin (Wotan) says,

> I ween that I hung / on the windy tree,
> Hung there for nights full nine;
> With the spear I was wounded, / and offered I was
> To Odin, myself to myself.[392]

It has been claimed that this point was adopted from Christianity. I think we can rule that out, however, because the "[offered] myself to myself" is not a Christian concept—the Christian concept is all about the I and you, about the relationship, with a pronounced Eros. In the East, one might be more likely to expect the God or *âtman* to say, "and offered I was [. . .]; myself to myself." But in the West that is unheard of. And yet it happened—we have the proof. But it is a primitive belief from a primitive time, in which the one-sided differentiation of the Western attitude was not yet present to the extent that it was in later centuries. On the contrary, I think it is something very ancient and primordial.

Now we will move on to the next invocation [of the "Anima Christi"]:

8. "Ne permittas me separari a te." (Permit me not to be separated from you.)

In this call appears an aspect that Przywara also stresses in particular: the absolute sovereignty of Christ.[393] That is how a god, a king, is addressed. One can only speak like that with an absolute ruler, one who has power over life and death. It is not "I don't want to separate myself," or "I could separate myself." Not that at all, but instead "Ne permittas"—"Do not allow it to happen." Here too, the ultimate power,[394] as you see, comes exclusively from the figure of Christ. "The person seems to be a god in this world."[395] Because of his creative power and all that he can achieve in the world. He can really make a lot happen. That's why many people

---

[392] *Hávamál* 139, in *The Poetic Edda* (Bellows, 1936), p. 60 (Germ.: *Die Edda*, p. 105). Cf. Jung, 1911–12, § 400; 1945, § 442, n. 60.

[393] "'that I may dwell in the house of the Lord' [Psalm 27:4]—where the Lord takes in and expels, forbids and allows. Yes, where even and especially the being-with-Him is entirely based on His permission. Yes, where my freedom to go to Him when I want is taken away, that even this depends on His permission. Yes, where I am so blessed in this restless captivity, so blessed that He is the Lord Almighty, that I beg Him never to grant this permission: do not permit me to leave you!" (Przywara, 1938, p. 9).

[394] ES has "Aktivität" (activity) instead of "Macht" (power).

[395] Przywara (1938), p. 9.

get the idea that we are godlike,[396] because of our technology, for example. But Przywara continues, "But he stands in their midst, he sees above him and below him, powerless, the chasm of the forces: the eternity of the spirit, the incalculability of nature. And both rampage through him as a battleground."[397] Przywara now calls this the suffering on the cross. We need to take a closer look at this notion. Here, Przywara places man in the center between the opposites of spirit and nature. We could also say spirit and substance, spirit and matter. That is one set of opposites. In the same meditation he also has another opposite: the person caught between heaven and hell.[398] This gives rise to the following constellation:

(moral opposite:)

Heaven

(cosmic opposite:)   Spirit   **+**   Matter

Hell

In the center is man. Heaven above, hell below. That would be the moral-ethical opposite. Alongside that is the cosmic opposite: spirit/nature (matter). So we don't just have an above and below, but also a right and left. This [**+** in the diagram] is a state of suspension between the opposites, which is the suffering on the cross.

In Przywara's notion, we see the glimmer of one of the original Christian ideas: namely, that the cross is a kind of cosmic symbol that stands on the boundary between heaven and hell; that is, right in the center of the world, so to speak. In this way Przywara considers man to be a central point, a meeting point of the great cosmic opposites, of the spiritual and anthropological opposites. The human being is a kind of uniting symbol; man in this form corresponds in a way to God as a prototype, or rather a copy, in which all opposites are also unified in God.[399] Thus, if

[396] RS has "ein göttliches Geschlecht" (a divine lineage) instead of "gottähnlich" (godlike).

[397] Przywara (1938), p. 9.

[398] Ibid.: "This truth is shown in the suffering: on the cross, helpless between heaven and earth, heaven and hell[.]"

[399] The scripts of RS and ES suggest that Jung attributed this statement to Przywara, which is incorrect. BH omitted this phrase.

the self comes to the person, or if we may understand Christ as a human being who has become a self, then he is in this crossed position and therefore the unifying symbol is the cross itself. That is why one so often hears the phrase "redeemed in Christ," or "in Christ's cross." The cross is the symbol for the uniting of the opposites, and Christ vanquishes the opposites. In him, the opposites are overcome. We cannot use the word "dissolved," since it is a harrowing process; instead we have to say the opposites are united or reconciled in him. He is the symbol of reconciliation.

With this realization and the image of the *suspensio*, the state of being suspended, with this acme of suffering, anguish, and abasement, the "Anima Christi" prayer reaches its climax.

We have discussed eight invocations. The first part is composed of

"Anima Christi, sanctifica me." (Soul of Christ, sanctify me.)
"Corpus Christi, salva me." (Body of Christ, save me.)
"Sanguis Christi, inebria me." (Blood of Christ, inebriate me.)
"Aqua lateris Christi, lava me." (Water from the side of Christ, wash me.)

These four invocations form the first verse: that is, the *praeparatio*— the preparation through the sanctification—saving,[400] inebriation, and purification—the *ablutio*. Then comes the *passio*, the suffering, or also the *penetratio*, the penetration of Christ or the penetration into Christ:

"Passio Christi, conforta me." (Passion of Christ, strengthen me.)
"O bone Jesu, exaudi me." (Oh good Jesus, hear me.)
"Intra tua vulnera absconde me." (Within your wounds hide me.)
"Ne permittas me separari a te." (Permit me not to be separated from you.)

These are in a way two stages that lead to the climax. Here we have a curious parallel to something we discussed in the last semester, namely the text of the *Shrî-chakra-sambhâra Tantra*, in which we also reach the climax in two stages.[401] And then something occurs, namely the next invocation. Now comes the third part, the actual *salvatio*, the actual salvation and deliverance, beginning with the ninth invocation:

"Ab hoste maligno defende me." (From the wicked foe, defend me.)

[400] LSM and ES have "Erleuchtung" (illumination) instead of "Errettung" (saving, deliverance).
[401] See *JMP*, vol. 6.

We find exactly the same thing in this Eastern text in which the defense against the destructive also comes after the two first sections. I want to jog your memories by presenting it again briefly:[402]

Shrî-chakra-sambhâra Tantra[403]	*Anima Christi*
Phase I, Thesis	I. *Praeparatio*
A. Shrî heruka aham	1. Soul of Christ, sanctify me
	2. Body of Christ, save me
	3. Blood of Christ, inebriate me
	4. Water from the side of Christ, wash me
B.	II. *Penetratio*:
1. Light and four colors	5. Passion of Christ, strengthen me
2. Ten directions	
3. Assimilation of all beings	6. Oh good Jesus, hear me
4. Emanation, absorbed in the self	7. Within your wounds hide me
	8. Permit me not to be separated from you
Phase II, Antithesis[404]	
A. Threat and defense (female devil)	III. *Salvatio*, redemption (devil)
Senses (delusion, rage, greed, avarice, jealousy)	9. From the wicked foe, defend me
Shakti, *mâyâ*	10. In the hour of my death, call me
a. Earth, "she who causes the fall"	
b. Water, "she who kills"	11. and bid me come to you,
c. Fire, "she who summons"	12. that with your saints I may praise you for ever and ever. Amen.
d. Air, "the lady of the dance"	
e. Ether, "she who has the lotus net"	

---

[402] The following diagram can only be found in ES.
[403] See Jung's lecture of 13 January 1939 (*JMP*, vol. 6, pp. 81–82).
[404] See Jung's lecture of 20 January 1939 (*JMP*, vol. 6, pp. 92–93).

The culmination of the first section is the acknowledgment of the *Shrî heruka aham*: "I am the sacred Heruka."[405] That simply means, "I am the divine figure. Heruka is the Lord in this whole meditation."

The second section culminates in the acknowledgment that now all strands are collected in the self, and that this self is again the Heruka. But all of that has come about through the meditator's own activity. Then comes the threat and the defense: namely, there is not a wicked foe, but a feminine being. Specifically, the meditating yogi must here defend himself against or ward off the one who causes the fall, the one who kills, who summons, who is the lady of the dance and who has the lotus net, namely the *mâyâ*, the deception, the illusion of the world in which one is entangled, and the more one is tangled up in it, the more one is cut off from one's own self. This entangling occurs through the attachment of the senses to illusory objects.

The actual devil who appears in this Buddhist meditation is female. She is Shakti, one who constructs a world, who is associated with the god, is his consort, his feminine aspect, but who also constructs a phantasmagoric world that is meant to be a reflection of the god. But if someone develops out of their own inner authority into an *âtman* or Shiva or Heruka, then they may fall into the trap of this illusion, because they have not yet attained perfection. And the trap is laid for them by this Shakti, the *mâyâ*.

In the West the devil is usually a male figure. And he has exaggeratedly masculine attributes: horns, cloven hoofs, or at least horse's hoofs, and is found on the Blocksberg[406] as you know; extremely masculine. He is modeled on the old fauns who don't exactly have a good reputation.

Now, how can it be that in the East the devil is female and in the West male? After all, in the legend of the Buddha it is Mara, the lord of this world. Exactly like in the New Testament, but without the side-helping of morals. He is a relatively conscientious devil, not so bad at all. The Mara is there to maintain the world's creation. Thus he has to use all means to turn the Buddha back to the world. He tries to seduce the

---

[405] See Jung's lecture of 16 December 1938 (*JMP*, vol. 6, pp. 70–71).

[406] Blocksberg, according to superstitious beliefs the name of a mountain where witches meet on Walpurgis night. The identification with the Brocken, the highest peak of the Harz mountain range, is a later fabrication, as is the specific night of 1 May. It is probably Goethe's famous scene in the first part of Faust that strongly links the name and the date in German consciousness: "To Brocken's tip the witches stream, / The stubble's yellow, the seed is green. / There the crowd of us will meet. / Lord Urian has the highest seat. / So they go, over stone and sticks, / The stinking goat, the farting witch." (Goethe, 2015, ll. 3956–61). See Peuckert (1956).

Buddha with a host of pretty *bayadères*.[407] But in this meditation, Shakti appears as the actual temptress, as the personification of the *mâyâ*, which is feminine.

There is a connection here with the curious divergence between the Eastern and Western attitudes: in the West a conscious, masculine attitude to the world, in the East a feminine, passive, resigned attitude. The world is full of suffering. The yogi denies the world, that is, he withdraws from it, closes in on himself, develops a strong masculine attitude that no longer cares at all about the world and rises above worldly suffering and pleasure, vice and virtue, temptation and enticement, in a completely unassuming[408] way.

In the West, the masculine consciousness is subject to a feminine attitude: namely, a devotion to Christ that is full of longing. The man is transformed into a feminine creature. That's why his devil is male—because his earlier masculine attitude, the exclusively masculine attitude, now works on him like the devil. It tempts him back into the world. Exactly like in the East, but in reverse: the earlier feminine attitude seduces the person back into worldly attachments.

If we want to use more psychological terms, we would say that the Westerner has an anima, that is a feminine unconscious, while the Easterner has an animus, an unconscious with a more masculine tone. And in fact the Eastern unconscious is different from the Western one. In Eastern terminology, there is no expression for the unconscious. In the whole Sanskrit language there is no word for it. Initially I had great difficulties making myself understood when I spoke with Eastern philosophers. You'd think that in the East, where people are so introspective, it would be possible. But then I realized that they call consciousness "bodh,"[409] referring to the bright consciousness. What they call the conscious mind, brightest spirit, is for us the unconscious. Thus they say that the highest consciousness is found in deep sleep, when we would say we are wholly unconscious. This peculiar reversal or contradiction in the Eastern attitude is of course due to this idiosyncratic order of things in the East.

The next invocation goes:

"In hora mortis meae voca me." (At the hour of my death, call me.)

---

[407] *Bayadère*, from French, designates a dancing girl especially associated with dance in southern Indian temples.

[408] RS has "ruchlos" (nefarious) instead of "anspruchslos" (unassuming).

[409] *bodh* (Hindi): "comprehension," is a derivative from Sanskrit *bodha*, also *bodhana*, meaning "awakening" or "enlightenment".

It is certainly not "I want to go to you"—I have to be called. And the same in the next invocation:

"Et iube me venire ad te," (And bid me come to you,)[410]

As if the person could not personally do anything about it. The person exists only in a state of completely resigned passivity characterized by hopeful yearning and wishing, totally feminine. As if the man's soul, which is actually feminine, ascribes total power to Christ in the hope that he will issue the command. One is ready to be rebuked by him for one's wrongdoing and dares at most to sigh and propitiate, that the great king might notice and call the poor mortal worm to him.

The last sentence goes,

"Ut cum Sanctis tuis laudem te, / In saecula saeculorum. Amen."

(That with your saints I may praise you / for ever and ever. Amen.)

Laudare Dominum, praise the Lord, is an expression we know very well. We hear it in sermons, hymns, and psalms, but we never stop and think about what it actually means.

It is an ancient institution, stemming from the courts of old. You have to imagine some Egyptian or Babylonian king in his court, always surrounded by devotees who are constantly singing his praises on harps and other instruments to propitiate him. The powerful of this earth are, after all, usually of human scale. They are not giants, in body or in spirit, but quite ordinary mortals. Merely through the fortune or misfortune of birth or the right connections, they are placed on such a high pedestal that they feel abject and scared up there and are plagued by feelings of inferiority. As a result, from very early in history there were court singers praising their leaders. You find them even in the very primitive courts of African chiefs. You cannot even meet such a chieftain without being propitiated by the head of the caravan or an emissary of the king who introduces you: "This is the great lord, the wise man, and he is a Mussulman and a Christian." They said that about me because I knew the Koran. "And this is the great King Maringa who has six hundred wives, three palaces, and a great army," and so on. That is the *laudare*, which first began as a courtly custom and was gradually transferred into the worship in which the Godhead is honored as an oriental prince. That is how our ideas about the

---

[410] Jung changed his previous German translation from "Und lass mich zu Dir kommen" (And let me come to you) to "Und befiehl mir zu Dir zu kommen" (And bid me come to you).

afterlife came about. Recall the countless images of the divine Godhead in which there are thousands of harpists on either side of God's throne permanently performing the *laudare*. This *laudare Dominum* has persisted down the centuries and become a standard phrase. Earlier it was an entirely conscious attempt, a conscious technique of propitiation, that is, of winning favor by elevating the monarch's self-esteem through praise so that he would be in a better mood. Great lords such as these are often bad-tempered if they are not sufficiently entertained by the huge claque that surrounds them. I know what I am saying sounds very heretical, but I think we ought to be aware of these things.

Lecture 7[411]

15 DECEMBER 1939

WE ACTUALLY FINISHED talking about the "Anima Christi" last time, but I'd like to say retrospectively a few more words about it today.

From our discussion, we were able to see the psychological significance of the Christ figure, at least in this prayer, as interpreted by authentic sources. I would like to remind you of the invocations once again. These are the "sanctifica me," "salva me," "inebria me," "lava me" (sanctify me, save me, inebriate me, wash me). Then the "conforta me," "exaudi me," "absconde me," "ne permittas me separari a te," "defende me," "iube me" (strengthen me, hear me, hide me, permit me not to be separated from you, defend me, bid me.) If you now translate these invocations into Christ's actions, the prayer would go, "Anima Christi sanctificat me"— "the *anima Christi* sanctifies me," "he saves me," "he inebriates me," "he strengthens me," "he defends me," and so on. These attributes clearly show the active significance of the Christ figure. I have said several times now that the Christ figure is actually the self: that is, that higher figure that comprises both the individual and the whole of humanity. Its *corpus mysticum* is the church, which is the body of Christ; it is Christ's vessel in which he appears on earth, his continuing appearance. He is therefore the *conglomerate soul*, to use the English expression, a conglomeration of the soul, like in India where the *hiranyagarbha*,[412] the golden seed or the golden child, is described as a *conglomerate soul*. It is also called womb.

---

[411] The text of this lecture is compiled from notes by LSM, ES, RS, and OK, as well as the English translation by BH.

[412] *Hiranyagarbha* (Sanskr.): "golden seed," "golden womb," mythological founder of the yoga tradition. According to the *Rig-Veda* he is the supreme lord of all beings, and the *Mahâbhârata* calls him "the higher mind." He is also identified with Brahma, who was born from a golden egg. The name is also seen as connected with an actual sage who wrote an early text book of yoga. The legend for image 59 of Jung's *Liber Novus* reads, "*hiranyagarbha*" (2009, p. 285). Cf. Jung's lecture of 17 February 1939 (*JMP*, vol. 6, pp. 141–42).

The *âtman* is also described as a *conglomerate soul*, as an activity that each individual unleashes in himself, because when, for example, in this meditation or invocation the believer enters into, is concealed, is hidden in the wounds of Christ, then he enters Christ's body. As Przywara says, he circulates with Christ's blood, sees with His eyes, hears with His ears, touches with His hands, so to speak.[413] If this happens, he is fully identical with the *corpus mysticum* of Christ, but of course only an approximation of it can occur in the mystical experience, or, it is assumed, after death. Thus the believer is part of this absolute ruler who defends, bids, permits and forbids, punishes, heals, and so on. He then takes full part in the Godhead. He himself is part of the divine epiphany. This participation in the Godhead is in perhaps curious contrast to the teachings of the Church about the immortality of the individual soul. The individual soul is a separate entity and it is difficult to postulate that it somehow ends in this way, that it is completely dissolved in the Godhead, because then it loses its individual immortality. It is then no longer an entity in itself, but merely a part. I cannot give you any information about what they think about that in the Church. But what we do know is that in the East, the idea of the individual soul is largely repudiated: it is denied in quite another sense. In Buddhism, at any rate, the individual soul is rejected as being an illusion. Instead the Buddha essence, the eternal Buddha, is understood as the only real thing, the only true transcendental reality. He is himself the *nirvâna* in which one as it were dissolves into eternal nothingness. That's why in the *sûtra* about the death of the Buddha it says that Buddha went into a state of complete non-existence from which there is no return or rebirth. It is the highest aim of release, to attain that state in which one no longer exists. Psychologically, a question remains open here: what actually happens with the individual soul and the *corpus mysticum*? It seems that the consequence would be that the individual soul becomes part of the Godhead and rules with Christ. That would fit quite nicely with our Western psychology, which is characterized by sharing in the fighting, conquering, and ruling whenever possible.

Now, in connection with our discussion of the "Anima Christi," I would like to make a small detour eastward. You will have already noticed how I described a meditation on the "Anima Christi"; in a way we meditated

---

[413] "This also includes the main methods of the exercises: from consideration (*consideracion*) to meditation (*meditacion*) to contemplation (*contemplacion*) and involving the senses (*traer los sentidos*): to feel and experience [. . .] from the inside: from within Christ to see with His eyes, to feel with His heart, to breathe with Him" (Przywara, 1938, p. 3).

together on the "Anima Christi." Not, however, in the strict Catholic form, because it's impossible for me to do that. But I did at least, to the best of my knowledge and ability, present the meditation in a manner that closely resembled the way a Jesuit would perceive it. I therefore used the work of Przywara as much as possible, as he is the best authority in this field. But here and there I added certain explanations or points of view, such as comparisons with the East that we simply cannot ignore if we are at all interested in the East. To my mind, one of the greatest sins of Europeans is that they do not have any intellectual interest in the East, or they have a false understanding of it. We are not alone on the earth. But that is of course the prerogative of those swaggering Europeans; they have always acted like buccaneers who believe they are God's chosen rulers of the world and simply look down pityingly on all that is foreign to them. I once asked a theologian, "What do you think about Buddhism?" His answer astonished me: "We don't need to think anything about it, it's nothing to do with us." Of course one can understand this answer from the point of view of the Christian who is convinced that his religion is the one truth, but from the point of view of a human being I think one can scarcely say with full confidence, "That is the eternal truth, of which I am convinced, my truth." Maybe it stirs you deeply, but if you really take other people seriously, you see that something also stirs them, and you must say, "We should listen to what it is." Because otherwise we cannot relate to them at all. That's why I always felt obliged to learn as much about Eastern psychology as I could, because I cannot afford to simply overlook the teachings of the East and stick only with our Western beliefs. We need to be able to take a critical look at ourselves, and we can hardly take a critical stance if we remain trapped in our Western psychological sphere. How can we criticize Europe if we cannot look at it from the outside? What do we know about Western people if we have never seen ourselves from outside, in particular through Eastern eyes? People's religions are the classic expression of their psychology. What a group of people believes, that is the thing. And if we in the West have the Christian religion, then that is the confession of our psychology, though naturally we do not regard it as such. That's a heretical view, but I don't care. But that's precisely why it is characteristic, because we do not realize that it is an expression of ourselves. And if we compare our religious ideas to those of the East, then we see that these statements are specific to us, and the Eastern ones to them. Thus, if people here in the West say they are Buddhists, that doesn't express who they are. It's only a facade. Not reality, just a label. But if people in the West are Christian, then of course "anima naturaliter

Christiana."[414] Yes, in the Western person. In the East, of course, the psychology is expressed by any of the Eastern religions, and the religious view fully expresses who a person is. If we now see that the ideas in the East are quite different, then that must mean something, because at the end of the day we all live on the same earth, and the earth is such a small vehicle that the Easterners are actually our next-door neighbors; we are actually not far away from them at all. They are people like us. They look a bit different, have a different skin color, but at base they feel the same emotions as we do and have a similar moral stance. And nevertheless, their religious beliefs are not compatible with ours. If we took it literally, we would have to say that the Eastern view is the utmost blasphemy.

Now I would like to read you a typical Eastern confession, specifically one of the old *Upanishads* and a section from the *Atharva Veda*. In this regard, I must note that the religious forms in India today are of course no longer directly expressed by the *Upanishads* or Vedic texts. These things are quite far from the experience of ordinary people, even though they are now being taught again in a considerable number of Indian colleges. All these universities have Sanskrit colleges where Vedic texts are studied. But quite apart from the fact that only a tiny fraction of the Indian population has read the *Upanishads*, the spirit of the religious teachings of the *Upanishads* is found across the whole of India; nothing in India is untouched by it. There, everything is permeated by everything else. Even the original Buddhism, which is a real Protestantism against the immense pantheon of Hinduism, is based entirely on the philosophy and practice of yoga.

In the East philosophy has always remained grounded; it is only in the West that philosophy became a verbose intellectual altercation. Nobody here thinks any more that a philosophy should first be lived by ordinary people. In the East, everyone is convinced of that. An old Indian man visited me once after he had been at an international philosophy congress in Paris.[415]

---

[414] "O testimonium animae naturaliter christianae!" (Oh testimony of the soul naturally Christian!) This phrase was coined by Tertullian (ca. 155/160–220 CE) in his *Apologeticus* (1844), 17.6 (=Patrologia Latina 1.377) to argue that the soul has a natural connection to the Christian God. From here derives the possibility that knowledge of God and a natural moral law are inherent in every human soul. Jung writes on Tertullian in *Psychologische Typen* (1921; Engl.: *Psychological Types*, 1923), §§ 8–21.

[415] Jung refers to V. Subrahmanya Iyer (1869–1949), who attended the Ninth World Congress of Philosophy in 1937 and visited Jung together with Paul Brunton in Küsnacht in 1937. When Jung traveled to India, they met again in Mysore. Their correspondence revolved around questions of Indian and European thought (see Iyer to Jung, 25 August, 1937 [JA], and Jung to Iyer, 16 September 1937 [Jung, 1973, vol. 1, pp. 235–36]). For Iyer's

It was his first time in Europe, and he had highly inflated expectations. He thought he would find the best European minds gathered there. He had prepared a good essay about what Indian people understood by truth.[416] He presented his paper, and was met by shaking heads all round; no one knew what the old man was talking about. I patted him on the shoulder and said, "Ah my friend, you don't know Europe. What you want is not understood here at all. You think what one lives is the truth?" [He said,] "There is no truth that is not lived!" And I said, "Yes, philosophy."

That's how Indian people think. Thus, when you read an Indian text, never forget that blood speaks. The person speaks, the man in the street speaks; a thought does not speak. Indian people do not think at all in the sense that we know it. When something like thoughts happen, these come to them. They are like signs that just appear, that the person does not cause. They do not fancy that they create the thoughts. But if here in the West a philosopher writes a book, he wouldn't believe me if I said to him that it came to him, that he didn't make it. But I would never say that, because it didn't just come to him—he thought it up, invented it, with great intellectual effort. If you watch a Chinese person writing some time, you'll notice something. It happens without any struggle. Not like here. With us, writing involves a great struggle, the whole arm is involved, we hold our breath, the whole body is stiff. The Chinese person makes brush-strokes by moving only the brush with two fingers and using vermicular movements, completely relaxed. Only the hand does it. They are not so stupid as to write with their heads. That's why our brains are so completely overstrained. When an Indian person thinks, it is not with his head. He is relaxed, sits cross-legged on a gazelle pelt under a tree. It is terribly hot and the words appear to him, they place themselves in his mouth like ripe fruits falling from the tree.

The ideas in the following verses are also extraordinarily different from our Western beliefs. I will read from the *Atharva Veda*, 10.8:

> 12. The infinite to every side extended,
>   the finite and the infinite around us,
>   These twain Heaven's Lord divides as he advances,
>   knowing the past hereof and all the future.

---

writings, see Iyer (1955). On the meeting in Küsnacht, see Bennet (1985), p. 78. See also Jung's lecture of 10 June 1938 (*JMP*, vol. 5).

[416] "Pure Philosophy in India" (Iyer, 1937).

16. That, whence the Sun arises, that whither he goes to take
his rest,
That verily I hold supreme: naught in the world surpasses it.

18. This gold-hued Haiisa's wings, flying to heaven,
spread o'er a thousand days' continued journey.
Supporting all the Gods upon his bosom,
he goes his way beholding every creature.

25. One is yet finer than a hair, one is not even visible.
And hence the Deity who grasps with firmer hold is
dear to me.

27. Thou art a woman, and a man;
thou art a damsel and a boy.
Grown old thou totterest with a staff,
new-born thou lookest every way.

28. Either the sire or son of these,
the eldest or the youngest child.
As sole God dwelling in the mind,
first born, he still is in the womb.[417]

You can find these texts in a slim volume by Paul Deussen, *Die Geheimlehre des Veda*,[418] well worth reading.

The other [text] is a philosophical text from the *Bridhadâranyaka-
Upanishad, First Adhyâya, Fourth Brâhmana*:[419]

1. In the beginning this was Self alone, in the shape of a person
[*purusha*]. He looking round saw nothing but his Self. He first said,
"This is I"; therefore he became I by name. Therefore even now, if a
man is asked, he first says, "This is I," and then pronounces the
other name which he may have. And because before [*pûrva*] all
this, he (the Self) burnt down [*ush*] all evils, therefore he was a person [*pur-usha*]. Verily he who knows this, burns down every one
who tries to be before him.
2. He feared, and therefore any one who is lonely fears. He thought,
"As there is nothing but myself, why should I fear?" Thence his

---

[417] Jung used the German translation by Deussen (1894), pp. 320–22; Engl.: Griffith
(1895), pp. 27–30.
[418] Deussen (1919).
[419] Jung: "That is the Deussen translation."

fear passed away. For what should he have feared? Verily fear arises from a second only.

3. But he felt no delight. Therefore a man who is lonely feels no delight. He wished for a second. He was so large as man and wife together. He then made this his Self to fall in two [*pat*], and thence arose husband [*pati*] and wife [*patnî*]. Therefore Yâgñavalkya said, "We two are thus (each of us) like half a shell." Therefore the void which was there, is filled by the wife. He embraced her, and men were born.

6. [. . .] This is the highest creation of Brahman, when he created the gods from his better part, and when he, who was (then) mortal, created the immortals. Therefore it was the highest creation. And he who knows this, lives in this his highest creation.

7. Now all this was then undeveloped. It became developed by form and name, so that one could say, "He, called so and so, is such a one." Therefore at present also all this is developed by name and form, so that one can say, "He, called so and so, is such a one."

He (Brahman or the Self) entered thither, to the very tips of the finger-nails, as a razor might be fitted in a razor-case, or as fire in a fire-place.

He cannot be seen, for, in part only, when breathing, he is breath by name; when speaking, speech by name; when seeing, eye by name; when hearing, ear by name; when thinking, mind by name. All these are but the names of his acts. And he who worships (regards) him as the one or the other, does not know him, for he is apart from this (when qualified) by the one or the other (predicate). Let men worship him as Self, for in the Self all these are one. This Self is the footstep of everything, for through it one knows everything. And as one can find again by footsteps what was lost, thus he who knows this finds glory and praise.

8. This, which is nearer to us than anything, this Self, is dearer than a son, dearer than wealth, dearer than all else. [. . .]

10. Verily in the beginning this was Brahman, that Brahman knew (its) Self only, saying, "I am Brahman." From it all this sprang. Thus, whatever Deva was awakened (so as to know Brahman), he indeed became that (Brahman); and the same with Rishis and men. The Rishi Vâmadeva saw and understood it, singing, "I was Manu (moon), I was the sun."

Manu is an old Indian lawgiver.

> Therefore now also he who thus knows that he is Brahman, becomes all this, and even the Devas cannot prevent it, for he himself is their Self.

Brâhman is the world god. *Âtman* is also world god. This is a didactic discourse.

> Now if a man worships another deity, thinking the deity is one and he another, he does not know. He is like a beast for the Devas. For verily, as many beasts nourish a man, thus does every man nourish the Devas. If only one beast is taken away, it is not pleasant; how much more when many are taken! Therefore it is not pleasant to the Devas that men should know this.[420]

And now another conversation, a didactic discourse of the Yâgñavalkya, *Third Adhyâya, Seventh Brâhmana*:

> 2. [. . .] The other said, "So it is, O Yâgñavalkya. Tell now (who is) the puller within."
> 3. Yâgñavalkya said, "He who dwells in the earth, and within the earth, whom the earth does not know, whose body the earth is, and who pulls (rules) the earth within, he is thy Self, the puller (ruler) within, the immortal."
> 4. "He who dwells in the water, and within the water, whom the water does not know, whose body the water is, and who pulls (rules) the water within, he is thy Self, the puller (ruler) within, the immortal."
> 5. "He who dwells in the fire, and within the fire, whom the fire does not know, whose body the fire is, and who pulls (rules) the fire within, he is thy Self, the puller (ruler) within, the immortal."
> 6. "He who dwells in the sky, and within the sky, whom the sky does not know, whose body the sky is, and who pulls (rules) the sky within, he is thy Self, the puller (ruler) within, the immortal."
> 8. "He who dwells in the heaven [*dyu*], and within the heaven, whom the heaven does not know, whose body the heaven is, and who pulls (rules) the heaven within, he is thy Self, the puller (ruler) within, the immortal."
> 15. Yâgñavalkya said, "He who dwells in all beings, and within all beings, whom all beings do not know, whose body all beings are,

---

[420] *SBE*, vol. 15, pp. 85–88.

and who pulls (rules) all beings within, he is thy Self, the puller (ruler) within, the immortal."

23. "[. . .] unseen, but seeing; unheard, but hearing; unperceived, but perceiving; unknown, but knowing. There is no other seer but he, there is no other hearer but he, there is no other perceiver but he, there is no other knower but he. This is thy Self, the ruler within, the immortal. Everything else is of evil." After that Uddâlaka Âruni held his peace.[421]

And last of all another section. *Fourth Adhyâya, Fourth Brâhmana:*

22. "And he is that great unborn Self, who consists of knowledge, is surrounded by the Prânas, the ether within the heart. In it there reposes the ruler of all, the lord of all, the king of all. He does not become greater by good works, nor smaller by evil works. He is the lord of all, the king of all things, the protector of all things. He is a bank and a boundary, so that these worlds may not be confounded."[422]

This last part shows how this great, all-encompassing *âtman* is thought of as a small being, *purusha*, a little man, a Tom Thumb living in the cave of the heart, hidden inside me as the tiniest of creatures. That is the *purusha*, the *âtman*, the unborn[423] creature that still lives in the mother's womb. There it is a seed, a *hiranyagarbha*. As the great being that covers and rules the whole world, the inner driver of all beings, it is the firstborn, or, using the Gnostic expression, the *monogenes*, the only begotten.

These texts show more clearly than I can how greatly the outlook differs between East and West. In the East, the world is an inner experience and not the external things we encounter; rather it is understood in the deepest sense as emanating from this inner creator. Even the world of the gods, even things that are greater than the creator, have emanated from this tiniest of creatures within each individual.

From a Western perspective, one might object that such a view could lead to excessive megalomania. We must answer that by remembering that there are certain statements of Christ that are particularly illuminating in this regard. For example he says, "Jesus saith unto him, I am the way, the truth, and the life: no man cometh unto the Father, but by me."[424] And in

---

[421] Ibid., pp. 133–36.
[422] Ibid., p. 179.
[423] BH has here instead "the great unborn Self."
[424] John 14:6 (*KJV*).

another place, "[H]e that hath seen me hath seen the Father."[425] With this he expresses something that corresponds substantially with Eastern wisdom. But we assume a god is speaking. At least, that is the orthodox notion. But if we consider it with that liberal Protestantism that[426] no longer maintains the divinity of Christ,[427] but sees him as a competent moral teacher who shows people how it goes and how to behave, like a kind of Sunday-school teacher, then such a *logion* cannot be anything other than a case of excessive megalomania. In this country, we cannot imagine a person who could nowadays seriously say, "I am the way, the truth, and the life." It is too objectionable; of course this liberal Protestantism falls down at such *logia*. Because if one refers to these things at all, one should take them seriously. Then one inevitably comes to the conclusion that this is either pathological hubris, or paranoia, or that a god is speaking. Those are our Western alternatives.

But could we not say that Christ perhaps spoke the language of India? An Indian person would accept such statements easily. Someone from India would feel much affinity with such things, specifically with people about whose humanity he is completely convinced. When he says about himself, "I am the truth," "I am the light of the world,"[428] he is not saying anything extraordinary. Rather he is saying a person is that, and alongside he is a swindler, a horse thief, and God knows what else. That is the curious thing,[429] that you find these statements in the dirt and dust. The most valuable pearls of Indian wisdom fall from the mouths of people who in our society would be shunned. It is so much embedded in the population, in all their language and gestures; everywhere there is this basic conviction, so much that it almost becomes meaningless. But at the highest levels of the Indian mind, these beliefs take on a significance that is hard to escape. But for that one needs to be in India, as it were. Our atmosphere doesn't allow for that. Here it is not done to talk in such a way. But Christ is a person who lived in the East. Why shouldn't he also sometimes speak an Indian language instead of Aramaic or Greek? Then it is no longer so astonishing; rather it is the human truth which is expressed one way in the West and another way in the East. Whether we believe that by entering the *corpus mysticum* we will also sit at the Father's right hand and rule with the *Rex gloriae*, or we say, "I am the *âtman*," it ultimately comes

---

[425] John 14:9 (*KJV*).
[426] RS adds here "leider" (unfortunately).
[427] This clause was reconstructed from BH's translation.
[428] John 8:12 (*KJV*).
[429] ES has "betrübende" (dispiriting) instead of "merkwürdige" (curious).

down to the same thing. It is a psychological predicate that in our innermost self we encounter a foundation that we perceive as the primordial foundation of existence, of the personality in general. Why that is, I cannot say; we'd have to ask a theologian. I can only confirm the psychological facts.

This concludes my presentation of the "Anima Christi" meditation. But I nevertheless still want to say a few words about the next part. We still need to look at the part called the "Fundamentum." That comes from Saint Ignatius himself. The meditation on the "Fundamentum," similar to the "Anima Christi," is a second pillar of the exercises, as it were.[430] Specifically, it is deconstructed into words and sentences. The meditator considers each part very thoroughly, by looking at each sentence and allowing the sentence to crystallize,[431] in order to fully absorb the meaning. The "Fundamentum" goes as follows:

> Creatus est homo ad hunc finem, ut Dominum Deum suum laudet ac reveratur, eique serviens tandem salvus fiat.[432]

The translation of the whole thing is:

> The human person is created to praise, reverence and serve God Our Lord, and by so doing to save his or her soul. The other things on the face of the earth are created for human beings in order to help them pursue the end for which they are created. It follows from this that one must use other created things in so far as they help towards one's end, and free oneself from them in so far as they are obstacles to one's end. To do this we need to make ourselves indifferent to all created things, provided the matter is subject to our free choice and there is no prohibition. Thus as far as we are concerned, we should not want health more than illness, wealth more than poverty, fame more than disgrace, a long life more than a short one, and similarly for all the rest, but we should desire and

[430] The reflection on the Principle and Foundation lasted until the Second Vatican Council. See Tetlow (1989), p. 1.

[431] RS has "und so den Satz herauszufordern versucht" (and thus tries to challenge the sentence) instead of "den Satz herausformen lässt" (allows the sentence to emerge/crystallize), and LSM has "sich davon herausfordern lässt" (allow oneself to be challenged by it).

[432] MHSI-MI, Versio vulgata, p. 164. Jung quoted from Latin translation of Ignatius's original Spanish text. The MHSI-MI gives three different Latin versions: the Versio vulgata (1547), the Versio prima (1540) and the Versio prima (1547). Jung seems to have followed the Versio vulgata. The Versio prima reads here as follows: "Homo est creatus ad laudandum Deum et ei exhibendum obsequium et reverentiam et ad salvandum his mediis animam suam" (MHSI-MI, p. 165).

choose only what helps us more towards the end for which we are created.[433]

You see already from this text that on the one hand it is a kind of philosophical anthropology and a basic attitude toward existence in general, and on the other hand it also indicates a path, a mode of conduct, the attitude which one should take toward the world or one's life, toward existence in general. Here we have a highly concentrated philosophy that is characteristic of the exercises and that must be thoroughly meditated on, as it is the foundation of the whole exercise.

We'll see each other again on 12 January. No lectures until then.

[433] *IPW*, p. 289.

Lecture 8[434]

12 JANUARY 1940

BEFORE THE VACATION I told you that we would today start discussing the "Fundamentum" of the *Exercitia spiritualia*. The meditation on the "Fundamentum" is usually done in the first week of the exercises. It is generally left up to the exercise leader whether to give it as a meditation task or to lead the meditation either at the beginning or in the course of the week.

We read the text briefly in the last session. Because we need to get into the text in more depth, the same as we did with the "Anima Christi," I want to read the text out again. So, in translation it goes,

> The human person is created to praise, reverence and serve God Our Lord, and by so doing to save his or her soul. The other things on the face of the earth are created for human beings in order to help them pursue the end for which they are created. It follows from this that one must use other created things in so far as they help towards one's end, and free oneself from them in so far as they are obstacles to one's end. To do this we need to make ourselves indifferent to all created things, provided the matter is subject to our free choice and there is no prohibition. Thus as far as we are concerned, we should not want health more than illness, wealth more than poverty, fame more than disgrace, a long life more than a short one, and similarly for all the rest, but we should desire and choose only what helps us more towards the end for which we are created.[435]

The "Fundamentum" begins with an assertion that presents an important principle. A whole attitude is present in one short sentence: namely,

---

[434] The text of this lecture is compiled from notes by LSM, ES, RS, and OK, as well as the English translation by BH.

[435] *IPW*, p. 289.

"Creatus est homo," "The human person is created." This is an anthropological statement of great psychological[436] significance. We should therefore reflect here for a moment on how we might react to such a statement.

In the discussion of the "Anima Christi," I deliberately did not use the "Annotationes" and "Explicationes," the annotations and explanations of Saint Ignatius, because these are drafted in medieval Latin. Instead I took the work of a modern commentator, Przywara, who fully follows the intention of his master in his exercise meditations and therefore gives us a shining example of how the meditation of the exercises is actually done. I will continue to follow Przywara's explanations here for the meditation on the "Fundamentum." But before we look at his work in more detail, I would like to mention a few considerations that may make us aware of how these old ideas relate to us.

You were able to see from Przywara's meditation how vividly alive these things are. They are alive. Many people still do these exercises today. They hold great importance in the Catholic church. Even if we are not Catholic, it is still useful and advisable to take some interest in these things, because there are many good reasons for them. But I don't want to go into the reasons in more detail today.

"Creatus est homo" means that man was created. Naturally one thinks here of the creation story in the Bible and turns one's back on such a claim with a smile. But it is foolish to dismiss it so easily. This "Creatus est homo" is actually a psychological expression, namely about whether people feel that they were created or not. You know that the natural sciences tell us that humans evolved. Not that humans did so actively[437]—it would be nonsensical to understand it like that—but that evolution is a natural process. After a long line of animal ancestors the human finally came into being. How it happened we do not know, at least not yet, and we probably still won't know in the future.[438]

How we ourselves actually feel in this regard is extraordinarily important, however. Do we have the feeling that we created ourselves? Or do we not feel that way? In general, one doesn't have this feeling, but rather one feels that one discovered oneself. Now, how did we discover ourselves? One day we became conscious of ourselves. We say, "This is my name, here I am"; we use the word "I." Did we just come about or were we made?

---

[436] ES has "philosophisch" (philosophical) instead of "psychologisch" (psychological).

[437] Trans. note: the German word for "evolve" is the reflexive verb *sich entwickeln*, literally "develop oneself," which is perhaps why Jung specifies this.

[438] RS noted "something along the lines of" in relation to this last clause.

Deciding that is quite another question, and a very difficult one at that. Our feelings give us no information about this at all. We do not feel that we were made as we are, but that we only discovered ourselves like that, with all our characteristics, talents, and imperfections. But we don't have the feeling that these things were in some way made part of or given to us on purpose, that some kind of intelligence is behind it and chose, selected, or intentionally put together this particular conglomerate, this mix. We might just as well feel that we became how we are by chance, a process of nature that led to us becoming a certain way. Our natural scientists do not give us any certainty there either. This question seems to be largely determined by whatever worldview we happen to have.

We initially find no indication in our own psychological feelings that there is any kind of intention behind our existence. What is behind it is something quite different. First we need to step back a bit and look for individual cases of people who have a great deal of life experience. If you ask them, "Do you have the feeling that everything that you are now simply came about by chance, or do you have the feeling that something in you was at work over a long period of time and made you what you are now?" you will find very many people, a surprisingly large number, who are convinced that something is at work that has guided them. They have the feeling of an inner purpose, inner guidance, that in a curious way made them they way they are now. Is this assertion simply a subjective fantasy, or is there any scientific evidence for it?

The answer to that has to be: what comes first is the unconscious. The unconscious psyche is older than consciousness. The child is at first unconscious, and gradually enters a state of consciousness. First there is an unconscious psyche, an animal psyche if you like. So consciousness comes out of an unconscious state. Things that we will know tomorrow that we cannot yet know today are perhaps already present in the unconscious. One can even find evidence of this in dreams: if you follow them for several months, you will find ideas coming up at a very early stage which cannot yet become conscious, and not until later do they suddenly break through into consciousness. Then one is quite justified in saying, "If the unconscious knows anything, it has already known it for a long time." Does the unconscious have awareness? We certainly don't know anything about that. It is a very difficult problem that I don't want to go into today.

But at any rate, we know that these ideas have been present for a long time. They have expressed themselves in dreams, symbols, actions, and relationships with others, have appeared covertly such that one often wants to say to people, "Do you realize what you are saying, what you are doing?" But no, they don't know. They just do it. The awareness doesn't come until much later. This is a fact that we can easily prove in various forms: namely, that an unconscious state precedes the conscious one, and that remains true throughout one's life, not only at the start. Contents, parts of the personality, opinions that will perhaps at some point play a very big role in a person's life, have been present for a long time before they come up, and can be objectively observed—just not by the person concerned, unless it is pointed out to them.

So if this fact is true, and according to everything we know empirically it really is true, we can say that consciousness is anticipated, is created. It comes out of an unconscious state: that is, from a very specific unconscious state that prefigures consciousness, that anticipates what the conscious mind will later finally come to clearly understand and recognize. It has already been thought before. Thus it is quite understandable if a great number of people who have lived a long and full life assure us that they have the feeling that they were anticipated, pre-understood, or guided by a higher intelligence. Whether there is in fact someone there who knows, that we don't know. It is possible that certain ideas[439] are inherently present, but no one knows them. But as I said, it is still debatable whether such a thing[440] is even possible. Of course, I personally do not approach such things with philosophical suppositions, but take a purely empirical approach. So if I were to discover such a case of a higher intelligence, it would be forever etched on my mind. You can bet your life on that, as the saying goes. But I have never come across such a case with absolute certainty, although I've occasionally had my suspicions.

This fact—that the unconscious anticipates us, prepares us, that it today contains the psychic contents of tomorrow, in a manner of speaking, and then kind of pushes them up so that tomorrow one says, "It has just occurred to me all of a sudden! I suddenly see what it means!"—that is the moment at which the unconscious manages to lift the pre-prepared material into consciousness, as it were. And this happens not only with individual incidents, but with the totality of the person, with the whole of a person's psyche. Our whole being, our whole character, is a discovery. We discover it. It has already been there. Maybe our parents have long been aware of it, but we were not. And then one day it suddenly becomes clear to us. We have finally understood it, although it was there for such a long time beforehand. This psychological fact may not prove the [truth of the]

---

[439] LSM has "Kräfte" (powers) instead of "Gedanken" (ideas or thoughts).
[440] RS has "Meinung" (opinion) instead of "so etwas" (such a thing).

feeling of having been created, but at any rate it makes it a significant possibility. This is of course an unpopular point of view, and an old-fashioned one. But it is valid.

If we understand the words "Creatus est homo" in this way, then of course our outlook changes considerably; because if we assume that everything that we are comes from our own consciousness, then we are entirely justified in feeling a diabolical hubris. Then we make claims such as "Where there's a will there's a way," and the like, and think we are the gods of this world. But unfortunately there is a multitude of different gods, not just one, and each tries as hard as they can to be the only god, which leads to all kinds of conflicts, as we well know. "There is not room for two suns in my heaven, I am the only one."[441] If on the other hand we understand this "Creatus est homo" correctly, then we tell ourselves that we are something that has come about, a product, that we are anticipated. We were there and did not know it. It was "known," only we do not know who knew it. This question must remain open.

If we hold this view, we are no longer so far removed from the old formulation that man was created, that the existence of the human psyche—I am not talking about our anatomy—was anticipated, that we were identified or imagined before we knew it. That is a psychological fact. I can fully subscribe to that and provide the necessary empirical evidence. That's why the declaration "Creatus est homo" seems very significant to me.[442] However, as I have already said, it must not be mixed up with the scientific viewpoint, as it is about mental and not physical existence.

---

[441] "Heaven cannot brook two suns, nor earth two masters" is attributed to Alexander III of Macedon—Alexander the Great—as his reply to King Darius III of Persia. In *Psychological Types*, Jung quotes from *Character as Seen in Body and Parentage* by Furneaux Jordan (1830–1911) to give an example for the extraverted man: "He has an incisive formula for everything that is put before him: either the thing is not true, or everybody knows it already. In his sky there is not room for two suns. If other suns insist on shining, he has a curious sense of martyrdom" (Jung, 1921, § 265). This is a slightly abridged version. Jordan actually wrote, "In the world of the busy passionless man there is not room for two Alexanders: in his sky there is not room for two suns. Seeing, however, that other Alexanders will thrust themselves not only into existence but also into notice, and that other suns insist on shining, he has a curious sense of martyrdom" (Jordan, 1890, p. 28).

[442] In his Eranos lecture of 1941, Jung referred the first line of the "Fundamentum": "It is not I who create myself, rather I happen to myself. This realization is of fundamental importance for the psychology of religious phenomena, which is why Ignatius Loyola started off his *Spiritual Exercises* with 'Homo creatus est' as their 'fundamentum.' But, fundamental as it is, it can be only half the psychological truth. If it were the whole truth, it would be tantamount to determinism, for if man were merely a creature that came into being as a result of something already existing unconsciously, he would have no freedom and there would be no point in consciousness." Jung (1942b), § 391.

Now, if there really is some intent, a particular purpose behind the existence of the psyche, then of course the question is, "What is it?" That's why Ignatius continues with "ut laudet Deum Dominum nostrum": claiming man was created in order "to praise God Our Lord". But we will put that aside for now and ask ourselves: psychologically, does the feeling that we were anticipated also lead to a feeling that we have a purpose? In other words, do we feel that life has meaning? From a psychological point of view, I must note here that the discovery or realization that we have been anticipated or preconceived is always accompanied by a feeling of meaning or purpose; we cannot precisely determine the meaning of life at that moment, but we feel it as something that is alive.

If I discover that I have been anticipated, it makes an enormous impression on me. The feeling of meaning or purposiveness is part of that, even if, as I said, we cannot precisely pinpoint what that meaning, the specific purpose, is. We might express it something like this: "It must mean something. What strange meaning can this have?" It seems extremely odd. Then in a series of dreams I see certain ideas gradually unfolding. I have been anticipated. I am like a plagiarism of myself, a copy of my unconscious anticipation. Immediately one has a feeling of meaningfulness, a sense of purpose, as if one's fate were mysteriously arranged. You don't keep asking for long what the meaning actually is, or what it is all for; you are just filled with the feeling of this meaning. You know, the essential decisions[443] are not made with clear formulations, but through emotional experiences that go much further and have a much greater influence on human life than our intellectual considerations. At the end of the day, it is much more important in life that a person is happy and content than that they have a particular intellectual standpoint. Anyone who is not an intellectual would not even care at all about this. One single live experience means much more. Psychology must be based on this fact and not on intellectual formulations, or it could be nothing but hot air.

Anyway, Ignatius continues by trying to formulate the purpose of human existence: namely, "laudare Dominum." You might recall that I already spoke about the *laudare* in a previous lecture.[444] It is an ancient notion of the royal court, the court of the oriental prince, in which the courtiers and flunkeys are careful to keep praising and glorifying their lord, to curry favor with the prince—because high-ranking folk like these,

---

[443] RS has "Entdeckungen" (discoveries) instead of "Entscheidungen" (decisions), and LSM has "Anschauungen" (opinions, assumptions).

[444] See lecture 6 (8 December 1939), pp. 124–25.

the monarchs with absolute power, are usually in a bad mood, as they are so isolated. Thus one has to be really careful what one says to them. They cannot be criticized; everything that is said must praise and glorify them. That's why we talk about Byzantinism.[445] It served to put the dangerous monarch in a good mood. This notion was passed on from Egyptian cults to all the Near-Eastern cults and thus over into Christianity. That's where the *laudare* comes from.

The same thing we saw in the "Anima Christi" meditation now makes a reappearance: namely, that absolute submissiveness and surrender to an absolute superior. We find in this attitude, that is, the assumption that man was created by an absolutely superior being with no higher judge, as Job says,[446] who must therefore be propitiated. One cannot do anything other than mollify this superior being, and Ignatius now formulates this in three different ways: *laudare*, praise; *revereri*, revere; *servire*, serve, like a slave, a servant who serves his lord. If you translate this into psychological terms, it means that the attitude proposed by Ignatius entails absolute surrender and submission to the unconscious—that is, to that authority which we in general completely disregard. We dismiss things as just unconscious ideas; everyone forgets that they would be unable to speak another word if the unconscious wasn't telling them what to say.

Here Ignatius tells us to take this attitude toward this anticipating unconscious, namely for a very specific purpose: "salvatio animae suae," to save one's soul. If one does not absolutely honor and submit to this source from which consciousness originates, from which consciousness is created, one loses one's soul. Then the connection with the soul is lost: that is, the connection with the unconscious is lost. Now, imagine if a psychotherapist today were to tell a patient, "You must submit to your own soul,[447] to the objective contents of the psyche that spontaneously appear in dreams." We would have to pack him off to Burghölzli[448]. That's what most reasonable people would think. You can't just surrender yourself to random notions; that is boundless subjectivism. But if we say, "God who

---

[445] Byzantinism, or Byzantism, is a term coined in the nineteenth century to denote an overly aristocratic and bureaucratic, hierarchical structured political and cultural system, as was then associated with the Byzantine Empire.

[446] Job 21:22: "Shall any teach God knowledge? seeing he judgeth those that are high" (*KJV*).

[447] LSM has "Ihrem Unbewussten" (your unconscious) instead of "Ihrer eigenen Seele" (your own soul), and ES has "Ihren Einfällen" (your ideas, what occurs to you).

[448] Burghölzli clinic, psychiatric hospital of the University of Zurich, founded in 1870. Its directors included Auguste-Henri Forel (1879–98) and Eugen Bleuler (1898–1927). Jung worked at the Burghölzli from 1900 to 1909. See Bernet (2013).

created us," then it is something different, then the formulation fits into our traditional schema. Then you can simply express yourself in traditional terms and you can't go wrong, although there have been plenty of people for whom it did go wrong. There have been a lot of very eccentric folk. You see that throughout history: most founders of sects were very odd fellows, though they were undoubtably pious people. They came up with such bizarre and dangerous ideas that the Catholic church has rightly prohibited people from having individual revelations. The Church decides in the last instance what is truth and what is a manifestation of the Holy Spirit. Otherwise it would be like during the Reformation. At that time, there were all kinds of *Schwärmer*:[449] Anabaptists and sectarians, each proclaiming their own truth until there was a complete Babel of competing voices. Just think of the Peasants' War.[450] And the Brethren of the Free Spirit:[451] pre-reformatory, cynical quasi-philosophers who took the view that the world is only mundane and transitory and therefore everything must be destroyed. They were like communists living at the expense of others. They beat up a harmless traveler, took his bag and told him, "We have to send your money into eternity, destroy it, because it is only worldly and means nothing." In such ways the basest of instincts are spiritually justified.

So there is great danger in submissiveness. When we invoke God, we think this danger is exorcised, because we, insofar as we are Christians,

---

[449] See n. 357.

[450] The German Peasants' War was an uprising of the peasants in several territories of the Holy Roman Empire between 1524 and 1526. Their demands for freedom from oppression by the aristocracy and clergy were based on Martin Luther's claim that a Christian was the servant of no one except Christ, as expressed in his pamphlet "On the Freedom of a Christian" (1520). The first riots took place in southwest Germany during the summer of 1524. At first Luther was sympathetic to the cause, though he rejected violence as a means to fulfill the peasants' demands (Luther, 1908 [1525]a), but as his plea for a peaceful solution was ignored, he changed his mind and supported the suppression of the revolt (Luther, 1908 [1525]b). Led by charismatic leaders such as the preacher and theologian Thomas Müntzer (ca. 1489–1525), a former adherent of Luther, the uprising initially succeeded in several German lands before it was finally crushed by the much better equipped troops of the nobility. High numbers of peasants were killed, with hardly any losses on the other side. Müntzer and other surviving leaders were captured, tortured, and executed. Due to his support for the ruling classes during the conflict, Luther's reputation suffered and never recovered completely. See also p. 210.

[451] "Brethren of the Free Spirit" is the name given to several loosely connected sects from the thirteenth to the fifteenth century, who were condemned as heretical by pope Clement V in his bull *Ad nostrum* at the Council of Vienne (1311–12). Their beliefs were based on the doctrine of personal revelation through the Holy Spirit (2 Corinthians 3:17) and potential mystical union with God during this life on earth. Most prominently, Meister Eckhart (1260–1328) was accused of this heresy, but died before he could be tried.

have completely forgotten our fear of God. We have forgotten that God is extremely dangerous. The old Church knew that. It was expressed in its symbols, which could be terribly shocking. For example, the rhinoceros is a symbol of God. Why? Because it is a very angry, bad-tempered, and dangerous animal. That's what the Old Testament God was like: a wrathful, violent God, who threw the world into disorder and through the love of a pure virgin was forced to come to peace in her womb and was thus transformed into a God of love. That's what one of the Church fathers said.[452]

So they were certainly aware of it. Nowadays we speak only of the loving God, but the Church knew otherwise and probably still knows it, although they make sure the sermons are a lot more soothing today. It's not exactly popular to talk about God's misdeeds, or, like Luther, of *Deus absconditus*, of a hidden God.[453] Then one cannot talk about who is the God of this or that country, and which one is better—rather the deity was always and is still a great danger for all religious people. There is a dark

---

[452] In his main work *Moralia, sive Expositio in Job* Pope Gregory I (ca. 540–604), also known as Saint Gregory the Great, commented on the *monoceros* (Septuagint) or *rhinoceros* (Vulgate) in Job 39:9–12 as follows: "Rhinoceros iste, qui etiam monoceros in Graecis exemplaribus nominatur, tantae esse fortitudinis dicitur, ut nulla venantium virtute capiatur; sed sicut hi asserunt, qui describendis naturis animalium laboriosa investigatione sudaverunt, virgo ei puella proponitur, quae ad se venienti sinum aperit, in quo ille omni ferocitate postposita caput deponit, sicque ab eis a quibus capi quaeritur, repente velut inermis invenitur." (This rhinoceros, which is called also the "monoceros" in Greek copies, is said to be of such great strength, as not to be taken by any skill of hunters. But, as those persons assert, who have striven with laborious investigation in describing the natures of animals, a virgin is placed before it, who opens to it her bosom as it approaches, in which, having put aside all its ferocity, it lays down its head, and is thus suddenly found as it were unarmed, by those by whom it is sought to be taken.) (Gregorius Magnus, 1878 [PL, vol. 76], 31. 15.29, p. 589; Engl.: 1844, vol. 3, p. 448).

[453] *Deus absconditus* (Lat.): "the hidden God," refers to the unknowability of the essence of God, as it is expressed in Isaiah 45:15: "Verily thou art a God that hidest thyself, O God of Israel, the Saviour" (*KJV*). In *De servo arbitrio* (*On the Bondage of the Will*) (1525), a refutation of Erasmus of Rotterdam's *De libero arbitrio diatribe sive collatio* (*Of Free Will: Discourses or Comparisons*; known as *The Freedom of the Will*) (1524), Luther differentiates between *Deus absconditus* and *Deus revelatus*: "I answer, as I said before,—we are to argue in one way, concerning the will of God preached, revealed, and offered unto us, and worshipped by us; and in another, concerning God himself not preached, not revealed, not offered unto us, and worshipped by us. In whatever, therefore, God hides himself and will be unknown by us, that is nothing unto us: and here, that sentiment stands good—'What is above us, does not concern us.' [. . .] For God Preached desires this:—that, our sin and death being taken away, we might be saved, 'He sent his word and healed them,' Psalm cvii. But God Hidden in majesty neither deplores, nor takes away death, but works life and death and all things; nor has he, in this character, defined himself in his word, but has reserved unto himself, a free power over all things" (Luther, 1823 [1525], pp. 157–58).

side to God that is also an enormous problem for religious people. Why does God allow the devil to exist, for example? Ah yes, we no longer speak of him. We no longer like to mention the devil, but speak rather of "dear God," and how he created the world so beautifully. "Omne bonum a Deo, omne malum ab homine."[454] Then it is us, *we* become the devil. That is also a diabolical arrogance—if we believe we are responsible for the other half of the world.

According to the old Church doctrine, the devil is the counterpart of Christ. He is autonomous and worldly. That is, the principle of evil is just as eternal, just as autonomous as the principle of good. The Church doctrine doesn't quite say that God intentionally created the devil, but it admits that the devil exists, and that he is the counterpart of Christ. By the way, even old Zarathustra had such an idea. There it is said that Ahura Mazda had a dubious thought, and that created Vohu Manah, the good word, the good disposition, the right attitude—that is, *logos*, and Angra Mainyu, the devil—that is, the doubt of God.[455]

There is also an alchemist who had the same idea. He says that on the second day of creation God created the *binarius*—the dyad—when he separated the upper and the lower waters.[456] The *binarius* is the devil,

---

[454] Lat.: "All that is good comes from God, all that is evil from man." Jung discusses this thought extensively in *Aion*, where he also speculates on its first expression: "The earliest authority of all for the later axiom 'Omne bonum a Deo, omne malum ab homine' is Tatian (second century), who says, 'Nothing evil was created by God; we ourselves have produced all wickedness.'" (Jung, 1951, § 81).

[455] Ahura Mazda (Ohrmazd in Pahlavi, Ormazd in Persian), "The Wise Lord," Indo-Iranian God: with the emergence of Zarathustra's teachings, Ahura Mazda becomes the one God who created the world of perfect order ("Mazdaism"). But the world is also the battleground between the Good Thought (Vohu Manah) and the Evil (Angra Mainyu, or Ahriman), where the righteous have to choose the side of the Good. Jung gave an introduction to Zoroastrian belief at the beginning of his seminar on Nietzsche's *Zarathustra* on 2 May 1934 (Jung, 1989 [1934–39], pp. 4–14): "Those two spirits, Vohu Manō and Angrō Mainyush, were together in the original Ahura Mazda, showing that in the beginning there was no separation of good and evil. But after a while they began to quarrel with each other, and a fight ensued, and then the creation of the world became necessary" (p. 7). And in letter to Erich Neumann of 12 August 1934, Jung wrote, "In Ahura Mazda, there were originally present in undivided form Ahura Mazda—the good word or the good disposition, and Ahriman—the evil one" (Jung and Neumann, 2015, p. 57).

[456] Jung refers to the alchemist and philosopher Gerhard Dorn (ca. 1530–84), also known as Gerardus Dorneus. Born in Mechelen (Habsburg Netherlands) he lived in Basel and Frankfurt. Dorn studied with Adam von Bodenstein, with whom he printed many Paracelsus manuscripts for the first time. He edited and translated Paracelsus's *Aurorae thesaurusque philosophorum* (1577). His own works include *Chymisticum artificium naturae, theoricum et practicum* (1568), and can be found in the first volume of the *Theatrum chemicum* (1602–21), which Jung studied on his journey through India in 1937–38. Jung discussed Dorn in connection with the *binarius* also in *Psychology and Religion* (Jung, 1938, § 104,

because it thrusts something in between that separates. *Binarius* separates, it destroys. That's why the second day of creation is the only day on which God did not say, "It is good." Really, if you go and re-read Genesis you will find that God did not say it was good on that day.[457]

This split between a good one and an evil one is actually resolved in the concept of God as he is the *coincidentia oppositorum*, the coming together of the opposites, the resolution of all opposites and the release from them. But insofar as he is that being in which the two are contained (*in potentia*), they can also *in actu* emerge from him.[458] This Christian notion is therefore a response to the old Persian idea.

The idea of God's dangerousness could be formulated thus: where the danger is greatest, God is closest by.[459] You find a similar formulation in a non-canonical dominical saying, in which Christ says, "He that is near me is near the fire. He that is far from me is far from the kingdom."[460] A very profound idea that also contains this darkness;[461] because fire is the epitome of the devouring and the destructive. It is also the devil, who is the lord of fire, who lives in fire, walks around like a roaring lion seeking

n. 88; § 120, n. 105) and "A Psychological Approach to the Dogma of the Trinity" (Jung, 1942a, § 262). Dorn wrote about the *binarius* in *De tenebris contra naturam et vita brevi*, which can also be found in the *Theatrum chemicum*, vol. 1 (p. 527).

[457] Genesis 1:6–8: "And God said, Let there be a firmament in the midst of the waters, and let it divide the waters from the waters./ And God made the firmament, and divided the waters which were under the firmament from the waters which were above the firmament: and it was so./ And God called the firmament Heaven. And the evening and the morning were the second day" (*KJV*).

[458] "Actus" and "potentia" are Scholastic translations of the Aristotelian concepts of *energeia* or *entelecheia*, and *dynamis*. "Potentia" refers to the capacity or potentiality to change, to act or to be acted upon, whereas "actus" is the fulfillment of this capacity. According to the Scholastic teachings, these are mutually exclusive, but present in every being. Only God as *actus purus* is the complete fulfillment without any potentiality: i.e., perfection.

[459] Cf. Friedrich Hölderlin's poem "Patmos": "Near is / And difficult to grasp, the God. / But where danger threatens / That which saves from it also grows" (Hölderlin, 2004, p. 567). Jung commented on this poem in "Wandlungen und Symbole der Libido" (1911–12, §§ 656–63). See Shamdasani (2012), pp. 12ff.

[460] The saying can be found in Origen's *Homiliae in Jeremiam* (1862), 20.3, p. 532. The complete passage reads as follows: "I have read somewhere that the Saviour said—and I question whether someone has assumed the person of the Saviour, or called the words to memory, or whether it be true that it is said—but *at any rate* the Saviour himself said: He that is near me is near the fire. He that is far from me is far from the kingdom" (Rhodes James, 1924, p. 35).

[461] ES has "Doppelheit" (duality) instead of "Dunkelheit" (darkness), and OK has "Totalität" (totality).

whom he may devour,[462] exactly like fire. There was much speculation about that in the Middle Ages. The lion in alchemy comes from that, for example.

It is therefore a burning problem: is a surrender such as Ignatius demands, a surrender to the foundation of the psyche's existence, even possible in practice? It is certainly possible in theory, as substantiated by the existence of all of Christianity. One can surrender to God. One has surrendered to God or to Christ. But it is a particular notion of God to which one has surrendered. You have not surrendered to *Deus creator*, God the Creator, but to an already evolved formulation of God, and one can only hope that despite this condition your prayer does indeed reach God. We could say a lot more on this point, but for now we will continue with the "Fundamentum."

If the purpose of my existence is that I surrender completely to God in service to him, and that this is necessary in order to save my soul, then this also gives rise to a particular attitude toward my fellow living creatures, toward the world in which I live. That is to say, if my purpose lies in this world, then this service to the Lord makes no sense at all. Because if my purpose is in this world, then I need to fulfill this earthly purpose. And that has become the modern view: we are here in order to function according to this or that purpose, to be a good citizen, to have a career, start a family, pay taxes, to serve the state wholeheartedly, with life and limb. The question is of course, "What is better?" Do we dedicate ourselves to the state or to God? You can't say, "That's no concern of mine."[463] It is my concern. The state's demand for totality is simply a derivative of the deity's demand for totality.

---

[462] 1 Peter 5:8: "Be sober, be vigilant; because your adversary the devil, as a roaring lion, walketh about, seeking whom he may devour" (*KJV*).

[463] Jung here uses a colloquial expression "Ich dreh die Hand nicht um," lit. "I don't turn my hand over"; i.e., "I don't want to make a choice."

Lecture 9[464]

19 JANUARY 1940

LAST TIME WE talked about the first part of the "Fundamentum," and we'll continue with that today. You will recall that the main idea of the first sentence of the "Fundamentum" is expressed through the "Creatus est homo". The second sentence then continues,

Reliqua vero supra terram sita, creata sunt hominis ipsius causa[465]

(The other things on the face of the earth are created for human beings)

From this sentence it becomes clear that in this view, not only is man something that has been created rather than simply come about, but so are all other creatures and things that populate the world and are found on earth. This statement can thus be extended to apply to the whole known universe—that things are not simply stumbled upon because they have come into being, but that they exist for a specific purpose. Namely, they are there to serve, to serve mankind. In this way, man is granted central significance in the Creation: the human being is the pinnacle, as it were, the goal of the Creation, the reason for which all things were created. Men are thus granted an exalted position here which they otherwise, for example from the scientific standpoint, do not have at all. From the standpoint of the natural sciences we can say that everything has come into being, it exists. It is certainly not to be understood that there should be

---

[464] The text of this lecture is compiled from notes by LSM, ES, RS, and OK, as well as the English translation by BH.

[465] MHSI-MI, Versio vulgata, p. 164. MHSI-MI, Versio prima reads, "reliqua autem omnia super terram existentia creata sunt ad hoc ut hominem iuvent ad prosecutionem finis ad quem conditus est" (p. 165). Translation: *IPW*, p. 289.

any kind of purpose behind it, nor that it is somehow arranged around mankind.

We laugh at the old view, saying scornfully that one might just as well say how wonderful it is that there is a river next to every town, what a wonderful job the Creator did. Of course it is easy to laugh at an idea like the "Creatus est homo." It's always easy to mock something, but real understanding is rather more difficult. We need not necessarily accept that man was created in the literal sense and that the other things were created for our benefit or to serve us. Rather, this statement describes a psychological attitude, an as-if: as if man was created, as if the things on earth served us, although no claim is made about the essence of the objects per se. I'm just putting that out there for reflection.

Now, supposedly all creatures are there to serve men, for a specific purpose. All things are created, says Ignatius,

ut eum ad finem creationis suae prosequendum iuvent[.][466]

(in order to help them pursue the end for which they are created.)

That is, not in order to make their earthly existence possible, to ensure they have meat and bread and wine, and so on, but in order that they achieve the purpose for which they have been created. And for what kind of purpose is man created according to this view? We already heard the answer in the first sentence: namely, "ut Dominum Deum suum laudet"— to praise God and revere him: in order, that is, ultimately to reach the royal court and there to serve the king. Of course, in a certain sense this is to be understood symbolically. We therefore need to get into the spirit a little and picture how someone such as Ignatius would have imagined this royal court.

We have a lot of material from the Middle Ages to help us. Art history gives us a lot of hints about medieval fantasies of the afterlife—because the royal court is the heavenly kingdom of God or the heavenly Jerusalem, where the *Rex gloriae*, the triumphant Christ, is enthroned, with the Trinity at the center, in place of the king. There are countless such paintings, I'm sure you've seen some of them. A particularly impressive depiction is

---

[466] MHSI-MI, Versio vulgata, p. 164. MHSI-MI, Versio prima reads, "reliqua autem omnia super terram existentia creata sunt ad hoc ut hominem iuvent ad prosecutionem finis ad quem conditus est" (p. 165). Translation: *IPW*, p. 289. Jung gave his own German translation of the Latin: "ihm zu helfen zur Erreichung des Zieles, wegen dessen er geschaffen ist" (to help him achieve the goal for which he has been created).

found in the "Paradiso" part of Dante's *Divine Comedy*. In the thirty-first and thirty-third cantos, there is a symbol that expresses this royal court, this special royal court of the *Regina caeli*, the Mother of Grace—it is the symbol of the white rose.[467] In Dante's vision, the angels and champions of God, the blood witnesses of Christ, the Church fathers, the saints, and so on arrange themselves as it were to form a wreath, and they form this heavenly flower in the center of which Dante finally also sees that three-colored circle which symbolizes the Trinity.

That is the image of the royal court. You also find it in the medieval rose windows in churches, where you see the *Rex gloriae* enthroned with the four Evangelists or their symbols, where Christ is enthroned on the four pillars of the four Evangelists. These circular images are called mandalas. And here we encounter a curious analogy between Eastern and Western thought: namely the image of a mystic flower that is the seat of the Godhead. We've already talked about that a great deal—about the *padma*, which means lotus, the lotus seat of the Buddha or some other Indian Gods. This *padma* has a female character. It is actually a female womb—*padma* is the hieratic word for that. You find the same thing in Dante, in the thirty-third canto, verses 7–9:

> In your womb was lit again that love
> By whose warmth, in the eternal peace,
> This flower has germinated as it is.[468]

And this rose also refers to the mystic rose of the thirty-first canto, where it says,

> In form then as of a shining white rose,
> The holy army of those whom, in his blood,
> Christ made his spouse, made its appearance to me[.][469]

Thus here the whole of the church, the *ecclesia sanctorum*, the community of the saints, is depicted, and in its center, in a manner of speaking in its womb, is contained the holiest of them all, namely the Godhead:

> In the profundity of the clear substance
> Of the deep light, appeared to me three circles
> Of three colours and equal circumference;

---

[467] Cf. *JMP*, vol. 6, pp. 172–73.
[468] Dante (1998 [1320]), p. 495.
[469] Ibid., p. 486.

And the first seemed to be reflected by the second,
As a rainbow by a rainbow, and the third
Seemed like a flame breathed equally from both.[470]

Such images of the goal, of the Godhead, were very likely also present in
Ignatius's mind—because they are the same images that we see over and
over again, throughout the Middle Ages, right up until today. You perhaps already know from Dante that the whole of heaven consists of a series of circles, and at the very top or the innermost, so to speak, is the
white rose [Fig. 3]. This corresponds precisely to the Eastern mandala,
where we also find the lotus in this central point, surrounded by the magical circles.

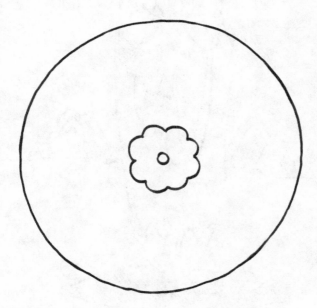

Funnily enough, I recently saw a picture, a Catholic work of modern
art, depicting the birth of Christ and the Christmas mystery. It shows a
snowy landscape with mountains in the background and a few houses. In
the foreground, in the snow, a plant is unfurling. It has four buds, and in
the middle is the calyx of the flower from which the Christ child is emerging, standing in the lotus [Fig. 4]. As far as I know, this kind of depiction

[470] Ibid., pp. 498–99.

is quite new. It could possibly also be a syncretic attempt to incorporate the lotus symbolism of the East into Church iconography.

In any case, we know that this basic notion of an archetype of the *finis* was common throughout the Middle Ages, namely the goal of entering this royal court, of reaching this figure which represents the king. Because Christ is this king, and he is so because of the mediation of the feminine, specifically of the great intercessor, the Mother of Grace, the *Mater Dei*. It is as if the *Rex gloriae* were surrounded by the love of the Mother of Grace, so that anyone who penetrates the various circles or spheres of heaven from outside, like Dante, plunges into the first sphere, which is spinning rapidly and successively advances as far as the innermost vision. This in turn corresponds exactly to the Eastern concept whereby the creator God—that is, Shiva—is in the center, surrounded by his female counterpart, Shakti.

Here, curiously, the central mystic conceptions of the East coincide with those of the West. As far as I know, it is not possible to prove that any direct contact took place which would enable us to say that the ancient Indian images had an influence on this central image in the West. It is unlikely, because we find such images not only in India and Europe, but also in the Mayan culture—to be precise, under the altar in a temple in Chichén Itzá, a second older altar was discovered, completely intact, and inside it a limestone vessel.[471] In this was a wonderful rose picture, a mandala, with four snakes guarding the horizon, which was made of three thousand turquoise gemstones. This is obviously the central mystery of this temple, which is in the shape of a *teocalli*, a terraced pyramid. At the deepest point in the inner sanctum is the mystery, the secret. So, in a way it is an image of the mysterious kingdom of God, which has exactly this structure, and in the center of which is this image.

So if this is the end toward which the efforts of a person undertaking the *exercitia spiritualia* are directed, it is quite obvious that the exercitant is striving for approximately the same thing as an Indian Tantrist or Lamaist: namely, to reach that seat of the Buddha in the center of the mandala, which is a symbol of the *âtman*, of the self. And all things are created for this purpose, that one might get there. That means one has to regard everything as if it only existed to enable this fruit to ripen: that is, that this self come into being and reach its place, the attainment of which is also a development process of the psyche. It follows from this that all things are created to this end, and as Meister Eckhart says,

All cereal nature means wheat,
all treasure nature means gold,
all generation means man.[472]

---

[471] Jung refers to this discovery also in his lecture of 15 December 1933 (*JMP*, vol. 1, p. 82) and in his seminar on dream analysis on 13 February 1929 (Jung, 1984 [1928–30], p. 115).

[472] Meister Eckhart: "Missus est Gabriel angelus (Luc. 1:26)," in Pfeiffer, 1857, p. 104; English translation as "The Angel Gabriel Was Sent" (1924, p. 80). Jung comments on this passage in *Psychological Types*, (Jung, 1921, §§ 425–26). See also Jung's lectures of 17 February 1939 and 9 June 1939 (*JMP*, volume 6, pp. 146 and 243).

This expresses the same idea. The consequence to be drawn from this, says Ignatius, is

> utendum illis vel abstinendum eatenus esse, quatenus ad prosecutionem finis vel conferunt vel obsunt.[473]

> (that one must use other created things in so far as they help towards one's end, and free oneself from them in so far as they are obstacles to one's end.)

Thus he derives from it an ethical mode of conduct or, we could say, a philosophical mode of conduct toward the world and toward the created things. Namely, Ignatius then says,

> Quapropter debemus absque differentia nos habere circa res creatas omnes (prout libertati arbitrii nostri subjectae sunt, et non prohibitae)[474]

> (To do this we need to make ourselves indifferent to all created things, provided the matter is subject to our free choice and there is no prohibition.)

This means: Ignatius infers from this necessity that man is created for a purpose, that all things are also put at man's disposal for this purpose, and one can only freely make use of them if one is indifferent to them, if the things actually mean nothing to one. You could almost imagine that this is a kind of Buddhist attitude to the world. You know already from my earlier lectures about how this attitude is cultivated:[475] interest is withdrawn from the world. The world is not just explained as *mâyâ*, but experienced as such, and the whole emotional relationship to the world becomes introverted, withdrawn into the individual, in order to there experience the maturation toward this center. This attitude in Ignatius, however, is not Buddhist, but more like a Stoic one: namely, *nihil datur.*[476] One should not let oneself be impressed by anything, but should ensure

---

[473] MHSI-MI, Versio vulgata, p. 164. MHSI-MI, Versio prima reads, "Ex quo fit quod homo eatenus eis uti debet, quatenus eum ad finem suum iuvant; atque ab eis abstinere, quatenus ad eum finem impediunt" (pp. 165, 167). Translation: *IPW*, p. 289.

[474] MHSI-MI, Versio vulgata, pp. 164, 166. MHSI-MI, Versio prima reads, "Quocirca opus est ut simus indifferentes ad amnia create, quoad concesum est libertati nostrae et non prohibitum" (p. 167). Translation: *IPW*, p. 289.

[475] See Jung's lectures of 1938–39 (*JMP*, volume 6).

[476] *nihil datur* (Lat.): "there is nothing," lit. "nothing is given."

one maintains indifference, *aequanimitas*,[477] equanimity. Ignatius also says, and we know from this that he didn't mean it in the Buddhist sense, that

ex omnibus ea demum, quae ad finem ducunt, eligere ac desiderare.[478]

(We should desire and choose only what helps us more towards the end for which we are created.)

This is of course not a Buddhist attitude, as this attitude favors certain things and rejects others; certain things or people are latched onto because they are necessary to achieve the goal. In the Buddhist attitude, on the other hand, nothing is necessary because all is illusion, *mâyâ*.

We have now finished our preliminary examination of the "Fundamentum." Next we come to the actual Jesuit meditation on the "Fundamentum" as it is done in the exercises, and which Przywara describes very thoroughly in his book *Deus semper maior*.[479] He also starts with the "Creatus est homo," that is, more precisely, with the "homo," and poses the question, "What is the human being?" In the meditations, as you saw when we looked at the "Anima Christi," almost every word is examined in great detail. I would like to give you some examples here to show how Przywara proceeds: he already stops at "homo." He says that man is a union of matter and spirit, actually composed of polar opposites.[480] Man is in a certain sense, as Przywara says, "the body become spirit,"[481] and in order that body can become spirit, the spirit must descend into the matter. Man is therefore also in a certain sense the "incarnation of the spirit."[482]

We can't just unthinkingly adopt this view wholesale. We have to ask ourselves, "Can we accept it? What does it mean: the body becoming spirit? Is it something we can experience? Can we see anywhere a body that has become spirit?" Yes, in the dogmatic tradition of the Church it is of course the case, because the *corpus Christi* has become spirit, the *corpus Christi*

---

[477] *aequanimitas* (Lat.): "equanimity": a central concept in the philosophical system of Stoicism. The Greek Stoics used the terms *apatheia* or *ataraxia*, referring to freedom from all passions.

[478] MHSI-MI, Versio vulgata, p. 166. MHSI-MI, Versio prima reads, "solum optemus et eligamus ea, quae magis conducunt nos ad finem propter quem creati sumus" (p. 167). Translation: *IPW*, p. 289.

[479] Przywara (1938), pp. 45–138.

[480] "Life experience shows that the human becomes most puzzling where the most extreme poles of the world meet: matter and spirit. In that the human is body and spirit, he becomes an entity" (Przywara, 1938, p. 50).

[481] Przywara (1938), p. 50.

[482] Ibid., p. 51.

has been transfigured, has become the *corpus glorificationis*. In the same way Mary's body—this view is not dogma, but is sanctioned by the Church—was directly received into heaven as *corpus glorificationis*. She is the only mortal, so to speak, to have this happen.[483]

The roots of this notion go back a very long way in the Church. A notion such as Przywara's naturally refers to this. But if one does not share this point of view, one has to ask oneself the question, "Is there a psychological experience that would somehow make this notion seem possible to us? Is there an experience that might underpin these assertions?" And I have to say, I could not demonstrate anything, directly, that would make such a notion seem possible somehow. I'm not talking about whether a body could actually transform directly into spirit, but about whether there is any kind of psychological occurrence or experience about which one could say, "It feels like that," as if a body had become spirit. True, we might say about a person that he has become very "*vergeistigt*," overly spiritual or intellectual.[484] But we don't mean his body. He only looks like that, a bit pale and emaciated, and terribly interesting, but we don't mean it literally. So it's not that kind of experience.

However, something we do know, in a quite quotidian and immediate way, is that man represents not the body becoming spirit [*Geistwerdung*], but a coming to consciousness [*Bewusstwerdung*] of the body: the person becomes conscious of the body. We know from medical experience that there are very many people who are not aware of their bodies, or only to a limited extent. They have no idea that they have some disease or physical ailment, or they do not even know what they look like. Those

---

[483] The Apostolic constitution *Munificentissimus Deus* (Lat.: "Most bountiful God") of 1 November 1950, written by Pope Pius XII, decreed *ex cathedra* the dogma of the Assumption of the Blessed Virgin Mary: "By the authority of our Lord Jesus Christ, of the Blessed Apostles Peter and Paul, and by our own authority, we pronounce, declare, and define it to be a divinely revealed dogma: that the Immaculate Mother of God, the ever Virgin Mary, having completed the course of her earthly life, was assumed body and soul into heavenly glory" (p. 44). There is no strong textual evidence for Mary's bodily assumption in the canonical scriptures, though it has been described in several apocryphal texts such as the *Liber requiei Mariae* (*Book of Mary's Repose*) from the fourth century, or the *"Six Books" Dormition Narratives* from the fifth.

[484] Trans. note: the German word "Geist" can be translated into English as both "spirit" and "mind," and incorporates aspects of both. This should be considered when reading this and the following lecture. In addition, Jung uses two related terms in this and the following paragraphs: *Vergeistigt* translates literally as "spiritual," but colloquially is a rather derogatory way of referring to someone who lives in the mind and is overly intellectual; Jung also uses the term *Geistwerdung*, which literally means "becoming spirit or mind."

are of course pathological cases, but there are people[485] who have to see their face in the mirror before they can speak, or who can completely forget about themselves physically, which can lead to serious health problems—they don't notice they're cold, for example. Or they are hungry but don't realize and think it's a psychological problem. Or they have a terribly unhealthy lifestyle and don't realize because they don't care about such things. So it is not to be taken for granted that a person is aware of their body. These unusual people have never properly experienced their body in reality. They only know in theory that they have a body. So when I become aware of my body to an extent, I translate the physical fact of the body into a mental experience. I have an image of my body. Gymnastics teachers will confirm that there are many people who have no idea about their musculature, or how they actually breathe.[486] And yet these are very important functions. Of course everyone knows that they breathe, but they don't know how wrongly they are doing it. They don't know that they're only breathing up here. Others know that. You can also see it in their posture. In the same way, many muscle groups are completely ungraspable for consciousness.[487] These people don't know how to innervate them.

But that is by no means spiritualization [Vergeistigung]; here we encounter a very dangerous misunderstanding: namely, calling this process of becoming conscious of the body Geistwerdung—"becoming spirit or mind." We think, in other words, that consciousness is the spirit, or we think that a conscious function, the intellect, for example, is the mind. Not a bit of it. Spirit, or mind, is something quite different. And we have indiscriminately adopted the three-part division of old: mind, soul, and body.[488] The soul is in the middle and does something or other here; the mind is what happens up here; the body is the raw material. Up there is your mind, as if consciousness were mind or spirit. I would thus initially quite cautiously say that man is not the body become spirit, but that awareness of the body means that a person knows who they are, how they are made, what they are called. No animal knows that. A dog does not

---

[485] RS has "ich hatte Patienten" (I had patients) instead of "es gibt Menschen" (there are people).

[486] Cf. Jung's lecture of 4 November 1938, in which he referred to Johannes Ludwig Schmitt's *Das Hohelied vom Atem* (1927) (*JMP*, vol. 6, p. 23).

[487] RS has "Deshalb sind viele Muskelgruppen durchaus unerreichbar" (That's why many muscle groups are completely unreachable) instead of "Ebenso sind viele Muskelgruppen für das Bewusstsein völlig unfassbar" (In the same way many muscle groups are completely ungraspable for consciousness).

[488] For a historical account of the concepts of soul and mind, see Makari (2016).

know that it is a dog, just as the stars do not know their names. Their names were thought up by astronomers.

And vice versa: the assertion that man is also an incarnation of the spirit is inaccurate as well. It's true that consciousness extends into the body and can have physical effects, but only to a very limited degree. There is a whole range of bodily functions that are never, under no circumstances, reached by consciousness. So only limited credence is to be given to this assertion.

We shan't go further into this problem of spirit and matter for now, but will continue following Przywara's contemplations. He now says that the two intersecting directions of spirit and matter cause a conflict, and refers to Galatians 5:17: "For the flesh lusteth against the Spirit, and the Spirit against the flesh: and these are contrary the one to the other: so that ye cannot do the things that ye would"[489] The ancient opposition between *pneuma* and *sarx*. He speaks of the "fall of the spirit into the chaos of the body."[490] He says the body should become spirit, and one asks oneself, whether in the end the spirit should also be body. He continues and says that the spirit rebels against the body. He even mentions an "uprising of the pure spirit against the humility of being bound to flesh,"[491] as if the spirit were suffering from a degree of hubris or arrogance and would not entertain the presence of the physical matter. He now actually switches to the antithesis: namely, whether the body also becomes spirit, and says that the matter of the body becomes God. It achieves divinity, or already has it, because in the body divinity appears as matter, so that through these contemplations the antithesis is actually canceled out to a large degree.

Now of course we have to ask ourselves again: does this polarity somehow exist in reality? Can we demonstrate it in psychological experience? Actually, this conflict does exist, between what we call mind or spirit, and what we call body. That is a long-known fact. There is no moral conflict where we cannot prove it; but whether the pairs of opposites in this conflict can be called spirit and matter is another question. We cannot, that is, directly experience spirit or mind. Initially it is simply the process of becoming conscious. The body is a mental something, nor can we experience

[489] *KJV.*

[490] "But the crowning darkness of the mystery of the salvation completes this revelation of the greater reality. For this reason the incarnate truth of God is submerged in the outward extent of physical suffering, and that is why the Holy Spirit, who fills the Church, is at the mercy of the flesh in order to atone in the way in which the sin was committed: in the fall of the spirit into the chaos of the body." (Przywara, 1938, p. 53).

[491] Ibid., p. 54.

matter directly, but would have to first ask modern physicists what matter actually is. We don't actually precisely know. You can read in the newspapers that matter consists of infinite mathematical formulas, which are therefore extremely abstract and difficult to imagine. Matter has disappeared into the realm of the inconceivable for us. It is no longer the density or weight of the *corpus*. That is a naive, antiquated view. Matter is something *toto caelo* unknown. We can only get an approximate idea of it. We have no idea whether modern physics has already progressed far enough to be able to make even an approximate assertion about the essence of matter.

And of course, the same is true of that which we call spirit or mind. It is definitely not what we call intellect or consciousness. Even the word "spirit" doesn't fully express it. We will come to what it actually means in a moment. We call something mental or spiritual when a psychological content has a certain quality that we designate as coming from the mind. In the same way, we call a certain quality of psychological experience material or physical if it has its origins in the body. What we imagine when we think of body or matter, and what we directly experience, is a psychic image. We only experience psychic images.[492] We have no direct experience of the things; that's why we need all kinds of tools to be able to establish to some extent their objective existence. All we have are psychological experiences of certain psychological conditions. We see colors and hear sounds, but there are no actual colors and sounds. They are physical mechanisms. There is the psychic phenomenon of the color, of the sound. So what we refer to as mental or spiritual is a translation of any kind of mechanism about which we are not sufficiently knowledgeable into a psychic phenomenon.

Namely, there are various words for "*Geist*" which reveal the original specific notions behind it. You know that the word for "spirit" in the New Testament, where it is used a lot, is *pneuma*. The original meaning of this word was simply "blowing," "breeze," "breath," "moved air"; by extension also "breath of life." It appears very often in the *Septuaginta*,[493] where

---

[492] In 1932, Jung formulated his understanding of psychic images as follows: "We perceive nothing but images, transmitted to us indirectly by a complicated nervous apparatus. Between the nerve-endings of the sense-organs and the image that appears in consciousness, there is interpolated an unconscious process which transforms the physical fact of light, for example, into the psychic image 'light.' But for this complicated and unconscious process of transformation consciousness could not perceive anything material" (Jung, 1932b, § 745). On the reality of psychic images, see Liebscher (2012), pp. 135–44.

[493] *Septuaginta* (Lat.): "seventy": abbreviation of *Versio septuaginta interpretum* (Translation of the seventy interpreters), known in English as the Septuagint. This is the

it actually simply means "life." It is often synonymous with the word *psyche*, soul. That has a similar origin: *psychros*, "cold," or *psychein*, "cool down," something that is "cooled down by a breath of wind," but it also means "desiccate," as the wind, when it is hot, can also dry things out. It also shares roots with the German words *pusten* or *blasen* [blow], which are also connected with breath. "Psychic" is that which breathes, so to speak. Thus in the Old High German translation of the Bible, the word "*Geist*", for example the Holy Ghost, is translated *Atum*, that is, *Atem* [breath]. Rightly so. It is a direct equivalent of the *âtman* in the East. That is also a breath, a sign of life.

The Latin word for *Geist* is *spiritus*. That also means "breath," and by extension, "soul." It comes from *spirare*, to blow, to aspirate. Then there is another word for spirit, namely *animus* and *anima*—*anima* is simply the feminine form. It fits with the Greek word *ánemos*, wind. This word is then found again in other languages, for example in Gothic: *usanan*, exhale; in Latin: *anhelare*, exhale, wheezing, rattling breath [*röcheln*]. The German word *röcheln* is onomatopoeic. It indicates the sound. Strangely, the same word is used for the sound dying people make when they breathe their last and exhale the soul [so "death rattle"]. In Swahili, the language of East Africa, it is called *roho*. That is a loanword from the Arabic *ruch*: that is, soul, spirit. It is connected with *rich*, the wind. These Latin, Greek, and Semitic words are simply different expressions for wind and breath. With the word *Geist* it is different. We'll look into that next time.

Latin name given to the earliest Greek translation of the Hebrew scriptures in the third and second century BCE. The name derives from the alleged number of translators involved. The Septuagint contains also the apocryphal or deuterocanonical scriptures.

Lecture 10[494]

LAST TIME WE began with Przywara's meditations, and we, initially at least, looked at how he deals with the word "man," *homo*, in the meditation. As we were examining this we came across the term *Geist*, and I told you my doubt about whether consciousness can rightly be called spirit. Consciousness is a representation, an imaging, and one can scarcely refer to consciousness as spirit. Neither can one say that the intellect is spirit— intellect is merely the capacity for thinking. And so we come to the question of what spirit actually is; or of which psychological experience is identified or expressed by this term. As a result, I initially tried to give you a definition through the etymology of those words that are used to express the experience of the spirit. We looked especially at the Greek word *pneuma* and the Latin words *spiritus* and *animus*. Today, we will look at the German word.

The German word *Geist* corresponds to the English *ghost*. It is related to the Norse word *geisa*: that is, "to rage." Here we see a new term that is not exactly identical with the soft breath of the *spiritus* or the *pneuma*. "Rage" indicates passion, fire or the like. It is also connected to the Gothic word *us-gaisjan*: that is, to agitate someone, get them into an emotional state, make them blow their top. We have a similar word in Swiss German: "'s isch zum Ufgeischte," as one says when a situation or a person is unbearable, when one gets into an intolerable emotional state. It corresponds to the English words *aghast* or *ghastly*. These particular origins of the word *Geist* are also seen in the general usage of the word and the associated metaphors. We say, for example, "geistsprühend" [sparkling wit], "Geistesblitze" [flashes of inspiration], or we talk about the fire or flames of the spirit. So you see immediately that *Geist* is associated with

---

[494] The text of this lecture is compiled from notes by LSM, ES, RS, and OK, as well as the English translation by BH.

enthusiasm or strong emotion; that is, with something fiery, flashing, even with light in general—the light of the spirit, for example.

These various images meet in the symbolism of the Pentecost miracle, as you will recall:

> And suddenly there came a sound from heaven as of a rushing mighty wind, and it filled all the house where they were sitting./ And there appeared unto them cloven tongues like as of fire, and it sat upon each of them./ And they were all filled with the Holy Ghost, and began to speak with other tongues, as the Spirit gave them utterance.[495]

The people who saw them said, "These men are full of new wine,"[496] as if they were drunk: in other words, they were in a state comparable to the effects of alcohol. That's why alcohol is also called "spirit," in all languages, the spirit of wine. That is also a spirit, of a particular kind. The volatile, hot, igniting feeling that surges through the blood when one drinks alcohol, that is spirit. That's why in Church symbolism the wine is called *spiritualis sanguis*, spiritual blood. The wine is the symbol of the blood and also of the spirit. These qualities of the term "spirit" also meet in this image.

So to sum up, we discovered from the Latin and Greek usages as well as from the Semitic languages—I mentioned the Arabic *ruch* which is associated with wind, corresponding to the Hebrew *ruach*—that these words always mean an animated or lively breeze, moving air or breath. *Pneuma* is not just air, but moving air. The Greek word for air is *aer*, while moving air or breath is called *pneuma*, and *psyche* also means a breath that is moving. The *atum*, the *spiritus sanctus*, the Holy Ghost, is therefore not *aer*, but *pneuma*. That's why it is also said that the Holy Ghost breathes between Father and Son.[497] It is a principle of life, just like the breath. And *spiritus* is also a sign of life. Thus in primitive imagery, the soul is the living breath. The last breath to leave the mouth of a dying person is the soul.

This sense of movement, of wind, also goes along with the word "rage." In German, we talk poetically about a "wütenden Windsbraut" [raging bride of the wind] or we say the "storm rages." That is the Greek *mainomai*: the passion, the ecstasy of an enthusiast who races like the wind, as if possessed by a wind demon which is propelling him forward. So this raging, this

---

[495] Acts 2:2–4 (*KJV*).
[496] Acts 2:13 (*KJV*).
[497] Cf. Dante's description of the Trinity cited in lecture 9 above, pp. 152–53.

racing ahead, is actually directly connected with the other image of the moving breath, except it is much stronger, expressed with much greater emotion.

German is a strangely devalued[498] language, isn't it? It is terribly hackneyed, which is why in my estimation it is much more advantageous to speak simply and unpretentiously in German, because the strong words are all well-worn and trite, and yet fraught with undomesticated barbaric life. The word *Geist* is thus actually a word of anger, in the same way that Wotan is an angry figure.[499] That is characteristic of the German mentality, which still gives expression to this barbaric condition of the psyche with considerable intellectual aptitude. German is a language that is still evolving in this regard, that has not completely freed itself from its primitive roots, in contrast to Latin, which has very fixed meanings. That's why German is the language most unsuited to philosophy, even though the Germans are the best philosophers. On the other hand, German is the best language for psychology, even though the Germans are, curiously, the very worst psychologists. But that is often the way, that unto him that hath shall not be given.[500]

Looking now at this word *Geist*, spirit, we see that it is a condition, a typical condition of mankind. If someone is lost in reverie, moved by something, carried away by the wind, compelled to move, animated, we talk of the spirit. So it is an augmentation of life and has nothing at all to do with the intellect or the like. A book such as Klages's *Der Geist als Widersacher der Seele* is relevant here.[501] Spirit has absolutely nothing to do with the intellect, but is an augmentation of life, a wonderfully elevated life even, as a consequence of which the phenomenon of the spirit in this sense always also meant possession by the spirit—because the primitive person cannot imagine this growth of life in any other way than that another soul, a spirit, has entered his soul, and is sitting on him, there on

---

[498] RS has "entwertende" (debasing, devaluing) instead of "entwertete" (devalued).

[499] Cf. Jung (1936b).

[500] This last paragraph was not included in the second edition (1959) of Barbara Hannah's translation.

[501] Ludwig Klages (1872–1956) was an influential German philosopher and psychologist as well as pioneer of graphology. Until 1904 he was a member of the Munich Cosmic Circle, a group of intellectuals around Alfred Schuler (1865–1923) promoting a return to pagan origins and a rejection of organized religion. His works include *Vom kosmogonischen Eros* (Of cosmogonic Eros) (1922) and *Der Geist als Widersacher der Seele* (The Spirit as the enemy of the soul) (1929–32), mentioned here by Jung. See Furness (2000), pp. 99–124, and Bishop (2017). On Jung's understanding of *Geist*, see his lecture at the Literary Society of Augsburg in 1926 (Jung, 1926).

the back of his neck. That's why they wear those amulets: because the unconscious is there, and I cannot see it. This spirit comes to me there and speaks through me, from behind, or from above through the fontanel, which according to Tibetan lore is where the soul also departs. That's why a person with an open fontanel always seems a bit odd, because the old channel of the soul is open and the soul can enter or leave. Or when someone dies, at the end of the death prayer the Lama makes a high-pitched sound that causes the skull to open and the soul exits through the air hole like a *miraculum* and separates from the body.

So the original idea of a spiritual state was that of possession by a spirit, by a breath-like creature. That is the original phenomenon. So if a primitive speaks unexpectedly in an elevated or strange way using uncommon words, he is immediately deemed *mana*,[502] or taboo, uncanny. People assume that he is a sorcerer, or is possessed, and make a big detour around him. For example, if someone speaks paradoxically or strangely, when someone insists that the flies danced, or a four-legged beast flew through the air, that proves that he is possessed. Because a sorcerer is always haunted by spirits.

These primordial ideas now clearly show us that the phenomenon of the spirit in the psyche causes an elevated state, or at least an unusual one. Or, to formulate it very cautiously, a change in the personality. This notion of spirit is, as you see, something quite different from the meaning one tends to associate with the term *Geist* in modern usage. But I am convinced that this is the original and actual meaning of *Geist*, that the *pneuma zoés* of the Old Testament, the spirit of life, is the true spirit. That is what people have always called spirit. And it is a condition in human beings. But what it actually is, in and of itself—that we have to be content leave to the realm of the unknown. This question is unanswerable. We only know that it is experienced in this way.

If we now apply the same critique that we have used for the term "spirit" to the term "matter," or "body," as would be fair, then we would also have to say, in this case, that body has nothing to do with matter. Matter or substance is an abstraction, in the past a philosophical term and

---

502 In "The Relations between the I and the Unconscious," Jung wrote about *mana* possession: "I therefore call such personality simply the mana personality. It corresponds to a dominant of the collective unconscious, to an archetype that has taken shape in the human psyche through untold ages of just that kind of experience. Primitive man does not analyze and does not work out why another is superior to him. If another is cleverer and stronger than he, then he has mana, he is possessed of a stronger power" (Jung, 1928a, § 388). Cf. Jung's lecture of 19 January 1934 (*JMP*, vol. 1, pp. 96–97).

now a scientific one, while body is a direct psychological experience of the soma. However, we cannot afford to get confused here. If you ask people today what the body is, they will give you a description of the anatomy or physiology which can be physically observed. But that is a scientific experience of the body, not a psychological one. The psychological experience of the body is how the soma is imaged in the psyche. That is quite another question: how I experience the body from within as a direct reality. After all, I am in my body. How does my body, which I myself am in, appear to me from the inside? If I examine this question in detail, I will discover very strange notions that have given rise to a series of the most curious symbols.

If you wanted to get an idea of how the body is experienced in the psyche, you would need to ask the yogis in India, or our medieval philosophers;[503] they know a thing or two about it. If you consider the body from the point of view of the psyche, you will be able to ascertain a sphere of consciousness up here,[504] with all kinds of strange sensations around it. Another center is in the heart area; before that there is one in the throat, and another one further down, in the belly.[505] These observations have not only been made by the yogis in India, but also by our medieval philosophers. In India the yogis meditated on them extensively. You too will realize that your anatomical knowledge tells you nothing about how you yourself fill your body. Indeed, you pervade your body as if with inner currents and thus you can flow into your limbs, which is how it is formulated in the *prâna* teachings of India.[506] If you follow these primordial images, if, for example, you say to yourself, "Let's assume there is something like

---

[503] ES has "Alchemisten" (alchemists) instead of "Philosophen" (philosophers).

[504] I.e., indicating probably the forehead, or just above the head: see next note.

[505] Tantric yoga differentiates between seven *chakra*s (wheels) containing the life energy or *prâna*. They are from the bottom to the top: the *mûlâdhâra-chakra* (root-foundation wheel) at the anus, the *svâdishtâna-chakra* (wheel of the self-base) at the genitals, the *manipura-chakra* (wheel of the jeweled city) at the navel, the *anâhata-chakra* (wheel of the unstruck [sound]) at the heart, the *vishudha-chakra* (pure wheel) at the throat, the *âjna-chakra* (command wheel) between the eyebrows, and the *sahasrâra-shakra* (thousand-spoke wheel), which is located outside of the physical body above the crown of the head. The chakras are connected through the the the central counduit along the spine, i.e., the *sushumnâ-nâdî*. The yoga practioner aims to awake the *kundalini-shakti* (serpent power), which lies dormant in the *mûlâdhâra chakra*, and raise it to the *sahasrâra-shakra*, where Shiva and Shakti are united. Jakob Wilhelm Hauer gave a seminar series on Kundalini yoga in the Psychological Club Zurich in 1932, which was accompanied by a psychological commentary by Jung (Jung, 1996 [1932]). There Jung gave a detailed account of the psychological meanings of the chakras. On the chakras, see Feuerstein (1997), pp. 67–69.

[506] See previous note.

a *prâna*," then you can achieve the oddest effects, innervate muscles that your consciousness would not have been able to reach any other way. For example you can warm up parts of your body that were cold, and such like. Feats like this, such as yogis can achieve, are nothing mystical at all; they are simply the application of the psychological *prâna* teachings. In this way you get an image of the human body that is *toto caelo* different from the anatomical image. That's why European physicians don't understand what Eastern doctors are talking about at all. They have this *prâna* concept, a system of channels that extend throughout the body. Modern doctors know, of course, that this is not anatomically true, but there is nothing mystical about the navel center: it is a functional center in the psyche, exactly as the heart area or the breath area is a psychological field. Certain things make us catch our breath. Some thoughts cause one to feel a pressure in the chest. In other cases, something presses on our stomach, gives us bellyache. This expresses the condition of the stomach, the activity of this particular center in the psyche.

So when we say "body," we are actually talking about how we experience the body. That has nothing to do with matter. Its relation to actual anatomy and physiology is very distant indeed. It cannot be identified. You can never prove there is a *prâna* channel that goes from the crown of the head all the way down to the big toe, and so in the West we say such teachings are complete nonsense. But *we* are the stupid ones, because we do not understand it. Pure and simple.

So the body is a condition, a psychological state, a peculiar kind of awareness. For example, if you think in your head—for now we'll say "think," but we could just as well talk about "psychic functioning"—it is quite different from when you do it with your heart. These two things are so different that for many people it is an incredible discovery to hear that one can also understand with the heart. Most people only function with this box up here[507] and have no idea that one can also comprehend things with the heart. I don't want to name names, but a very well known and famous man discovered that religion is not only a matter of the head, but also of the heart. We could go even further, couldn't we? If I say to a Negro[508] that one can understand the world through the gut alone, I'm not telling him anything new. For them, something is only a thought if it is felt in the belly. That's where their thoughts are and they also think down there—a Pueblo once said to me, "The Americans are all crazy because

---

[507] LSM added that Jung pointed to his eyes.

[508] LSM has "Inder" (Indian, i.e., person from India) instead of "Neger" (Negro).

they think in their heads." But thinking is done in the heart. The Homeric Greeks thought it was in the diaphragm: that's why intellect was called *phren*, that is, the diaphragm. We still use it today in "schizophrenia,"[509] to mean a mental splitting of the personality—we consider the personality to be located in the head, but it actually means diaphragm-split.[510]

Perhaps we should quickly investigate why Negroes, for example, think with their bellies. Now, we can assume that the abdomen or the stomach was the very first center to demand conscious attention, because food didn't just fly into people's mouths. That is probably also the reason why the stomach is still an organ of the psyche. The slightest psychological reactions cause all kinds of stomach complaints.

A little higher than the belly is the breathing function, and here we see symptoms such as heart complaints or breathing difficulties. Nearly all neurotic people have breathing problems, irregular or too-shallow breathing which they have to interrupt with deep intakes of breath and big sighs. Their breathing is inhibited because their soul is in this region around the heart. It causes enormous tension around the chest. The next center would then be around the mouth. It is not very clear, but in India they make this distinction. Thought connected with speech is located here, and you know how people can develop stutters and similar difficulties. And the next center is here in the head.

So, "body" and "spirit" are psychological states, conditions of psychic functioning. "Body" tells us just as little about what "matter" is as "spirit" tells us about whatever it is that is behind the word "spirit", behind the condition. It in no way tells us whether "spirit" is a spirit or, I don't know, a divine being. We only have this experience, which we express in this way. We have bodily conceptions and bodily experiences, and we also have conceptions of the spirit and conditions of the spirit, and these we perceive with consciousness.

Thus Przywara's meditation is actually incomplete, in that it gets stuck in certain predicated terms: that is, the term "spirit" and the term "matter." In reality, this contradiction certainly does not exist to such a great degree in the soul itself. In a way, we tear this contradiction apart when we

---

[509] The concept of schizophrenia was formulated by Eugen Bleuler in his seminal study *Dementia Praecox oder die Gruppe der Schizophrenen* (1911; Engl.: *Dementia Praecox, or the Group of Schizophrenias*,1950). He introduced it for the first time in a presentation entitled "Die Prognose der Dementia Praecox" (The Prognosis of dementia praecox) at the Deutsche Verein für Psychiatrie in Berlin in 1908. See Apelt-Riel (2009) and Bernet (2013).

[510] The last sentence of this last paragraph and the next two paragraphs can only be found in the script of OK.

say, "Here is spirit, down there matter, and a tremendous tension in between." That's not how it is in us *eo ipso*; rather, within us is a body that
can be experienced psychologically, a *prâna* body, a *subtle body*, and there
are states of sublimity, of ecstasy, of animation, of supernatural animation, and that is spirit. So in the same way that spirit is not spirit, then
body is also not matter, but both are actually modalities of the psyche.

Przywara then goes on to say that the person is actually a "medium
formale et materiale"—a medium of formal and material nature—and
here we can agree with him again. The formal is the spirit, the material is
the body. Man is a strange psychological unit of body-experience and
spirit-experience. It is an undivided oneness, which is only torn into two
parts when the intellect is at work. In other words, we think that the nature of our spirit-experience is wholly different from that of our body-
experience, and as a result this splitting occurs. I don't mean to say that
this split did not occur, or that it is nonsense that it occurred. If we were to
say that, we would deny the entire spiritual development of mankind. This
contradiction had to come about, the chasm had to be ripped open, or else
nothing would ever have been recognized, because it is only through differentiation that we understand.[511] If things are together, if white and
black are one and the same, we cannot recognize anything. And now Przywara
says that man, as a "medium formale et materiale," through his unified
nature portends the one who is the unity of everything that was ripped
apart in the Creation, and that is of course God.

Przywara now says literally about man,

> If, then, [man] as the center is objectively the analogy of God and
> subjectively there to proclaim God as the absolute center, then his
> activity is possible only insofar as he, incapable of clinging to himself,
> hangs completely in God (adhaerere, inhaerere, cohaerere Deo).[512]

This word "hanging" he gets from Ignatius's annotations. It is the "adhaerere, inhaerere, cohaerere Deo": "adhere to God, hang in him, cleave to
him." He says, "He is man, insofar as he is in God."[513] This unity, this

---

[511] Jung had entertained this thought already in *Liber Novus*: "If we do not differentiate, we move beyond our essence, beyond creation, and we fall into nondifferentiation,
which is the other quality of the Pleroma. We fall into the Pleroma itself and cease to be
created beings. We lapse into dissolution in nothingness. This is the death of the creature.
Therefore we die to the same extent that we do not differentiate. Hence the creature's essence strives toward differentiation and struggles against primeval, perilous sameness. This
is called the *principium individuationis*" (Jung, 2009, p. 347).

[512] Przywara (1938), p. 69.

[513] Ibid.

coincidentia oppositorum, this coming together of the opposites in the human soul, this psychic essence of man, is a metaphor, an allegory so to speak, or an analogy of God, because in God the opposites are eliminated. From this the purpose of man also emerges: through his own unity, to proclaim and represent the unity of God.

And in what condition, then, is man? Well, in fact, as an analogy of God he has a likeness to God, a likeness to the unity. But man is *creatus,* created. As a created being, man is not of himself, but is dependent on God. God is not only our *causa exemplaris,* our prototype, but also our *causa efficiens,* the efficient cause, on which we are completely dependent. Man is contained entirely in God, as it were, and this state is described by Przywara as a "hanging." And this hanging also refers—I'm getting ahead of myself here—to the hanging on the cross. It is a state of lack of freedom, a condition that is not determined by oneself, but by the producer, by the cause, namely by God himself. Because God is "in His essence the respective absolute center."[514]

And he continues, "Body and spirit 'rightly' belong together, insofar as man is 'rightly' in God."[515] So if the person is correctly suspended in God, then he is also right in himself: then body and spirit, that is, the conceptual poles, are rightly joined with each other. This unity is ensured by the *unum*[516] that is God—because God is the only way of being-in-oneself, says Przywara.[517] This being-in-oneself [*In-sich-Selbst-Sein*] is of course the epitome of "being oneself" or "existence of self" [*Selbst-Sein*]. God is the "existence of self." God is the self. He is the actual self, and insofar as man is congruent with God, then man is also an image of this self. Here you have the *âtman* lore in purest Catholic terms. God is thus *causa efficiens*: that is, the efficient cause, the "is" of all things. "Quod dat esse rei." That which gives the thing its existence. He is the actual being, the actual reason for being, the thing that guarantees existence at all. No existence outside of the divine. There is a direct correlation here with the Indian teaching, "I am the *âtman,* I am the world." The concept of God as the *causa exemplaris,* the prototype, with man as the copy is a Platonic idea that every yogi could accept easily: because the personal *âtman* is after

[514] Ibid.
[515] Ibid.
[516] RS has *medium* instead of *unum.*
[517] "God thus reveals Himself in humans, inasmuch as they are the center between matter and spirit, as He who absolutely penetrates everything by being absolutely in Himself, and is absolutely in Himself by absolutely penetrating everything" (Przywara, 1938, p. 69).

all the miniature *âtman*, the tiny creature living in my heart, no bigger than a thumb, but which at the same time is also the *âtman* that covers the whole world and contains everything in it. So up to this point we find complete concordance, except for Przywara's notion that man "hangs" in God. Instead of man being the free, uncomplicated, plant-like emanation[518] of God, there is a condition of compulsion, a state of suffering, because the hanging is a state of *suspensio in Deo*, a state of being suspended—and that is agony, a veritable torture. It is indeed a copy, but an agonizing suspended copy.

Curiously, there was an ancient mystery cult in which this notion became reality, with an annual festival celebrating it. It was the cult of Attis. Attis's mother Cybele loved him and suddenly made him go crazy, whereupon he castrated himself under a spruce into which his spirit transferred.[519] So every year at the time of the festival, a spruce was cut down and carried to Cybele's cave. A picture of the god was pasted on this spruce: the tree, that is, represented the god. The tree is a child of Cybele. Cybele is nature. If we think in Eastern terms, Attis is the spruce and stands in the womb of nature; he is the whole of nature itself. He is the purest expression, the purest image of Mother Nature. If, on the other hand, this image of a son of god[520]—that is, of Attis—is fixed to the tree, it is an expression of the *suspensio*, the state of being suspended, and of the agonizing death of Attis, whose corpse, so to speak, is then returned to his mother, namely for the resurrection. The cave of course symbolizes a grave. Life is buried like a grain of wheat in the earth's womb, whence it grows again. That was the mystical[521] idea in the Eleusinian mysteries, in the Attis cult, and suchlike.

But Przywara makes it even clearer. He says that the person as a unification of the active opposites, spirit and matter for example, is a crossing:[522] he uses the word *Kreuzung*. That is, two different tendencies, the somatic and pneumatic, cross each other in him like two express trains passing on the railway tracks. That is of course also a state of tension, of being suspended between two poles. Isn't that the same as the ancient depiction that we find in the Mithras cult, of the tragic death of the god Mithras,

---

[518] RS has "Erscheinung" (appearance, manifestation) instead of "Wirkung" (emanation, effect).

[519] This sentence was only recorded by LSM.

[520] ES has "Sonnengottes" (sun-god) instead of "Sohn Gottes" (son of god).

[521] LSM has "kultische" (cultish) instead of "mystische" (mystical), and ES has "Mysterien-Idee" (mystery idea).

[522] Przywara (1938), p. 69.

which takes place between the opposites?[523] Have you ever seen an altarpiece from the Mithras cult showing the *tauroktonos*?[524] The bull collapses as Mithras the matador plunges the sword into its throat. I remember one picture showing this scene. In the middle is the scene of the slaughter, flanked by *dadophoroi*, torchbearers: on one side, a torchbearer holds the torch up high, a kind of Eros in Phrygian garb; on the other side is another *dadophoros*, with the torch down low. The ascent and descent, like in the Heddernheimer Museum.[525] Up there is the sunrise, Helios driving up into the sky with his panting stallions, while on the other side, Luna descends. Day and night. It demonstrates that this sacrifice takes place at high noon: that is, between the opposites. It is the same as the image of the crucifixion: Christ on the cross between the two thieves. One will be with him in paradise, the other in hell—one goes up, the other down. These are the opposites between which Christ is crucified. These opposites are in a way played out within the person, and that's why Przywara calls it a crossing. The suspension between the poles he describes as a split or rift, and that is none other than a conflict between the opposites.

You don't find anything like this in India. Conflict is not part of Buddhism. Conflict is illusion. It consists of the opposites from which you are supposed to free yourself. *Nirdvandva* is freedom from the opposites. They are only *concupiscentia*.[526] I desire the world, all is illusion, and if I stop desiring, if I know with absolute knowledge that it is illusion, this whole *Nidana* chain, this chain of causality that leads ultimately to death and the entire sum of suffering, ceases. Buddhists in a way refuse to take part in the conflict.

For Przywara, the conflict is central. Here we see again an expression of this Western attitude of ours that is quite different. Our attitude to the world is extraverted. The world is desirable and beautiful; one can do and achieve something. The world is not a vale of sorrow. Yes, of course we complain about things—and in the very next moment say, "Then we'll improve it." We are hopeful, convinced that tomorrow everything will be

[523] Cf. Jung (1942a), §§ 342–43.

[524] *tauroktonos*: see n. 376.

[525] Heddernheim is a district of the German city of Frankfurt, which was the historical site of the Roman settlement of Nida. Excavations in the nineteenth century found the remains of three Mithraic temples. The findings were housed in the Archaeological Department of the Historical Museum of Frankfurt until 22 June 1937, when they were moved to the newly founded Museum für heimische Vor- und Frühgeschichte (Museum of native pre- and early history, since 2002 the Archaeological Museum Frankfurt).

[526] See n. 366.

better. *Reculer pour mieux sauter.*[527] While in India they say, "What non-sense! Nothing will ever change." And they don't have this split. We have this rift inside of us. For Indian people, it is external and was written off long ago. But we have given up having anything to do with this inner split. That's why we always have to locate it outside of ourselves. If we hear or read about a criminal who has been judged for his crime, we are happy to hear that someone else did something wrong and was caught—thank God it wasn't us.

---

[527] *Reculer pour mieux sauter* (Fr.): "draw back in order to jump further."

Lecture 11[528]

2 FEBRUARY 1940

WE HAVE ALREADY looked at Przywara's meditation on the first part of Saint Ignatius's "Fundamentum," and talked specifically about Przywara's understanding of mankind: his metaphysical position, as it were. As you heard, he considers man to be a *medium formale et materiale*, a medium between the *formale*, which refers to spirit, and the *materiale*, matter. Thus, according to Przywara, man is a likeness of God, who himself is a union of the great cosmic opposites. So you see that in his meditation Przywara views God as a uniting symbol. I have dealt with the concept of the uniting symbol in another context. If you are interested in learning more I recommend the fifth chapter of my book *Psychological Types*.[529] There I write about the symbol that is a *medium formale et materiale*.

So according to Przywara, man, as a union of opposites, is a likeness of God. Man is analogous to God and as such is actually in a certain sense the same as God. However, this particular identity relationship, if one may say so, is very problematic, because the state depicted by Przywara is far from being a state of identity,[530] rather it is a state of suspension in God, an *adhaerere, inhaerere, cohaerere Deo*, and an agonizing suspension at that. Because man is at the same time a conflict. Przywara calls it a rift, or split, as I mentioned last time. Man is actually not so much a union of opposites as a conflict of opposites. The contact of the opposites that takes place in man is not harmonious—it is something discordant. And yet man is completely encapsulated in God, hangs in God as it were, and represents God. The person is an image or copy of God. As a result, one would have to say that if man is a copy of God, the human condition is also a

---

[528] The text of this lecture is compiled from notes by LSM, ES, RS and, OK, as well as the English translation by BH.

[529] The fifth chapter of *Psychological Types* contains the section "The Significance of the Uniting Symbol" (Jung, 1921, pp. 189–220).

[530] LSM has "Ebenbild" (image or likeness) instead of "Identität" (identity).

copy of God. But Przywara doesn't give any more information about that. This problem only comes up once more, a bit later on. We'll talk about it then.

In any case, the copy that is at that same moment suspended in God is actually also substantially and essentially the same as the Godhead. Man only exists because he is dependent on God. God is the *causa efficiens* and the *causa exemplaris*.[531] Without God, men would not exist, and their form is dependent on the form of God; because God is man's *causa exemplaris*. Thus even the essence of man is in a way divine in nature. That is of course a very important point. Because here we have a concordance with the Eastern teaching, "I am the *âtman*, I am the world." But this teaching is not included in the Christian tradition—instead it is obfuscated, it is extraordinarily problematic, as I said. Nevertheless, we have proof in the Holy Scripture of the inner relatedness of man to the Godhead. Remember that part in the Gospel of John where it says,

> Jesus answered them, Is it not written in your law, I said, Ye are gods?/ If he called them gods, unto whom the word of God came, and the scripture cannot be broken;/ Say ye of him, whom the Father hath sanctified, and sent into the world, Thou blasphemest; because I said, I am the Son of God?/ If I do not the works of my Father, believe me not./ But if I do, though ye believe not me, believe the works: that ye may know, and believe, that the Father is in me, and I in him.[532]

So quite without a doubt he calls humans gods. This point refers to the Psalm 82: "I have said, Ye are gods; and all of you are children of the most High."[533] This psalm begins with the words, "God standeth in the congregation of the mighty; he judgeth among the gods."[534] I turned to the Vulgate for this verse, as I can't read Hebrew. It follows the Septuagint, the Greek-Jewish translation of the Old Testament. There it says, "Deus

---

[531] The Aristotelean differentiation of four different causes was an important thought in Scholasticism. According to Aristotle, things change due to a *causa materialis, causa formalis, causa efficiens*, or a *causa finalis*. The *causa efficiens* refers to a change or movement initiated by a thing apart from the thing affected by this change. Saint Thomas Aquinas (1225–74) added a fifth cause, the *causa exemplaris*, whereby God is the exemplary cause of his own efficacy. God is the *summum bonum* (highest good) toward which the human strives. The *causa exemplaris* of all beings is Jesus Christ.

[532] John 10:34–38 (*KJV*). Jung quoted from the Luther Bible edition of 1912.

[533] Psalm 82:6 (*KJV*). Jung quoted from the Luther translation.

[534] Psalm 82:1 (*KJV*). Jung again quoted from the Luther translation.

stetit in synagoga deorum in medio autem Deus deiudicat":[535] "God stands in the congress of the Gods, but in the middle he judges the Gods." So, to judge or make a judgment about someone. God is apparently here thought of as one who stands in the middle of the congress of Gods and judges his colleagues, his co-gods, as it were.

So we clearly see that this statement "Ye are gods" actually refers to the idea of gods and not to what is usually said, that it was the judges. That is the usual explanation: that the judges in Israel were referred to as gods. That is also true of course. It says that clearly in Exodus,[536] but Christ is not using the word in this sense. That's why he is also able to say of himself that he is the Son of God. When he says, "He that hath seen me hath seen the Father,"[537] he clearly means he is of the same essence as the Godhead. When he says to the disciples, "Ye are gods," he means it. It is quite beyond doubt that in Christian teaching the divine nature of men is completely valid.[538] However, as I have said, it is curiously obfuscated, in that Przywara says that this suspension in God could cause men to abuse their position in quite a diabolical way: namely, by claiming to be like God.[539] He evidently means that this suspension in God is also an identification with God that a person might also misuse in order to claim God-like qualities. Now, if a copy says, "I am similar," of course it can do that, but naturally it can also misuse it in the psychological sense: for example, if a drop of water in the ocean says, "I am the ocean." The water

---

[535] Psalm 81:1 (Biblia sacra vulgata [Vulgate]).

[536] For instance in the case of Exodus 22:8–9, *KJV* translates *elohim* as "judges": "If the thief be not found, then the master of the house shall be brought unto the judges, to see whether he have put his hand unto his neighbour's goods./ For all manner of trespass, whether it be for ox, for ass, for sheep, for raiment, or for any manner of lost thing which another challengeth to be his, the cause of both parties shall come before the judges; and whom the judges shall condemn, he shall pay double unto his neighbour." Compare this with the New Revised Standard Version: "If the thief is not caught, the owner of the house shall be brought before God, to determine whether or not the owner had laid hands on the neighbor's goods./ In any case of disputed ownership involving ox, donkey, sheep, clothing, or any other loss, of which one party says, 'This is mine,' the case of both parties shall come before God; the one whom God condemns shall pay double to the other." In his German translation, Luther used the plural "Götter" (gods).

[537] John 14:9 (*KJV*).

[538] RS has "geläufig" (common) instead of "gültig" (valid).

[539] Przywara (1938), p. 71: "That is then the consummated rupture, and this beyond all measures of nature, in the supernatural mystery of original sin: since man, who, in the mystery of participation in the divine nature, bears the God-center in the middle of his crossing, abuses this most inward and intimate 'hanging in God' for the greedy seizure of 'being like God,' and therefore falls prey to the worse rift, and is torn and torn apart by the demonic (for to wish to seize God is actually something diabolical)."

drop is part of the ocean, not the ocean itself, but nevertheless the nature of this part is essentially and substantially the same as the ocean. This idea also corresponds to a point from Augustine that is often used in medieval texts: "Deus est circulus cuius centrum est ubique, circumferentia vera nusquam":[540] "God is a circle whose center is everywhere but whose circumference is nowhere." And this center that is everywhere is of course in every person, and the circumference that is nowhere is the infinite perimeter.

Now, if there is an identification of this kind, then of course the possibility of diabolical misuse also arises: namely, that the droplet assumes it is the ocean, or the grain of sand in the Sahara believes it is the whole Sahara desert. That is what those who utter such things are always accused of. Because the devil is the *simia Dei*, the ape of God, an imitator of God. Apparently the most imperfect, agonizing, conflicted human condition is undoubtedly the particular condition of mankind. If someone has no conflict, they simply don't know it yet, but think their gut or their stomach in general is causing these symptoms. Of course they think they have nothing of the sort, but that's just self-deception. In reality one is never quite right if one doesn't have any doubt about oneself. Such a person would be mistaken, that's for sure. Doubt is generally a higher state than certainty. Because it is in doubt that the opposites meet, whereas in certainty the other leg is missing, there's always a limping one-sidedness.

Man, as a creature of conflict and doubt, needs a savior. That's why Przywara says that God repairs the rift through Christ's crucifixion.[541] What is noteworthy here is how this word "crucifixion" fits with the intersection

---

[540] "God is an infinite sphere whose centre is everywhere, whose circumference is nowhere." Jung quoted the phrase also in letters to Max Frischknecht (8 February 1946) and Günther Däss (12 July 1947) (Jung, 1973, vol. 1, pp. 412 and 471). He wrongly attributed it to Augustine. Copenhaver (1992, p. xlvii) and Bishop (2002, p. 81) have identified it as the second maxim of the twelfth-century hermetic text entitled *Book of Propositions or Rules of Theology, Said to be by the Philosopher Termegistus*, also known as the *Book of the Twenty-Four Philosophers*. Marcilio Ficino (1433–99) gave ten different interpretations of it in the *Tractatus de Deo et anima vulgaris* (1457). Jaffé and Adler in Jung (1973), vol. 2, p. 18, n. 8, comment that the phrase "Deus est sphaera infinita, cuius centrum es ubique, circumferentia vero nusquam" can also be found in the *Itinerarium mentis ad Deum* (The mind's road to God), a work that is attributed either to Bonaventura (1221–74) or Giordano Bruno (1548–1600). In his essay *The Fearful Sphere of Pascal* (1962), Jorge Luis Borges described the conceptual history of this metaphor from Xenophanes to Bruno. See also Jung's lectures of 12 May 1939 (*JMP*, vol. 6, p. 202) and 23 February 1940 (this vol., p. 214).

[541] Przywara (1938), pp. 71–72: "But the answer of God in the redemption is then that God himself steps into this rift to be torn and torn apart in order to defeat the 'prince of this world' and to free men from their bondage to him[.]"

of the opposites within people. This will be confirmed, as we shall see. The *crucifixio Christi* is known to signify redemption. I must admit that, despite my Christian upbringing, I have never understood why the *crucifixio* should mean redemption. I thought I must be particularly stupid, but in my almost sixty-five years of life I have met quite a number of other people who didn't understand it either. One says it without thinking and hears it often, but one never really understands why the act of someone else being nailed to a cross should heal the conflict. Because that's how it is supposed to be: because of our imperfection, Christ was nailed to the cross. Przywara says clearly, "Man is the crucifixion of God." The human is the hanging on the cross, and is thus to an extent identical with it, with this suffering of God's son, the suffering of God. This expresses quite clearly that this human suffering is not just our own imperfection, our own suffering, but that this suffering is also present in God. It is the suffering of God that is revealed in the figure of Christ. Where does the suffering come from? From the conflict. So the conflict is in the Godhead. That is a thought that should not be spoken.

When the suffering is so great that the atonement required is the *crucifixio*, one naturally asks what caused it. What is the crime for which the son of God had to suffer this punishment? Evidently the sinfulness[542] of men, which through the death of the son becomes conscious and atoned for. Our debt is paid. We are then released from this debt through the crucifixion of the son of God.

Now, it is said that Christ was innocent. Only the guilty party should suffer the punishment, but here the innocent one takes the punishment on behalf of the others. If we consider Christ from the human perspective, not the dogmatic one, the question arises: what is the psychological debt of Christ that caused him to be punished? What was missing in his life? Where did he incur debt? We can say it in one word: he was no animal. That was his failure: that he did not live the animal side of human nature. What is men's crime? It is precisely that they are animals, that they are carnal, that they live as animals, which keeps them unconscious. That is the debt of men that has to be and is discharged by the atoning death of Christ. Because the conflict within man is after all this conflict between *materiale* and *formale*. The *materiale* is the flesh, the *formale* is the spirit. These are the opposites that rage inside men: namely, the principled, form-giving nature of the spirit, as opposed to the formlessness

---

[542] ES has "Schuldhaftigkeit" (culpability) instead of "Sündhaftigkeit" (sinfulness), and RS and LSM have "Unvollkommenheit" (imperfection).

and intemperance of simply blindly drifting along. This opposition is not answered by remaining at the level of the usual instinctual man, who exists as instinctively as an animal that experiences no conflict. Or the conflict is pushed aside, and as a result all spirituality or intellectual thinking is also foregone. Those who pride themselves on living instinctively and having no conflict are simply ignoring their inner humanity. But those who make the opposite mistake—living only in the mind—are punished from the other side.

Przywara calls these opposites that meet in man the timbers of the cross that join in the middle from right, left, above, and below. That for him is the symbol of the opposites that agonizingly combine in the human being in the form of conflict and in the image of Christ. That's why one often says "the cross" instead of "Christ"—"the cross redeemed us." It is the expression of a symbol. Przywara says that the crossing, the intersection of the opposites, is the redemption. In other words, those who are unaware of the conflict, who are only spiritual or only material, are not redeemed. Only when people are in this state of uncomfortable doubt or conflict are they redeemed.

Of course, we do not think we are redeemed when we are in this state of doubt or conflict. We think, "This is all wrong,"—and that's when it is exactly right. Because there's no other way to reach a higher consciousness than by experiencing some pain or suffering. No one ever undertook anything[543] when they were feeling fine. One has to get into a wretched state before one will do something. That is the great psychological meaning of the glorification of suffering in Christianity, and that is what we have to criticize in Buddhism—that they leave out the conflict.[544] *Nirdvandva* means, "I am free of the opposites, neither right nor left, neither up nor down." The yogi thus grows up into a higher unconsciousness which is called *bodhi*, meaning "enlightenment" or "consciousness." In the West, we assume the yogis are all engrossed in a realm of higher consciousness, but they have simply entered a trance-like state and return with a feeling of bliss, as if after a deep sleep. That is not consciousness, but unconsciousness. And it is certainly true that if you can get yourself into an unconscious

---

[543] RS has "Der Mensch hat sich noch nie in einen anderen Zustand versetzt" (No one ever shifted into a different state) instead of "Der Mensch hat noch nie irgendetwas unternommen" (No one ever undertook anything), and ES has "Der Mensch hat noch nie etwas geändert" (No one ever changed anything).

[544] OK has "dass er den Konflikt weglegt" (lay aside the conflict) instead of "dass er den Konflikt weglässt" (leave out the conflict), and ES has "Leiden" (suffering) instead of "Konflikt" (conflict).

state you feel revitalized, like when Antaeus touches the earth.[545] I am reminded here of the parallels in the myth of Antaeus, who was a giant and the son of Poseidon and Gaia. He forced all strangers to wrestle him, and in every case won and killed them. Every time he touched his mother, the earth, he gained renewed strength. Finally Heracles managed to overcome him by holding him up in the air until he suffocated.

It is not that a state of conflict is always the most desirable thing— sometimes this state can be so destructive that one wishes one could free oneself from these opposites and sink back down into an unconscious state where nothing matters in the least. That is the great thing about Indian people, that they have learned that so thoroughly. But they should use words we understand and say that the state they attain is unconsciousness, not consciousness. Buddhism is a bit different in this regard, as Buddha is also conscious of something that transcends consciousness, and that cannot be anything other than "no consciousness." It is different from consciousness.

So as you see, Przywara regards man himself, his psychological existence which is essentially conflictual, as the cross. Man is not just crucified, he is the actual cross—like in the old Christian depictions where Christ is not nailed to the cross, but stands in front of the cross with arms outstretched because he himself is the cross.[546] I have seen one of these crosses. It's from around the eleventh century and shows Christ pulling the nails out of the cross and walking away from it. It is very unusual. It's held in the Germanisches National Museum in Nuremberg.

Przywara says,

> By God as savior descending into man, His countenance appears in the real man in-between, the *soul* as the midpoint between pure body and pure spirit. But by Him as savior descending into man as the rift, His countenance appears in the *soul*, insofar as it is to be *saved from being lost (salvar)*—i.e., God appears in the guise of the "rift as cross."[547]

This means that the soul is a cross. That is true in the fullest sense of the word. The human soul is a cross. Also in the figurative sense if we say it is a cross with this psychology. Because *crux* also means "torment." This becoming conscious, this recognition of the conflicted nature of man, is a

[545] The rest of the paragraph can only be found in OK.
[546] The rest of this paragraph can only be found in OK.
[547] Przywara (1938), p. 73 (including emphasis).

cross to bear. That's why we'd rather ignore it. We don't want to recognize our faults, lest we discover something unpleasant that causes a conflict, and that would be a cross. And we completely forget that the opposite that we carry inside ourselves—that that is also me. The other in me is also part of me, and if I recognize that, then it is a cross, a crucified state, because I am suspended between the opposites. Then I am thrown into doubt, I no longer know what to do. That's precisely how it is: you feel doubtful, and when you do something you can only hope that it happens from both sides. Not only spirit, not only matter, but something alive. And that which is alive is never absolutely sterile and pure, but is somewhat murky. Przywara says ultimately that God himself appears on the cross. So God himself is also this cross. God himself is a torment. God is a cross for us, a cross imposed on us. And if we realize the conflict within us, if, that is, we consciously accept the conflict, then we accept the cross, and this cross is God himself. As Nietzsche says, "You sought the heaviest burden and you found *yourself*."[548] He might just as well have said, "You found God." This encounter with oneself is the encounter with God. This other is me and at the same time it is God. People in India understand that without any problem. Whatever I encounter is me, it is *âtman*, it is my essence. But what the Indian person doesn't say is that this encounter is the most painful thing, that we are our own most painful experience. We don't want to understand that here either, and in India it is rejected in order that one can be free of this torment. Of course, there are good reasons for that in Indian psychology. You can't resent the Indians for wanting to escape these opposites. But with us it is not like that. We are supposed to become aware of our own inner opposites, but we must also doubt ourselves.

If, according to Przywara's meditations, we have to call the experience of conflict an experience of God, it is understandable that he proclaims, using the words of Holy Saturday no less, "O happy fault, which gained for us so great a Redeemer!"[549] It's not just a *façon de parler*[550] when one

---

[548] From Nietzsche's poem "Zwischen Raubvögeln" (Amid Birds of Prey), in Nietzsche (1891) (*KSA*, vol. 6, pp. 389–92; Engl.: 1945, p. 45). Jung also quoted this poem in "Wandlungen und Symbole der Libido" (1911–12, § 469) and "The Relations between the Ego and the Unconscious" (1928a, § 373).

[549] Przywara (1938), p. 73: "But then more deeply it means: everything standing in the reality of the cross is right insofar as it leads to the praise of God, as in the Exultet of Holy Saturday original sin and Good Friday become one psalm: 'O happy fault, which gained for us so great a Redeemer!'"

[550] *façon de parler* (Fr.): "manner of speech, way of speaking."

says that suffering is a cross to bear. It *is* a manner of speaking, but in saying it one is also saying that suffering is actually God himself. It is like in the legend of Saint Christopher:[551] Christopher wants to carry a child over the stream, but when he is in the water, the child gets heavier and heavier and he can hardly reach the other side. Then he realizes that he was carrying the Lord himself. This Lord, this child, is also Christopher himself. So Przywara now sees the fact that man is crucified with Christ between heaven and hell as being the actual meaning of human existence. Man is in reality only in the cross, created by Christ. Christ makes it so that the person is only real in the cross. Przywara refers here to the Epistle to the Ephesians: "For we are his workmanship, created in Christ Jesus unto good works, which God hath before ordained that we should walk in them."[552] Namely, we are his product. We are the product of Christ: that is, in other words, the symbol of Christ teaches people that they themselves are a cross, that they themselves are sufferers, that they are in a state of conflict and that that which they are afraid of, namely the conflict, is themselves. Those who avoid the conflict, avoid themselves.[553]

Now we are actually finished with Przywara's meditations on the "Fundamentum." Of course, there is lots more one could say about his meditations, but that would take us too far. I just wanted to touch on the main points. Now we just have to look briefly at the third section of the "Fundamentum":

It follows from this that one must use other created things in so far as they help towards one's end and free oneself from them in so far as they are obstacles to one's end.[554]

With that, a thought is again expressed that was already intimated at the start with the "Creatus est homo." That is, that men are in this state of suffering, in this state of conflict, for a very specific purpose and goal, so that a very particular ethical stance also seems logical to them; in fact is even enjoined of them: namely, only to use that which is necessary to reach their purpose, and to let go of that which may prevent them reaching that purpose.

And now the "Fundamentum" continues,

---

[551] Saint Christopher, a martyr killed in the third century, is the patron saint of travelers.

[552] Ephesians 2:10 (*KJV*). Przywara wrote, "Lifting of the deception of unbroken progress, rise of the truth of the cross: that we 'are' only out of mercy and 'are' only in the cross: 'created in Jesus Christ'" (1938, p. 76).

[553] OK has "schaut" (looks at) instead of "scheut" (avoids).

[554] *IPW*, p. 289.

To do this we need to make ourselves indifferent to all created things, provided the matter is subject to our free choice and there is no prohibition. Thus as far as we are concerned, we should not want health more than illness, wealth more than poverty, fame more than disgrace, a long life more than a short one, and similarly for all the rest, but we should desire and choose only what helps us more towards the end for which we are created.[555]

The main accent is put on the end for which we are created. And what is this goal? You know what the goal is in the Christian symbolism or Christian faith. Psychologically, based on what we have just discussed, it is initially the awareness of the conflict. From that, from the conviction that the conflict is our truth, it should follow that we also want this conflict, that we can say yes to it. When we can say yes, the goal also emerges: through the conflict alone we reach a higher level of consciousness—in that we know not just one of us, but also the other.

This increase in the state of consciousness is always the secret of all cultures. All culture is increased consciousness. All barbaric culture, everything primitive, is characterized by a lower state of consciousness: namely, by a consciousness that is still completely caught up in the life of the drives, in which nothing becomes conscious unless it is shoved under one's nose by a drive: that is, in which we are still completely caught up and trapped in the emotions of our drives. A higher state of consciousness, however, always means reining in the drives, control, mastery of the emotions. Not complete suppression, but control, specifically a control that allows people to exist as lively creatures despite their world of drives and despite their emotionality. Culture that is only a prison is not culture. Discipline for discipline's sake is not culture. Culture means a possible expression of drives and emotionality within the limits of what is reasonable, for individuals and for humanity. Culture is not disciplinarianism, asceticism, suppression; culture is giving nature freedom within a certain measure, within human bounds. Those people who are merely in thrall to their emotions, their illusions, their drives, and are dragged along by them, might just as well be a carriage in a train or a sheep in a flock. That is not culture. Culture is much more a consciousness that has a certain power, namely a power that is equal to the blindly emotional and libidinal impulses, and that, like a benevolent father, tolerates them to an extent, so long as they do not overstep certain limits. But if the drives exceed those

[555] Ibid.

limits, that paves the way to unconsciousness: so into a lower state of culture, a destructive state, and that is the devil—because the devil destroys all works of the Godhead, and the Godhead is, as you just heard, the suffering, the conflict, the cross. And so Christianity was, for example, a moment in the history of mankind at which a higher level of consciousness was reached. If you compare the other religions that were contemporaneous with Christianity, you'll see the difference quite clearly.

The Dionysian element in the ancient world was a glorification of the emotional, the libidinal, the uninhibited. It was a kind of lowering, a letting-oneself-go into the most unbridled unconsciousness. We see this in particular in the cult and legends of Dionysus with those frenzied females tearing apart live animals with their teeth. These are things that actually happened, not just fables. These cults have been maintained until this day in Morocco, under the guise of Islam: the whirling dervishes are remnants of the old cult of Dionysus. That's why Dionysus's retinue consists of satyrs, creatures with cloven feet or horse-like hooves, who represent simply the idea of the half-man, half-animal—which is how people in antiquity were. That's why they were so beautiful. Well, in reality they weren't so nice, but nevertheless they created immortal works and an ideal of beauty that we can only envy. But you know the best cabbage always grows on the dung heap. In Pompeii, for example, there was only one single *water closet*, and the rest you can imagine. I'll leave you to picture the result yourselves.[556]

The ancient world was built on social conditions that were truly without equal. The awful state of those times was worse than anything seen since—until today. Three-fifths of the population were slaves, a dreadful situation which the old Romans were very well aware of and tried to ameliorate with all kinds of people-friendly legislation, enfranchisement, and so on. But it didn't help. Even the first Christian bishops still had house slaves. It wasn't until the advent of Christianity that things changed, but the transformation came from within, not through external laws or social measures. Each person received the center of God—not just emperors, kings, or aristocrats. With Christianity, each person had the divine soul inside them, and each person was granted dignity. That's what finally led to the downfall of the ancient world.

[556] In contrast to Jung's claim, ancient Pompeii had an elaborate water system and most of the houses were equipped with lavatories built over lavatory pits. When flushed with a bucket of water, the lavatory pit discharged into a cesspit near the house. On the drainage system of Pompeii, see Poehler (2012).

Lecture 12[557]

LAST TIME, WE finished looking at Przywara's modern Jesuit meditations on the "Fundamentum." I read you the meditation on his anthropology, namely on his view of man as an analogy of God. God, in Przywara's conception, is a union of the opposites. The Godhead contains the opposites, encompasses them, and has unified them within itself, while man is stretched taut between these opposites. Man is also the opposites as *pars totius*.[558] Man as part of the Godhead takes part in the whole being, in the substantial essence of the Godhead, and consequently also in the opposites, and these opposites mean conflict. That is why man is primarily a creature of conflict. We are taut with tension so to speak. We hang between the opposites and are therefore analogous to the suffering God who is presented to the world in the figure of Christ—because in Catholic theology Christ is, as you know, at once true God and man. Therefore, Christ is also a representation of the opposites contained in God. He is the solution, the uniting of the opposites, but at the same time in his true human nature he is also suspended in the opposites. He is crucified. Because the cross is the perfect expression of the pairs of opposites that combine into one point, so to speak, and Christ with his suffering is stretched out over this point. Christ therefore represents God in his state of suffering. God is also an affliction: to be precise, an affliction within man, because he is the suffering man. And thus man is actually in turn an analogy of Christ insofar as he suffers, but only insofar as he suffers. As God is the *causa exemplaris* of man suspended between the opposites, Christ is not only the *causa exemplaris*, but also the *causa efficiens*. We are created in Christ,[559]

---

[557] The text of this lecture is compiled from notes by LSM, ES, RS, and OK, as well as the English translation by BH.

[558] *pars totius* (Lat.): "part of the whole."

[559] Ephesians 2:10: "For we are his workmanship, created in Christ Jesus unto good works, which God hath before ordained that we should walk in them" (*KJV*).

and created by him,[560] as it is said; that is, from the suffering man, from the human which Christ is.

You must always keep this idea in mind as we continue with the other parts of the *Exercitia spiritualia*. In connection with the "Fundamentum" and as *praeparatio*, by way of preparation and introduction, there is also an Ignatian prayer that gives a classic impression of the attitude of the meditator or exercitant who is preparing to undergo the exercises. Once again, it is a Latin prayer. It begins,

> Suscipe, Domine, universam meam libertatem. Accipe memoriam, intellectum atque voluntatem omnem. Quicquid habeo vel possideo, mihi largitus es: id tibi totum restituo, ac tuae prorsus voluntati trado gubernandum. Amorem tui solum cum gratia tua mihi dones, et dives sum satis, nec aliud quicquam ultra posco.[561]

> (Take, Lord, and receive all my liberty, my memory, my understanding, and my entire will all that I have and possess. You gave it all to me; to you Lord I give it all back. All is yours, dispose of it entirely according to your will. Give me the grace to love you, for that is enough for me.)

This prayer shows you the attitude that is characteristic not only of a person undertaking the *exercitia*, but also the general formulation of religiosity in the West: namely, this surrender to the figure that one sees before one. The Easterner would say, "What you see before you is a thought figure. It's a figure created through your meditation, a creature from your thoughts,"—which for the Easterner is nonetheless real, for the Easterner, in identifying with the *âtman*, is the world-creating being. People in the East can thus from their own minds produce figures that are real, even though they are thought beings. Their gods are, as they well know, thought-figures, and yet they really are gods. We Westerners cannot understand that at all, because we assume that if Christ is not really—*vere, realiter et substantialiter*[562]—standing in front of us, there is nothing. We cannot imagine that we could also create such a figure, albeit under certain conditions. These conditions may not be expressly formulated, but they are

---

[560] Colossians 1:16: "For by him were all things created, that are in heaven, and that are in earth, visible and invisible, whether they be thrones, or dominions, or principalities, or powers: all things were created by him, and for him" (*KJV*).

[561] The Latin version Jung uses here is from MHSI-MI, Versio vulgata, p. 308. Translation: *IPW*, p. 329.

[562] See n. 191.

present in the teachings of the East: one cannot simply create any old figure; it has to be one that is somehow present in the essence of man. But what is this essence in the East? It is the *âtman*. I can imagine the *âtman*, because I *am* the *âtman*. Western people do not know that, do not know that they are imagining their essence. But from the meditations it becomes clear that as *pars totius*, as part of the Godhead, the meditator has the ability to imagine this thought creature. That is the purpose of icon worship in the Church. It is a means of concretization, to help people have the ability to clearly imagine these figures. Exactly like in the East, where the images per se mean nothing, but are merely *yantra*s, tools, to help one imagine the thought figures, and the thought figure is the real thing.[563]

So people in the West give their whole being, their whole physical existence, so to speak, to this other creature standing in front of them, and of course one can hardly say without becoming blasphemous that it is perhaps a thought being. For people in the East, it is quite obvious. For us, it causes our brains a great deal of trouble, because we think that that which we create with our mind is nothing, simply air. Why? Because it cannot be proven with chemical formulae or weighed on the scales. But it is nonetheless a reality, it is a reality just like any plan a person might come up with to build a bridge or design a locomotive. That is not real either, it only exists in the designer's head. Not until it is constructed in metal and stands before us do we say it is real. But for someone in the East, it is real immediately.

Thought creatures are entirely real. If, for example, we hear of people with strange ideas we think we can simply say, "That's illogical, it's totally unreasonable! Just send someone over and tell them!" And then we wonder why that's no use at all. Only well-meaning ignoramuses believe it's possible to set other people on the right path just by telling them what to do. They would never dream of doing it. They are possessed, and this possession is a reality. But we are so stupid that we think that if someone is possessed they are possessed by air, that it is nothing, just nonsense. But possession is an absolute fact. The usual methods are no use at all in such cases. You can't talk people out of it. Mere talking gets you nowhere. These are psychic realities[564] that cannot be criticized with the usual methods. They are psychological facts, albeit ones that do not fit into our usual

---

[563] Jung drew his knowledge of the *yantra* mainly from Heinrich Zimmer's book *Kunstform und Yoga im indischen Kultbild* (1926) (Engl.: *Artistic Form and Yoga in the Sacred Images of India*, 1984). See Liebscher's introduction to *JMP*, vol. 6 (pp. lx–lxiii).

[564] See n. 492.

schema. But who told you that was the only right one? If there's enough time left, we still might learn someting.

This prayer demonstrates how absolutely Jesuits tried to surrender in order to make it through the exercises. You can easily imagine that even if one only partially achieves this attitude, the whole undertaking of such an exercise sequence is a very serious business that takes hold of people at the deepest level. Not, however, because one has to tell oneself unpleasant things and it is arduous, but because one is dealing with symbols that are suitable expressions for the innermost essence of man, that strike a chord somewhere deep inside. And at the end of the day, that is the reason such exercises exist at all, and why they can exert such a great influence on a person's mentality.

The order of the individual exercises differs depending on the place and the time. I've already said a bit about that. The sections we've been talking about, which I treated as a kind of introduction, can also be meditated on at other points in the exercises. As I said, the exercise leader is free to and indeed is supposed to individually tailor the sequence, and depending on the exercitant's abilities may bring one or the other section forward or leave it until later. So the order is not absolutely set in stone, although the overall content is strictly formulated. When all the exercises are done, all these individual parts will have come in somewhere. Usually the *examen generale et particulare* forms the introduction to the actual exercises, which, as you will have noticed, we have still not come to. This *examen* is an examination of one's own conscience that one undertakes in order to purify and prepare oneself. I want to use an old Jesuit introduction to explain a few points here.[565] We don't have time to go into great detail.

So, the intention is that the soul will be purified through a scrupulous examination, a scrupulous investigation of one's own condition, that is, of one's whole psychic make-up. It is a kind of mental analysis of one's own mind. The criteria set are naturally the traditional standards established by the Church doctrine about what is sinful, what is good, and so forth. So it says, "The soul is purified by the acknowledgment of the inner roots of vice in order that they be eradicated."[566] That also includes carefully noting individual occurrences in which these bad characteristics have been displayed, and noticing the specific conditions under which such things

---

[565] Izquierdo (1695).
[566] Izquierdo (1695), p. 23: "Purificatur anima cognoscendo internas radices vitiorum, ut extirpentur; notando externas occasiones casuum, ut caveantur."

happen, so that they can be avoided. So in a way you have to look at your whole life from this angle in order to put all your faults, anything which might be deemed sinful, under the microscope, so that they can be rooted out.

The form under which this examination of conscience is to take place is also prescribed. Firstly the timing of each individual event has to be established: When did it happen? Where? In relation to what? And then one has to undertake to avoid this sin, and one can do that by deciding not to commit this sin for a whole morning long, not even slightly, and in the afternoon checking whether or not anything of the kind did indeed happen in the morning. Now, if despite this careful research and monitoring it is not possible to eradicate something straight away, the *examen particulare* follows: that is, a particular examination of conscience with regard to this case. In this case the exercitant has to examine in detail how it happened that this sin, or at least the temptation to sin, came near again. Izquierdo says that those who take it seriously may even carry a string of little beads and every time they stray again they make note of it by pushing one bead to the other side, like an accounting of individual *défaillances*.[567] Or they keep a notebook in which they mark lines to show how often in a day they had bad thoughts or other lapses. This is all done as scrupulously as possible and, as I said, like keeping an actual ledger of accounts.

This *examen generale et particulare* is generally the preparation for the first exercise. It is called the "meditation with the three powers on the first, second and third sins." Specifically, it is the exercise on mortal sin. What does "mortal sin" mean? The Church distinguishes between *peccatum mortale et veniale*, mortal sin and venial sin. The first is the serious kind of sin, while the second is the kind of sin that arises from ignorance, indifference, or foolishness. *Peccatum mortale* is an intentional sin in which one knowingly contradicts God. One deliberately puts oneself in opposition to God. Our author, a seventeenth-century Spanish Jesuit says about that, "There is actually only one single mortal sin, which consists in putting one's goal in the creature and not in God."[568] That goal is the one we already talked in regard to the "Fundamentum." So in other words, it means that if you set your human goal above the spiritual goal of attaining God or of being reintegrated into the Godhead, you commit a mortal

---

[567] *défaillances* (Fr.): "failures."
[568] Izquierdo (1695), p. 33: "Est autem unicum dumtaxat, scilicet peccatum mortale: nam hoc ponit ultimum finem in creatura, & non in Deo."

sin. "No God, no heaven, no grace can now help the man who commits such mortal sin, and thus we should direct our human hate toward this enemy."[569] This is the end, then, which the exercises serve.

So you see, according to this view, the vast majority of Western humanity would be in this state of *peccatum mortale*. Come now, it's no laughing matter. Now, let us for a moment try to ventilate this view: here is a doctrine which, however many millions adhere to it, is contradicted to such a huge extent by the behavior and attitude of countless millions of other people. This of course means an enormous psychological difference between the people who are aligned with and adhere to such thinking, and the others who emphatically do not have this attitude, who have absolutely no idea of anything of the sort. Insofar as this conception really is the Christian view, and has been since time immemorial—namely, that man's goal is in God and not in the creature—then we can state emphatically that the great majority of Western humanity has fallen by the wayside. In fact, they are all fiendish brutes. Well, are they or are they not? We will see about that. If Russia, for example, saw the attainment of God's grace as its sole goal, there would have been no Finnish war and other such atrocities.[570] So if we strictly apply the genuine Christian teaching, we would have to say that Christianity has actually ceased to be a world religion. That's simply incontrovertible.

This meditation on the *peccatum mortale* takes place in three stages. That's why they are called the first, second, and third sins: first, one meditates on the sin of the angels. It begins in the metaphysical realm. The "sin of the angels" refers to the insurrection of Lucifer against the *monarchia Dei*, the autocracy of God, and the subsequent fall of the angels. This is followed by the contemplation of the sins of the first parents, Adam and Eve. And then comes the third stage: the contemplation of one's own

---

[569] Ibid.: "Atque adeo, vel unico stante in homine peccato mortali, nec Deus, nec Coelum, nec Salutatio pro illo est. Quapropter contra hunc inimicum totum nostrum odium, & bellum est impendendum."

[570] On 30 November 1939, the Soviet army invaded Finnish territory, marking the beginning what is known as the Winter War between the USSR and Finland. The conflict lasted until 13 March 1940, when the Moscow Peace Treaty was signed. Initially, the Finnish army inflicted substantial losses on the Soviet troops. It was only after the Soviet army had increased its capacity and changed tactics that it was able to break through the Finnish defense lines. Its successful offensive was launched on 1 February 1940. The war ended with considerable territorial losses on the Finnish side, though Finland kept its sovereignty, and presented a humiliating display of the alleged military might of the USSR. The invasion of a sovereign state by the Soviet Union led to international condemnation and the expulsion of the USSR from the League of Nations on 14 December 1939.

sinfulness. This is followed by the colloquy: a conversation, that is, with whichever of the divine figures the individual chooses. We have already talked about that.

Now we want to look at this meditation a bit more closely, using the old text. So the first sin is a primordial sin, a sin that occurred even before the creation of man, and that was the sin of the fallen angels.

> God created all angels, whom he blessed with countless perfections, in both grace and nature. [. . .] But a large number of them [out of hubris or *superbia*; CGJ] rebelled and committed mortal sin. [. . .] And God then transformed these angels into demons. From the most wondrous creatures he created the most foul, and his most loving friends became his most hateful enemies.[571]

Here we also have to ask ourselves, "What does this mean? How does a person come to make such a statement? Is it merely a fabulation or does it mean something psychological?" If we reduce it to the psychic connections, it means that even before human consciousness arose, a split occurred in those powers that were pre-conscious: that is, that are in our disposition, that lie in the unconscious. So an absolute global contradiction was already present in the unconscious disposition, as if between angels and demons. It is notable that angels always come in multiples—for example, choirs of angels. The angel as an individual does not exist. They are completely collective beings. That's why there also cannot be individual monks, only monasteries; because monks belong to the angelic orders, they represent the choirs of angels on earth. That means, therefore, that these psychic entities are collective in nature. And that also indicates that man, before developing an "I" consciousness, must be a collectivity, not yet aware of individual psychic existence. The human being is initially an instinctive creature. There is not yet the psychology of mother and father, family, clan, and environment. There is not yet an individual psychology, in the same way as the infant does not have its own psychology, but still a collective one. You can see that clearly in the dreams of early childhood, which are very unchildlike, because they consist of mythological material. They contain things that children cannot possibly know, but that quite naturally stream out of the human mind, rather like magma

---

[571] Izquierdo (1695), p. 34: "Creavit Deus omnes Angelos ornatos innumeris perfectionibus tum naturae, tum gratiae. [. . .] Superbijt magna pars eorum, & in peccatum mortale ceciderunt. [. . .] Ex Angelis convertit in Daemones. Ex pulcherrimis creaturis fecit foedissimas. Ex charissimis amicis Dei odiosissimos inimicos."

that bubbles up from the depths of nature and corresponds to the whole constitution of the brain. A natural functioning of a not-yet-conscious psyche, a natural brain function that produces such forms, the way particular flowers grow from the seed of a particular plant, the way crystals follow the laws of crystallography, or a chick pecks its way out of the shell, or ducklings take to the water, and so on. And the human mind also begins to function in this way in accordance with its disposition,[572] and this disposition is collective. You can see this in the dreams of very young children, but also later, specifically often in those who are mentally ill, where the whole psyche swells up to the surface, bringing things that the ordinary mortal knows nothing about, thank goodness. Then the most astonishing mythological images can emerge, such as are found in the literatures of all peoples[573] and epochs. They are in effect the same thoughts and connections, sometimes literally so.

The small child is under no circumstances a *tabula rasa*,[574] or completely blank sheet of paper. The writing on the page is done in invisible ink, but the page is not blank. You know, like that ink that only becomes visible when you go over it with that special stuff. But when something happens in life that fits what is written there, then the lettering becomes visible.

So, in primordial times this split in the material occurred. It is of course none other than the opposites manifesting in man, the opposites that are already present before there is consciousness. That is, the opposition between above and below, angels and demons, is already present in the child from the beginning. Well, that is the Christian predication. That is the actual psychological meaning of a myth such as the fallen angels—it is none other than the divine nature which, as it unfolds in a person, necessarily reveals this contradictory nature, exactly as in the Christian legends this contradictoriness was revealed in Christ. As a result, Christ's image,

---

[572] RS has "Konstitution" (constitution) instead of "Disposition" (disposition).

[573] RS has "Länder" (countries) instead of "Völker" (peoples).

[574] See also Jung's lectures of 3 November 1933 (*JMP*, vol. 1), pp. 20–23, and 17 November 1933 (*JMP*, vol. 1), p. 45: "Our consciousness perceives the outer world; it is an organ of perception. But behind our consciousness there stands a perceiving subject, and this is no *tabula rasa*. This subject is not simply another exterior, but instead it comes endowed with a background, with whose help it is able to interpret perceptions in the first place. Human children are not born with empty brain capsules, but instead with a complete brain, created for eons. Consequently, every child is born with a predetermined assumption of the world, of which it is not conscious, but which is nevertheless at work. Failing this innate opinion, we would be unable to grasp the world at all. There is no escape from this psychic background with which we enter life, it can only be accepted. Endowed with it, however, we must comprehend the world according to this disposition."

the image of the crucified one, is the exemplar for man which the person has to imitate in the *imitatio Christi*, because only then is he whole and able to unite the opposites of human nature, which then leads to redemption. But we haven't discussed that yet.

When I say, "God is the contradictoriness itself," I am just formulating Przywara's meditation. But Przywara also knows the other side, because God is also the unifying force. Now, this conflict that exists a priori in man is the original sin. That is the sin that has always been there, for all time. Thus it is already the *privatio justitiae originalis*, the privation of the original justice of men, which then made itself apparent when the first parents were banished from paradise. In the sin of the first parents; the fall of the angels was repeated. One can say that in some way, despite the fact that God, according to Church doctrine, created the first people in the state of *iustitia originalis*, original justice, this metaphysical event nevertheless played out again, so that they too had to fall and be ejected from paradise.

The text firstly speaks of the fall of the angels and the terrible punishment that was visited upon these fallen angels. The author says,

> If God punished those creatures with such a horrible and everlasting punishment for all eternity because of one single mortal sin, what can the mortal being expect for his mortal sin, for his erring?[575]

This meditation must now be completed by incorporating the five senses: one imagines the condition of the angels in great detail, visualizes this extremely violent event as clearly as possible, and imagines the hellish punishments that follow, down to the smallest detail.

Then comes the contemplation of the second sin, its second occurrence, namely the sin of the first parents. So,

> God created Adam and Eve in his grace and friendship and blessed them with *iustitia originalis* and they were in a condition that was free of death and all the horrors of punishment. He placed them in the paradise of pleasure, in *Paradisum voluptatis*.[576]

---

[575] Izquierdo (1695), p. 34: "Si igitur talis Deus creaturas tales tam ingenti, & nunquam in aeternum finienda poena punivit propter unicum peccatum mortale; quis non hinc mortales culpae perspicit infinitam malitiam?"

[576] Ibid., p. 35: "Creavit Deus Adam, & Evam in in gratia, & amicitia sua, ornatos dono Iustitiae originalis, & a morte, omnia; malo poenae exemptos. Posuit eos in Paradiso voluptatis."

As you know, they were not able to resist the snake's powers of persuasion and did indeed eat from the tree of knowledge. They thereby knowingly contradicted God's command:

> And so Adam and Eve were deprived of the *iustitia originalis* for themselves and for their descendants and sentenced to death, exposed to the pain, weaknesses and other miseries of this world, and thrown out of paradise.[577]

The meditator again has to imagine this precisely, including all the details, and again mentally recreate the event.

Then comes the third punishment, namely the one God uses to punish man, who is in a state of mortal sin.

> It is enough that a person with one single mortal sin dies, that he is thrown into the all-consuming flames where he is burned for as long as God shall exist, as the faith [or the doctrine of the Church; CGJ] teaches us.[578]

That is, for all eternity. It is the eternal punishment of hell:

> That never-ending ocean of pity (*pelagus miserecordiae*). He has now condemned those creatures for whom He hung His only begotten son on the cross to burn in the fire which He has kindled for eternity, with no mercy but rather with pleasure because He then has the opportunity to see how His infinite righteousness extends for all eternity. [CGJ: Then he proclaims:] Oh terrible wickedness of mortal sin that is worthy of such a punishment.[579]

It is rather unusual for this aspect of the loving God to make an appearance, isn't it? One can hardly continue to call him a loving God. He looks on, "rather with pleasure," at how they all burn in hell, and for all eter-

---

[577] Ibid.: "Adam, & Eva pro se, & pro suis descendentibus Iustitia originali privati sunt: damnati ad mortem: expositi doloribus, infirmitatibus, caeterisque huius Mundi miseriis: eiectie Paradiso[.]"

[578] Izquierdo (1695), p. 36: "Licet enim cum uno solo moriatur homo, tandiu in poenam eius intra voraces illas flammas arsurus est, quadiu Deus est extiturus, ut Fides docet."

[579] Ibid.: "Illudque immensum misericordiae Pelagus creaturae a se factae, tamq; dilectae, ut pro ea unigenitum suum Filium e Cruce suspenderit, ignem, quo comburitur, flatu suo est accensurus in aeternum, ut ait Isaias, absque ulla commiseratione, potius cum gaudio, quod ibi videat exerceri suam infinitam Iustitam. O peccati mortalis horribilissima malitia, quae tanto supplicio digna est!"

nity at that. Here a *Deus absconditus*,[580] a terrible God, is unveiled. It is the unveiling of the contradictory nature of God, who is a loving father as long as there is still some sign of hope for these rogues, the human beings. But woe betide them if they do not obey him; then he is a terrible God, who can send people to eternal damnation and even enjoys seeing them burn in the fire. This conception of God does not fit with our Protestant view at all.

---

[580] See n. 453. RS has "*Deus terribilis*."

Lecture 13[581]

16 FEBRUARY 1940

I TOLD YOU last time about the meditation on the *peccatum mortale*. Today I want to give you an overview of the first week's meditations, and then we'll return to the *peccatum veniale*.

The first exercise includes the meditation on the sins of the angels, the sins of the first parents, and lastly one's own sins. This meditation is followed by a colloquy, a dialogue with one of the divine figures, generally at the end of each exercise. The purpose of this colloquy is to make the meditator particularly aware of the divine presence in the exercises. By talking to another party, as it were, the effect is naturally much more vivid than if one simply turns inward to meditate. In addition, this colloquy does not just take place with the divine figure, but also with the exercise director, a soul guide who supervises the exercises and gives the necessary instructions, talks with the exercitant about the meditation, points out any mistakes, and hears the confession. These methods and circumstances ensure that the meditation on the sins is certain to make a deep impression on the meditator. The aim is of course to make the meditation a deeply personal experience. The meditators do not dream, for example, but hear themselves speaking before a witness, which makes the whole exercise more dramatic and impressive.

The second exercise relates to the *examen generale*—that is, a general examination of one's own sins, and as usual this meditation is divided into separate points. The first point involves putting on trial, as it were, the various sins committed during the course of one's life. In order to picture things as realistically as possible, this must be imagined as a kind of court hearing. You imagine yourself standing before a judge or jury and acknowledging your misdeeds. These must be recounted with

---

[581] The text of this lecture is compiled from notes by LSM, ES, RS, and OK, as well as the English translation by BH.

all the relevant details, giving the time, the place, and all the individual circumstances.

The second point involves precisely weighing up each individual misdeed, from a moral perspective as well as all the other possible angles, naturally also in regard to religious truths.

The third point is a comparison of one's own sinfulness and the corruption of humanity in general with the lives of the saints and the innocence and purity of the angels, whose particular merit lies in not committing any sins. The angels have the characteristic of "non posse peccare."[582] The bad angels sinned only once, in a fundamental fashion, and the whole company immediately tumbled down to hell. There they were transformed into evil demons, and have not been able to do anything but sin ever since.

Then one also compares oneself to the purity of God himself and thereby realizes one's own odiousness. Then, again point by point, one has to imagine what God is like, the God against whom one has sinned, and one has to exclaim with wonder that God has put up with the angels, with mankind, and with one's own nature all this time despite all this sinfulness.[583]

At the end of these points, there is another colloquy in which, as usual, only the meditator speaks. It is actually not really a colloquy, but an address that the meditator gives to any of the divine figures and in which one praises the divine mercy and proposes a list of good intentions which one promises to keep to henceforth.

Now comes the third exercise. This consists firstly in repeating once again the colloquy that took place in the two previous exercises. So there is now another colloquy which is to be made with "Our Lady" so that she will advocate for the speaker with Christ. The *Beata Virgo*, the "sacred virgin," is chosen as an intercessor for the sinner for a very particular reason: namely, that according to the Church, she, body and soul, ascended to heaven after her death. She is therefore the first dead person ever to be received in heaven with her body, meaning she naturally has a special relationship with us mortal, carnal men and will therefore understand sinners particularly well. That's the only conclusion we can draw, or at

---

[582] Saint Augustine differentiates between four states of man's relation to sin: 1.) man before the Fall from paradise: able to sin, able not to sin ("posse peccare, posse non peccare"); 2.) man after the Fall: not able not to sin ("non posse non peccare"); 3.) reborn man: able not to sin ("posse non peccare"); 4.) glorified man: unable to sin ("non posse peccare"). According to Augustine, the good angels have the same state as the saints in heaven, unable to sin, i.e., "non posse peccare."

[583] RS has "Verworfenheit" (depravity) instead of "Sündhaftigkeit" (sinfulness).

least it's the generally accepted view. Consequently, she is an advocate *par excellence*. And then one has to ask her to grant one recognition of one's own sins, of the extent to which one's previous way of life was wrong, and finally also of the vain, transient, and fleeting nature of the world.

Then follows a colloquy with Christ, who will essentially then be one's intercessor with the Father. So you see, it takes place in stages. Then comes a colloquy directly with the Godhead, the Father, and specifically to ask for the same three things: recognition of one's own sinfulness and depravity, recognition that one's previous attitude was wrong, and complete recognition of the transience and superficiality of the world.

The fourth exercise that follows consists of repeating the third exercise. So you see that in these exercises the reflection on the sins is recapitulated in all possible forms, in order to make a particularly lasting impression on the meditator. So, it consists again of imagining the wickedness,[584] corruption, depravity, and odiousness within oneself, and in which one would be lost *eo ipso* were one unable to beg for God's grace.

Now, bringing this meditation to its climax, comes the fifth exercise. This is the meditation on hell, which occupies a very special position, if one may say so. It is done in incredible detail. The meditator has to imagine very precisely and concretely the length, breadth, and depth of hell. In the *oratio*, the prayer, one even has to ask God to give one a very precise and clear sense of what it is like to be punished in hell.

The first point to be meditated on is thus a very precise and concrete visualization of the great fires and the multiple and varied ways in which the damned suffer.

The second point is an equally sensate process, in which one imagines the wailing and blaspheming of the damned, the sounds that ring out around hell.

The third point involves smelling the smoke, the burning sulfur, the putrescence, the stench of feces and rotting matter emanating from what are, after all, corpses.

In the fourth point, one vividly imagines a bitter taste which represents the pangs of conscience or bitterness that one would feel if one were damned to hell for eternity and looked back on one's life and had to say to oneself, "I messed up in all those idiotic ways and now I am lost forever."

---

[584] RS has "Verlorenheit" (state of being lost) instead of "Verruchtheit" (wickedness).

And finally comes the sense of touch, imagining how it would feel to burn in this fire. We'll pick up a few more points about the hell meditation from our old Jesuit friend Izquierdo later.

The finale is a colloquy with Christ again, this time about the terrible impression that you have of hell, about the fate of eternal damnation, and you give thanks that you have not sunk so far even though you actually deserved such a fate long ago due to your corrupt and depraved nature.

That is the content of the first week. Perhaps I should also tell you about the general circumstances during such an exercise week. During the period when one is completing the exercises, one should exclude, if possible, all thoughts that are not directly related to the exercises.[585] Specifically, from the time you wake up until you go to sleep, all thoughts relating to anything worldly must immediately be suppressed, and only things which are related to the purpose of the exercises should be allowed to become conscious, in fulfillment of the Ignatian instruction that we should only choose that which is useful for our goal. It is about training the ability to concentrate and to discipline our impulsive instinctual and capricious nature.

If one prays during the exercises,[586] it should always be done while imagining that Christ, God the Father, or the Virgin is looking on, so that one always has the feeling of a presence, that one is never alone, as it were, but is always being monitored by the eternally watchful eye of the Godhead. *In concreto*, this is done in such a way that the exercise director goes into each individual detail, examines it, and holds the meditator to account.

The meditations themselves can be done in various positions, depending on personal preference. This could be sitting, lying, or standing, walking to and fro, or kneeling. After each exercise, one has to examine again how the exercise went, whether everything went *rite*, exactly according to the instructions, and *lege artis*, or whether any point was overlooked. To aid concentration, the meditations should be done in a darkened room. The curtains should be drawn or the shutters closed. Laughing is not allowed. Of course, one may also encounter other people, although the meditations are done alone. When one meets others, one may not look them in the eye,

---

[585] RS has first "Examina" and then "Examen" (examination) instead of "Exerzitien" (exercises).

[586] RS again has "Examina" (examination).

apart from on greeting, and if possible one should not talk to them, in order not to have other thoughts.

The necessary feelings of regret should be cultivated with acts of self-penance, such as fasting, sleep deprivation, and flagellation. The flagellation is optional: it is left up to the individual whether to do it. But sometimes flagellation is used. There are many people, even clergymen, who do the small exercises and simply cannot take the large exercises, psychologically. I've met a few Catholic clerics who said they had not been able to get through it, because they were so affected that they became severely depressed and were pushed to the limit even physically. You can easily imagine that happening, because it's a terribly aggressive thing. Of course, if you just listen to a lecture about these things and have never done them yourself, it's hard to picture. You can't put yourself in the state of mind that you might be in if you were really to seriously consider your own sins. I must say, I have not done these exercises, but I am blessed with a pretty good imagination and can picture how it might be. But I have also seen what it is like when someone takes these things seriously. These people want to take it seriously, and it is a serious business for them; otherwise they wouldn't subject themselves to it, and if they do, it is clear that they will be moved to their core.

Hopefully I've managed to give you an impression of the extraordinarily impressive way in which one becomes aware of one's own sinfulness. I would like to support that with a few points from Izquierdo's meditation book, specifically about the *peccatum veniale*—I already translated a few bits about the *peccatum mortale* before.

> They [the *peccata venialia*] include sins that happen due to careless-ness, from *imbecilitas* or lack of attention, and even perfect people are not completely immune to these sins. Other *peccata venialia* are done out of real evil [. . .]. The first point in the meditation is to get a deep impression of the strictness with which God also punishes venial sins. Indeed, he keeps that terrible imprisonment in *Purgato-rium* [the purgatorial fire] ready as punishment. [. . .] The second point contemplates how much one should actually fear the venial sins. [. . .] They are punished by God with terrible punishments in-volving not just physical suffering and persecution but also— mainly—spiritual punishments: for example, being subjected to temptations which then cause the affected person terrible troubles, then unrest, pangs of conscience, desolation, darkness, aridity [e.g.,

like a thirsty animal deprived of water, that is, of the grace of God; CGJ], and finally, privation of the peace and calm that are always the fruit of a good conscience.[587]

These, then, are the sacred punishments that God hands out.

Then one considers how great is the evil even of venial sin, because the consequences to which it can ultimately lead are similar to those of *peccatum mortale*. [. . .] One must therefore consider as deeply as possible the consequence of venial sin. Namely, it is a *spiritualis aegritudo animae* (spiritual sickness of the soul) which causes the same effects as a physical illness has on the body. That is, it generates stultification and lack of strength with which to resist temptations. It also generates a weariness with regard to spiritual matters; [there is no longer any willingness, there is resistance; CGJ] to prayer and to the colloquy (*conversatio*) with God, a weakness, weariness, and laziness preventing one turning to the spiritual path: [. . .] and thus this spiritual sickness from the venial sin now disposes one to the death of the soul, namely to *peccatum mortale*, to mortal sin. That is what we have to fear the most about venial sin [that it leads to *peccatum mortale*; CGJ].[588]

---

[587] Izquierdo (1695), pp. 43–46 (with regard to variations between Izquierdo's text and Jung's translation, see n. 266): "Duplex est genus peccatorum venialum. Alia enim committuntur ex negligentia, imbecillitate, aut parva advertentia: a quibus ne Perfecti quidem immunes sunt. Alia committuntur ex malitia [. . .]. Primum punctum erit. Considerare rigorem Deus punit peccata venialia. Siquidem ad illa praecipue punienda horribilem carcerem Purgatorii paratum habet. [. . .] Secundo ponderabo, quantum horrorem de peccatis venialibus debeo concipere: [. . .] Punit praeterea Deus peccata venialia saepe in hac vita multis modis. Iam poenis corporalibus infirmitatum, dolorum, persecutionum, &c. Iam spiritualibus maioribus; ut sunt permissiones tentationum, quae valde affligunt, inquietudines, turbationes conscientiae, desolationes obscuritates, siccitates, demum privationes, illius pacis, ac tranquilitates, quae fructus est bonae conscientiae."

[588] Izquierdo (1695), pp. 46–48: "Secundum punctum erit. Animadverte, quam magna est malitia peccati venalis considerati secundum se; quamvis ea dicatur, & sit parva comparata cum malitia peccati mortalis. [. . .] Tertium punctum erit, considerare, quomodo peccatum veniale spiritualis aegritudo animae est: sicque illi eos propotionaliter praestat effectus, quos aegritudo corporalis solet praestare corpori: nimirum imbecillitatem, defectumque virium ad exercendas virtutes, & ad vincendas tentationes: taedium rerum spiritualium, orationis, & conversationis cum Deo: debilitatem, lassitudinem, & pigritiam ad deambulandum per viam spiritus: [. . .] ita aegritudo spiritualis peccati venialis est dispositio ad mortem animae, scilicet ad peccatum mortale. Et hoc est, quod in illo debemus plus timere, & horrere."

There are also a few other points worth mentioning about the meditation on hell. Namely, similarly to what I told you before, he describes how one should carefully visualize the place when meditating on hell:

One has to imagine a great cavern, which one pictures in one's mind and which in reality is at the center of the world [presumably of the earth; CGJ], full of sulfurous fire in which the damned are submerged like fish in the depths of the ocean. And one must say the prayer and beg God to grant one a vivid fear of descending to such a place. And if love[589] is not sufficient to turn one away from such a fate, then at least let fear prevent it./ The punishments in hell consist in principle of the *privatio gloriae* [the privation of glory, the withdrawal of glory; CGJ], which the damned forgo.[590]

This is is of course the *gloria Dei*. The glory is the emanation of God, his merciful fire, which these damned souls forgo.

As Saint Thomas teaches, the punishment is unending, because it robs one of the infinite goodness that is God, the possession of which is the privilege of the Blessed. Thus Saint Chrysostom also says that a thousand hellish fires combined still would not reach the scale of the punishment of the damned, namely the *privatio Dei* [that is, the state of being removed from God; CGJ] because God is the center of the soul [the innermost point toward which the soul is oriented and pulled; CGJ], and this pull is infinitely greater than that of other things to their center, e.g., the limbs that are attached to the body[.]

So he says that the arms, legs and head are less drawn to the body than the soul is to that center which it carries in itself.

And thus the separation from this center, the tearing off, causes infinitely more pain than if a living person's limbs were torn off.[591]

---

[589] OK has "Reue" (regret) instead of "Liebe" (love).

[590] Izquierdo (1695), p. 73: "Magna concavitas mente conspecta, quae revera est in centro Mundi, plena igne sulphuris, quo Damnati submersi sunt uti in profundo maris pisces submersi sunt aqua. Petitio autem. Postulare a Deo vividum cadendi in eum locum timorem; ut quando a cadendo in peccatum non me deterreat amor, detterat saltem timor./ In primo puncto considerabo peonam Damni, quae consistit in privatione Gloriae, qua Damnati carent."

[591] Izquierdo (1695), pp. 73–74: "Et, ut docet S. Thomas, est poena infinita: quia privat bono infinito, quale Deus est, & possessione, qua ipsum possident Beati. Unde ait Chrysostomus, mille ignes Inferni simul iunctos, non fore tantae poenae Damnatis, quantae est privatio Dei. Quoniam Deus est centrum animae, ad quem ea habet post hanc vitam inclinationem

This point is essential. *In puncto* hell, Izquierdo is now particularly graphic. At the time when this text was written, the seventeenth century, the Jesuit sermons and missions played a particularly large role, especially through the small exercises, as I mentioned in the historical introduction, which were generally led by wandering preachers, while the large exercises were only performed by clerics or particularly pious men. Izquierdo now talks about meditating on the hellish apparitions using the senses:

The sense of sight is tormented by this evil light of the infernal fire [. . .]. The sense of sight is plagued by demonic figures that take the form of lions, tigers, bears, snakes, dragons, and other terrible beasts, and also the putrid corpses of the damned and other frightful and abominable creatures that are imprisoned there./ The sense of hearing is tormented by the constant noise of hellish hammering, of raging cries, moans, lamentations, screams of the damned, by quarreling, blaspheming, cursing, and all kinds of other dreadful and shocking sounds. [. . .]/ The sense of smell is tormented by an unbearable stench, by the smoke of the fire and the sulfurous fumes, and by the awful reek of the rotting bodies of the damned, worse than the stench of as many festering cadavers of dogs all piled up together in an airless place./ The sense of taste is tormented by permanent hunger and raging thirst for which there is no relief. There is only one thing to eat, *absinthium* [wormwood, that is the bitterness; CGJ]. And to drink, bile [. . .]./ The sense of touch, incorporating the whole body, is plagued by this sulfurous fire in which the damned are completely submerged. Oh ignorant sinner, if you cannot bear to hold one finger in the flame of a candle for the briefest of moments, how will you bear being submerged from head to toe in the flames of hell for all eternity? [. . .]/ The inner sense is plagued by an acute perception of pain and by sad and terrible fantasies that are imagined over and over again [. . .]. The *appetitus sensitivus* [that is, intellectual pursuits, human desire; CGJ] consists of a tempestuous longing that is never fulfilled. There are afflictions and fears. The intellect is full of misapprehensions. It is imbecilic and fatuous, sees nothing else and is directed only at perceiving the enormity of the infernal punishments [. . .]. The will is doggedly fixed on evil and is afraid of reaching the good that

---

incomparabiliter maiorem, quam habent ceterae res ad suum centrum, & membra eiusdem corporis ad mutuam unionem. Atque ita non potest non illa pati violentiam, ac dolorem de sui a tali centro aeterna avulsione incomparabiliter maiorem, quam patiuntur membra eiusdem corporis, quando ab se invicem avelluntur[.]"

one cannot reach, and afraid of the evil that one cannot avoid [. . .]./ The mind is plagued by fantasies that it constantly generates, feeds, and incubates, and from which the worm of remorse hatches [that voracious worm of conscience, pangs of conscience; CGJ]. The Holy Scriptures say of this worm that it will never die. [. . .]/ As Saint Gregory says, in hell the wretched creature suffers a death without death, an end without end, because death always lives and the end always begins. [. . .] Because these damned souls are eternal, their imprisonment is also everlasting, the fire is everlasting.[592]

This is how Izquierdo, our Jesuit Father from the seventeenth century, suggests we might contemplate hell.

Before we get into the meditations of the second week, we have to ask ourselves—from a historical and psychological distance—what this concept of sin is all about. Why does a sense of their own sinfulness have to be so drummed into people? There are probably historical reasons for it. This form of the exercises is medieval, not modern, and we are thus in the realm of medieval psychology, in which the Church had a lot to be guilty about. In Spain alone, from the burning of heretics. It was a dreadful and

---

[592] Izquierdo (1695), pp. 76–79: "Sensus visus torquebitur luce illa maligna ignis Infernalis. [. . .]; figuras scilicet, quas Demonia assument Leonum, Tigrium, Ursorum, Serpentum, Draconum, aliarumque ignearum bestiarum: foedissima iamtum omnia corpora Damnatorum: & alia, quae in eo carcere teterrimo horribilissima./ Auditus torquebitur continuo illo Infernalium Malleatorum strepitu: rabiosis fletibus, planctis, lamentis, clamoribusque Damnatorum: querelis, blasfemiis, maledictionibus: alliisque ingratissimis, ac inordinatissimis sonibus. [. . .]/ Olfactus torquebitur intolerabili foetore tanti ignis, & fumi sulphuris: foetore horribili tot corporum Damnatorum, qui totidem canum mortuorum foetore longe gravior erit; eorumque stricte coniunctorum in loco nullam habente respirationem./ Gustus torquebitur perpetua fame, sitique rabiosa, in quarum levanum dabitur miseris Damnatis pro cibo absynthium, pro potu autem aqua fellis [. . .]./ Tactus, qui in toto corpore residet, torquebitur ab igne illo sulphureo, quo Damnatus totus submersus erit. O amens peccator! Si hic non potes sufferre, ut vel unum digitum tuum tangat flamma lucernae per breve tempus; quomodo ibi sufferes, ut totum a capite ad pedes tangat flamma Inferni, tanto crude delior, per integram aeternitatem? [. . .]/ Sensus internus torquebitur vehemente apprehensione dolorum, qua fixa in illis graviores faciet; tristissimisque, & horribilibus phantasmatibus, quae semper imaginabitur [. . .]. Appetitus sensitivus erit mare quodam tempestuosum desideriorum non implendorum, moerorum, afflictionum, & angustiarum. Intellectus erit plenus erroribus; hebes pro caeteris, & solum perspicax ad percipiendam magnitudinem tum poenae Inferni susceptae iam [. . .]. Voluntas erit obstinata in malo: anxia semper pro bonis, quae non potest consequi, & a malis, quae non potest vitare [. . .]./ Memoria, etsi aliis poentiis simplicior sit, erit orige maioris Damnatorum poenae: siquidem in ea gignendus, nutriendus, & fovendus est edax ille conscientiae vermis, de quo dicit Scriptura sacra, quod non morietur. [. . .]/ Nam ut Gregorius dixit. In Gehenna miseris erit mors sine morte, & finis sine fine: quia mors semper vivit, & finis semper incipit. [. . .] Quia ii sunt aeterni, carcer est aeternus, ignis est aeternus[.]"

dark time, rooted to a large degree in the barbarity and unconsciousness of the time, a barbarity which until recently we thought we had risen above. But now we have discovered a few things in this regard, thank God. Maybe it will get even better, but we have become slightly more enlightened in this respect. Hitherto we looked down on the Middle Ages with regret: a terrible time—it did these awfully uneducated and ignorant people a lot of good when a missionary came and hauled them over the coals to give them a bit of a shock about themselves and their spiritual fate.

This form of meditation on hell is of course very medieval, and one tends to disregard something like that with a smile. But I must stress that even in the most modern form of the exercises, sinfulness plays a significant role. We must ask why it is that people have to be made to feel their own sinfulness so keenly. We know that we are, unfortunately, not gods, and that it is terrible to tell children they will burn in hell if they don't obey their papa. That plants an inferiority complex in them. One should therefore instead tell them more often that they are good. "Tout est bien, sortant des mains de l'Auteur des choses."[593] You just have to tell them that, then they'll all be good people, amenable and appreciative. Now just give that a try. These ideas, which came in with the French Revolution and our dear Rousseau, are still floating around. Of course, it is very nice to be friendly to people when you first meet them. It is also better to treat the other person like a gentleman before you put the boot in. But, you have to ask: is it any use? And is it really true? As we have recently read in the newspapers, people also have quite different backgrounds.

All people, even the most primitive, provided one approaches them in the right way, are awfully nice in ordinary circumstances. I once spent time with a primitive tribe;[594] we spent the whole evening enjoying ourselves and dancing around the fire together. They were extremely charming. They thought we were very nice people. We thought they were, too. Two days later, an Englishman came upon the same people. He approached them the wrong way and snarled at them. So they speared him. That could have happened to us, too. We were just three White fellows,[595] with only one gun. That's why one hears such contradictory reports about the primitives.

---

[593] The first book of the pedagogical treatise *Émile, ou De l'éducation* (1762; Engl.: *Emile*, 1911), by the Genevan philosopher Jean-Jacques Rousseau (1712–78) opens with the line, "God makes all things good; man meddles with them and they become evil."

[594] See n. 169.

[595] OK has "Europäer" (Europeans) instead of "Weiße" (Whites).

Some say the Papuans[596] are the slyest dogs going, with not a trace of loyalty and faith or anything good, and others say they are the most lovable children—yes, they are like children. They are terribly nice, but also diabolical; they abuse animals and all sorts. If a child has a bad upbringing and grows up in an abusive atmosphere, as is the case in many families, you will find that this child abuses others. Only the abused become abusers. Then they torment animals and other people, and then those sweet children are bad kids. It's a fact of nature: men are not just good, they are also bad. And if we want to know the truth, we must know that we are not only capable of being good-natured. One doesn't harm others, one treats them well. On the one hand, we are capable of great virtue; if we are well brought up we are astonishingly good at self-denial, but on the other hand, we can also do the most terrible, unbelievable things—like machine-gunning people, women and children even, as we keep reading about at the moment. Those who do such things are not bad people, they're just normal folk like you and me. But they have gotten above themselves, have gone beyond their bearings, just like others who show the highest virtues have also gotten above themselves. And we must remember that we are not simple creatures, but have a background that stretches infinitely farther than we can perceive with normal consciousness.

[596] Only RS refers specifically to the Papuans here, inserting "von den Papuas" ([Some say] of the Papuans [that]).

Lecture 14[597]

23 FEBRUARY 1940

IN THE PREVIOUS session, we looked at the idea of sin as it appears in the Ignatian exercises. In the first week's meditations, sin plays a key role, sin and the dreadful punishment thereof. The exercises of the first week are intended to give the participant an absolutely unforgettable grasp of sin and its consequences. As I told you, many people who do these exercises find the experience almost unbearable and often suffer real damage. It is no wonder that such meditations—especially when done with such intensity—can have extremely deep, long-lasting, and potentially damaging effects on those with more sensitive temperaments. But these side effects are not our concern here; our focus is on the content of the ideas.

Seeing the intensity with which the idea of sin and the punishment resulting from sin is emphasized, one finds oneself asking why they go to such incredible lengths. If we approach it from the dogmatic standpoint, from the concept of original sin that says we are already corrupted in embryo, so to speak, such an exercise is understandable, a logical step. But if we examine the psychological question, namely, to what end such a strong emphasis on sin should serve, we encounter a different problem. And that is the following: if sinfulness has to be impressed on us to such a great extent, the other side of the coin is that the human tendency to sin must be just as great; that is, that men have a certain diabolical hubris that is inimical to God, a certain likeness to God that continually makes them want to do the things that are forbidden. And we cannot say that men have a certain tendency to merely unintentionally break rules somehow; it is more that they have an almost organic tendency to arrogance, to hubris.

---

[597] The text of this lecture is compiled from notes by LSM, ES, RS, and OK, as well as the English translation by BH.

But what happens when awareness of one's sinfulness is inculcated in this way? The individual is crushed, personhood suppressed, one's existence or dignity is invalidated. One becomes deeply convinced that one is corrupted and lost from the start, that one is constantly tempted to stray from the righteous path into meaninglessness and absurdity, and that one is only capable of achieving a state worthy of grace if one makes the greatest of efforts.

This quashing or deflation of the human spirit is counterpoised with an equally strong tendency to inflation. Now, we are not talking about conscious resolutions here, such as "I want to sin," "I choose to sin," "I want to be like God," or "I am like God." It is not about such convictions—rather, it is a psychological phenomenon. Namely, if people are not humbled to their core, then they will slip into divine likeness without realizing it. That comes from men's lack of domestication, with a primordial barbarism that tends them toward one extreme or the other: deprecation or overestimation of themselves.[598] Not that they want that; it simply happens—they slip into hubris or into the most extreme and undignified self-deprecation.

These exercises, this whole historical stage of development of Christianity in fact, are specific to their time, inextricably linked to a particular epoch. One could say that these exercises particularly describe an epoch in which humanity's self-conceit, intellectual hauteur, and godlike qualities began to become dangerous. It is like that other phase in the history of ideas, a bit before this time, in the fourteenth and fifteenth centuries, when there was the persecution of heretics, witch hunts, people being burned alive en masse, and so on. That was a time during which doubt crept in, in which hubris took the form of all sorts of challenges to religion. The expansion of knowledge about the world led to all kinds of speculations. It was a time of great voyages of discovery, and with the enlargement of the known world came the idea that the world might not actually be as flat as was thought, that the earth might revolve around the sun and not the other way around. These early beginnings of the natural sciences awakened certain religious doubts, and then began the burning of heretics and suchlike, long before the Reformation. The Reformation was then a heretical movement that brought this epoch to an end, as it were,

---

[598] OK has "Selbstvernichtung oder Überheblichkeit" (self-destruction or arrogance/hubris) instead of "Selbstentwertung oder Selbstüberwertung" (self-deprecation or self-overestimation).

and caused a schism, a split in the Church, that has endured to this day. So it is a weakening of Christianity in the true sense.

This tendency, this high-handedness of human reason, was the trigger for the intense suppression that took place. The Ignatian exercises, therefore, and indeed the Jesuit order in general, are simply a further consequence of the schismatic disintegration of the Church. The Jesuits are the *milites Christi*, the soldiers of Christ, whose vocation is to destroy or overcome the enemies of Christ. The purpose of the exercises was also to instill greater discipline in the ranks of the Church's members—a real retaliation against the schism of the Reformation. The Reformation itself was an uprising against the absolute authority of the Church, an intense promotion of human reason in the face of pure authority. And along with it, a bit of that hubris, that arrogance of men, revealed itself, and was also quickly followed by a revolutionary mood that deeply permeated the population. Think of the terrible peasants' revolt[599] at the time of Luther, which was then suppressed with dreadful ferocity. These are simply some of the other effects. So long as human beings are insufficiently domesticated— they suffer, that is, from a barbaric lack of self-control, they without fail fall prey to pairs of opposites. If they are believers, they lose themselves completely to their faith. They are called the virtuous ones. But they might also lose themselves in complete self-denial: completely cease to exist as individuals. Or they will push the whole problem aside and abandon themselves to their infantile drives, like Thomas Müntzer[600] and other such people, the Anabaptists causing riots, and so on.

The fact is that a dark force, a driving force so to speak, always takes possession of people, and then they simply get swept up in it and everything becomes crazy. When they are in the barbaric state, people are unable to maintain a sensible idea; instead they flog it to death. Then every time it leads to a catastrophe, and then one thinks that when that is suppressed, the situation will improve. But of course the same old story repeats itself, just in a different guise. One may even doubt whether it is even possible for men ever to be governed by reason—whether people will ever actually completely come to their senses. I wouldn't blame you for thinking that it will simply go on like this for ever. But if we want to be more optimistic, we might hope that after something particularly idiotic things would improve.

[599] See n. 450.
[600] See ibid.

What we see historically, however, is the opposite. We flip from white to black and from black to white, and when the cycle is completed it starts over again from the beginning. That we know from history, and we also know that human consciousness has significantly increased in breadth and scope. But have we thereby become morally better? There's no doubt about it: morally, things have not improved. The best inventions, methods, and ideas are harnessed for destruction in the most diabolical ways, which doesn't exactly bode well for the future. But I am convinced that this kind of thinking is actually incorrect. We should learn to think differently. We should deal more with our own problems and less with the problem of the eleven thousand virgins who actually have nothing to do with us.[601] It's no use asking, statistically, what things will be like in twenty years. Then there'll be a whole load of other people. We are alive today, and it is about us. This way of looking at things, that deals with hundreds of thousands and millions, is no better than a neurosis, in that one simply escapes one's own problems. But if you deal with your own problems, you'll have enough to keep you going for a lifetime and you won't need to worry about how things will be for other people in twenty or fifty years.

So these enormous conflicts, this to and fro between hubris and depreciation, are actually symptoms of a lack of domestication. Such extremes are actually unnecessary, as we'll see later. I'll read you something from India about that later.

Sin, as it is historically described, is in the first instance a deviation from a law, from a divine command. That concords more or less with the Old Testament standpoint. Before that, there was no sin as such. In antiquity, for example, the concept of sin was unknown; instead they spoke of clumsiness and foolishness, or of great hubris which led one to perhaps offend this or that god—imprudence in dealings with powerful beings. But that was not perceived as a sin. In ancient Egypt, the concept of sin as we understand it did not exist either. Instead they had a rite called the negative

---

[601] Jung refers to the legend of the Romano-British Christian Saint Ursula from the fourth century. According to a medieval story, Ursula traveled from Britain to marry the pagan governor Conan Meriadoc of Armorica. She took with her eleven thousand handmaidens, with whom she went on a pilgrimage to Rome before her marriage. But they only made it to Cologne, which was besieged at the time by the Huns, who captured and beheaded the virgins, while Ursula was shot dead with an arrow. The main place of veneration of Saint Ursula is Cologne, where her tomb can be found. But there is also a tradition of Ursula-worship in Basel, where Jung spent his youth. It is said that Ursula and the eleven thousand virgins passed through the city on their way to Rome. This legendary event is commemorated in the street-name Elftausendjungfern-Gässlein (Eleven thousand virgins alley).

confession, which dying people had to recite: "I have not stolen the widow's belongings, have not lied or deceived. I have not stolen the cow." So only, "I have not. . . ." Of course, the thinking behind it is to reinforce that I haven't done anything stupid that could offend this or that god or community. But there is no mention of a moral conflict.

The concept of sin is essentially a product of the Old Testament, and means the transgression of a command. In Christianity itself it is thus no longer about the law: that is, that one has broken laws—that was only reintroduced more recently, in Protestantism—but about whether or not one has acted against the love of God and against other people. And as you heard, our Spanish source Izquierdo gave a good definition of sin: namely, there is only one sin, and that is the mortal sin, "because this always puts the goal in the creatural and not in God."[602] So those who put their goal, the *finis* that we know about from Ignatius, in what is created—either created by man or by God, so in things that can be perceived with the senses, natural things, and so forth—are committing mortal sin. Because the unique and sole justification for man's existence is that he has his goal in God; in other words, that his whole life must be conceived in such a way as to be directed toward God, and not to anything creatural. Thus according to this view, sin is a deviation from God, and not the transgression of a commandment—for example, the commandment of love. Sin is rather the act of withdrawing from the Godhead.

What is the Godhead, according to the Jesuit conception? We saw it with Przywara and talked about it at length: namely, the Godhead is a union of the opposites, the uniting of the split. The split, when developed, is a conflict, which is why the union takes place in the cross. That's why Przywara says that God appears on the cross. He manifests himself through the Christ figure hanging on the cross. Those who wish to become one with God can only do it through the *imitatio Christi*, the imitation of Christ,[603] by taking on the cross, taking on the conflict of the universal opposites, and putting themselves in the middle as it were, in front of the cross. Or, if we think from the perspective of Christ, as Przywara does, we say that we are on the cross with Christ.[604] That is a literal translation of the original Spanish text of Ignatius.[605] Thus God empirically appears, in a manner of speaking. He has shown himself to the world as the cross,

---

[602] Izquierdo (1695), p. 33: "nam hoc ponit ultimum finem in creatura, & non in Deo."

[603] See n. 109.

[604] Przywara (1938), p. 72.

[605] Jung probably refers here to paragraph 53, a colloquy at the end of the first exercise during the first week: "Imagining Christ our Lord before me on the cross, make a colloquy"

as the instrument of martyrdom, as an affliction, and insofar as Christ takes on his suffering, he manifests God, makes God visible. So you see that the suffering between opposites, the collision of opposites, is actually the manifestation of God, according to this view. Of course, the cross, as well as the Godhead, is now not only an affliction, the Passion of Christ or that to which the *imitatio Christi* submits; the cross also symbolizes the redemption—because the blood of Christ that is spilled for us is an elixir, the *medicina catholica*, the universal cure. It is the water of ablution, the water of purification in which we are cleansed of the blackness of our sins and healed of our affliction of being far from God. In the cross is thus also salvation, in that the person who is placed on this cross or who bears the conflict stands in the middle between the two great universal opposites, and is therefore also saved. Thus the separation from God is a separation from the cross, and the separation from the cross is a deviation from God. In other words, if one manages to some extent to get out of this conflict, no longer to suffer it, one is cut off from God and is in the state of *peccatum mortale*.

Now it is quite clear that the suffering God who appears in Christ is a reflection of the human being. In the *imitatio Christi*, I try to make myself one with the Passion of Christ. If I succeed, I am the suffering Christ, so to speak, but in the sense that I surrender myself so fully to Christ that I completely disregard myself, completely cast aside this unworthy I and give it to Christ, in order that my I enters into his body through the stigmata of Christ. I am completely absorbed by his body, such that I no longer live, but Christ lives in me.[606] Thus I am transferred, through my own abnegation, into Christ. It is not I who am Christ, but there was once an I, my I, that entered Christ and what now lives is Christ. That is what Christ actually means. And as he is the second figure in the Godhead, he is actually the innermost core, the innermost experience of mankind. Where he is in a state of complete surrender, where he can no longer have illusions about anything, he is in this conflict, and there he is God. There was once a mystic who said quite rightly about Christ's words on the cross "My God, my God, why hast thou forsaken me?"[607] that Christ was at

---

(*IPW*, p. 296). The original Spanish manuscript reads, "Ymaginando a Xρo nuestro Señor de lante y puesto en cruz, hazer un coloquio" (MHSI-MI, p. 192).

[606] See Galatians 2:20.

[607] "And at the ninth hour Jesus cried with a loud voice, saying, Eloi, Eloi, lama sabachthani? which is, being interpreted, My God, my God, why hast thou forsaken me?" (Mark 15:34; Matthew 27:46). Here Jesus addresses God with the words of Psalm 22: "My God,

that point the true God, because if God had left him then there was no more God outside of him. You see, it is the same idea.

Curiously, shortly after Ignatius, living almost at the same time, there was a German mystic who expressed these ideas in a rather wonderful way—Angelus Silesius.[608] I'm going to read out a few of his verses that relate directly to this problem:

> 1.5.   I know not what I am, what I know I am not,
>   A thing and not a thing, a circle and a dot.

Here he uses the Augustine symbol of the Godhead.[609] God is a circle whose center is everywhere and whose periphery is nowhere. So Angelus Silesius, in his childlike modesty and humbleness, has become God himself, as he is a dot and a circle. And in another verse,

> 1.10.   I am as big as God, God is so small, like me.
>   God cannot be above me, I cannot below God be.

> 1.6.   Should I my final goal and primal source discover,
>   I must myself in God and God in me recover
>   Becoming what He is: a shine within His shine,
>   A word within His Word, by God be made divine.

> 1.204. No thing seems high to me, I am the highest thing,
>   Because God without me, remains Himself lacking.

> 3.135. Quite without measure is the Highest, as we know,
>   And yet a human heart can wholly Him enclose.

And last of all he says,

> 5.354. Flee not oh Christ the cross, you must endure the pain,
>   That the kingdom of heaven you might thereby attain.[610]

---

my God, why hast thou forsaken me? why art thou so far from helping me, and from the words of my roaring" (*KJV*).

[608] Johann Angelus Silesius (1624–77), born Johann Scheffler into a Lutheran family, converted to Roman Catholicism in 1653 and probably adopted the name Angelus Silesius after a Spanish mystic of the sixteenth century. In 1661, he was ordained as a priest and in the years to follow he became an outspoken advocate of the Counter-Reformation. His most famous collection of poems is known by the title of the second edition as *Cherubinischer Wandersmann* (1657; Engl.: *The Cherubinic Wanderer*, 1986). Cf. Jung's lecture of 9 June 1939 (*JMP*, vol. 5, pp. 244–45).

[609] Cf. Jung's lectures of 12 May 1939 (*JMP*, vol. 6, p. 202) and 2 February 1940 (this vol., p. 178).

[610] Angelus Silesius (1657). Jung quoted the aphorisms from the German edition of 1924. English translations of 1.5, 1.204, and 5.354 by CS for this volume; 1.10 by Werner

In these verses, Angelus Silesius expresses in a perfectly simple way everything we have said about Przywara and about the meditations of Ignatius. You see clearly in these words that Christ is none other than the projected self of the human being, the "something greater" in the person, the part that contains this I, the part in which this I can dissolve. The purpose of the exercises is after all to dissolve the I in this greater figure. In other words, and here we see the other side of the cross symbolism, the I thereby enters the state of resolution or redemption, that is, that state in which the opposites merge into one. Now, as I have mentioned several times already, it is totally characteristic of the West that this development has to take place through an intense life process, while in the East that is not the case at all. There, in contrast, the development process unfolds in quite a different way—through renunciation of suffering, avoidance of misery; so, quite the opposite, you might say. But the underlying thoughts are actually the same, and in that regard I'd like to read you a passage from the *Dhamma-kakka-ppavattana Sutta*, eleventh volume of the *Sacred Books of the East*:[611]

Reverence to the Blessed One, the Holy One, the Fully-Enlightened One.

1. Thus have I heard. The Blessed One was once staying at Benares, at the hermitage called Migadâya. And there the Blessed One addressed the company of the five Bhikkhus,[612] and said,

2. "There are two extremes, O Bhikkhus, which the man who has given up the world[613] ought not to follow—the habitual practice, on the one hand of those things whose attraction depends upon the passions, and especially of sensuality—a low and pagan[614] way (of seeking satisfaction), unworthy, unprofitable, and fit only for the worldly-minded—and the habitual practice, on the other hand,

Pelz (2001); 1.6 and 3.135 by Maria Schrady (1986). See also Jung (1921), § 432. For the BH edition, Mary Mellon translated the verses into English (BH, vol. 2, p. 249).

[611] *Dhamma-kakka-ppavattana Sutta* (*Foundation of the Kingdom of Righteousness*), *SBE*, vol. 11, pp. 146–59. Jung read out his own German translation of the English. Cf. his lecture of 11 November 1938 (*JMP*, vol. 6, pp. 28–29), in which he also quoted and interpreted this passage.

[612] *SBE* comment: "These are the five mendicants who had waited on the Bodisat during his austerities, as described in 'Buddhist Birth Stories,' pp. 88, 89."

[613] *SBE* comment: "Pabbagito, one who has gone forth, who has renounced worldly things, a 'religious.'"

[614] *SBE* comment: "Gamma, a word of the same derivation as, and corresponding meaning to, our word 'pagan.'"

of asceticism (or self-mortification), which is painful, unworthy, and unprofitable.

3. "There is a middle path, O Bhikkhus, avoiding these two extremes, discovered by the Tathâgata[615]—a path which opens the eyes, and bestows understanding, which leads to peace of mind, to the higher wisdom, to full enlightenment, to Nirvâna!

4. "What is that middle path, O Bhikkhus, avoiding these two extremes, discovered by the Tathâgata—that path which opens the eyes, and bestows understanding, which leads to peace of mind, to the higher wisdom, to full enlightenment, to Nirvâna? Verily! it is this noble eightfold path, that is to say,

> Right views;
> Right aspirations;
> Right speech;
> Right conduct;
> Right livelihood;
> Right effort;
> Right mindfulness;
> and Right contemplation.

"This, O Bhikkhus, is that middle path, avoiding these two extremes, discovered by the Tathâgata—that path which opens the eyes, and bestows understanding, which leads to peace of mind, to the higher wisdom, to full enlightenment, to Nirvâna!

5. "Now this, O Bhikkhus, is the noble truth concerning suffering.

"Birth is attended with pain, decay is painful, disease is painful, death is painful. Union with the unpleasant is painful, painful is separation from the pleasant; and any craving that is unsatisfied, that too is painful. In brief, the five aggregates which spring from attachment (the conditions of individuality and their cause) are painful.

"This then, O Bhikkhus, is the noble truth concerning suffering.

---

[615] *SBE* comment: "The Tathâgata is an epithet of a Buddha. It is interpreted by Buddhaghosa, in the Samangala Vilâsinî, to mean that he came to earth for the same purposes, after having passed through the same training in former births, as all the supposed former Buddhas; and that, when he had so come, all his actions corresponded with theirs. 'Avoiding these two extremes' should perhaps be referred to the Tathâgata, but I prefer the above rendering."

6. "Now this, O Bhikkhus, is the noble truth concerning the origin of suffering.
"Verily, it is that thirst (or craving), causing the renewal of existence, accompanied by sensual delight, seeking satisfaction now here, now there—that is to say, the craving for the gratification of the passions, or the craving for (a future) life, or the craving for success (in this present life).
"This then, O Bhikkhus, is the noble truth concerning the origin of suffering.

[. . .]."

24. Thus spake the Blessed One. The company of the five Bhikkhus, glad at heart, exalted the words of the Blessed One. And when the discourse had been uttered, there arose within the venerable Kondañña the eye of truth, spotless, and without a stain, (and he saw that) whatsoever has an origin, in that is also inherent the necessity of coming to an end.

25. And when the royal chariot wheel of the truth had thus been set rolling onwards by the Blessed One, the gods of the earth gave forth a shout, saying,
"In Benâres, at the hermitage of the Migadâya, the supreme wheel of the empire of Truth has been set rolling by the Blessed One— that wheel which not by any Samana or Brâhman, not by any god, not by any Brahma or Mâra, not by any one in the universe, can ever be turned back!"

26. And when they heard the shout of the gods of the earth, the attendant gods of the four great kings (the guardian angels of the four quarters of the globe) gave forth a shout, saying,
"In Benâres, at the hermitage of the Migadâya, the supreme wheel of the empire of Truth has been set rolling by the Blessed One— that wheel which not by any Samana or Brâhman, not by any god, not by any Brahma or Mâra, not by any one in the universe, can ever be turned back!"[616]

I wanted to mention that again so that you can see how the idea of the quaternity also comes up here, but in the reverse order. The cross is characterized by the four points. It is the Christian form of the ancient *quaternitas*.

---

[616] *Dhamma-kakka-ppavattana Sutta*, SBE, vol. 11, pp. 146–49, 153–54.

Western people enter the unity of God from outside, via the quaternity, while Eastern people descend from the unity of the divine being into the quaternity. The truth of the Buddha is uncovered from the unity, and is then taken up by the gods of the earth, the lower psychic centers, and finally placed above the lower quaternity which represents the earth. And thus the realm of truth descends into the world of illusion and suffering, while Western people emerge from the world of illusion and suffering and ascend to the cross, to the quaternity, and to the unity. The East has a completely opposite perspective. The Eastern path is different from the Western one, in that while we move from the outer world up into the inner world, Eastern knowledge[617] moves from the unity of the Holy Spirit down, as it were, into the world. Because the wheel that is set in motion, which you can see on all Buddhist temples, the wheel of *dharma*, represents the Buddha's teaching that is set rolling across the world and that brings redemption from a world of illusion and suffering. But the underlying ideas and symbols are essentially the same. So these clearly must be general human ideas.

With these considerations and in concordance with this meaning of Christ as the bridge, the mediator to the Godhead, the second week of exercises then begins with a meditation on the kingdom of Christ. This is primarily concerned with the fate of Christ, and the purpose of the exercise is to bring the figure of Christ close to the meditator, exactly like with the sin and damnation and eternal hellfire: namely, Christ as the savior, the redeemer, who through his crucifixion provides a model for the union of the opposites.

[617] RS has "Gnosis" instead of "Wissen" (knowledge).

Lecture 15[618]

1 MARCH 1940

LAST TIME WE finished our examination of the first week of the exercises and we come now to the second week. From now on, we can summarize things a bit more briefly, as we have already discussed many of the following ideas in the introductory parts of the exercises.

The subject of the second week is the contemplation of the kingdom of Christ and Christ as Lord of the world. That is, it is a matter of considering the personage of Christ and his redemptive significance for mankind and the world as a whole. This contemplation is the logical progression of what we discussed before. It will certainly have become clear to you that in the meditation on the "Anima Christi" and the "Fundamentum," and then in the contemplations of the first week, one particular idea became ever clearer: that man stands in a unique relationship to God, namely to the God-become-man who appears as a reflection of man, so to speak, although of course dogmatically speaking is not actually such. One might rather say that the human being is to an extent a distorted reflection of this universal or eternal man. Thus in the second week there follows, logically, the contemplation of the image, the image of the incarnated God and his earthly existence—that is, his historical existence.

The first contemplation or exercise thus begins by precisely picturing, that is, actively imagining, how Christ came into being. Specifically, this incarnation does not begin with the birth, but with the events in the *pleroma*: that is, in the fullness. That's an expression that Paul uses occasionally.[619] It is that spiritual sphere, if one may say so, in which the world has

---

[618] The text of this lecture is compiled from notes by LSM, ES, RS, and OK, as well as the English translation by BH.

[619] Saint Paul uses the word *pleroma* (Gk. πλήρωμα): "fullness," to describe God's perfection, the fullness of his being, as in Colossians 1:19: "For it pleased the Father that in him should all fulness dwell," or Ephesians 3:19: "And to know the love of Christ, which passeth knowledge, that ye might be filled with all the fulness of God." It is also applied to

not yet come into being. It is an existence of possibilities, the spiritual pre-existing possibilities of the world, out of which the seeds of the world emerged. One might say that this notion is to an extent also found in primitive cultures in ideas about the world of the ancestors: that is, the world from which the forebears came and in which they abide, the place from which they emerged to create the world by transforming themselves into things. They did not create the things, but in a peculiar way transformed themselves into the things.

To give an example: the ancestor who represents the rain. This creature's head is represented by the clouds, its hair is the rain, its body is the pouring torrential rain. Its feet are the places where the raindrops bounce off the ground. These are Australian ideas. And this creature has now transformed itself into this form. It is actually invisible, half animal, half man, cloud or rain. The things in the world that we can see or touch were not created by this being—rather the creature actually transformed itself into these things. In this way, for example, the archer's bow came about. The archery ancestor and his wife transformed themselves into a bow, but still kept their original form too. It would not be possible to make a bow if this archery ancestor had not existed. His head is at the top, that is the tip of the bow, and the fibers of the bowstrings are his hair; at the bottom is his foot, and the bowstring that hangs on the bow is his wife who hangs around his neck. This couple are the ancestors that transformed themselves into the bow, and this is how animals and humans and all creatures that exist came about. Esoteric teachings identify all the places on the globe where the ancestors lived, where they traveled, what they did at this or that spot. There are countless legends about which only some people know and others do not. For example, the rain totem: the old men who belong to the rain totem group know all the stories about the rain ancestor: what he did, where he lived, and so on. And the same is true for the

---

Jesus Christ as in Ephesians 4:13: "Till we all come in the unity of the faith, and of the knowledge of the Son of God, unto a perfect man, unto the measure of the stature of the fulness of Christ," or Colossians 2:9 "For in him dwelleth all the fulness of the Godhead bodily." In Ephesians 1:23, Paul speaks of the church as "his body, the fulness of him that filleth all in all" (New Testament citations from KJV). The meaning of the term changes in Gnosticism, due to its closeness to Greek philosophy, to "state of completeness in contrast to deficiency, or of the fulness of real existence in contrast to the empty void and unreality of mere phenomena" (Lock, 1902, p. 2). Jung gives a detailed account of his understanding of the pleroma in the first of the *Septem Sermones ad Mortuos* (1916; Engl. transl. *The Seven Sermons to the Dead*, 1925), a Gnostic tract he published under the name of the Basilides of Alexandria, first written down in his black notebooks in January 1916 (see Jung, 2009, pp. 509–14).

other strange and unimaginable kinds of ancestors. These are actually ideas in the Platonic sense: ideas that pre-exist and that have become things that can be perceived through a process of transformation. A primordial idea, then. The primitives call this pre-existing world *altjira*.[620] That word also means "dream." So we can say that this *altjira*, this realm of the ancestors, is identical with the dream world: in other words what we would call the unconscious. This pleroma, this fullness, should also be understood in this way—that is, that the world's existence has been preconceived, a preconception in which everything is contained but is *in potentia*, as possibilities. Everything can arise from it.

And thus at the start of the meditation on the incarnation one has to imagine clearly how the three persons of the Trinity look down on the earth from heaven and see that the earth is full of people who are all heading directly to hell. They look down and consult as to what is to be done to somehow put a stop to this lamentable state of affairs, and come to the conclusion that the second person of the Godhead must incarnate himself as a man, in order to end the terrible situation on earth.

You see—this very naive-sounding idea is modeled on the old pattern, isn't it? It is conceived in a way that is similar to how primitives think. If the rice won't grow properly, if the rice is in a poor condition, you fetch a man, an expert, from the rice totem group who knows all the rice legends, who knows how the rice ancestor originally transformed into rice, how rice came to exist. There are masses of strange legends about. And then you build a hut for the rice expert in the rice field, and there he tells the rice how the rice ancestor originally made the rice so that the rice remembers how it originally came into being and grew so nicely. When the rice remembers this, it turns out well again. Thus by telling the rice clearly how it actually came to be, a bad harvest can be averted.

This idea is found again in the origins of Christianity, where there was the notion that the man Jesus had always existed and that he still remembered

---

[620] *Altjiranga mitjina*, "the eternal dream-time" or "the Dreaming," refers in the mythology of some Australian aborigines to a concept of sacred time or time belonging to the gods. The French anthropologist Lucien Lévy-Bruhl (1857–1939) translated *altjiranga mitjina* or *churinga* as "les éternels incréés" (Lévy-Bruhl, 1935, pp. 48–49). Jung came across the concept when he read Lévy-Bruhl's *Les fonctions mentales mentales dans les sociéties inférieures* (1910) in preparation for his "Wandlungen und Symbole der Libido" (1911–12). Lévy-Bruhl borrows the concept from Baldwin Spencer and F. J. Gillen's *The Native Tribes of Central Australia* (1899) and Carl Strehlow's *Die Aranda- und Loritja-Stämme in Zentral-Australien* (1907–20). Jung discussed the concept in his *Children's Dream Seminar* (2008 [1936–40]), p. 151. Cf. also his lecture of 13 January1939 (*JMP*, vol. 6, p. 91), and Jung 1936–40. See Shamdasani, 2003, pp. 295–97.

the pleroma, the state in which he had still held conversations with God. He still somehow remembered his discussions with God. And he is now the one who comes to men and whose figure reminds them of what the human being originally was and was meant to become: because men have forgotten where they actually came from. They have forgotten the *homo creatus*, forgotten the creator, and believe that everything they do is initiated by themselves and not by their ancestors, and that's why everything goes wrong.

Thus the purpose of Christ's manifestation is interpreted as being to remind men of what they originally were before they were put on earth, when the human, the *anthropos*, lived in heaven. The Gnostic texts then elaborate in a very complicated fashion, and with many variations, upon how this primordial human came into being when the events that preceded the entire existence of the world were in the pleroma, which is the fullness. Christ therefore serves to remind men of what they originally were, so that they recognize themselves in this image.

Thus in the Ignatian meditations one imagines that Christ's incarnation has begun, corresponding to the start of the Gospel of John in which it says that the *logos* has always existed, has always been with God, and that all things were made by the same, and without the same "was not any thing made that was made."[621] So in a way he is thought of as an executive organ of the Godhead. The person meditating therefore has to vividly imagine this process, imagine the Godhead discussing the fate of the world.

And now the human existence of Christ begins, in that one imagines how Gabriel comes down to visit the *Beata Virgo*, how she lives in a little cottage near Nazareth, and how he enters the door of the house. Now all the local geographical details also have to be imagined, even so far as to picture Nazareth being situated in the province of Galilee. All knowledge that the meditator already has must be recalled in order to picture the scene in as much specific detail as possible. Then all those events follow that we know from the Bible stories.

Then follows the second exercise: contemplation of the nativity, again with all the details. The nativity story begins with the *Beata Virgo* leaving Nazareth with Joseph and making her way to Bethlehem for the census. One has to imagine how the heavily pregnant Mary, in her ninth month, is heaved on to the donkey. And to be on the safe side she also takes a

---

[621] John 1:2–3: "The same was in the beginning with God./ All things were made by him; and without him was not any thing made that was made" (*KJV*).

maid with her, as one does, and a cow so that they'll have enough milk when the baby comes. You have to meditate on it in such incredible detail. Then the journey has to be imagined, step by step. What a long way it is. How many kilometers it is from Nazareth to Jerusalem. You have to imagine all the different Judean hills you'd have to cross—Jerusalem is about a thousand meters above sea-level—how steep the path is, the incidents that might occur along the way. And then you arrive tired at that cave in Bethlehem where, according to legend, the birth of Christ took place. It is not simply an ordinary stable, but a cave of the sort that do actually exist in Bethlehem. They are still used today to house goats. Bethlehem has many such caves—the Church of the Nativity now stands on the site of the so-called nativity cave. The church is an old Byzantine building and later excavations found it to be on the site of a temple of Adonis. The choir of the church dates back to the fourth century. Adonis was another dying-and-rising son of a deity.[622]

So then the meditator has to enter this cave and attend the whole labor and birth and observe all that happens there, with the donkey, the cow, and the people. And when all that has been thoroughly meditated on, there comes a further exercise, which consists in picturing once again a) the incarnation, Christ's coming into being before his existence on Earth, and b) the actual birth of Christ, so that every detail sticks.

And when that has been done, it is all repeated again, and then comes another exercise in which the whole preceding meditation is undertaken yet again, this time using the five senses. So the whole process is practiced using each individual sense—sight, hearing, touch, taste, and smell. So you see that the aim of this enormous imaginative effort is for the meditating person to be transplanted into the situation, for it to feel almost real, because the meditator has made it real, and thereby made himself real in such a situation. The meditator is transformed, in other words, through this process, so that the experience takes root in him as if it were his own story: that is, as if he were Joseph, Mary, or the maid. Then he is this whole situation. He transforms himself directly into the situation through such contemplation.

---

[622] Saint Jerome stated in his epistle 58 that prior to the construction of the Church of the Nativity the same ground had been consecrated to the worship of Adonis, which had taken place after the birth of Christ. James Frazer disputed Saint Jerome's statement in chapter 33 of *The Golden Bough*, claiming the existence of an earlier pagan worship at this site. According to Ricciotti (1941, p. 276) the Adonis cult in Bethlehem was probably instigated by Hadrian in the second century, to efface Christian worship there.

On the second day of the second week comes the meditation on the presentation at the temple and then the flight into Egypt. This is repeated twice and then performed again using the five senses.

On the third day, the meditator contemplates Christ's childhood. We don't actually know any concrete details about his childhood years. They are therefore amplified through active imagination, with the special instruction to imagine what an absolutely obedient child Jesus was. A boy who was extremely obedient to his parents because he was thereby fulfilling God's will, and who later was just as obedient to God. In this meditation, the exercitant of course again identifies strongly with the obedience of Christ, with the figure of Christ. The Christ figure is assimilated directly.

In curious contrast, there then comes that dramatic turning point in Jesus's life when the obedient boy visits Jerusalem with his parents for Passover and disappears, and is later found talking with the scribes in the temple. When his mother comes to fetch him and admonishes him he says, "How is it that ye sought me? wist ye not that I must be about my Father's business?"[623] In other words, "Woman, what have I to do with thee?"[624] He rejects his mother here, in a way. Then obedience to his mother, to his parents, is replaced with obedience to God, and in a manner that hurts her feelings. This lack of respect for one's parents, for one's own mother, is a sacrilege against the commandment to honor your father and mother. Here he apparently did not honor her, but set his own vocation against obedience to his parents. That is a decisive moment, even in the lives of individuals who do not have lofty aspirations. This separation from the absolute authority of father and mother is something that happens to every single one of us. Both these contrasting aspects, these important aspects, also have to be repeated twice [by the exercitant] and then practiced again using the five senses.

Then we come to the fourth day: the meditation on the two standards. That is the classic term used. Specifically, these are the two armies that are characterized by two ensigns: the army of Christ on one side and on the other the army of Lucifer, that renegade angel whose arrogance led to his fall from God and banishment to hell. These two figures are imagined alongside each other as commanders of two enemy armies. Here we see the army officer in Ignatius coming out. He imagined the battle against

---

[623] Luke 2:49 (*KJV*).

[624] John 2:4 (*KJV*). These are the words Christ said to Mary at the beginning of his ministry at the marriage of Cana.

the powers of evil in militaristic form. These are the *milites ecclesiae*, the soldiers of God, of the Church. Christ is now imagined here as the general of his army that gathers on a wide plain outside Jerusalem, while Lucifer gathers his legions in the region of Babylon. There sits Lucifer the commander on a throne of fire and smoke enveloped by the vapors of hell. And here he is now surrounded by his officers, the chief demons, and he sends them around the world to recruit soldiers. And Lucifer gives an address haranguing his deputies and instructing them how they should go about corrupting men to recruit them for the demonic foreign legion. Of course this part has to be conjured up freely using one's own imaginative powers as we do not have any references in the Holy Scripture.

Christ, on the other hand, sits near Jerusalem in a pleasant spot on a hill surrounded by his officers, his general staff. The first of these are the twelve apostles. They are the generals. He sends them out into the world to recruit people, and also addresses them. As you know, for this part there is certain basic information in the Holy Scripture on which the meditation can be based, but by and large the creative imaginative power of the meditator is given free rein.

When one meditates on all that, this preparation for the final war is then brought into relation with one's own I. You are yourself there, at Babylon and on the Jerusalem plain, as an observer, and you realize then that you are also called to take part in this battle. Therefore you hold a colloquy with the *Beata Virgo*, the great intercessor. You ask her to speak for you to the Lord, that you might be received under his standard. You offer yourself as *miles Christi*. Now it could happen, and that is the reason why so many people go to hell, that someone is not sure which side they ought to choose. In this war one cannot remain neutral—please don't be tempted to draw historical parallels here—which is why a contemplation now follows about the different types of people. There are three types, and they are characterized in a most banal way: each has ten thousand ducats. This is the old example. Now each has to decide. How will they decide when they hear the call of these commanders? The first would like to give up his attachment to the ten thousand ducats, but will not do it until he dies. The second wants to be free of his attachment to the money, but also wants to keep it. This kind of person never comes to a conclusion. The third also wants to give up the attachment. This person is also willing to give up the possession entirely, not just the attachment, but the actual possession of the money, if that is what God and reason want. So, in other words, if this person believes he has received a clear instruction from God he will give it up, and if reason commands it he would also do so. That is specifically Ignatian: if it corresponds to God *and* reason. Ignatius is an extraordinary rationalist. In all his decisions, the will of God must be taken into account on the one hand, and human reason on the other. Decisions must be very carefully considered, with Jesuit precision, in order that one does not let oneself be led only by the will of God, but also by reason, so that one clearly understands why God's will is leading one in a certain direction. It cannot merely be suggestion or fancy; it is important to check whether it is reasonable. This kind of decision-making is absolutely necessary in such a case, because otherwise you would have no criteria for what God decides to do with you. Because the internalizing of God's will is an intuitive act that afflicts men. You feel forced to decide about something. Is this intuition you feel coming from God or from the devil, or somewhere else?

That is exactly like the problem that concerned the old Church teachers: whether dreams were sent from God, were whispered by demons, or were the result of digestive processes, of physiology. Initially one had no criteria in this respect other than reason: that is, the criterion of the Church that allows that they could be "somnia a Deo missa."[625] The Church thus says that if the contents of these dreams are in accordance with the teachings and moral laws of the Church, they can be accepted as having been sent by God. But if the dream is not in accordance with Church doctrine, then of course it is from the devil.

Consequently there are cases in which one might be in doubt about whether a dream was sent by God or the devil. There's an amusing story about the Egyptian Saint Anthony,[626] the historical accuracy of which I cannot vouch for. It is in Anatole France: when Saint Anthony had been in the desert for twenty years, he was already a very holy man. Then one evening he heard a knock at the door. A stranger stood outside and Anthony asked him what he wanted. The stranger replied, "Anthony, you are very holy, you have earned great merit, but I know a man in Alexandria who is holier than you." Saint Anthony was very disappointed to hear that; he immediately packed his suitcase and set off for Alexandria to meet this other holy man in order to learn his exercises and practice that he might earn greater merit. Even saints have a certain ambition with regard to saintliness. So he arrived in Alexandria and began searching for a cobbler named Armonius. This was supposed to be the holy man's name, but he

---

[625] *somnia a Deo missa* (Lat.): "dreams sent by God."
[626] Saint Anthony (ca. 251–56), often referred to as "the Great," a Christian hermit from Egypt, seen as the father of monasticism.

couldn't find him anywhere. On the third day, finally someone told him, "He's down there in the cellar." There he came upon a quite ordinary cobbler. Anthony said to him, "The angel of the Lord told me that you are a holier man than me." The cobbler said, "I don't know anything about that." Anthony said, "What is your practice?" The other shook his head and said, "I have nine children and have to earn a living for them. That's what I do." Saint Anthony couldn't believe his ears. Finally he clapped his hand to his forehead and said, "It must have been the devil after all."[627]

This case illustrates how despite the best efforts of human reason, potentially difficult problems can arise. Then one has to say that church teachings are very good, they encompass a lot; but what if God should resolve to do something that is not provided for in the doctrine—for example, put out a new publication? He hasn't published anything new for the last two thousand years. A Newer Testament for example. Then where would we be? With what doctrine could we orient ourselves then? It's a serious question. It just sounds so scholastic. But if you think through these things psychologically, you'll notice something.

Now, the meditations on the life of Christ, from his baptism until Palm Sunday, continue until the twelfth day. They conclude with an exercise on humility, namely about Christ as God's servant who took the burden of the world and its sins upon himself and did not shy away from humbling himself or being humbled right down into the dirt. In this way, the contemplation leads, one could almost say, in an unexpected but totally logical way into the meditation on one's choice of vocation. That is, not only has the Godhead allowed himself to be born and appear in a human body, but he has also been humbled into the dirt, has allowed himself to be ridiculed and tormented, has led a wretched life in the dirt of the earth. God became fully human, became like me. What should I do now? What is my vocation? How do I live? This question leads directly to considering one's own way of life; specifically, to a meditation on one's profession—for example, saddler, carpenter, or soldier. And thence comes the meditation on the manner in which one lives one's life, namely how one practices one's profession, to what end or for what purpose one is a soldier. Is it done in

---

[627] Anatole France (1844–1924), pseudonym for François-Anatole Thibault, French writer and journalist, who was awarded the Nobel Prize for Literature in 1921. Jung's library contained a number of books by France. Although the figure of Saint Anthony features in texts such as the novel *Thaïs* (1890), the specific adaptation of the well-known motif of Saint Anthony and the cobbler which Jung recounted in the lecture could not be located in France's work. On France, see Bancquart (1994).

relation to the creature, or does one do it with the Godhead in mind: that is, *ad finem*?[628]

And then follows the contemplation of one's own life from the viewpoint of absolute humility and absolute obedience. In other words, do you go about your life with the same humility, obedience, surrender as Christ did? Now you start to get the measure of yourself: where you dodged something, chose the easier option, neglected your duties, stuck to the routine, deceived others, lied to yourself, all those daily occurrences. In this way, you trawl through your own life comparing it with the life of Christ. As a result, the most intimate merging of the life of Christ with the life of the individual naturally takes place, so that the exercises enable you to live life with the totality with which Christ lived his life. That then comes very close to the thought that Christ is actually a role model for life, that he is an image held up to men to remind them of their true nature. Because the true nature of men never appears if they do not live totally. If a person ducks out of life, swindling here or finagling there, he slinks his way through existence always remaining slightly invisible. No one really knows what he is like. He is clever enough not to cause offense. He avoids this and that, not because he is particularly moral or respectable, but merely somewhat cowardly. It is also comfortable—hugely so—to be respectable, or to dodge one's authentic self for the sake of some agenda. Then people say, "He was a respectable man." He gets a nice obituary, but it was actually all a sham. The meditations are getting rather profound here, aren't they?

---

[628] *ad finem* (Lat.:) "toward an end."

Lecture 16[629]

8 MARCH 1940

LAST TIME WE discussed the second week. I told you that the main focus was on the life of Christ up to and including Palm Sunday, and that this contemplation leads to contemplation of one's own way of life, starting with one's choice of profession. Specifically, by considering the life of Jesus, which followed a consistent thread leading to his tragic end, a process of self-reflection begins. You cannot engage with the life of another person in such a thorough manner without your own life somehow being drawn into it. One always measures one's own experience. Without wanting to or intending to, one draws one's own life into the meditation. It is therefore only logical that, at the end of the meditation, suddenly one also contemplates the way in which one conducts one's life, one's decisions, plans, and intentions.

And if you now consider your own life from the perspective of the life of Christ, it can only happen in one sense: namely, in terms of the totality—because the aim of the meditation is to induce one to identify completely with the life and the person of Christ and to review and examine one's own life in terms of the *imitatio Christi*. This is a critical point: the question of the *imitatio Christi*. Should it be an imitation of the life of Christ such that one even gets the stigmata, like Saint Francis, or does it mean that each person should live life to the full, in their own way, until the bitter end, as Christ did? Those are two very different paths. It is clear that for medieval and more recent Christianity it was certainly a matter of the *imitatio Christi*, not about living one's life *sine imitatione*—without imitation.

In any case, if in the sense of the *imitatio Christi* one lives and conducts one's life in such a way that it corresponds to an imitation of the

---

[629] The text of this lecture is compiled from notes by LSM, ES, RS, and OK, as well as the English translation by BH.

life of Christ, then it is a matter of taking up the cross—either in the almost literal sense of the cross of Christ, or alternatively taking up one's own cross, namely one's own conflict. If, in the sense of the *imitatio*, the cross of Christ is taken up, then the conflict which is richly described in the New Testament arises. It is the conflict of Christ with the world and the flesh. If, on the other hand, it is one's own cross, then initially we lack a definition, because the conflict is a more individual one. Life that is lived fully in one sense or the other leads to suffering from conflict. In any event, if the conflict is taken up, if life is lived fully in either sense, then a suffering in the conflict occurs from which there emerges a corresponding reformation of one's own way of life, in which henceforth the aspect of one's own conflict is accepted. After all, initially we all try to live our lives as conflict-free as possible. There is a certain liberal view which we also see in the kind of "joyous Christianity" in which one is friendly with everyone, always good-tempered, always smiling, and one is relieved of all conflicts because Lord Jesus Christ took on all the conflicts so I don't have any. That of course is no *imitatio Christi*; rather it is a way of dodging one's own conflict.

It is thus entirely logical that the third week of the exercises is devoted to contemplating the Passion of Christ. [630] The first contemplation includes how Christ sent two disciples from Bethany to Jerusalem to prepare the Last Supper, and then also made his way there with the other disciples and how he, after enjoying the Paschal lamb and the Last Supper, washed their feet, gave them his flesh and blood, and held a sermon, after which Judas left to go and betray Jesus.

The second contemplation is of how Christ and his disciples descended from Mount Sion, where they had held the Last Supper, to the Valley of Josaphat; how he then left eight of them at a place in the valley and went with the other three to the garden on the Mount of Olives where he withdrew to pray to the Father, then woke his three disciples from their sleep; how then his enemies fell to the ground at the sound of his voice; how Judas gave him the kiss of peace; how Peter cut off Malchus's ear and Christ restored it; how Christ was then arrested and taken away.

We don't need to go into detail here. We already mentioned all the essential main points, when we discussed the "Anima Christi." We already covered a good portion of this meditation there. You must not imagine, however, that such shortcuts are also taken in the actual exercises—on the contrary, in the third week, the Passion is examined down to every

---

630 The rest of this paragraph and the next can only be found in OK.

last detail. In order to influence the mood even more, the exercitants have to fast during this time. The rules stipulate particular care in eating and drinking. Bread is considered safe enough, but everything else must be greatly restricted. One has to meditate even when eating, while picturing Christ and the disciples eating supper together in Emmaus. That is essentially the content of the third week.

The fourth week relates to everything that happened after Christ's death; the main meditation is on the meeting between Christ and his mother after his resurrection. These exercises are referred to as "Exercitia de amore Dei," exercises on divine love, but this designation only applies for laypersons. In this final week, however, there is also a second meditation or a second aspect of these contemplations that is intended for the members of the Jesuit order.

I first want briefly to discuss the simple meditation—that is, the one that laypersons also do, following the old instructions of that Spanish monk Izquierdo. So, in this last exercise the subject is divine love. This is connected with the meditation on the meeting of Christ and his mother, which is about maternal love on the one hand, and filial love on the other. This meditation is done in order to awaken love, in the first order divine love. The following points must be meditated on:

> I first recall to mind all the beneficence that God has shown me. Above all, the beneficence of the Creation. [. . .] Then the beneficence of preservation [that God has kept me alive until now; which includes that continuous influence of the omnipotent God who keeps me alive, because if this influence did not take place continuously, I could not live for a moment; CGJ]. [. . .] Then comes the beneficence of redemption. Which includes the advent of the Son of God into the world [. . .]. And further, the aid of the grace in which we partake [through the Church; CGJ]. [. . .] And then we recall all the particular individual beneficence that God has shown me [in the course of my life; CGJ]. [. . .] I also have to observe the excellence of the giver in terms of the multitude and magnitude of the beneficence and the infinite intensity of the love from which the beneficence flows to me.[631]

---

[631] Izquierdo (1695), pp. 112–13 (again, with regard to variations between Izquierdo's text and Jung's translation, see n. 266): "In primo puncto ad memoriam traham beneficia mihi facta a Deo. Nimirum beneficium Creationis. [. . .] Beneficium Conservationis. Ad quod pertinent influxus continuatus Omnipotentiae divinae [. . .]. Beneficium Redemptionis. Ad quod pertinent Adventus Filii Dei in Mundum [. . .]. Auxillia gratiae, quae nobis

The second point in the meditation is,

> [t]he manner in which God inhabits all creatures, how he inhabits the elements, how he lives in the trees and gives them life, in the animals, how he gives them the ability to sense, and in men to whom he also gives intellect [that is, intelligence; CGJ], and also in me by giving me existence, life, feelings and comprehension. And moreover, how in his temple, which is created in his image, he has bestowed on everything supernatural gifts through which one believes in, loves, honors, and worships God.[632]

You see again here this conception of the absolute dependence of men on the creative primordial source, on the Godhead. It is thus actually a psychological observation that can also be understood very scientifically: namely, that we are dependent on the correct functioning of our unconscious, of our whole life and of our dispositions, without which we cannot do anything at all. So faithful Christians or Catholics who understand these things literally will have a conception that absolutely corresponds with the reality of nature. That is a great advantage, because then one essentially has the right attitude. But if you imagine you live from your consciousness or intellect, then you live downward from up here, and that is not right because it is against nature. Consciousness is the happy result of natural life, but nowadays we like to reverse this eternal basic truth. We think we can do everything we want, that we can pit our intelligence against nature. But that is simply very bad for our physiological health and unhygienic for our nervous systems. Thus I permit myself to consider these metaphysical things from the medical side. That explains, for example, why it is that when people can make peace with their God, they feel a lot better in their nervous and physiological systems. Then they function properly. When we are against nature, the body cannot thrive either.

---

comparavit. [. . .] Beneficia denique omnia particularia, quae mihi particulatim contulit Deus [. . .]./ Ponderabo excellentiam Datoris: multitudinem, ac magnitudinem beneficiorum: intensionem infinitam amoris, a quo illa manarunt[.]"

[632] Izquierdo (1695), p. 114: "[Considerare,] quomodo Deus habitat in omnibus creaturis. In elementis, dando eis esse: in arboribus dando eis vivere: in animalibus, dando eis sentire: & in hominibus, dando eis praeterea intelligere: atque ita in me, dando mihi esse, vivere, sentire, & intelligere. Et insuper, ut in templo suo ad suam similitudinem facto; ornatoque supernaturalibus donis. Quibus creditur, amatur, veneratur, & colitur."

The third point is,

the way in which God works in all creatures, how he labors [. . .] in the heavens, elements, trees, animals, fruits, and also in me.[633]

So it is a precise observation and realization of the work of God in individual creatures and also in me. And it is specifically to be understood that all things that befall me are the effects of that other from whom I am also derived. This view also fits perfectly in the psychological sense, because if my unconscious does not cooperate with me, I cannot even formulate my next sentence, for example, because all the sentences I utter have already been preconsciously prepared and flow into my speech. If then the preconscious functioning[634] of the unconscious is disturbed, I find myself unable to remember things; for example, I might even have written a name in my notes, but if the unconscious decides to confuse me, it escapes my mind completely. I am entirely dependent on whether the unconscious labors in me or not, or, in metaphysical language, whether God labors in me or not. If that is understood properly, it means once again one has a kind of attitude that is simply practical: it is *mentally hygienic*[635] to consider things in this way. Because then I always give more attention to my unconscious, to how it is functioning, to whether it is moving with me or what it is actually producing. That's why the psychiatrist has to ask, "What did you think then? What occurs to you about that?" The patient has long been receiving signs from the unconscious, has maybe had dreams. And look there! They were all there, but this patient was not the kind of person who paid attention to how God labored, worked in him; instead he believed he could sail on by using his head, and thereby capsized.

These truths in metaphysical form are somewhat difficult for modern people to stomach, but if we can stomach them despite the metaphysics, we have to ask whether the psychology behind them is not actually completely healthy. Then we might make some discoveries.

In the fourth point, one has to "consider the way in which all created goods derive from the uncreated."[636] That is, how everything that is

---

[633] Izquierdo (1695), p. 115: "[Considerare,] quomodo Deus laborat (hoc est se gerit, ac si laborarit) in omnibus creaturis. In Coelis, elementis, arboribus, animalibus, fructibus, &c. & in me ispo."

[634] RS has "Kooperieren" (cooperation) instead of "Funktionieren" (functioning).

[635] Jung used the English phrase "mental hygiene."

[636] Izquierdo (1695), p. 116: "Considerare, quomodo omnia bona creata descendunt ab increatis."

man-made, all the great, good, and beautiful things that people make, actually come from the uncreated. That is simply a continuation of the other meditation. Insofar as I am convinced that all my conscious contents spring forth from the unconscious, I can also accept that all human achievements ultimately stem from unconscious patterns. That's a Platonism, but it corresponds precisely to the structure of the psyche.

And then, at the end, Izquierdo speaks of love for God and says that "he who so loves finds nothing that he could love so much other than God."[637] So if one follows this belief and this insight, then one understands that the highest goal of man lies in loving most of all this power that completely carries him. That is the end of the meditations for laypersons.

Now we come to the second part, namely the meditations that are specifically for the *milites ecclesiae*, the soldiers of the Church—that is, the members of the Societas Iesu. This confrontation of Christ with his mother takes place after death. In a way, this event takes place in the afterlife, although his mother is alive. Christ, however, has already become a ghost at this point, an incorporeal being, and meets his mother after his resurrection. What occurs is therefore somewhat supernatural. Psychologically, that always means something that actually occurs in the unconscious. It is connected to the fact that the mother has a dual significance.

Not for nothing did our old friend Izquierdo here insert a meditation for laypersons with the purpose of making them aware of all they owed to the Godhead: that is, that metaphysical background. He thereby expressed an idea which is represented in the symbol of the mother: namely, that the confrontation with the mother is a return to the source. The mother of Christ is the origin of Christ. He came out of her. She is the mother soil from which he grows. As the source, she is a symbol of that from which Christ always emerges, the ground on which Christ always stands. And this ground on which one stands is in psychological terms the unconscious soul. On it we stand, on it we repose. It flows into us. It is the creator of our consciousness, and in this sense Christ is confronted with his mother, with his source. This idea is taken up in the meditation for laypersons, but there the mother is replaced by the Godhead.

That happens in the Jesuit meditation too, but it also goes further, specifically in that the meditation on the background involves not only contemplating the good things God has done for me, but also considering the background, in the sense of the mother, in more detail. It is as if the meditation were trying to break through into a psychological contemplation

---

[637] Izquierdo (1695), p. 117: "qui sic amat, nihil iam invenit, quod amet, nisi Deum."

and trying to understand this background in a different way, not just as the active, willing creator God, but also as a maternal nurturing being. There is a connection here with the peculiar nature of the Christ image, that androgynous, masculine-feminine nature which I spoke about earlier in a different context. This dual-gendered characteristic is connected with the nature of the unconscious. The unconscious is neither masculine nor feminine, but something more. It oscillates between these qualities. That's why the old non-Christian creator gods are generally hermaphroditic. All these gods of the Gnostic, Greek, or Indian traditions are generally hermaphroditic because the psychological background—which is after all our sole model for such cosmogonic speculation—has a hermaphroditic character: the human being, that is, is hermaphroditic in nature. It is only a matter of which genes are in the majority that determines whether a child is a boy or a girl. But the opposite-sex genes do not disappear. They are always there. That's why each man has a female side and each woman has a male side. There are people in whom the ratio is almost equal. Thus we can see why there are some very masculine women and some very feminine men. These things also determine homosexuality, provided it is not just a *développement arrêté*.[638] But in addition there are also true hermaphrodites.

In any case, this hermaphroditic nature plays a significant role in the Jesuit meditation, although it is not considered with such rigid determination, as these things are prudently not thought through to their ultimate conclusion. That would be too *shocking*. One cannot necessarily allow oneself to admit such things: that's why I also hesitated to attach such *termini*[639] to them.

This confrontation of Christ with the mother means psychologically that the image of the whole person as he is comes into confrontation with his mother, with his unconscious: either in its divine form, as with the *exercitia de amore Dei*, or in its feminine form, as in the meditation on the feminine aspect, on the mother aspect. It should actually be written in the exercises that the subject here is this feminine aspect which corresponds to the nature of Christ. He could not appear in the background as

---

[638] *développement arrêté* (Fr.): "arrested development." In "Marriage as a Psychological Relationship," Jung wrote, "The normal man is a fiction, although certain generally valid laws do exist. Psychic life is a development that can easily be arrested on the lowest levels. It is as though every individual had a specific gravity, in accordance with which he either rises, or sinks down, to the level where he reaches his limit. His views and convictions will be determined accordingly" (Jung, 1925, § 343; Engl.: *CW* 17).

[639] *termini* (Lat.): "terms."

an androgynous being if the background did not actually have this quality. The Christ image would not have such a quality if it was not drawn directly from its matrix: that is, from the divine couple, from father and mother, as the Gnosis says.

That's where the androgynous nature of Christ comes from. The Jesuit meditation, however, says nothing about this aspect, but says the mother is the Church, *ecclesia mater*. Thus the second professional part of this meditation is on the Church. And its form is prescribed by Ignatius in his *Regulae ascendium cum ecclesia*—rules for feeling with the Church, or the right attitude to hold toward the Church.

We will now look together at the Ignatian exercise rules, that is, the rules that are given in the "Annotationes" [additional material] laying out how these exercises are to be done. I'll have to translate some parts of it for you.[640] These parts are characteristic of the spirit of the Societas Iesu:

> Rules to follow in view of the true attitude of mind that we ought to maintain [as members] within the Church militant.[641]

So feeling or thinking with regard to the Church:

> *Rule 1* Laying aside all our judgments, we ought to keep our minds open and ready to obey in everything the true bride of Christ our Lord, our holy mother, the hierarchical Church.

> *Rule 2* We should praise confession made to a priest, and the reception of the Blessed Sacrament once a year, much more its reception once a month, and very much more its reception once a week, given the duly required dispositions.

> *Rule 3* We should praise frequent attendance at mass; also hymns, psalms, and long prayers, whether in or out of church; [. . .]

> *Rule 4* We should praise greatly religious life, virginity, and continence, and we should not praise matrimony to the same extent as any of these.

> *Rule 5* We should praise the vows of religion—obedience, poverty, and chastity—and other vows of perfection made voluntarily; [. . .]

> *Rule 6* We should praise the cult of the saints, venerating their relics and praying to the saints themselves, praising also the stations,

---

[640] BH states that Jung translated into German from the Latin.
[641] *IPW*, p. 356.

pilgrimages, indulgences, jubilees, dispensations, and the lighting of the candles in the churches.

Rule 7 We should praise the decrees about fasting and abstinence [. . .]

Rule 8 We should praise the decoration and architecture of churches, also statues, which should be venerated according to what they represent.

Rule 9 Finally we should praise all the precepts of the Church, being ready to seek arguments in their defence and never in any way to attack them.

Rule 10 We should be more inclined to approve and praise the decrees and regulations of those in authority, and their conduct as well; for although some of these things do not or did not in the past deserve approval, more grumbling and scandal than profit would be aroused by speaking against them [. . .]. In that way people would be become hostile towards authority, either temporal or spiritual. [. . .]

Rule 11 We should praise both positive theology and scholastic theology[.][642]

Then one has to show one's unanimity (*unanimitas*) with the Church. We must be in conformity with the Church.

Rule 13 [W]e must always maintain that the white I see, I shall believe to be black, if the hierarchical Church so stipulates; for we believe that between Christ Our Lord, the bridegroom, and the Church, His bride, there is the same Spirit who governs and directs us for the good of our souls because it is by the same Spirit and the Lord of us all who gave the Ten Commandments that our holy mother Church is directed and governed.[643]

So, because Christ is the Lord of the Church and because the Church, the *sponsa*, his bride, is derived from the same Holy Ghost that also governs us, we must believe what the Church says: even if we see white, we must believe it is black.

---

[642] *IPW*, pp. 356–57.
[643] Ibid., p. 358.

The next rule says,

Rule 14 Even granting as perfectly true that no one can be saved without being predestined, and without having faith and grace, nevertheless much caution is needed in the way in which we discuss and propagate these matters.[644]

Namely,

Rule 15 We must not make a habit of talking too much about predestination [. . .] that simple people are not led into error, as sometimes happens with them saying, "It is already decided whether I am to be saved or damned, so whether I do good or evil can change nothing."[645]

So that's why one should not talk too much about predestination.

Rule 17 Similarly we must not talk of grace at such length and with such insistence[.][646]

In order, namely, that no poison is generated that stultifies people's attitude to free will so that they say, "Well what can I do? It's no use whether I decide this or that if grace doesn't come from above."

The eighteenth rule, the last, relates to divine love, namely that we should serve God out of purest love, and that we should also fear the Divine Majesty, however, because that will greatly help one escape from mortal sin. Specifically, one must fear God with the fear of the son, that is, with a childlike fear. Interestingly, it is not an *amor filialis*, but a *timor filialis*, which indicates the dual nature of the Godhead. God is not only to be loved, but also to be feared. So if God is the *summum bonum*, he is only love, but apparently God also has another side that is to be feared.

You see in these *regulae* those things that the Jesuits are accused of: namely, that they have a rather artful way of dealing with the truth. They are after all the *milites ecclesiae*, who may only say and do things that are in concordance with the welfare of the Church. And insofar as the Church is not just a mystical institution but a legal, worldly one (it extends into this world, hence the significance of the church state), it takes part in global politics, and it is well known that one cannot do politics without lying.

---

[644] Ibid.
[645] Ibid.
[646] Ibid.

A Protestant reviewer of the exercises says, in conclusion,

> The Ignatian method is not lacking in psychological perspicacity and didactic calculation that even tips over into craftiness, but it does lack above all the character of "discretio," a sensitive discernment and adaption to the spirits who are to be led—or better said: to be educated, that "discretio" which the wise educator Benedict of Nursia demanded as the main requirement of the abbot, i.e. of the spiritual father.[647]

In this respect, the Benedictine orders are organized in a much more considerate and less "militaristic" fashion.

> The consequence of this Ignatian intolerance in recognizing and permitting only their own methods is actually also a widespread hardening into the schematic across the whole Catholic life of edification, the so-called inner asceticism. Even in this area in which previously individualistic, varied mysticism reigned free, all individuality has died out and been expunged since the preeminence of the Jesuit system. Aridity prevails everywhere, and has extended deep into sermons and Christian teaching. Catholicism has Ignatius to thank for that, though he probably did not mean it so.[648]

Even within the Catholic church there is actually considerable opposition to the Jesuit system. But because it's a practice that can be taught, a method that can be taught to anyone, and an effective one at that, then it is of course highly valued, because it can be schematically applied. But the Benedictine *discretio*, and thereby also individuality, falls completely by the wayside. And it begins precisely at that point where Ignatius (and one cannot blame him for that, but this is where the Jesuit order remains at the medieval level) does not think the matter right through and instead translates "the mother" as Church. This is understandable, if one considers the weakness of human nature.

But we will see that in the Middle Ages, and even earlier, a movement arose that placed value precisely on that which lies within man—namely on that Augustinian[649] point that is the punctiform image of the fullness of the Godhead—and tried to find the individual path, in opposition to the Church's attempt to subsume the whole of the human soul into its institution.

---

[647] Funk (1913a), p. 35.
[648] Ibid.
[649] Cf. n. 540. RS has "individuelle lebendige" (individual living) instead of "Augustinischen" (Augustinian).

Winter Semester 1940/41
(Lecture 3)

Lecture 3[650]

22 NOVEMBER 1940

TODAY WE ARE going to recapitulate the *Exercitia spiritualia* of Saint Ignatius. The exercises were invented by Saint Ignatius, but there's also some history behind them. They had precursors. They emerged from two sources, namely from the prayer and meditation exercises of the so-called Devoti[651] who directed spiritual exercises in monasteries centuries earlier. That is one of the sources. The other source is Islam. At the end of the eleventh century, there was a great theologian and scholar, Al-Ghazâlî, who died in 1111.[652] This theologian is the real spiritual father of Islam. He initiated the whole mystical development within Islam. He created exercises that were spread out over three or four weeks for the faithful to practice and deepen their mystical life.

Ignatius structured his exercises in the form of military drill rules. He himself had originally been an army officer, and as he lay in his sick bed after being wounded he became acquainted with spiritual books from which he got the inspiration for the exercises. These exercises take place over four weeks. Those are known as the large exercises. There are also smaller three-day exercises, but they are no more than sermons by missionaries, whereas the large exercises are really and truly meditations.

The actual meditations are preceded by the *praeparatio*, the preparations. Here two main texts are meditated on: the "Anima Christi" and the

[650] Jung used the third lecture of the winter semester 1940/41 for a recapitulation of his lecture series on the *Exercitia spiritualia*. The editor decided to add this lecture to volume 7 of Jung's lectures series in order to provide a coherent theme for each volume. The text of the lecture is compiled from notes by RS, ES, LSM, and OK, in conjunction with Louise Tanner (LT) and the English translation of BH.

[651] See n. 116.

[652] See pp. 62–63.

"Fundamentum." The "Anima Christi" is an old Church prayer to the soul of Christ. The Latin version goes,

> Anima Christi, sanctifica me.
> Corpus Christi, salva me.
> Sanguis Christi, inebria me.
> Aqua lateris Christi, lava me.
> Passio Christi, conforta me.
> O bone Jesu, exaudi me.
> Intra tua vulnera absconde me.
> Ne permittas me separari a te.
> Ab hoste maligno defende me.
> In hora mortis meae voca me,
> Et iube me venire ad te,
> Ut cum Sanctis tuis laudem te
> In saecula saeculorum. Amen.

> (Soul of Christ, sanctify me.
> Body of Christ, save me.
> Blood of Christ, inebriate me.
> Water from the side of Christ, wash me.
> Passion of Christ, strengthen me.
> O Good Jesus, hear me.
> Within your wounds hide me.
> Permit me not to be separated from you.
> From the wicked foe, defend me.
> At the hour of my death, call me
> and bid me come to you
> That with your saints I may praise you
> For ever and ever. Amen.)[653]

This prayer is then meditated on line by line; in previous lectures we examined the meditation process in detail. We have an excellent example and explanations in a modern work by the Catholic theologian and Jesuit Erich Przywara.[654] Three volumes have been published to date. There you can gain an impression of the incredible precision with which these lines are meditated on. His elaborations on the "Anima Christi" and the

---

[653] This translation is from *Finding God in All Things: A Marquette Prayer Book*, pp. 90–91. For the translation by John Henry Newman, see n. 276. Jung read out a German version (also given at n. 276) that was probably his own translation.

[654] Przywara (1938).

"Fundamentum" are actually the best part of the whole book. You will find there all the impressions you need of Przywara's theology and ultimately also of Ignatius's, as he weighs up the meaning of every word, as it were.

The purpose of this meditation is that the idea and form of the Christ figure—that is, the anima—is pictured through active imagination so vividly that one is in a manner of speaking transported into the presence of this image that actually exists, and ultimately absorbed into it, so to speak. That means that the believer—we can no longer say yogi here—disappears completely into the self-created figure which of course, according to the official or orthodox view was not, however, created by the believer: because Christ is an eternal presence, which the meditator simply makes visible to himself through the imagination. In a way, he simply supports his already existing conviction of the absolute existence of Christ, and through such an intimate and strenuous engagement with this figure, the meditator's own being or soul is gradually transferred into the idea and form of Christ. And as a result, the human being is elevated, which after all is the ultimate purpose of such a meditation.

As Przywara says, "Thus it is the perfect wholeness": namely, the wholeness of this perfect God-man, a unity of "spirit and flesh, God and creature."[655] Those are Przywara's own words. Christ appears in this meditation as a wholeness, not only of the person but also of the Godhead, insofar as he is simultaneously *verus Deus* and *verus homo*, according to the Church formula. So: true God and true man at the same time, an all-encompassing figure in the fullest sense of the word; namely, a figure that surrounds the human being and encloses it fully within itself.

Now as you already heard, this figure corresponds to the Eastern figure of the *purusha*, *âtman*, or Mahâsukha, which is the example we discussed last time, the figure of the mystical Buddha. It is the idea of a being that completely encompasses the conscious man, a being that at the same time also raises up and elevates men to a wholeness which they would not be capable of on their own. This elevated and greater being that encompasses man is known in the Indian definition as the transcendent self of human beings: not an I, but something beyond the I, a transcendent subject. In Christian mysticism—not in Jesuit mysticism but according to Paul or John—it is the Christ in us, the "inner Christ," to whom we relate "as the grape to the vine."[656] We are part of this whole, perfused by the blood

---

[655] Ibid., p. 5.

[656] John 15:1–8: "I am the true vine, and my Father is the husbandman./ Every branch in me that beareth not fruit he taketh away: and every branch that beareth fruit, he purgeth

of Christ. We share in his life, and it flows through us. We breathe as it were with his breath and as a result we are entirely Christ, and yet we are also parts.

Naturally, the Eastern conception differs here. In the Eastern view, it is the yogi who becomes Buddha. Here it is the exact opposite. Man becomes Christ insofar as Christ takes man into himself. Christ is the agent, he stands before the believer, draws him in, and embraces him. It is not the believer who embraces Christ. Although such expressions [as "the inner Christ"] may crop up, that is not the intention. It is only meant like that in the East. There, that is, there is no subject present other than the yogi. The Buddha does not even exist any more. In the East, it is blasphemy to say there is still a Buddha. Buddha has entered *nirvâna*, entered the state of non-existence, and has thereby demonstrated his perfection, shown that he was able to bring about his complete dissolution.[657] If you think that the Buddhist worship before a Buddha statue is actually directed at this Buddha, you are completely mistaken. The Buddha no longer exists, whereas in Christianity it is the opposite. Christ exists, and that's why in these exercises the person is transferred into the form, as it were, into the whole of this transcendent subject, and disappears as a human being. That is after all the purpose of these exercises: namely, to make the subjective I-person disappear, because it is that person who always willfully rebels against the discipline of the Church.

Now, this notion which I have just tried to explain to you is not some invention of Saint Ignatius; no, these are ideas that have been present in the Church for ages, and not just in the Church, but also in the activities of antiquity that took place outside the Church. I'd like to read you a section from the *Philosophoumena* of Hippolytus in this regard. He was one of the Church fathers and died as a martyr in the year 235 CE. He was a presbyter in Rome, later becoming a bishop of a schismatic group that split from the main church due to disputes about the Godhead of Christ

---

it, that it may bring forth more fruit./ Now ye are clean through the word which I have spoken unto you./ Abide in me, and I in you. As the branch cannot bear fruit of itself, except it abide in the vine; no more can ye, except ye abide in me./ I am the vine, ye are the branches: He that abideth in me, and I in him, the same bringeth forth much fruit: for without me ye can do nothing./ If a man abide not in me, he is cast forth as a branch, and is withered; and men gather them, and cast them into the fire, and they are burned./ If ye abide in me, and my words abide in you, ye shall ask what ye will, and it shall be done unto you./ Herein is my Father glorified, that ye bear much fruit; so shall ye be my disciples" (*KJV*).

657 RS has "das absolute Nicht-Sein" (the absolute non-existence) instead of "seine vollkommene Auflösung" (his complete dissolution).

and ecclesiastical discipline. He wrote a great number of theological works, including commentaries (his *Commentary on the Prophet Daniel* being the oldest preserved biblical commentary), essays opposing the Gnostics, a paper on the calculation of the Easter dates, and a chronicle of ecclesiastical law and dogmatic works. His writings were widely disseminated in the ancient world.[658] He was an opponent of Pope Callixtus.[659] That was part of the Church's *chronique scandaleuse*. The two of them had an unholy quarrel. It was one of those cases where an introvert and an extravert rub up against each other, and for that reason it's particularly interesting. Hippolytus was hushed up by the Roman church, but his texts survived in Greek. A Greek man rediscovered them on Mount Athos in the [eighteen-]forties.[660] Hippolytus is one of the main sources of our knowledge of Gnostic, para-Christian systems, which are all derivations from that whole spiritual movement from which Christianity also originally emerged. Hippolytus says,

> And you shall receive the kingdom of heaven, you who, while you sojourned in *this* life, knew the Celestial King. And you shall be a companion of the Deity, and a co-heir with Christ, no longer enslaved by lusts or passions, and *never again* wasted by disease. For you have become God: for whatever sufferings you underwent while being a man, these He gave to you, because you were of mortal mould, but whatever it is consistent with God *to impart*, these God has promised to bestow upon you, because you have been deified, and begotten unto immortality. This constitutes *the import of the proverb*, "Know yourself"; i.e., discover God *within yourself, for* He has formed you *after His own image*. For with the knowledge

---

[658] Only OK has the last three sentences here.

[659] Callixtus (or Callistus) I was the bishop of Rome from around 218 until his death as a martyr in 222. During his papacy, he extended the forgiveness of sins to all kinds of transgressions, including adultery and murder, for which he was fiercely attacked by Hippolytus (ca. 170–235 CE): "And he first invented the device of conniving with men in regard of their indulgence in *sensual* pleasures, saying that all had their sins forgiven by himself. For he who is in the habit of attending the congregation of any one else, and is called a Christian, should he commit any transgression; the sin, they say, is not reckoned unto him, provided only he hurries off *and attaches himself* to the school of Callistus." (Hippolytus, 1886, 10.7, p. 131) The controversy ended with Hippolytus being declared rival bishop of Rome, the first antipope.

[660] Minoides Minas discovered a number of manuscripts at Mount Athos in 1842, amongst them *The Refutation of All Heresies*, which has been widely acknowledged as having been authored by Hippolytus (Engl.: 1886).

of self is conjoined the being an object of God's knowledge, for you are called by *the Deity* Himself.[661]

As you see, this formulation is very dangerous, as it could lead one toward all sorts of peculiar ideas. But this kind of avowal is very typical of the early Christian ideas. You'll find similar in Paul's epistles, and Hippolytus here refers to 1 Corinthians 13:12, where it says, "For now we see through a glass, darkly; but then face to face: now I know in part; but then shall I know even as also I am known."[662] Hippolytus takes this part literally, as it were. This inner relatedness with God, this reciprocal relationship through relatedness, was an idea originally present in Christianity and was not actually lost until much later.

I would like to read you something else, but it is Gnostic rather than Christian. It comes from another highly valuable document left to us by Hippolytus: the letter from Monoïmus, the Arab, to Theophrast. Monoïmus is not known otherwise, apart from through the work of Hippolytus. In this letter Monoïmus writes,

> [S]eek for Him from (out of) yourself, and learn who it is that absolutely appropriates (unto Himself) all things in you, and says, "My God (is) my mind, my understanding, my soul, my body." And learn from whence are sorrow, and joy, and love, and hatred, and involuntary wakefulness, and involuntary drowsiness, and involuntary anger, and involuntary affection; and if you accurately investigate these (points), you will discover (God) Himself, unity and plurality, in yourself, according to that title, and that He finds the outlet (for Deity) to be from yourself.[663]

This is a conception of the religious phenomenon as something absolutely psychological. He even goes so far as to say that God himself has his origin in man. That of course is in stark contrast to the truth of the Church: that he is a counterpart, a real "thou"; whereas here, God is not actually a "thou," but is rather my innermost essence. This teaching certainly tends in the Eastern direction. Monoïmus was an Arab. It is not out of the question that around this time, perhaps the first century, influences from the East had already spread westward. Indeed, there are also other reasons that make it quite likely. In the second century before Christ there were Buddhist monasteries in Persia. And in Hellenic-Egyptian literature there

---

[661] Hippolytus (1886), 10.30, p. 153.
[662] *KJV*.
[663] Hippolytus (1886), 8.8, p. 122.

are a few very striking ideas that probably have a connection with India. In India too, there are a few things that indicate links with the West, but we don't know exactly how old these influences are. This whole question is still very much in flux; we do not yet have sufficient information to properly evaluate these transmissions.

The interesting thing about this text is that the Godhead is made responsible for all involuntary mental phenomena. So, for example if people fall asleep without meaning to, or are unable to sleep, or have unwanted fits of anger or sadness, it is not their own action, but is "a Deo missum": sent by God. We say, "Don't be so lazy! Don't fall asleep! Pull yourself together!" as if one could tell God what to do, according to Monoïmus. This view contains a very important perspective on assessing human emotions. You all know that it is tremendously difficult to overcome emotions, to have complete mastery over them, as one says. It is impossible to do so without eventually doing oneself harm in the process. Habitual suppression of emotions is dangerous in certain circumstances; you could even say life-threatening. It's not just that the emotions then fester—such suppression can cause an actual infirmity to develop, because you are internally compressed by the affects that never come to the surface, and it is then hugely cathartic when you can finally let loose. And this over-empowerment of mental phenomena, the might of all psychological experiences that come to us, becomes the criterion for this inner Godhead, this willful arbitrary Godhead.

Now to the "Fundamentum." The "Fundamentum" is a text that Ignatius puts at the start of his exercises. I'll give you the German[664] version here:

> The human person is created to praise, reverence and serve God Our Lord, and by so doing to save his or her soul. The other things on the face of the earth are created for human beings in order to help them pursue the end for which they are created. It follows from this that one must use other created things in so far as they help towards one's end, and free oneself from them in so far as they are obstacles to one's end. To do this we need to make ourselves indifferent to all created things, provided the matter is subject to our free choice and there is no prohibition. Thus as far as we are concerned, we should not want health more than illness, wealth more than poverty, fame more than disgrace, a long life more than a short one, and similarly

[664] I.e., Funk (1913a), p. 135.

for all the rest, but we should desire and choose only what helps us more towards the end for which we are created.[665]

The "Fundamentum" is so named because it is the ideological and psychological[666] foundation of the exercises, intended to make exercitants aware of the purpose of human life. In contrast, that is, to our biological notion that men's purpose lies within themselves, in this view man is created for a specific purpose and end. The purpose is the *laudare Dominum*, to praise the Lord at the heavenly court in the mold of the royal courts of the Orient, to belong to the circle surrounding the Lord, to be part of God's world, a grape on the vine which has to return to the vine. That is the purpose of human life and of mankind, and is also the foundation of the whole of Christian morality, I mean this Jesuit morality: namely, to use created things only to the extent that they serve to reach this goal. In Przywara, there is at this point an extensive meditation on the nature of God and the relationship of man to God. That is to say, he talks about God as the *unio oppositorum*, the union of the opposites. In God all opposites are united; in man they have fallen apart. Man is a conflict. That's why mankind is in a sad state, in need of redemption. The redemptive thing is the unity, and that unity is God. Przywara says that the conflict, the rift, is where the symbol of the cross enters in. That is this figure, namely the intersection: +. The symbol of the union of the opposites. And the thing that unites, the unity itself, is the Godhead. And so man meets the Godhead, as it were, in the center of the cross, as Przywara says, in that man is the manifested opposite, but God is the unity of the opposites. In the act of redemption, the human being becomes one, as God is one. The symbol of the cross is actually for Przywara really the symbol of God, of the essence of God. God is a cross. That is a very profound formulation: namely, that God himself is the suffering that is inflicted on men, in the sense that man is not God, is not unified, but is split in two and suffers from the longing and need to recover that unity. That gives the split in the human soul an unprecedentedly novel and important meaning. But even that is not new, as luckily we have a very interesting text from antiquity, namely the "Erinnerungen des Heiligen Johannes an Jesum," from Hennecke's collection *Neutestamentliche Apokryphen*. You can also find it in *Dokumente der Gnosis* by Schultz:[667]

---

[665] *IPW*, p. 289.

[666] ES has "philosophische" (philosophical) instead of "psychologische" (psychological).

[667] Jung quotes from the "Erinnerungen des Heiligen Johannes an Jesum" (John's recollections of Jesus) in Wolfgang Schultz's *Dokumente der Gnosis* (1910), pp. 202–13; here

And the Lord stood before me in the middle of the cave and illuminated it and said, "John! For the masses below in Jerusalem I am crucified and stabbed with lances and sticks and drink vinegar and bile. But to you I say, and listen to what I say, 'I promised you I would come up on to this mountain so that you would hear what the pupil must learn from the teacher, the man from God.'"[668]

This scene takes place during the crucifixion on Golgotha. John is transported to the top of the mountain where this revelation takes place. We see here once again the symbol of the mountain: "Do you wish to see Christ transfigured? Ascend this mountain; learn to know yourself."[669]

And with these words he showed me a cross with timbers of light, and around this cross a great crowd of figures flowing through each other with fluctuating forms. And it had one single form and the same appearance.[670]

This "crowd" refers precisely to the multiplicity of the psychological entities in the human being, and here it has one single form, namely the human form. Many things are combined within man and form a multiplicity. That's why the writer Carl Spitteler once called the "multiplicity of his soul" the "peoples of his soul."[671]

---

pp. 207–8. The German translation by Edgar Hennecke of the *Acta S. Johannis* in his *Neutestamentliche Apokryphen* (Hennecke, 1904; Engl.: *New Testament Apocrypha*, 1963) varies significantly from that of Schultz. The English translation of Schultz's German text here is by CS.

[668] Schultz (1910), pp. 207–8.

[669] Richard of Saint Victor (1979), p. 136. See Jung's lecture of 15 November 1940 (*JMP*, vol. 6, pp. 284–88).

[670] Schultz (1910), p. 208.

[671] In his novel *Imago* (1906), the Swiss author and Nobel laureate Carl Spitteler (1845–1924) wrote, "There at home, before the front door, he turned in the direction of her apartment and spread his arms wide: 'Imago,' he said, calling her name. 'No, more than Imago, because your majesty is ennobled with the pathos of corporeality. Theuda and Imago combined in a single person.' Then, charging into his room, he gathered all the *peoples of his soul* 'Children! Great news. You may love her; love without condition or caveat, without measure and without limitation, the more intensely, the more intimately the better. Because she is noble, and she is good.' The permission was met with a thunderous cry of joy; the whole Noah's ark danced around him. And more and more bands of figures, about whose existence he had had no idea, came cheering out of the shadows carrying blazing torches and bedecked with garlands. He smiled as he watched the celebration, and he too was overjoyed about his permission—like a king who after many years of fierce resistance finally allows a constitution and is overcome by the undreamed-of gratitude of the people" (Spitteler, 1945 [1906], pp. 371–72. English translation here by CS; emphasis added).

Above the cross [please note that it says *above* the cross; CGJ] however, I saw the Lord with no form, rather merely as a voice, not the
voice that we were used to but a voice that was sweet and gracious,
a truly divine voice, which said to me, "John! Someone has to hear
this from me, because I need one who will hear it. This cross of light
will soon be called word by me for your sakes, soon spirit, soon
Jesus, soon anointed one, soon door, soon way, soon bread, soon seed,
soon resurrection, soon son, soon father, soon breath of spirit, soon
life, soon truth, soon faith, soon grace. And it has these names for
the sake of the people; but in reality it is the boundary of all things,
actually conceived and proclaimed to us, and for that which is solidified it is the sure release of all bonds, and the harmony of wisdom. Because the harmony of wisdom involves powers of the right
and left, forces, dominions, daemons, threats, rages, slanderers, Satan
and the lowest root from which the essence of all created things
originates."[672]

That is the rhizome, the root, the elements, the chaos from which everything came about, the matter, the *hyle*.[673]

Now this cross (stake), which solidified everything by means of *logos* and separated the things of formation from the things below, but
afterward expanded into the All, is not the wooden cross you will
see when you descend from here [the vision was on Golgotha; CGJ].
Also I, whom you now do not see but whose voice you hear, am not
the one who is on the cross; I was taken for he who I am not, without being the one I was for the many. Rather, what they will say
of me is instead ignoble and unworthy of me. And if even the place of
rest [that is, paradise; CGJ] is neither seen nor described: how much
less will one be able to look on me, the Lord.[674]

The uniform crowd around the cross is the lower humanity [that is
the part of mankind that is in need of redemption; CGJ]. And you
see it in the cross, even if not in uniform appearance; and it would
never be completely consolidated by the descending *logos*. But if the

[672] Schultz (1910), p. 208.
[673] The term *hyle*, originally Greek for "wood," was used by Aristotle to denote the
basic underlying substance of all that is physical. The *hyle* only comes into existence when
form is attached to it. Roman philosophers used the concept of "materia" instead.
[674] Schultz (1910), pp. 208–9.

essence of mankind and the descending crowd is completely grasped by the *logos*, convinced by the power of my voice as you hear it now, then I will no longer be who I am now. Because until you do not call yourself mine, I am not what I am. But if you hear me, pause as soon as you have heard me, as I do; and I will be the one I was as soon as you, like me, are with me. Because this rests with you. The multitude, however, and above all those who are far removed from the secret, despise and recognize me rather as I am wholly with the Father and as the Father is with me.[675]

I did not suffer, therefore, from anything they will say of me. But also that suffering which I showed you and the others in the dance I want to hear described as secret. Because who I am when you look, that I have already shown you. But who I really am, only I know and no other. Let me then keep mine, and be content to see yours through me. But to look at me in reality is, as I told you, impossible.[676]

You hear that I suffered; but I did not suffer. And you hear that I did not suffer; but suffer I did! I was whipped and no strikes hit me; hanged, but I was not strung up. The blood that flowed out of me did not flow; and all the things they say about me are not true, and the things they do not say are things I did suffer. But I want to give you a hint about what that is: because I know that you will understand. So think of me as of the word's praise, the word's flagellation, the word's blood, the word's wound, the word's connection, the word's suffering, the word's solidification, the word's death. And through these boundaries I describe MAN. Reflect on the words, then you will also understand their Lord, and the MAN as three and what he suffered.[677]

This most noteworthy text demonstrates the ways people have thought about these matters even as far back as the early days of Christianity. Of course, Przywara doesn't refer to this text, as it is not in the canon. I don't know whether he had it in mind at all, but actually it contains all the ideas that Przywara also expresses in his meditation.

Now regarding the sequence of the Ignatian exercises, as I already told you, they are split into four weeks. The first week is spent meditating on

[675] Ibid., p. 209.
[676] Ibid.
[677] Ibid., pp. 209–10.

the three aspects of sin: the sin of the angels and the insurrection of Lucifer against God, the disobedience of Adam, and one's own sinfulness. This is usually followed by a conversation known as a colloquy: that is, a dialogue between the exercitant and the Godhead. But it is a one-sided conversation. Only the believer speaks, God does not speak. Nothing is mentioned about that. Then there is a thorough meditation on one's own sins, and then the colloquies are repeated, then the exercises again, and finally there is a meditation on hell, in which hell is imagined down to the finest detail. The anguish of hell must now, says Ignatius, be experienced with all one's senses, seen, heard—the cries of the damned—smelt—the stench of sulfur, smoke. Finally, the burning of the fire must be felt, and this goes on for days.

In the second week is the meditation on the kingdom of Christ, the incarnation, and the nativity, which must also be imagined using the senses so that it penetrates every sense, it is felt, seen, heard, smelt, tasted. Then comes the meditation on the circumstances of Christ's life, especially the great battle of the principle of good, personified by Christ, against Satan. There are Persian prototypes of this: for example, Gayômard, the Persian god-man who clashed with the forces of darkness. Of course, that was long before Christianity. Here we see the enactment of these battles with Ahriman, the god of darkness and of suffering. It is the eternal battle between dark and light.[678] That must be thoroughly meditated on in order to make it conscious in one's mind.

The third week therefore logically follows with a meditation on the Passion of Christ. This suffering is again the result of experiencing the conflict. This week involves fasting and mortification.

In the fourth week comes the "Exercitium de amore Dei," the exercise on the love of God, in which God enters this conflict as redeemer and lovingly takes the person back into his fold. This is followed by the meditation on the epiphany of Christ after his death, which underscores the transcendence of this subject and to an extent draws man, through identification with this Christ figure, up out of the temporal and into eternity. Last of all are the famous rules, "Regulae ad sentiendum cum ecclesia,"

---

[678] Gayômard, according to Zoroastrian tradition, is the primal human being. Created by Ahura Mazda (The Wise Lord), he was the first to accept his religious doctrine. He lived three thousand years in peace before the onslaught of Evil (Ahriman). While his companion the primeval ox died instantly after Ahriman's attack, Gayômard continued to live for a further thirty years. From the seminal fluid of the dying giant originated the first human couple, Mašya and Mašyāne, forty years later. After Gayômard's death, Ahriman attacked fire (mingling it with smoke) and the cosmic battle between good and evil began.

on thinking and feeling in the Church, about bringing one's attitude of mind into accord with the intentions of the Church. Here Ignatius goes so far as to say that "the white I see, I shall believe to be black, if the hierarchical Church so stipulates."[679] And this demonstrates precisely the accusation that is leveled at the Jesuits, that they go against their own judgment.

[679] *IPW*, p. 358.

Abbreviations

BH	Barbara Hannah, ed. (1959) *Modern Psychology: Notes on Lectures Given at the Eidgenössischen Technischen Hochschule, Zürich, by Prof. Dr. C. G. Jung*, October 1933–July 1941, compiled and translated by Elizabeth Welsh and Barbara Hannah, 3 vols (Zurich: privately published).
CW	C. G. Jung (1953–83): *The Collected Works of C. G. Jung*, ed. Sir Herbert Read, Michael Fordham, and Gerhard Adler, trans. R.F.C. Hull, executive director William McGuire, 20 vols and 2 supplementary vols (Bollingen Series 20) (New York: Pantheon; Princeton, NJ: Princeton University Press)
ES	Eduard Sidler
GW	C. G. Jung (1958–94): *Gesammelte Werke*, ed. Lena Hurwitz-Eisner, Lilly Jung-Merker, Marianne Niehus-Jung, Franz Riklin, Elisabeth Rüf, and Leonie Zander, 20 vols (Zurich: Rascher; Olten: Walter)
IPW	Saint Ignatius of Loyola (1996): *Personal Writings: Reminiscences, Spiritual Diary, Select Letters including the Text of* The Spiritual Exercises, trans. with introduction and notes by Joseph A. Munitiz and Philip Endean (London: Penguin Books).
JA	C. G. Jung Papers Collection, ETH-Bibliothek, ETH Zurich University Archives
JL	Jung Library Küsnacht
JLN	Jung's Lecture Notes from the C. G. Jung Papers Collection, ETH-Bibliothek, ETH Zurich University Archives (JA)
JMP	*Jung's Lectures on Modern Psychology Delivered at the ETH Zurich*, ed. Ernst Falzeder, Martin Liebscher, Sonu Shamdasani, and Christopher Wagner, 8 vols (Philemon Foundation) (Princeton: Princeton University Press, 2018–)

JOHA   Jung Oral History Archive, Countway Library of Medicine, Harvard Medical School, Boston

KSA   Friedrich Nietzsche (1988 [1967–77]): *Sämtliche Werke: Kritische Studienausgabe*, compiled under the general editorship of Giorgio Colli and Mazzino Montinari, second revised edition, 15 vols (Berlin: De Gruyter)

KJV   *King James Version* of the Bible

LSM   Lucie Stutz-Meyer

LT   Louise Tanner

MHSI   Monumenta Historica Societatis Iesu

MHSI-MI   José Calveras and Cándido de Dalmases, eds (1969): *Sancti Ignatii de Loyola exercitia spiritualia: Textuum antiquissimorum nova editio lexicon textus hispani* (Monumenta Historica Societatis Iesu 100: Monumenta Ignatiana, Seria Secunda: Exercitia Spiritualia. S. Ignatii de Loyola et eorum directoria) (Rome: Societas Iesu)

OK   Otto Karthaus

RE   Saint Ignatius of Loyola: *Reminiscences, or Autobiography of Ignatius Loyola*, as heard and written down by Luís Gonçalves de Câmara, trans. with an introduction and notes by Philip Endean; in *IPW* (see above), pp. 1–64

RS   Rivkah Schärf, later Schärf-Kluger

SBE   Max Müller, ed. (1879–1910): *Sacred Books of the East*, 50 vols (Oxford: Clarendon Press)

Bibliography

Aldama, Antonio de (1990): *The Constitutions of the Society of Jesus: The Formula of the Institute, Notes for a Commentary*, trans. Ignacio Echániz (St. Louis: The Institute of Jesuit Sources).

Angelus Silesius, Johann (1657): *Cherubinischer Wandersmann: Sinnliche Beschreibung der vier letzten Dinge; Sämtliche poetischer Werke*, vol. 3, ed. Hans Ludwig Held (Munich: Allgemeine Verlagsanstalt, 1924); English translation (1) as *Angelus Silesius: The Cherubinic Wanderer*, trans. Maria Shrady, with introduction and notes by Josef Schmidt and a preface by E. J. Furcha (New York: Paulist Press, 1986); (2) as *The Wanderer: Epigrams of a European Mystic*, trans. Werner Pelz (Sheffield: Cairns Publications, 2001).

Apelt-Riel, Susanne (2009): "Der Briefwechsel zwischen Ludwig Binswanger und Eugen Bleuler von 1907–1939 im Spannungsfeld von Psychoanalyse und Psychiatrie in der ersten Hälfte des 20. Jahrhunderts." Dissertation, University of Tübingen.

Bailey, Ruth (1969–70): "Unpublished oral interviews with Miss Ruth Bailey" (interviewer Gene F. Nameche). Archived in the C. G. Jung Biographical Archive at the Countway Library of Medicine, Harvard University.

Becker, Kenneth L. (2001): *Unlikely Companions: C. G. Jung on the Spiritual Exercises of Ignatius of Loyola* (Leominster: Gracewing; New Malden: Inigo).

Bellows, Henry Adams, trans. (1936): *The Poetic Edda* (Princeton, NJ: Princeton University Press); German: *Die Edda: Die Lieder der sogenannten älteren Edda*, ed. and trans. Hugo Gering (Leipzig: Bibliographisches Institut, 1892).

Bennet, E. A. (1985): *Meetings with Jung: Conversations recorded during the years 1946–1961* (Zurich: Daimon).

Bernet, Brigitta (2013): *Schizophrenie: Entstehung und Entwicklung eines psychiatrischen Krankheitsbildes um 1900* (Zurich: Chronos).

Bettenson, Henry, ed. and trans. (1956): *The Early Christian Fathers: A Selection from the Writings of the Fathers from St. Clement of Rome to St. Athanasius* (Oxford: Oxford University Press).

Bhikkhu Bodhi, trans. (2000): *The Connected Discourses of the Buddha: A Translation of the Saṃyutta Nikāya*, vol. 1 (Somerville, MA: Wisdom Publications).

Bishop, Paul (2002): *Jung's Answer to Job: A Commentary* (Hove: Brunner-Routledge).

——— (2017): *Ludwig Klages and the Philosophy of Life: A Vitalist Toolkit* (London: Routledge).

Bancquart, Marie-Claire (1994): *Anatole France* (Paris: Éditions Julliard).

Böminghaus, Ernst (1927): *Die Aszese der Ignatianischen Exerzitien. Ihr Sinn und Wert im Lichte heutiger Fragen und Bedürfnisse* (Freiburg im Breisgau: Herder).

Burkert, Walter (1962): *Weisheit und Wissenschaft: Studien zu Pythagoras, Philolaos und Platon* (Nuremberg: Hans Carl); English translation as *Lore and Science in Ancient Pythagoreanism*, trans. Edwin L. Minar (Cambridge, MA: Harvard University Press, 1972).

Burnet, John (1892): *Early Greek Philosophy* (London: Adam and Charles Black).

Burleson, Blake (2005): *Jung in Africa* (New York: Continuum).

Buonaiuti, Ernesto (1908 [1907]): *The Programme of Modernism*, trans. A. Leslie Lilley (London & Leipzig: T. Fisher Unwin).

—— (1936): "Die Exerzitien des Hl. Ignatius von Loyola," in *Westöstliche Seelenführung*, Eranos Yearbook 1935 (Zurich: Rhein Verlag), pp. 304–22.

—— (1939): "Maria und die jungfräuliche Geburt Jesu," in *Gestalt und Kult der "Großen Mutter,"* Eranos Yearbook 1938 (Zurich: Rhein Verlag), pp. 325–63.

—— (2008 [1945]): *Pellegrino di Roma: La generazione dell'esodo* (Rome: Alberto Gaffi).

Busch, Johannes (1886): *Des Augustinerpropstes Johannes Busch* Chronicon Windeshemense *und* Liber de reformatione monasteriorum, ed. Karl Grube (Halle: Otto Hendel).

Câmara, Luis Gonçalves da (2004 [1904]): *Remembering Iñigo: Glimpses of the Life of Saint Ignatius of Loyola; The* Memoriale *of Luís Gonçalves da Câmara*, trans. with introduction, notes, and indices by Alexander Eaglestone and Joseph A. Munitiz (St. Louis: The Institute of Jesuit Sources).

Cisneros, García[s] Ximénes de (1876 [1500]): *A Book of Spiritual Exercises, and A Directory for the Canonical Hours [Ejercitatorio de la vida spiritual]* (London: Burns and Oates).

Copenhaver, Brian P., ed. (1992): *Hermetica: The Greek* Corpus Hermeticum *and the Latin* Asclepius *in a New English Translation, with Notes and Introduction* (Cambridge: Cambridge University Press).

Creuzer, Georg Friedrich (1810–12): *Symbolik und Mythologie der alten Völker, besonders der Griechen*, second revised edition, 4 vols (Leipzig: Leske [vols 1 & 2]; Darmstadt: Heyer and Leske [vols 3 & 4]) (continued from vol. 5 [1819–23] by Franz Joseph Mone).

Cumont, Franz Valery Marie (1894–99): *Textes et monuments figurés relatifs aux mystères de Mithra* (Brussels: H. Lamertin); English translation (from second revised French edition) as *The Mysteries of Mithra*, trans. Thomas J. McCormack (Chicago: Open Court Publishing Co., 1903).

Dante (Alighieri) (1998 [1320]): *Divine Comedy*, trans. C. H. Sisson (Oxford: Oxford University Press).

De Quincey, Thomas (2013 [1821]): *Confessions of an English Opium Eater, and Other Writings* (Oxford: Oxford University Press).

Dieterich, Albrecht (1903): *Eine Mithrasliturgie* (Leipzig: B. G. Teubner).

Deussen, Paul (1894): *Allgemeine Geschichte der Philosophie mit besonderer Berücksichtigung der Religionen*, vol. 1.1: *Allgemeine Einleitung und Philosophie des Veda bis auf die Upanishad's* (Leipzig: F. A. Brockhaus).

—— (1897): *Sechzig Upanishad's des Veda* (Leipzig: F. A. Brockhaus).

—— (1919): *Die Geheimlehre des Veda: Ausgewählte Texte der Upanishad's* (Leipzig: F. A. Brockhaus).

Eusebius (1999): *The Church History: A New Translation with Commentary*, ed. and trans. Paul L. Maier (Grand Rapids, MI: Kregel).

Evans-Pritchard, Edward E. (1965): *Theories of Primitive Religion* (Oxford: Oxford University Press).

Exposcit debitum (1937 [1550]): *Constitutiones Societatis Iesu* (MHSI), vol. 1 (Rome: Societas Iesu), pp. 23—33.

Feuerstein, Georg (1997): *The Shambhala Encyclopedia of Yoga* (Boston, MA: Shambhala).

Finding God in All Things: A Marquette Prayer Book (2005) (Marquette: Marquette University Press).

Fludd, Robert (1629–31): *Medicina catholica, seu Mysticvm artis medicandi sacrarivm*, 2 vols (Frankfurt: William Fitzer).

Franz, Marie-Louise von (1959): *Die Visionen des Niklaus von Flüe* (Studien aus dem C. G. Jung Institut 9) (Zurich: Rascher).

—— (1970): *A Psychological Interpretation of the* Golden Ass *of Apuleius* (New York: Spring Publications); German translation as *Die Erlösung des Weiblichen im Manne: Der* Goldene Esel *des Apuleius in tiefenpsychologischer Sicht*, trans. Gisela Henney (Frankfurt: Insel, 1980).

Freud, Sigmund (1921): *Massenpsychologie und Ich-Analyse*, in Sigmund Freud, *Gesammelte Werke*, eleventh edition, vol. 13 (Frankfurt am Main: Fischer, 2010), pp. 71–162; English translation as *Group Psychology and the Analysis of the Ego*, in *The Standard Edition of the Complete Psychological Works of Sigmund Freud*, ed. James Strachey, vol. 18 (London: Hogarth Press, 1955), pp. 67–144.

Funk, Philipp (1913a): *Ignatius von Loyola* (Klassiker der Religion 6) (Berlin: Protestantischer Schriftvertrieb).

—— (1913b): *Von der Kirche des Geistes: Religiöse Essays im Sinne eines modernen Katholizismus* (Munich: Verlag der Krausgesellschaft).

Furness, Raymond (2000): *Zarathustra's Children: A Study of a Lost Generation of German Writers* (Rochester, NY: Camden House).

Gandhi, Mohandas Karamchand (Mahatma) (1962): *The Essential Gandhi: An Anthology of His Writings on His Life, Work, and Ideas*, ed. Louis Fisher, with a preface by Eknath Easwaran (New York: Vintage Books).

—— (1993): *An Autobiography: The Story of my Experiments with Truth* (Boston, MA: Beacon Press).

Geiger, Wilhelm, ed. and trans. (1922): "Nidâna-Samyutta," in *Samyutta Nikâya: Die in Gruppen geordnete Sammlung aus dem Pâli-Kanon der Buddhisten, zum ersten Mal ins Deutsche übertragen von Wilhelm Geiger*, vol. 2.1 (Munich: Oskar Schloss).

Goethe, Johann Wolfgang von (2015): *Faust: Parts I and II Complete*, trans. A. S. Kline (Poetry in Translation), available at https://www.poetryintranslation.com/klineasfaust.php (accessed 9 April 2022).

Gregorius Magnus (1878): *Liber moralium, sive Expositio in librum B. Job*, in *Sancti Gregorii Papae I*, in Patrologia Latina, vols 75–76, ed. Jacques-Paul Migne (Paris: Garnier Fratres), pp. 509–1162; 1–781; English translation as

Morals on the Book of Job by Saint Gregory the Great, 3 vols (Oxford: John Henry Parker; London: J.G.G. and J. Rivington, 1844), available online at https://www.ecatholic2000.com/job/untitled-53.shtml (accessed 9 April 2022).

Grenfell, Bernard P. and Arthur S. Hunt (1898), eds and trans.: *The Oxyrhynchus Papyri*, part 1 (London: Kegan Paul, Trench & Hübner).

Griffith, R.T.H. (1895): *The Hymns of the Atharva-veda*. Benares: Lazarus & Co.

Guyon, Jeanne-Marie Bouvier de La Motte (2007 [1685]): *A Short and Easy Method of Prayer*, trans. Thomas D. Brook (New York: Cosimo Classics).

Harlan, Elizabeth (2004): *George Sand* (New Haven, CT: Yale University Press).

Hegardt, Bernhard (1937): *Religion och själsträning: En studie i jesuiternas andliga övnigar* (Stockholm: Natur och Kultur).

Hegel, Georg Willhelm Friedrich (1977 [1802]): *Faith and Knowledge*, ed. and trans. Walter Cerf and H. S. Harris (Albany, NY: State University of New York Press, 1977); German edition: *Glauben und Wissen oder Reflexionsphilosophie der Subjektivität in der Vollständigkeit ihrer Formen als Kantische, Jacobische und Fichtesche Philosophie*, in G.W.F. Hegel, *Werke in 20 Bänden*, vol. 2: *Jenaer Schriften 1801–1807* (Frankfurt am Main: Suhrkamp, 1970).

Heine, Heinrich (2007 [1834]): *On the History of Religion and Philosophy in Germany*, ed. Terry Pinkard, trans. Howard Pollack-Milgate (Cambridge: Cambridge University Press); German edition: *Zur Geschichte der Religion und Philosophie in Deutschland*, in *Heinrich-Heine Säkularausgabe*, vol. 8: *Über Deutschland 1833–1836; Kunst und Philosophie*, compiled by Renate Francke (Berlin: Akadmie Verlag, 1972), pp. 125–230.

Hennecke, Edgar, ed. (1904): *Neutestamentliche Apokryphen* (Tübingen & Leipzig: J.C.B. Mohr); English translation as *New Testament Apocrypha*, ed. Wilhelm Scheemelcher and R. McL. Wilson, 2 vols (Philadelphia: Westminster Press, 1963).

Hilliard, Kevin (2011): *Freethinkers, Libertines and Schwärmer: Heterodoxy in German Literature, 1750–1800*, ed. Martin Liebscher (London: Institute of Germanic and Romance Studies).

Hippolytus (1886): *The Refutation of All Heresies*. In *The Ante-Nicene Fathers*, vol. 5: *Fathers of the Third Century: Hippolytus, Cyprian, Caius, Novatian*, ed. A. Cleveland Coxe, trans. J. H. MacMahon (Buffalo, NY: Christian Literature Publishing Co.), pp. 9–163.

Hoerni, Ulrich (2019): "Foreword: C. G. Jung's Activities at ETH Zurich," in *C. G. Jung: History of Modern Psychology; Lectures delivered at ETH Zurich*, vol. 1: *1933–1934*, ed. Ernst Falzeder (Princeton, NJ: Princeton University Press), pp. vii–xviii.

Hölderlin, Friedrich (2004): *Poems and Fragments*, trans. Michael Hamburger (London: Anvil Press Poetry).

Hostie, Raymond (1955): *Du mythe à la religion: La psychologie analytique de C. G. Jung* (Paris: Desclée de Brouwer).

Iyer, V. Subrahmanya (1937): "Pure Philosophy in India," in *Travaux du IXᵉ Congrès International de Philosophie*, vol. 9: *Analyse reflexive et Transcendance II* (Paris: Hermann & Cie).

—— (1955): *The Philosophy of Truth, or, Tatvagnana: A Collection of Speeches and Writings* (Salem: Court Press).

Izquierdo, Sebastián (1695): *Praxis exercitiorum spiritualium* (Rome: Typis Ioannis Francisci Buagni).

Jordan, Furneaux (1890): *Character as Seen in Body and Parentage* (London: Kegan Paul, Trench and Trubner).

Jung, Carl Gustav (1905): "Über spiritistische Erscheinungen," in *Basler Nachrichten*, 12–17 Nov., pp. 311–16; *GW* 18, pp. 317–34; English translation as "On Spiritualistic Phenomena," *CW* 18, pp. 293–308.

—— (1911–12): "Wandlungen und Symbole der Libido: Beiträge zur Entwicklungsgeschichte des Denkens," *Jahrbuch für psychoanalytische und psychopathologische Forschungen* 3–4, pp. 120–227 ("Erster Teil" [First part], 1911) and pp. 162–464 ("Zweiter Teil" [Second part], 1912); English translation as *Psychology of the Unconscious: A Study of the Transformations and Symbolisms of the Libido; A Contribution to the History of the Evolution of Thought*, trans. Beatrice M. Hinkle (New York: Moffatt Yard & Co., 1916; London: Kegan Paul, 1917); *CW*, supplementary volume B.

—— (1916): *Septem Sermones ad Mortuos* (private print); English translation as *The Seven Sermons to the Dead Written by Basilides in Alexandria, the City Where the East Toucheth the West*, trans. H. G. Baynes (London: private printing, 1925; reprinted, London: Stewart and Watkins, 1967).

—— (1921): *Psychologische Typen, GW* 6; English translation as *Psychological Types*, trans. H. G. Baynes (London: Kegan Paul; New York: Harcourt, Brace & Co., 1923); *CW* 6.

—— (1925): "Die Ehe als psychologische Beziehung," in *Das Ehebuch*, ed. Graf Hermann Keyserling (Celle: Niels Kampmann); reprinted in Jung (1931c), pp. 275–95; *GW* 17, pp. 213–30; English translation as "Marriage as a Psychological Relationship," (1) trans. Theresa Duerr, in *The Book of Marriage* (New York: Harcourt, 1926); (2) trans. H. G. Baynes and Cary F. Baynes in Jung (1928d), pp. 189–203; *CW* 17, pp. 187–204.

—— (1926): Geist und Leben," *Form und Sinn* 2 (2), pp. 33–44; English translation as "Spirit and Life," trans. H. G. and Cary F. Baynes in Jung (1928d), pp. 77–98; *CW* 8, pp. 319–37.

—— (1927): "Die Frau in Europa", *Europäische Revue* 3, pp. 481–99; republished in *Neue Schweizer Rundschau* (Zurich, 1929); *GW* 10, 135–56; English translation as "Woman in Europe," trans. H. G. Baynes and Cary F. Baynes in Jung (1928d), pp. 164–88; *CW* 10, pp. 113–33.

—— (1928a): "Die Beziehungen zwischen dem Ich und dem Unbewussten," *GW* 7, pp. 127–50; English translation as "The Relations between the Ego and the Unconscious," *CW* 7, pp. 227–41.

—— (1928b): "Die Struktur der Seele," *Europäische Revue* 4, pp. 125–135; revised and expanded in Jung (1931c), pp. 144–75; *GW* 8, pp. 161–82; English translation as "The Structure of the Psyche," *CW* 8, pp. 139–58.

—— (1928c): "Das Seelenproblem des modernen Menschen," *Europäische Revue* 4, pp. 700–715; revised and expanded in Jung (1931c), pp. 401–35; *GW* 10, pp. 91–114; English translation as "Spiritual Problems of Modern Man," in Jung (1931d), pp. 226–54; *CW* 10, pp. 74–94.

—— (1928d): *Contributions to Analytical Psychology*, trans. H. G. Baynes and Cary F. Baynes (London: Kegan Paul, Trench, Trubner & Co.).

—— (1929): "Kommentar zu *Das Geheimnis der Goldenen Blüte*," in Wilhelm and Jung (1929), pp. 1–66; *GW* 13, pp. 11–63; English translation as "Commentary on *The Secret of The Golden Flower*," trans. Cary F. Baynes, in Wilhelm and Jung (1931), pp. 77–138; *CW* 13, pp. 1–56.

—— (1931a): "Der archaische Mensch", *Europäische Revue* 7, pp. 182–203; revised and republished in Jung (1931c), pp. 211–47; *GW* 10, pp. 67–90; English translation as "Archaic Man," in Jung (1931d), pp. 143–74; *CW* 10, pp. 50–73.

—— (1931b): "Die Entschleierung der Seele," *Europäische Revue* 7, pp. 504–22; revised version published as "Das Grundproblem der gegenwärtigen Psychologie" in Jung (1934c), pp. 1–32; *GW* VIII, pp. 371–92; English translation as "The Basic Postulates of Analytical Psychology," in Jung (1931d), pp. 200–225; revised in *CW* 8, pp. 338–57.

—— (1931c): *Seelenprobleme der Gegenwart* (Zurich: Rascher).

—— (1931d): *Modern Man in Search of a Soul*, trans. W. Stanley Dell and Cary F. Baynes (London: Kegan Paul, Trench, Trubner & Co.).

—— (1932): "Ulysses," *Europäische Revue* 8, pp. 547–68; reprinted in Jung (1934c), pp. 132–69; *GW* 15, pp. 121–50; English translation as "Ulysses: A Monologue," trans. W. Stanley Dell, *Spring* (1949) (Analytical Psychology Club of New York journal), pp. 1–20; and in *Nimbus* 2 (1) (1953), pp. 7–20; *CW* 15, pp. 109–34.

—— (1932b): "Wirklichkeit und Überwirklichkeit", in *Querschnitt* 12 (12); *GW* 8, pp. 419–23; English translation as "The Real and the Surreal," *CW* 8, pp. 382–84.

—— (1933a): "Bruder Klaus," *Neue Schweizer Rundschau*, New Series 1 (4), pp. 223–29; *GW* 11, pp. 329–34; English translation as "Brother Klaus," *CW* 11, pp. 316–23.

—— (1933c): "Editorial," *Zentralblatt für Psychotherapie und ihre Grenzgebiete* 4 (3), pp. 139–40; *CW* 10, pp. 533–34.

—— (1934a): "Seele und Tod. Von der Psychologie des Sterbens," *Europäische Revue* 10, pp. 229–38; republished in Jung (1934c), pp. 212–30; *GW* 8, pp. 443–56; English translation as "The Soul and Death," trans. Eugene H. Henley, *Spring* (1949) (Analytical Psychology Club of New York journal); *CW* 8, pp. 404–15.

—— (1934b): "Rejoinder to Dr. Bally," ("Zeitgenössisches"), *Neue Zürcher Zeitung* 437/443 (13/14 March); *CW* 10, pp. 535–44.

—— (1934c): *Wirklichkeit der Seele* (Zurich: Rascher).

—— (1935): "Über die Archetypen des kollektiven Unbewussten," in *Ostwestliche Symbolik und Seelenführung*, Eranos Yearbook 1934 (Zurich: Rhein-Verlag), pp. 179–229; *GW* 9.1, pp. 11–49; English translation as "Archetypes of the Collective Unconscious," *CW* 9.1, pp. 3–41.

—— (1936a): "Yoga and the West," in *Prabuddha Bharata*, vol. 41.2, trans. Cary F. Baynes (Advaita Ashrama, Mayavati Almora, Himalayas), pp. 170–77; *CW* 11, pp. 529–37; German: *GW* 11, pp. 531–39.

—— (1936b): "Wotan," in *Neue Schweizer Rundschau* 3 (11); *CW* 10, pp. 203–18.

—— (1938): *Psychology and Religion: The Terry Lectures of 1937* (New Haven, CT: Yale University Press); *CW* 11, pp. 3–106; German translation as *Psychologie und Religion*, trans. Felicia Froboese (Zurich: Rascher, 1940).

—— (1939): "Geleitwort" to Daisetz Teitaro Suzuki, *Die große Befreiung: Einführung in den Zen-Buddhismus* (Leipzig: Curt Weller & Co.), pp. 7–37; English translation as "Foreword to Suzuki's *Introduction to Zen Buddhism*," *CW* 11, pp. 538–57.

—— (1940): "Die verschiedenen Aspekte der Wiedergeburt," in *Die Symbolik der Wiedergeburt in der religiösen Vorstellung der Zeiten und Völker*, Eranos Yearbook 1939 (Zurich: Rhein), pp. 399–447; revised and extended as "Über Wiedergeburt," in *Gestaltungen des Unbewussten* (Psychologische Abhandlungen 7) (Zurich: Rascher, 1950), pp. 39–94; *GW* 9.1, pp. 125–61; English translation as "Concerning Rebirth," *CW* 9.1, pp. 113–47.

—— (1942a): "Zur Psychologie der Trinitätsidee," in *Trinität, christliche Symbolik und Gnosis*, Eranos Yearbook 1940/41 (Zurich: Rhein Verlag), pp. 31–64; extended and revised as "Versuch einer psychologischen Deutung des Trinitätsdogmas," in: *Symbolik des Geistes* (Psychologische Abhandlungen 6) (Zurich: Rascher, 1948), pp. 323–446; English translation as "A Psychological Approach to the Dogma of the Trinity," *CW* 9, pp. 107–200.

—— (1942b): "Das Wandlungssymbol in der Messe," in *Trinität, christliche Symbolik und Gnosis*, Eranos Yearbook 1940/41 (Zurich: Rhein Verlag), pp. 67–155; extended and revised in *Von den Wurzeln des Bewusstseins: Studien über den Archetypus* (Psychologische Abhandlungen 9) (Zurich: Rascher, 1954), pp. 217–350; *GW* 11, pp. 217–312; English translation as "Transformation Symbolism in the Mass," *CW* 11, pp. 201–96.

—— (1944): *Psychologie und Alchemie* (Psychologische Abhandlungen 5) (Zurich: Rascher); English translation as *Psychology and Alchemy*, *CW* 12.

—— (1945): "Zur Psychologie des Geistes," in *Der Geist*, Eranos Yearbook 1945 (Zurich: Rhein Verlag), pp. 385–448; revised and published as "Zur Phänomenologie des Geistes im Märchen," in *Symbolik des Geistes* (Zurich: Rascher, 1948), pp. 3–70; *GW* 9.1, pp. 221–70; English translation as "The Phenomenology of the Spirit in the Fairy Tales," *CW* 9.1, pp. 207–54.

—— (1946) "Nachwort," in *Aufsätze zur Zeitgeschichte* (Zurich: Rascher, pp. 117–47; *GW* 10, pp. 255–73; English translation as "Epilogue," in *Essays on Contemporary Events*, trans. Elizabeth Welsh (London, 1947), pp. 73–90; *CW* 10, pp. 227–43.

—— (1951): *Aion: Untersuchungen zur Symbolgeschichte; Mit einem Beitrag von Marie-Louise von Franz* (Psychologische Abhandlungen 8) (Zurich: Rascher); again as *Aion: Beiträge zur Symbolik des Selbst*, *GW* 9.2; English translation as *Aion: Researches into the Phenomenology of the Self*, *CW* 9.2.

—— (1952): "Synchronizität als ein Prinzip akausaler Zusammenhänge," in *Naturerklärung und Psyche* (Studien aus dem C. G. Jung Institut 4) (Zurich: Rascher), pp. 1–107; *GW* 8, pp. 457–553; English translation as "Synchronicity: An Acausal Connecting Principle," *CW* 8, pp. 417–519.

—— (1954a): "Der philosophische Baum," in *Von den Wurzeln des Bewusstseins: Studien über den Archetypus* (Psychologische Abhandlungen 9) (Zurich:

Rascher), pp. 351–469; *GW* 8, pp. 271–376; English translation as "The Philosophical Tree," *CW* 8, pp. 251–349.

—— (1954b): "Die Visionen des Zosimos," *GW* 8, pp. 65–121; English translation as "The Visions of Zosimos," *CW* 8, pp. 57–94.

—— (1955–56): *Mysterium Coniunctionis*, *CW* 14.

—— (1962): *Memories, Dreams, Reflections*, recorded and edited by Aniela Jaffé, trans. Richard and Clara Winston (New York: Pantheon Books).

—— (1973): *Letters*, selected and edited by Gerhard Adler, in collaboration with Aniela Jaffé; trans. R.F.C. Hull. Vol. 1: 1906–50; Vol. 2: 1951–61 (Princeton, NJ: Princeton University Press).

—— (1984 [1928–30]): *Dream Analysis: Notes of the Seminar Given in 1928–1930*, ed. William McGuire (Princeton, NJ: Princeton University Press).

—— (1987): *C. G. Jung Speaking: Interviews and Encounters*, ed. William McGuire and R.F.C. Hull (Bollingen Series 97) (Princeton, NJ: Princeton University Press).

—— (1989 [1934–39]): *Nietzsche's* Zarathustra: *Notes of the Seminar Given in 1934–39*, ed. James L. Jarrett, 2 vols (Princeton, NJ: Princeton University Press).

—— (1996 [1932]): *The Psychology of Kundalini Yoga: Notes of the Seminar given in 1932 by C. G. Jung*, ed. Sonu Shamdasani (Bollingen Series 99) (Princeton, NJ: Princeton University Press).

—— (1997 [1930–34]): *Visions: Notes of the Seminar Given in 1930–1934*, ed. Claire Douglas (Princeton, NJ: Princeton University Press).

—— (2008 [1936–40]): *Children's Dreams*, ed. Maria Meyer-Grass and Lorenz Jung, trans. Ernst Falzeder with the collaboration of Tony Woolfson (Philemon Series) (Princeton, NJ: Princeton University Press).

—— (2009): *The Red Book: Liber Novus*, ed. Sonu Shamdasani (London: W. W. Norton).

—— (2012): *Introduction to Jungian Psychology: Notes on the Seminar on Analytical Psychology Given in 1925*, ed. William McGuire, updated with a new introduction by Sonu Shamdasani (Philemon Series) (Princeton, NJ: Princeton University Press).

—— (2020): *The Black Books 1913–1932: Notebooks of Transformation*, ed. Sonu Shamdasani, trans. Martin Liebscher, John Peck, and Sonu Shamdasani (Philemon Series) (New York: W. W. Norton).

—— and Aniela Jaffé (forthcoming): *Protocols for Memories, Dream, Reflections*, ed. Sonu Shamdasani (Philemon Series) (Princeton, NJ: Princeton University Press).

—— and Karl Kerényi (1941): "Das Göttliche Kind: In mythologischer und psychologischer Beleuchtung," *Albae Vigiliae* 6–7; and "Das göttliche Mädchen: Die Hauptgestalt der Mysterien von Eleusis in mythologischer und psychologischer Bedeutung," *Albae Vigiliae* 8–9; extended version published as *Einführung in das Wesen der Mythologie. Gottkindmythos; Eleusinische Mysterien* (Amsterdam: Pantheon Akademische Verlagsanstalt, 1941; Zurich: Rascher, 1951); English translation as *Essays on a Science of Mythology: The Myth of the Divine Child and the Mysteries of Eleusis*, trans. R.F.C. Hull (Bollingen Series 22) (Princeton, NJ: Princeton University Press, 1969).

—— and Erich Neumann (2015): *Analytical Psychology in Exile: The Correspondence of C. G. Jung & Erich Neumann*, ed. Martin Liebscher, trans. Heather McCartney (Philemon Series) (Princeton, NJ: Princeton University Press).

—— and Richard Wilhelm (1929): "Einleitung zu Tschang Schen Schu: Die Kunst, das menschliche Leben zu verlängern," *Europäische Revue 5* (1929), pp. 530–56.

Kant, Immanuel (1838 [1766]): "Träume eines Geistersehers, erläutert durch Träume der Metaphysik," in *Immanuel Kants Sämmtliche Werke*, ed. Karl Rosenkranz and Friedrich Wilhelm Schubert, vol. 7: *Kleine anthropologisch-praktische Schriften*, ed. Friedrich Wilhelm Schubert (Leipzig: Leopold Voss), pp. 31–107; English translation as *Dreams of a Spirit-Seer, Illustrated by Dreams of Metaphysics*, ed. Frank Sewall, trans. F. Goerwitz (London: Swan Sonnenschein & Co.; New York: The Macmillan Co., 1900).

Kautzsch, Emil, ed. (1899): *Textbibel des Alten und Neuen Testament* (Tübingen: J.C.B. Mohr).

Klages, Ludwig (1922): *Vom kosmogonischen Eros* (Munich: Georg Müller).

—— (1929–32): *Der Geist als Widersacher der Seele*, 3 vols (Leipzig: Barth).

Koepgen, Georg (1939): *Die Gnosis des Christentums* (Salzburg: Otto Müller).

Le Bon, Charles-Marie Gustave (1895): *Psychologie des foules* (Paris: Félix Alcan); English translation as *The Crowd: A Study of the Popular Mind* (London: The Macmillan Co., 1896).

Leisegang, Hans (1924): *Die Gnosis* (Leipzig: Alfred Kröner Verlag).

—— (1940): "Das Mysterium der Schlange," in *Die Symbolik der Wiedergeburt in der religiösen Vorstellung der Zeiten und Völker*, Eranos Yearbook 1939 (Zurich: Rhein Verlag), pp. 151–250.

Lévy-Bruhl, Lucien (1910): *Les fonctions mentales dans les sociéties inférieures* (Paris: Felix Alcan); English translation as *How Natives Think*, trans. Lilian A. Clare (London: Allen & Unwin, 1926).

—— (1935): *La mythologie primitive: Le monde mythique des Australiens et des Papous* (Paris: Felix Alcan).

Leppin, Volker, Fernando Enns, and Ralf Stroh (2011): "Enthusiasts (Schwärmer)," in *Religion Past and Present* (*RPP*) *Online*, available at http://dx.doi.org/10.1163/1877-5888_rpp_COM_024772 (accessed 9 April 2022).

Liebscher, Martin (2012): *Libido und Wille zur Macht: C. G. Jungs Auseinandersetzung mit Nietzsche* (Basel: Schwabe).

—— (2020): "C. G. Jung and the Berneuchen Movement: Meditation and Active Imagination in Jungian Psychotherapy and Protestant Spiritual Practice in the 1930s," in *Medical Humanity and Inhumanity in the German-Speaking World*, ed. Mererid Puw Davies and Sonu Shamdasani (London: UCL Press), pp. 85–113.

—— (2021): "Introduction," in *C. G. Jung: Psychology of Yoga and Meditation; Lectures Delivered at the ETH Zurich, October 1938 to June 1939 & November 1940*. (Philemon series ETH Lectures, vol. 6 [*JMP*]) (Princeton, NJ: Princeton University Press), pp. xlv–lxxi.

Luther, Martin (1823 [1525]): *On the Bondage of the Will: Written in Answer to the Diatribe of Erasmus on Free Will*, trans. Henry Cole (London: Printed by Bensley for Simpkin and Marshall).

—— (2006 [1520]): *Von der Freiheit eines Christenmenschen* (Gütersloh: Gütersloher Verlagshaus); English translation as *The Freedom of a Christian*, trans. W. A. Lambert, revised by Harold J. Grimm, in Martin Luther, *Three Treatises* (Minneapolis: Fortress Press, 1970), pp. 261–90.

—— (1908 [1525]a): "Ermahnung zum Frieden auf die Zwölf Artikel der Bauernschaft in Schwaben," in *D. Martin Luthers Werke: Kritische Gesamtausgabe Weimar* (*Weimarer Ausgabe* [*WA*]), vol. 18 (Weimar: Hermann Böhlaus Nachfolger), pp. 279–334; English translation as "Admonition to Peace: A Reply to the Twelve Articles of the Peasants in Swabia," in *Luther's Works*, vol. 46, ed. Jaroslav Pelikan (Minneapolis: Fortress Press, 1967), pp. 17–43.

—— (1908 [1525]b): "Wider die räuberischen und mörderischen Rotten der Bauern," in *D. Martin Luthers Werke: Kritische Gesamtausgabe Weimar* (*Weimarer Ausgabe* [*WA*]), vol 18 (Weimar: Hermann Böhlaus Nachfolger), pp. 344–61; English translation as "Against the Robbing and Murdering Hordes of Peasants," in *Luther's Works*, vol. 46, ed. Jaroslav Pelikan (Minneapolis: Fortress Press, 1967), pp. 49–55.

Lock, Walter (1902): "Pleroma," in *A Dictionary of the Bible, Dealing with Its Language, Literature and Contents*, ed. James Hastings, vol. 4: *Pleroma-Zuzim* (New York: Charles Scribner's Sons), pp. 1–2.

Ludolph of Saxony (1374): *De vita Christi* (Strasbourg and Cologne); English translation as *The Life of Jesus Christ*, trans. Milton T. Walsh, 4 vols (Athens, OH: Cistercian Publications).

Maier, Michael (1617): *Symbola aureae mensae duodecim nationum* (Frankfurt: Lucas Jennis).

Makari, George (2016): *Soul Machine: The Invention of the Modern Mind* (New York: W. W. Norton).

Mauburnus, Johannes (1494): *Rosetum exercitiorum spiritualium et sacrarum meditationum* (Zwolle: Peter van Os).

Mead, Goerge Robert Stow (1919): *The Doctrine of the Subtle Body in Western Tradition: An Outline of What the Philosophers Thought and Christians Taught on the Subject* (London: J. M. Watkins).

Mertens, Michèle (2006): "Greco-Egyptian Alchemy in Byzantium," in *The Occult Sciences in Byzantium*, ed. Paul Magdalino and Maria Mavroudi (Geneva: La Pomme d'or), pp. 205–30.

Müller, Herman (1898): *Origines de la Compagnie de Jésus* (Paris: Fischbacker).

Neumann, Erich (1952): "Eros und Psyche: Ein Beitrag zur seelischen Entwicklung des Weiblichen," in Apuleius, *Amor und Psyche* (Zurich: Rascher), pp. 75–217; English translation as "The Psychic Development of the Feminine: A Commentary on the Tale of Apuleius," trans. Ralph Manheim, in Apuleius, *Amor and Psyche* (New York: Pantheon Books, 1956), pp. 57–161.

Nietzsche, Friedrich (1882): *Die fröhliche Wissenschaft*, in *Sämtliche Werke: Kritische Studienausgabe* (*KSA*), vol. 3, ed. Giorgio Colli and Mazzino Montinari (Berlin: de Gruyter, 1988), pp. 343–651. English translation as *The Gay Science: With a Prelude in Rhymes and an Appendix of Songs*, trans. and with commentary by Walter Kaufmann (New York: Vintage Books, 1974).

—— (1883–85): *Also sprach Zarathustra*, in *Sämtliche Werke: Kritische Studienausgabe* (*KSA*), vol. 4, ed. Giorgio Colli and Mazzino Montinari (Berlin: de

Gruyter, 1988); English translation as *Thus Spoke Zarathustra*, trans. R. J. Hollingdale (Harmondsworth: Penguin Books, 1961).

—— (1887): *Zur Genealogie der Moral*, in *Sämtliche Werke: Kritische Studienausgabe (KSA)*, vol. 5, ed. Giorgio Colli and Mazzino Montinari (Berlin: de Gruyter), pp. 245–412; English translation as *On the Genealogy of Morality*, ed. Keith Ansell-Pearson, trans. Carol Diethe (Cambridge: Cambridge University Press, 2006).

—— (1889): *Götzendämmerung, oder Wie man mit dem Hammer philosophiert*, in *Sämtliche Werke: Kritische Studienausgabe (KSA)*, vol. 6, ed. Giorgio Colli and Mazzino Montinari (Berlin: de Gruyter, 1988), pp. 55–161; English translation as *Twilight of the Idols, or How to Philosophize with a Hammer*, in The Anti-Christ, Ecce Homo, Twilight of the Idols *and Other Writings*, ed. Aaron Ridley and Judith Norman, trans. Judith Norman (Cambridge: Cambridge University Press, 2005), pp. 153–230.

—— (1891): *Dionysos-Dithyramben*, in *Sämtliche Werke: Kritische Studienausgabe (KSA)*, vol. 6, ed. Giorgio Colli and Mazzino Montinari (Berlin: de Gruyter, 1988), pp. 375–411; English translation by R. J. Hollingdale as *Dithyrambs of Dionysus* (London: Anvil Press, 1984).

Origen (1862): *Homiliae in Jeremiam*, in *Origenis opera omnia* Patrologia Graeca, vol. 13, ed. Jacques-Paul Migne (Petit-Montrouge: Imprimerie Catholique), pp. 253–513.

Paul, Jean (Johann Paul Friedrich Richter) (1845 [1796–97]): *Flower, Fruit and Thorn Pieces of the Married Life, Death and Wedding of the Advocate of the Poor Firmian Stanislaus Siebenkäs*, trans. Edward Henry Noel (London: William Smith). German edition: *Siebenkäs* [full title: *Blumen-, Frucht- und Dornenstücke oder Ehestand, Tod und Hochzeit des Armenadvokaten F. St. Siebenkäs im Reichsmarktflecken Kuhschappel*] (Frankfurt am Main: Insel Verlag, 1987).

Peter of Alcántara (1556): *Tratado de la oración y meditación* (Madrid: Hijos de Gregorio de Amo, 1917); English translation as *Treatise on Prayer and Meditation*, trans. Dominic Devas (London: Burns, Oates & Washburn, 1926); German translation as *Das goldene Büchlein über die Betrachtung und das innerliche Gebet*, trans. Philibert Seeböck (Würzburg, 1900).

Peuckert, Will-Erich (1956): "Der Blocksberg," *Zeitschrift für deutsche Philologie* 75, pp. 347–55.

Pfeiffer, Franz, ed. (1857): *Deutsche Mystiker des vierzehnten Jahrhunderts*, vol. 2: *Meister Eckhart* (Leipzig: Göschen); English translation, with some omissions and additions, as *Meister Eckhart*, trans. C. de B. Evans (London: Watkins, 1924).

Pfister, Oskar (1910): *Die Frömmigkeit des Grafen Ludwig von Zinzendorf: Ein psychoanalytischer Beitrag zur Kenntnis des religiösen Sublimierungsprozesse und zur Erklärung des Pietismus* (Schriften zur angewandten Seelenkunde 8, ed. Sigmund Freud) (Vienna, Leipzig: Franz Deuticke).

Philo of Alexandria (1941): *On the Contemplative Life, or Suppliants*, in *Philo in Ten Volumes and Two Supplementary Volumes*, vol. 9, with an English translation by. F. H. Colson (Loeb Classical Library 363) (Cambridge, MA: Harvard University Press), pp. 112–70.

Pius XII (1950): *Munificentissimus Deus* (Apostolic constitution defining the dogma of the Assumption), *Acta Apostolicae Sedis*, vol. 42, pp. 753–73.

Plutarch (1878): *Plutarch's* Morals, *Translated from the Greek by Several Hands, Corrected and Revised by William W. Goodwin, with an Introduction by Ralph Waldo Emerson*, 5 vols (Boston, MA: Little, Brown, & Co.).

Poehler, Eric (2012): "The Drainage System at Pompeii: Mechanisms, Operation and Design," *Journal of Roman Archeology* 25 (1), pp. 95–120.

Pratt, Tim and James Vernon (2005): "'Appeal from this fiery bed . . .': The Colonial Politics of Gandhi's Fasts and Their Metropolitan Reception," *Journal of British Studies* 44 (1), pp. 92–114.

Preisendanz, Karl, ed. (1928–31): *Papyri graecae magicae: Die griechischen Zauberpapyri*, 2 vols (Stuttgart: Teubner); English translation as *The Greek Magical Papyri in Translation, including the Demotic Texts*, ed. Hans Dieter Betz (Chicago: University of Chicago Press, 1986).

Przywara, Erich (1932): "Jude, Heide, Christ," *Europäische Revue* 8, pp. 470–76.

——— (1938): *Deus semper maior: Theologie der Exerzitien*, 3 vols, vol. 1: "Anima Christi," "Annotationen," "Fundament," "Erste Woche" (Freiburg im Breisgau: Herder).

——— (1964): *Logos: Abendland, Reich, Commercium* (Düsseldorf: Patmos, 1964).

Purcell, Mary (1970): *The Quiet Companion: The Life of Peter Faber, S.J., 1506–46* (Dublin: Gill and Macmillan).

Rahner, Karl (1968): "Laudatio auf Erich Przywara," in *Gnade als Freiheit: Kleine theologische Beiträge* (Freiburg im Breisgau: Herder), pp. 266–73.

Regimini militantis ecclesiae (1938 [1540]), *Constitutiones Societatis Iesu* (MHSI), vol. 1 (Rome: Societas Iesu) pp. 24–32.

Rhodes James, Montague, ed. and trans. (1924): *The Apocryphal New Testament* (Oxford: Clarendon Press).

Ribadeneira, Pedro de (1572): *Vita Ignatii Loiolae* (Naples [Neapoli]: Societatis Iesu); Spanish translation as *Vida del P. Ignacio de Loyola, fundador de la religión de la Compañía de Jesús. Escripta en latín por el Padre Pedro de Ribadeneyra de la misma Compañía y aora nuevamente traduzida en romance, y añadida por el mismo autor. Dirigida al illustre y reverendiss. señor don Gaspar de Quiroga, cardenal y arçobispo de Toledo, inquisidor general, etc.* (Madrid: Alonso Gómez Impresor de su Majestad, 1583); English translation as *The Life of Ignatius of Loyola*, trans. Claude Pavur (Boston, MA: The Institute of Jesuit Sources, 2014).

Ricciotti, Giuseppe (1941): *Vita di Gesù Cristo* (Vatican City: Tipografia Poliglotta Vaticana); English translation as *The Life of Christ*, trans. Alba I. Zizzamia (Milwaukee, WI: The Bruce Publishing Company, 1947).

Richard of Saint Victor (1979): *The Twelve Patriarchs; The Mystical Ark; Book Three of the Trinity*, trans. with an introduction by Grover A. Zinn, preface by Jean Châtillon (London : SPCK).

Rohan, Anton Karl Prinz (1923): *Europa: Streiflichter* (Leipzig: Der neue Geist Verlag).

——— (1932a): "Einige Bemerkungen zum Italienischen Faschismus," *Europäische Revue* 8, pp. 665–68.

—— (1932b): "Einige Bemerkungen zur Judenfrage," *Europäische Revue* 8, pp. 453–59.

Rosignoli, Carolo Gregorio (1737): *Guldener Denck-Ring. Das ist: Merck-würdige Begebenheiten und wunderbarliche Würkungen der vortrefflichen Exerzitien des Heil. Ignatii* (Augsburg [Augspurg] and Dillingen: Joh. Caspar Bencard).

Rousseau, Jean-Jacques (1762): *Émile, ou De l'éducation* (Jean Neaulme: The Hague); English translation as *Emile*, trans. Barbara Foxley (London: J. M. Dent & Sons, 1911).

Sand, George (1929): *The Intimate Journal of George Sand*, ed. and trans. Marie Jenney Howe (New York: Loring & Mussey).

Schelling, Friedrich Wilhelm Joseph (1977 [1815]): *Schelling's Treatise on "The Deities of Samothrace": A Translation and an Interpretation* [*Über die Gottheiten von Samothrace*], introduced and translated by Robert F. Brown (Missoula, MT: Scholars Press).

Schultz, Wolfgang (1910): *Dokumente der Gnosis* (Jena: Eugen Diederichs).

Schulz, Matthias (2010): "Der Europäische Kulturbund," in *Europäische Geschichte Online*, ed. Institut für Europäische Geschichte (Mainz). Available at http://ieg-ego.eu/de/threads/europaeische-netzwerke/politische-netzwerke/europa-netzwerke-der-zwischenkriegszeit/matthias-schulz-der-europaeische-kulturbund (accessed 9 April 2022).

Serina, Florent (2017): "Carl Gustav Jung en France au XXᵉ siècle: Histoire d'une reception." PhD thesis, Université de Lausanne.

Shamdasani, Sonu (1990): "A Woman called Frank," *Spring: Journal of Archetype and Culture* 50, pp. 26–56.

—— (2003): *Jung and the Making of Modern Psychology: The Dream of A Science* (Cambridge: Cambridge University Press).

—— (2012): *C. G. Jung: A Biography in Books* (New York: W. W. Norton).

Sherry, Jay (2010): *Carl Gustav Jung: The Avant-Garde Conservative* (New York: Palgrave Macmillan).

Sourvinou-Inwood, Christiane (2003): "Festival and Mysteries: Aspects of the Eleusinian cult," in *Greek Mysteries: The Archaeology and Ritual of Ancient Greek Secret Cults*, ed. Michael B. Cosmopoulos (London: Routledge), pp. 25–49.

Spencer, Baldwin and F. J. Gillen (1899): *The Native Tribes of Central Australia* (London: MacMillan).

Spitteler, Carl (1945 [1906]): *Imago*, in Carl Spitteler, *Gesammelte Werke*, ed. Gottfried Bohnenblust, Wilhelm Altwegg, and Robert Faesi, vol. 4 (Zurich: Artemis), pp. 267–435.

Stegmaier, Werner (2013): "Oh Mensch! Gieb Acht! Kontextuelle Interpretation des Mitternachts-Lieds aus Also sprach Zarathustra," in *Nietzsche-Studien* 42 (1), pp. 85–115.

Stöckli, Alban (ed.) (1933): *Die Visionen des seligen Bruder Klaus* (Einsiedeln: Benzinger Verlag).

Strehlow, Carl (1907–20): *Die Aranda- und Loritja-Stämme in Zentral-Australien* (Frankfurt am Main: Joseph Baer).

Suzuki, Daisetz Teitaro (1927): *Essays in Zen Buddhism: First Series* (London: Luzac & Co.).

—— (1933): *Essays in Zen Buddhism: Second Series* (London: Luzac & Co.).

—— (1934a): *Essays in Zen Buddhism: Third Series* (London: Luzac & Co.).

—— (1934b): *Introduction to Zen Buddhism* (Kyoto: Eastern Buddhist Society); German translation, with a foreword by C. G. Jung, as *Die große Befreiung* (Leipzig: Curt Weller & Co., 1939).

Swedenborg, Emanuel (1758): *De caelo et ejus mirabilibus et de inferno, ex auditis et visis* (London: s.n.); English translation as *Heaven and Its Wonders and Hell from Things Heard and Seen*, trans. George F. Dole (West Chester, PA: Swedenborg Foundation, 2001).

Tassi, Ildefonso (1952): *Ludovico Barbo (1381–1443)* (Rome: Edizioni di storia y letteratura).

Tertullian (1844): *Apologeticus adversus Gentes pro Christianis*, in Patrologia Latina, vol. 1, ed. Jacques-Paul Migne (Petit-Montrouge: Imprimerie Catholique), pp. 257–536.

Tetlow, Joseph A. (1989): *The Fundamentum: Creation in the Principle and Foundation* (Studies in the Spirituality of the Jesuits 21.4) (St. Louis: The Seminar on Jesuit Spirituality).

Theatrum chemicum, præcipuos selectorum auctorum tractatus de chemiæ et lapidis philosophici [. . .] (1602–61), 6 vols (Oberursel: Lazarus Zetzner).

Thiede, Werner (2001): *Wer ist der kosmische Christus? Karriere und Bedeutungswandel einer modernen Metapher* (Kirche–Konfession–Religion 44) (Vandenhoeck & Ruprecht: Göttingen).

Uhsadel, Walter (1966): *Evangelische Seelsorge* (Heidelberg: Quelle & Meyer).

Voragine, Jacobus de (2012 [1260]): *The Golden Legend: Readings on the Saints*, trans. William Granger Ryan, with an introduction by Eamon Duffy (Princeton, NJ: Princeton University Press).

Volz, Pia Daniela (1990): *Nietzsche im Labyrinth seiner Krankheit: Eine medizinisch-biographische Untersuchung* (Würzburg: Königshausen & Neumann).

Waterworth, J., ed. and trans. (1848): *The Council of Trent: The Canons and Decrees of the Sacred and Oecumenical Council of Trent* (London: Dolman).

Weizsäcker, Carl Heinrich von, trans. (1875): *Das Neue Testament* (Tübingen: Laupp'sche Bunchhandlung).

Widengren, Geo (1974): 'Einige Bemerkungen über die Methoden der Phänomenologie der Religion', in: *Selbstverständnis und Wesen der Religionswissenschaft*, ed. Günter Lanczkowski (Darmstadt: Wissenschaftliche Buchgesellschaft).

Wilhelm, Richard and C. G. Jung (1929): *Das Geheimnis der Goldenen Blüte: Ein chinesisches Lebensbuch, Übersetzt und erläutert von Richard Wilhelm, mit einem europäischen Kommentar von C. G. Jung* (Munich: Dornverlag); English translation: Wilhelm and Jung (1931).

—— (1931): *The Secret of the Golden Flower: A Chinese Book of Life, Translated (into German) and Explained by Richard Wilhelm with a European Commentary by C. G. Jung*, trans. Cary F. Baynes (London: Kegan Paul).

Zerbolt, Gerard, of Zutphen (1908): *The Spiritual Ascent: A Devotional Treatise, with a life of the author by Thomas à Kempis*, trans. J. P. Arthur (London: Burns & Oates).

Zimmer, Heinrich (1926): *Kunstform und Yoga im indischen Kultbild* (Berlin: Frankfurter Verlagsanstalt); English translation as *Artistic Form and Yoga in the Sacred Images of India*, ed. and trans. Gerald Chapple and James B. Lawson (Princeton, NJ: Princeton University Press, 1984).

Index

active imagination, xiii, xv, xlvii, xlviii, 52, 245
Adam, 58, 58n239, 112, 191, 194–95
Adler, Alfred, xiii, xxxix
Adler, Gerhard, xxxi
Ahriman, 254, 254n678
Ahura Mazda, 147, 147n455, 254n678
Albertus Magnus, 23, 23n155
alchemy: Freemasons and, 27; lectures on, xvii; parallels to meditation exercises in, 17–23; serpent and cross as symbol in, 32; transformation series, 53–58. See also *lapis philosophorum*
Alexander the Great, 142n441
Al-Ghazâli, 61–63, 243
Allah, 62
Amitâyur-dhyâna-sûtra, xv, xlvii
Anabaptists, 145, 210
Analytical Psychology Club, Los Angeles, xxi
androgyny, 114, 117, 236. *See also* hermaphrodites
angels, sins of, 191–94
Angra Mainyu (also Angrō Mainyush), 147, 147n455
"Anima Christi" (prayer), xlvii, lviii, lxvi, 77–88, 98–136, 243–45
anima Christi (soul of Christ), 78, 81, 84, 126
Antaeus, 181
Anthony, Saint, 226–27, 226n626
Apuleius, lxii, 6, 6n97
Aquinas, Thomas, 23n155, 176n531
Arabic mysticism, 61–64, 243
Aristotle, 176n531

arrested development, 105, 235, 235n638
Asclepius, lxiv, 32–33, 33n181
Atharva Veda, 129, 130–31
âtman: Christ likened to, 87, 93, 98, 115, 245–46; mandala as symbol of, 155; as universal and individual essence, 19n141, 88–89, 96–98, 103, 115n387, 127, 133–36, 162, 171–72, 176, 182, 186–87, 245
Attis, 172
Augustine, 178, 178n540, 198n582, 214, 239
Australia, 220
Avalon, Arthur (Sir John Woodroffe), xv

Baeck, Leo, lvi, lvii
Bailey, Ruth, 52n225
Bally, Gustav, xxix, lvii
Barbo, Ludovico, 12, 12n119
Barth, Karl, xxxi, lvii
Bavaud, Maurice, xliii
Baynes, Cary, xxi
Baynes, Helton Godwin ("Peter"), 52n225
Becker, Kenneth, lviii; *Unlikely Companions*, xlix
Beckwith, George, 52n225
Beirnaert, Louis, lxvi, lxvin84
Belur Mutt (also Math) monastery, 80, 80n287
Benedict of Nursia and Benedictine orders, 239
Besant, Annie, 88n309
Binswanger, Kurt, ix–x
Binswanger, Ludwig, liv, 307n363
Binswanger, Otto, 307n363
Blavatsky, Madame, 34n185